Y0-CBA-374

AFTER THE LONG VIGIL, THE IMPACT OF THIS BOOK WILL BE FELT!

The shocking, vibrant drama that unfolds here is more than the story of two wrongly executed Americans. It is the story of all of us—of our country caught up in the destructive forces of mindless fear, of a government crippled from within by opportunists and hate-mongers, and of a cherished system of justice that was dealt a violent blow through the vindictive judgment of a ruthless few.

"Terrifying . . . a soul-shattering experience."
—Brett Halliday

By John Wexley

* In collaboration

THE JUDGMENT OF JULIUS AND ETHEL ROSENBERG

John Wexley

BALLANTINE BOOKS • NEW YORK

ISBN 0-345-24869-4

Manufactured in the United States of America

First Ballantine Books Edition: November 1977

TO THOSE WHO WALKED

Early in January, 1953, thousands of men and women traveled to Washington, D. C., from all parts of the United States to picket the White House during the clemency campaign in behalf of the Rosenbergs.

It was bitterly cold, but the marchers continued their vigil throughout the night, changing shifts every two hours as they had done for many days and nights.

While watching the picket line, this writer asked a black policeman assigned there what he thought of the effort. He replied:

"All I can say, sir, if I was waiting in a death cell, I would sure like to have someone walk for me."

"To remain silent when your neighbor is unjustly persecuted is cowardice; to speak out boldly against injustice, when you are one against many, is the highest patriotism."
—*Abraham Lincoln*

ACKNOWLEDGMENTS

In the original edition of this book there was a special tribute to Emanuel Bloch for his epic fight in behalf of justice. Today, it is a privilege to repeat this tribute. Our long talks about the case were invaluable; also those with his colleague Gloria Agrin. My thanks again to Albert Kahn, co-publisher with Angus Cameron; and long-due thanks to Carl Marzani who joined them; also to Andor Braun, who did the design of the original edition as a labor of love.

Fortunately, with this revised edition I can restate my gratitude to Angus Cameron for my good fortune in having had an editor so "undivided." Now, twenty years later, he has responded again with equal élan. My thanks too to William Reuben, courageous author of the *National Guardian* articles on the case.

And to Marshall Perlin, attorney, who has been dedicated to the good fight for two decades, my profound thanks. Also, to Bonnie Brower, and secretary Lucy Walker, for their help. And to all those at Ballantine Books, my deep appreciation.

Finally, a renewed salute to my wife, Katharine, for all she has done to make this book possible. My debt to her, especially for her insistence on simplicity, is a great one.

J. W.

CONTENTS

AUTHOR'S NOTE

The purpose of writing this book originally was simply stated—to make known the truth about the world-famous Rosenberg case. Today, as we will show, many of the hidden and suppressed facts which we presented over twenty years ago have been confirmed. In addition, we will present quite startling new material. At all times I have relied on documentation and reliable sources. The Chronology of Events should aid in following the sequence of legal moves and to set the historical frame of reference.

In order to analyze the Government's case in the most impartial way, I have followed the objective summary of evidence quoted in full from the *Columbia Law Review*. Thus every important point, favorable or unfavorable to the defendants, is accurately presented.* Concerning this summary, a special index follows the Synopsis of the Government's case. References to the Rosenberg trial record, available at the U.S. Federal Courthouse in New York City, will be indicated by "R" or "Record."

In this revised edition, several passages of peripheral material have been omitted. This has afforded space to deal with many of the disclosures recently released by the FBI and other government agencies as well as for developments taking place subsequent to the original edition. Many of these are in the Addenda to each chapter following Notes and References.

It is, however, in the new section "The Letter 'W',"

* As witness to this effort, despite critical reservations, there have been these comments in the *New York University Law Review*, Vol. 31, April, 1956: "Mr. Wexley has obviously done a monumental research job. . . . brilliant, painstaking analysis of the government's case. . . . Wexley analyzes in minute detail the events of the trial and the circumstances surrounding it."

that I deal with the most important document released thus far. This is the "Pollack" memorandum ordered by the U.S. Attorney General in 1956 to "counter-act" the impact of this book and to find answers to its charges that the Government's case was a political frame-up. Here is how the Washington *Post* of November 14, 1975, describes this memorandum:

. . . One of the most controversial documents to result from the Rosenberg case [and one that] has never been made public before in its entirety.

The lengthy Pollack memo was inspired by publicity for a book published in 1955—*The Judgment of Julius and Ethel Rosenberg,* by John Wexley—which involved a strong attack on the government's conduct of the case.

In view of the fact that this 112-page document was prepared by a staff of Justice Department lawyers with full access to *all* the FBI files, it must be regarded as the Government's definitive "White Paper" on the Rosenberg-Sobell case. Hence there arises the question: Why is it that *none* of the much-hinted at and long-withheld "overwhelming" evidence proving the guilt of the Rosenbergs is produced in this document? Surely, since it was prepared as the official handbook on the case to combat the effect of this book on the public, secretly or otherwise, one would expect such conclusive evidence to be presented.

But, on the contrary, as will be seen, the document is a perfect instance of the fable about the Emperor's clothes. The repeated claim by J. Edgar Hoover, Judge Kaufman and the former prosecutors (Saypol, Lane, Cohn, et al.) that the Government is in possession of this "overwhelming" evidence is now proven to be a lie as naked as the Emperor was. Moreover, not only does the memorandum fail to "counteract" our charges, but in its desperate efforts to cover up the glaring "holes" exposed in this book, there are revealed others even more glaring. In the new material, the role of Harry Gold as an FBI puppet, strongly suggested in the original edition, will now be seen quite plainly.

Other new material in "The Letter 'W'" will show the result of this writer's recent investigation of the "sky platform project" as well as the disclosure of the secret, high-level conference in Washington held a month *before* the trial with the decision to apply the death sentence as a torture device "to break this man Rosenberg." Also included is an analysis of Louis Nizer's effort to present Harry Gold as a *bona fide* spy in his book supporting the Government's case.

Finally, in "The Letter 'W'," we have laid special emphasis on the climate of fear which existed at the time of the Rosenberg case, the peak of the McCarthy Era, a climate almost impossible for today's average reader to imagine were it not for the revelations of "Watergate" and the Congressional investigations of our intelligence agencies. The code of expediency adhered to by Nixon, Hoover and their zealous followers who would have led us to a police state has given us a mirror image of the political attitudes of all those officials responsible for the Rosenberg tragedy.

No longer is there the unquestioning acceptance of the motives and morality of our highest officials. What was unthinkable in the 1950's is now one of the nation's primary concerns. Today, the challenge inherent in Justice Hugo Black's protest to the executions of the Rosenbergs without a review of the Record by the Supreme Court, is one we are no longer hesitant to accept. Let us therefore "review the Record. . . ."

JOHN WEXLEY
October, 1977

CHRONOLOGY OF EVENTS

1945

Aug. 6   First atomic bomb dropped on Hiroshima; dead: 78,150.

Aug. 9   Second atomic bomb dropped on Nagasaki; dead: 73,884.

1949

Sept. 23   President Truman announces that an atomic explosion had taken place in the Soviet Union.

1950

Feb. 3   Dr. Klaus Fuchs, German-born British nuclear physicist, arrested in England on basis of a voluntary confession that he had transmitted atomic information to the Soviet Union. Fuchs tried and sentenced to fourteen years, March 1.

May 23   Harry Gold, a hospital laboratory chemist in Philadelphia, arrested on basis of a voluntary confession that he had been the courier in the United States in 1944–45 between Fuchs and Russian Vice Consul Yakovlev, who had returned to Russia in 1946.

June 15	David Greenglass, a machinist, formerly a soldier at the Los Alamos Atomic Project, arrested for having been an accomplice of Gold in 1945.
June 16	Julius Rosenberg, owner of a small machine shop in New York City, brother-in-law of Greenglass, questioned by FBI and released the same day.
June 25	Outbreak of the Korean War.
July 17	Julius Rosenberg arrested on charges of having conspired to commit espionage with Greenglass and Gold in 1944–45.
July 29	Abraham Brothman, a chemical engineer and former employer of Gold, arrested on charges that he and Gold had conspired to obstruct justice by lying to a Grand Jury during an investigation in 1947.
Aug. 11	Ethel Rosenberg, wife of Julius and sister of David Greenglass, arrested on same charges as her husband.
Aug. 18	Morton Sobell, former college classmate of Julius Rosenberg, while on a trip to Mexico with wife and children, abducted by Mexican secret police and "deported" across the Texas border, arrested by the FBI on charges of having conspired to commit espionage with Rosenberg.
Nov. 13 to 22	Trial of Brothman before Judge Irving R. Kaufman. Prosecution: U.S. Attorney Irving H. Saypol, assisted chiefly by Roy M. Cohn. Principal witnesses: Harry Gold and Elizabeth Bentley. Brothman convicted and sentenced to seven years on Nov. 28.

| Dec. 9 | Harry Gold sentenced in Philadelphia to thirty years. |

| Mar. 6-29 | Trial of Rosenbergs and Sobell before Judge Irving R. Kaufman. Prosecution: Saypol, etc. Principal witnesses: David and Ruth Greenglass; Max Elitcher, a former classmate of Rosenberg; Gold, and Bentley. Verdict: Guilty. |
| Apr. 5 | Ethel and Julius Rosenberg sentenced to death in the electric chair by Judge Kaufman, with date of execution set for week of May 21, 1951. Morton Sobell sentenced to thirty years. David Greenglass sentenced to fifteen years on April 6. |

1952

Feb. 25	Conviction of the Rosenbergs and Sobell affirmed by U.S. Circuit Court of Appeals. (Judges Swan, Chase, Frank.)
Oct. 13	Supreme Court declines to review the case, Justice Black dissenting.
Nov. 21	Judge Kaufman fixes second date of execution for week of Jan. 12, 1953.
Dec. 10	Motion for a hearing for a new trial based on evidence of perjury and unfair trial argued before Judge Sylvester Ryan. Motion denied; stay of execution denied.
Dec. 30	Motion to reduce sentence argued before Judge Kaufman on grounds that sentences were "cruel and excessive" and unprecedented since charges were not treason and indictment did not include "intent . . . to injure the U.S."

Dec. 31	Court of Appeals affirms Judge Ryan's denial of motion for hearing for a new trial.

1953

Jan. 2	Judge Kaufman denies motion for reduction of sentence.
Jan. 5	Motion for stay of execution denied by Court of Appeals.
Jan. 10	Petition for Executive Clemency to Truman; executions stayed until five days after determination by President.
Jan. 20	Truman leaves office, and petition for clemency passes to Eisenhower.
	Clemency appeals in U.S. attain unprecedented height of three million letters and telegrams to White House.
	Direct appeals by Dr. Albert Einstein, Dr. Harold C. Urey, 3,000 Protestant ministers, etc.
Feb. 11	Eisenhower refuses clemency.
Feb. 13	Appeals by Pope Pius XII for clemency renewed.
Feb. 16	Kaufman sets third execution date for week of March 9.
Feb. 17	Court of Appeals headed by Judge Learned Hand stays execution pending action by Supreme Court.
Feb. 22	New York *Times* survey reports Rosenberg case "TOP ISSUE IN FRANCE." Appeals for clemency from clergy, statesmen, scientists, writers from many countries.
May 25	Supreme Court declines for second time to review case, Justices Black and Douglas dissenting.

May 29	Kaufman sets fourth execution date for week of June 15.
June 8	Motion for a hearing for a new trial argued before Judge Kaufman on basis of new evidence proving perjury and subornation of perjury by the prosecution. Kaufman refuses to grant hearing that same afternoon; refuses stay of execution.
June 10	Motion for new trial argued before Circuit Court of Appeals. Kaufman decision affirmed and stay of execution denied.
June 15	Supreme Court declines for third time to review case and refuses stay of execution. Vote is 5 to 4.
June 16	New appeal, on ground that Atomic Energy Act of 1946 should have applied to the case, filed with Justice Douglas. Second clemency petition to Eisenhower.
June 17	Douglas grants stay of execution stating that substantial question is involved whether defendants were correctly tried under the Espionage Act of 1917.
June 18	Clemency appeals to Eisenhower by organizations representing millions in England, Germany, Italy, France, etc.
	Mounting protests at U.S. embassies by thousands. Direct appeals to Eisenhower from President Auriol of France, Edouard Herriot, former Premier Faure, etc.
	Supreme Court called into unprecedented session. Justices recalled from vacations to hear argument on Douglas stay regarding applicability of Atomic Energy Act. Execution automatically

delayed pending Supreme Court decision.

June 19   Supreme Court vacates Douglas stay by vote of 6 to 3 (Frankfurter joining Black and Douglas). Eisenhower rejects second clemency plea.

Execution of the Rosenbergs, scheduled for 11 P.M., moved up before sundown to avoid desecration of the Sabbath.

Union Square meeting of 10,000 people to protest execution of the Rosenbergs. Simultaneously, in many nations, hundreds of thousands voice last-minute protest.

Julius Rosenberg executed at 8:02 P.M.

Ethel Rosenberg executed at 8:08 P.M.

June 20   Published text of Justice Black's dissent discloses that the Supreme Court "had never reviewed the record of this trial and therefore never affirmed the fairness of this trial."

THE JUDGMENT
OF JULIUS
AND ETHEL
ROSENBERG

THE LETTER "W"

If the reader should wonder at this strange title, it may be well to start with its strange source—a secret "memorandum" kept under tight lock for almost two decades by the Internal Security Division of the Department of Justice until its recent release under the Freedom of Information Act.

To begin with, since the memorandum is an unprecedented attack directed chiefly, as stated, against "the book entitled *The Judgment of Julius and Ethel Rosenberg* by John Wexley," one might say, it amounts to a clandestine war declared and conducted by the Attorney General of the United States upon an American writer's published work in direct violation of the First Amendment.

The formidable document was prepared by an intradepartmental team working almost a full year (November 13, 1956, to November 7, 1957) under the supervision of one Benjamin F. Pollack, a "veteran Justice Department attorney," and has become known as the "Pollack report."

In the report, we find its genesis explained in these unabashed terms: "The ensuing memorandum has been prepared in reply to an advertisement in the Book Review Section of the New York *Times* of November 4, 1956" which "contained favorable comment on the [Wexley] book" and which "gave concern to the office of the Attorney General. . . ."

As an example of this "favorable comment" the report quotes from the "commendation" given the book by Elmer Davis "of the American Broadcasting Company and wartime Chief of the OWI":

Assuming that the record is here correctly cited (and I have no reason to suppose that it is not) I cannot believe the testimony of Elitcher and the Greenglasses, or much if any of that of Harry Gold.

Thus, there was the concern of the Attorney General that the famous commentator (among the other notables quoted in the advertisement *) not only accepted the trial record documentation in this book as correct, but had found *all* of the principal Government witnesses unworthy of belief. Accordingly, we see the Attorney General's express order given to the Internal Security Division:

to make a thorough study of the Wexley book and to make an appropriate reply thereto . . . to determine the accuracy of the serious charges made in that book against high government executives and judicial officials.

Moreover, as the report warns,

In view of the pressure exerted by our representatives in foreign governments where the Wexley book has been prominently circularized, it was considered advisable to make a study and prepare a report, the contents of which would serve to counteract such propaganda.

Whereupon, after elaborating on the effect the book was having on a "great many good-hearted but gullible people who did not know the facts or the real issues," we find Mr. Pollack concluding Chapter 1 (the first of 51 chapters) as follows:

Since Wexley's book is the prime weapon in the hands of the Communists it is essential that it be analyzed extensively. Such an analysis will prove that it is a Communist propaganda instrument of the most diabolical type.

One might argue that this is undeserved tribute, placing this book in the same Satanic league with the writings of Marx, Lenin, and Mao, but no matter. As for our title, "The Letter 'W,' " it has been borrowed

---

* Lord Bertrand Russell; Judge James H. Wolfe, former Justice of the Supreme Court of Utah; Judge Patrick O'Brien, former Attorney General of Michigan; and Professor Francis D. Wormuth of the *Western Political Quarterly*.

from Mr. Pollack's explanation in the report: "In referring to Wexley's book, the letter 'W' will be used."

•

In 1957, when I first learned of this report, I never dreamed I would live to see it, or that there would ever be exposed the most serious political scandal in American history—Watergate. Which brings us to a Now and Then comparison between the frames of reference we must deal with in understanding the Cold-War hysteria which produced the Rosenberg case. In the original edition of this book, there is a prophetic passage regarding the death sentences imposed by Judge Kaufman and "the unreasoning hate which dictated his entire conduct of the trial."

Evidently, it does not occur to Kaufman that some decades hence Americans might tire of the tension diet of McCarthyism and . . . that the dogma of fear engulfing the country in the 50's might happily be dispelled by the 60's and 70's.

To be sure, not entirely dispelled, but what is thinkable now was then unthinkable. History, to an astonishing extent, has become my collaborator, and much of what I had been forced to conclude (lacking the power of subpoena) as to what actually had taken place behind forbidden doors has been compellingly confirmed. Today, old assumptions about the morality of our intelligence agencies are no longer valid. Today, we are no longer shocked to learn that the CIA was allied to the Mafia in conspiring to assassinate leaders of other countries, or that "Lawlessness under the guise of national security [was] almost commonplace" during the period involved in the Rosenberg case. As reported in the New York *Times* of October 10, 1975:

Forgery of letters, anonymous threats and other forms of coercion became standard tools in the FBI's counter-intelligence operations.

At the Watergate hearings, we observed the U.S. Attorney General and the President's chief advisors

3

justifying their criminal acts by the attitude expressed by one of the White House aides: "Anyone who opposes us we will destroy. As a matter of fact, anyone who doesn't support us we will destroy."

All of this was only a few years ago, and we are still numbed by the extent of the deception revealed by these officials in their own taped phrases. Even so, it is difficult to convey what it was like a quarter-century ago during that period of national paranoia which began with the outbreak of the Korean War and provided the basis for our slide into the quagmire of the Vietnam War.

During that period, the height of McCarthyism, to entertain any suspicion openly of a J. Edgar Hoover was akin to the archaic definition of Treason in the English Courts—"imagining the death of the King." How could one dare suggest that the United States Attorney, Irving Saypol, honored as the "nation's Number One legal hunter of top Communists," or that his chief assistants, Myles Lane and Roy Cohn, would do anything questionable to the Rosenbergs' convictions? These were all honorable men, trusted watchdogs guarding our freedoms, vigilantly sniffing out the enemy within.

In short, it was a time when most Americans, manipulated into dread fear of an inevitable atomic attack by the Soviet Union, came to accept everything stated by the Government as gospel truth. It was a time of illusion and myth. There was a desperate need for implicit faith in the Establishment. We had just "lost" China, and World Communism was still regarded as monolithic. It would be many years before the first loss of innocence, before the rebellious wearing of long hair, the burning of Watts, and the killings of the Kent students, before the revelations in the Pentagon Papers and the duplicity surrounding the Gulf of Tonkin Resolution. Not until the late sixties did Senator Fulbright, its author, realize that he and the nation had been "had."

All of these things we know now would have been inconceivable in the 1950's; all of this was before the White House Horrors and the "Fall." And yet. much could have been perceived even then, despite the

4

blinding malaise of anti-Communist paranoia which Richard Nixon had been exploiting throughout his career. As Vice-President, this was his apologia for McCarthyism on television as footnoted in this book from a report in *Time,* March 22, 1954:

Some Red-hunters feel that Communists deserve to be shot like rats. Well, I'll agree . . . but remember this. . . . You have to shoot straight, because . . . you might hit someone else who's trying to shoot rats, too.

It was, ironically, Nixon falling victim to his own demagogy which led eventually to his undoing, but even in 1957, this "ideological fervor" became the dominant theme in the Pollack report. There is, perhaps, no better illustration of this, the "real issue" in the Rosenberg-Sobell case, than in Pollack's own words:

A major specific charge that Wexley makes is that the admission of evidence of Communist sympathies . . . was unfair and unjust because it . . . inflamed the jury against the defendants. . . .

And here is Pollack's justification of such evidence, drawing the conclusion that Julius Rosenberg and Morton Sobell, as college students, were *already* committed to a career of espionage:

There is ample proof in the Departmental files that they were both active members of the Young Communist League at the City College of New York. Wouldn't that be an indication of their possible conspiracy to act further together in the cause of Moscow?

To help complete our frame of reference, it may be worth noting Pollack's repeated objections with regard to illegal FBI practices:

To be sure, the FBI needs no defense on the question of concocting evidence, but just the same, brazen statements by Wexley casts doubt on every word in his book.

The charge of coercion and inducement is invented by Wexley for the purpose of slanting the facts. . . . Wexley charges wire-tapping by the FBI. There is no proof of wire-tapping anywhere. It is a fabrication on Wexley's part.

Such loyalty to his FBI associates may be commendable but it was not blind. What we know today concerning the "standard tools" used by the FBI for the past "30 years" was old hat in the Internal Security Division at the time of the Pollack report.

In the opening chapter of this book, "The Anatomy of Frame-up," we have analyzed the various elements which comprise a political frame-up. With "so many participants" and with the political atmosphere conditioning them, there need not be any "master-mind" deliberately plotting a grand strategy. Each participant, wed to the morality that anything done to the enemy (suspected or accused Communist) is legitimate, plays his little part, frequently with no conscious intent to do anything wrong.

Fortunately, with confessions from all those "loyal zealots" who played their parts in the Watergate conspiracy, often without specific orders, not only has history confirmed this analysis, but there is also the long-hidden Pollack report shedding further light on the cover-up in the Rosenberg case.

•

When we recall the traumatic events which led to the Nixon downfall, there come to mind those impassioned denials of wrongdoing by Nixon's defenders. The "smoking gun" was what they demanded. And then, suddenly it was disclosed: the secret tape in which Nixon himself is heard agreeing to use the CIA to halt the FBI's investigation of Watergate.

Ever since I first learned of the Pollack report, I had been perplexed. It had been brought to public attention in a most curious way, by giving "a single publication exclusive rights to exploit it." I am quoting this from an editorial of November 2, 1957, in *The Nation,* called "Preview of a White Paper." It was referring to a cover story published on October 29, 1957, in the magazine *Look* titled: "Exclusive: The Atomic Bomb and Those Who Stole It."

In the *Look* article, this book had been singled out as the principal target for attack with the implied promise that the Justice Department was ready to "reopen the files to prove again that the Rosenbergs were justly convicted," and that "previously unreleased facts" would shortly be made public. The article was written by one Bill Davidson, who says that he "worked along with Pollack during much of his investigation" and that

Look was given access to the extensive data that went into the Government report, of which this article is an exclusive preview.

Exclusive preview! Surely an explicit statement, obviously made with official approval. One would expect that the report would soon be released in its entirety or, as *The Nation* demanded, that copies would be made "available for inspection by the press."

However, despite the fanfare, the promised White Paper was never released for objective examination. Why, I often wondered, with all that advance ballyhoo, had the report been kept under such tight wrap? Now, finally, we have the answer: Like the secret Nixon tape, the Pollack report reveals its own "smoking gun." There, buried amidst all the rhetoric and pejorative accusation, is the tell-tale evidence of the cover-up so determinedly concealed for over two decades.

To demonstrate this, let us turn to the most crucial area in the Government's case, the one dealing with our original findings of the "FBI-inspired forgery" of Harry Gold's hotel registration card and the Santa Fe Railroad timetable documenting that his alleged train trip from Albuquerque to New York City was "impossible" and therefore a "provable perjury."

For our on-the-scene investigation of the Albuquerque episode, the chapter "All Is Not Gold . . ." will provide a step-by-step analysis. Concerning the hotel registration card, we will come to that presently, but right now let us see why Gold's return trip to New York City was impossible.

According to his testimony at the Rosenberg trial, he had taken a train from Albuquerque on Sunday, June 3, 1945, which arrived in Chicago on Tuesday, June 5. However, his prearranged rendezvous with his Russian superior in New York City had been for that Tuesday evening, precisely at 10 P.M. To verify this,

I had obtained a Santa Fe Railroad timetable of June, 1945, and by checking the connecting trains to New York, found, as indicated in this book:

That no train leaving Chicago on Tuesday . . . could have gotten Gold into New York before June 6, or Wednesday morning!

In short, then, Harry Gold's testimony about his June 5 rendezvous with Yakovlev, during which he swears he transmitted the secret information from Fuchs and Greenglass, *is a provable perjury!*

Now, to clarify why this is the most crucial area in the Rosenberg case: First, because Gold was the *only* witness produced by the prosecution to corroborate the Greenglass testimony that a crime involving atomic espionage had indeed taken place. Second, because it was *only* in Gold's testimony regarding the famous "Jello-box" * meeting with the Greenglasses that the name "Julius" was brought in to connect the Rosenbergs to the alleged conspiracy.

In other words, we are dealing here *not* with some minor discrepancy, but with the most gaping hole in the Government's case—the alleged episode which begins with Gold receiving the atomic secrets in Albuquerque and ends with their delivery to his Russian contact in New York. That it goes to the very heart of the case can be seen in the record as the chief prosecutor, Saypol, sums it up for the jury:

Harry Gold, who furnished the absolute corroboration of the testimony of the Greenglasses, forged the necessary link in the chain that points indisputably to the guilt of the Rosenbergs.

The necessary link? Or, as analysed in this book, the *weak* link in the so-called chain and the one which succeeded in shattering both the chain and the complacency of J. Edgar Hoover, who, only a few days after the book's publication, considered punitive action. In the inventory of the FBI files on the Rosenberg case, there is this item:

_____
* Although the actual trademark is "Jell-O," we have followed the simplified version "Jello" as spelled in the court record and in the *Columbia Law Review*.

Memo dated May 27, 1955, from Director FBI to AAG [Assistant Attorney General] Olney re possible libel in Wexley book on Rosenbergs.

And, judging from several similar items in the inventory, there can be little doubt that the book, and its exposure of Gold as a classic case of "pseudologia phantastica" (or, more simply, a compulsive liar acting out his own phantasies), had opened a can of fish-hooks at FBI headquarters. For on August 22, 1955, we find no less than *137* pages of:

Photostatic copies of excerpts of the book, "The Judgment of Julius and Ethel Rosenberg," sent from FBI Director to AAG Olney.

What evidently contributed to Mr. Hoover's concern were not only our findings dealing with Gold's unbelievable testimony, but also those exposing his psychopathic history.* For, after all, it was Hoover who was chiefly responsible for the public's acceptance of Gold as the self-proclaimed American courier for Dr. Fuchs.

To proceed chronologically from Hoover's memo of May 27, 1955, something else happened to give him even greater concern. Only one day after this book's official publication date on June 16, 1955, it had served to destroy Gold's credibility as a *bona fide* spy before a Federal jury in Dayton, Ohio. On that day, Gold, the chief prosecution witness in a perjury trial of a former air-force lieutenant colonel named Benjamin Smilg, was cross-examined and, with the aid of this book, completely discredited.

There is a dramatic story of how the book, fresh off the press, was rushed down from Cleveland to Dayton by a young man driving through the night to deliver it to Smilg's attorney, a veteran criminal lawyer named Michael F. Hopkins; how the attorney eagerly studied the chapters dealing with Gold until dawn so that he could confront him the next day in cross-examination; how Hopkins made a laughing-

* See *Addenda* following Chapter 3 with reference to the official psychiatric summary of Gold made in 1950 reported in the New York *Times,* December 6, 1975.

stock of Gold by questioning him about his phantasied wife and two children, about an imaginary real-estate man who had stolen his wife's affections, about Gold's poignant visits to watch his children from afar as they played in the schoolyard; and how all of this was sheer fiction told by Gold to associates and friends over a period of many years. And further, quoting from passages I had selected from the Brothman trial during which Gold had admitted his prodigious talents at deception,* how Gold was asked:

Q. [Hopkins]: Did you make this statement: "It is a wonder that steam didn't come out of my ears at times"?
A. [Gold]: It really is remarkable that it didn't occur.
Q. Because of the lies you told?
A. I had gotten involved into one of the doggonest tangles. . . .
Q. You lied for a period of six years?
A. I lied for a period of sixteen years, not alone six.

Space does not permit several other points in the book with which Hopkins hit Gold, but the Dayton jury, fortunately hearing what the jury at the Rosenberg trial had *never* heard, returned a verdict of acquittal. Gold's credibility had been destroyed. Never again did the Justice Department dare to trot him out to convict anyone on the "enemies lists" of the fifties, or thereafter. The risk was too great that some defense counsel might delve deeper, might cross-examine Gold concerning the Hilton hotel card and the Santa Fe timetable, and thereby set off the keg of dynamite Mr. Hoover and so many uneasy officials were sitting on.

To continue our chronology, here is what happened as a result of the debacle in that Dayton courthouse. The Senate Internal Security Sub-Committee (also known as the Eastland Committee) had become dis-

---

* See Chapter 3 describing the Brothman trial of November, 1950, the "try-out" for the Rosenberg trial four months later, with Kaufman the same judge, Saypol the same prosecutor, and Gold the star witness.

turbed about Mr. Hoover's "atom spy courier." Not only because of Gold's admitted lying for some sixteen years, but specifically because of the "impossible" train trip. Since some or all of the Senators on the committee were aware of this book, many copies of which had been sent to leading members of Congress by the National Committee to Secure Justice for Morton Sobell, it may be assumed that the significance of the timetable (with its photostat in the Appendix) * was brought to their attention either by Senator Eastland or the committee's chief counsel, Robert Morris.

In any event, on April 26, 1956, Harry Gold was ordered by the Senate committee to be brought from his cell in Lewisburg Federal Prison by U.S. marshals to be interrogated in Washington. And, as we will see shortly from the Senate transcript, there was an obvious invitation given Gold to have him patch up the hole he had dug himself into at the Rosenberg trial. However, let us return to the "exclusive preview" in *Look*.

As a measure of how vital the timetable challenge was to the Justice Department, we see it presented by *Look* as its opening assault on "one of the main points in Wexley's book":

Gold testified that he obtained information about the atomic bomb . . . [and] left Albuquerque . . . for New York by train on Sunday evening, June 3, 1945. He testified that he then gave the information to Soviet Vice Consul Anatoli Yakovlev in New York City on Tuesday, June 5.

Wexley builds much of his case around these dates. Using the evidence of railroad timetables, he insists that Gold could not possibly have reached New York by train before Wednesday morning (June 6)—and that therefore his entire testimony was concocted and invalid.

However, it took Pollack exactly three days to demolish this point in the Wexley argument. First, Pollack noted that Gold never testified that he made the entire trip by train.

Let us pause right here to note that Gold's testimony at the Rosenberg trial clearly implies that his *entire*

* See Appendix 11.

11

trip to and from New Mexico was made by train. There is no mention of traveling any other way, save by bus between Santa Fe and Albuquerque. Similarly, in J. Edgar Hoover's May, 1951, *Reader's Digest* account based on "the confidential files of the FBI," there is not the slightest hint of any plane travel.

Let the reader, as we proceed, bear this in mind. For, as will now be shown, Gold's testimony before the Senate committee confirmed that his alleged return to New York City was *entirely* by train. Here is his *sworn* testimony taken verbatim from pages 1035–1036 of the Senate report ("Scope of Soviet Activity in the United States") published by the Government Printing Office in December, 1956. Gold is describing what he did after receiving the atomic secrets from Greenglass in Albuquerque on June 3, 1945:

MR. GOLD: . . . And when I returned to New York City, I told Yakovlev about it.

MR. MORRIS: Now, before you go back to New York, Mr. Gold, will you tell us what Greenglass gave you?

MR. GOLD: He gave me a number of sheets containing at least 2 or 3 sketches and a few pages of explanatory material.

MR. MORRIS: And you took [this] with the material that Fuchs gave you and proceeded back to New York?

MR. GOLD: That is correct.

MR. MORRIS: Did you go by train or did you fly?

MR. GOLD: I went by train.

MR. MORRIS: And when you returned to New York, what did you do with the material?

MR. GOLD: Wait now. I've got to get this straight. Some of these—you see, I was over this about 6 years ago. The events actually happened 11 years ago, and there is a tendency to blur.

What I want to say now is my present recollection. I want to say, as I recall it now, it is certainly not going to be an exact duplication as far as the minutest details go. I am just trying to think, how did I get out of Santa Fe that particular time? [*Note:* This should read Albuquerque—not Santa Fe.] That particular time I went by train. I hated waiting, but I went back by train. I am trying to remember. I remember why I didn't fly. I was running short of funds.

MR. MORRIS: Now, did you have a prearranged meeting with Yakovlev back in New York?

MR. GOLD: Yes, we did.

Not only do we see these thrice repeated responses from Gold that he "went back by train" to New York, but also, his explanation: "I remember why I didn't fly. I was running short of funds." This last point is almost exactly the same as that in the *Reader's Digest* article by Hoover concerning Gold's trip to New Mexico, that he "was low, as usual, on funds."

And so, here we have Gold sticking closely to his original tale given at the Rosenberg trial about the "impossible" trip by *train*. Whether or not Gold was shown the timetable is of little consequence. To inquire into the intricate workings of a mind like his would be fruitless. As suggested in this book, a pathological liar, with Gold's admitted history of successful deception, comes to believe "his own phantasies almost as promptly" as he invents them.

In any event, having seen Gold's sworn denial of any plane travel, let us turn back to the *Look* cover-up as Davidson triumphantly presents Pollack's "painstaking detective skill":

He visited Gold in his cell . . . and was told by the ex-spy that he had traveled by train only from Albuquerque to Chicago on the Santa Fe Railroad's *California Limited*.

From Chicago, said Gold, he took a United Air Lines plane to Washington "at about 9:30" and completed the trip to New York by train, leaving Washington late in the afternoon. A check of the FBI files confirmed to Pollack that this was the same story Gold had told on July 10, 1950, after he was arrested.

Let us examine this last bit of sleight of hand. First, since Pollack had available at the Justice Department *all* the FBI files on Gold, why did he need "three days to demolish . . . the Wexley argument"? Second, how could Gold have told the FBI in 1950 that he had flown from Chicago, when in 1956, he swears that he did not fly because he was "running short of funds"? One can only conclude that this "same story," purportedly discovered in the FBI files *after* Pollack had refreshed Gold's memory, belongs in the same category with the forged hotel card presented in court in 1951 to prove Gold's presence in Albuquerque in 1945.

Pollack's next step, according to *Look,* was to check with United Air Lines. Yes, he was told, there had been a flight leaving Chicago for Washington at 9:30 A.M. on Tuesday, June 5, 1945.

This was the last piece of evidence that Pollack needed to complete his puzzle. . . . By taking the train from Washington at 4:00 P.M., he [Gold] reached New York in plenty of time for his meeting with Soviet Vice Consul Yakovlev at 10 P.M. that night.

One can easily be misled by this attempt to counteract the railroad timetable with a plane schedule. The fact that planes were flying from Chicago to Washington in 1945 is *not* "evidence"; there exists no vestige of proof that Gold had been aboard one of them. Why did not Pollack ask Gold in his cell to explain his Senate testimony that the trip had been entirely by train? No such normal question can be found in the *Look* version or in the Pollack report. Indeed, we do not know for a fact that the interview with Gold as described by Pollack actually took place. There is no official record, and Gold was not under oath. On the other hand, we do have the official record of Gold's sworn statements before the Senate committee.

Here, then, emerges one of the important answers to why the Justice Department report was never made public. It contains the Senate testimony showing that Gold did *not* fly, that he traveled *only* by train. In other words, the "smoking gun." It had to be buried. Had it been released to the press, it would have invited comparison with the trial record, with the *Look* version, and with this book. In short, by this unique arrangement with *Look* to present a quasi-official version of the report, the Justice Department could have its cake and eat it. It could keep the smoking gun concealed and, at the same time, plug the gaping hole revealed by the timetable.

And yet, sheer common sense exposes the *Look* version of Gold's detour by plane as but another fiction glibly added to that in his testimony at the Rosenberg trial. For example, why is there no mention of any effort by Gold to fly *directly* to New York? The answer is obvious. It would have been too easy—too pat. As in a TV thriller, there had to be some difficulties the spy had to overcome in his dramatic race against time for the split-second rendezvous in New York.

But it was still wartime in June of 1945. Both plane and train travel during World War II presented the most serious delays and uncertainty. Big-city airports were jammed with waiting passengers, sleeping on benches and floor, hoping to obtain a seat. And even when their turn came, the seat was in jeopardy. According to a recent check with a District Operation Manager who had worked at the Midway Airport in Chicago during those years, I found these facts confirmed as follows:

You were subject to a priority system and could be bumped just before departure for a higher-priority passenger. As I recall it was an A, B, C, D system:

"A" was more or less Presidential orders; "B" was civilian or military on urgent business; "C" was, I believe, emergency military travel and "D" was for everyone civilian or military just hoping to get a seat. The priority office, I believe, was run by the military and had offices in most large cities.

How, then, could Gold, as Pollack claimed, so easily and immediately obtain a seat on that 9:30 A.M. flight to Washington, D.C.? Indeed, such a plane would be carrying even more VIP's, government and military officials, than a plane to New York, and the planes were much smaller than those of today. Moreover, both departure and arrival were, more often than not, delayed, sometimes for hours. As to Gold's alleged train trip from Albuquerque to Chicago, few trains, if any, left on time and most of them were late in arriving. It is even doubtful that the *California Limited* arrived in Chicago at the scheduled time of 7:30 that wartime Tuesday morning.*

•

Concerning Gold's alleged visit to Albuquerque, which is analyzed in ensuing chapters, let us focus on the famous Hilton registration card and see how the Pollack report deals with our charge that it was nothing less than an "FBI-inspired forgery." Here is how Pollack presents Gold's trial testimony describing his arrival in Albuquerque on Saturday evening, June 2, 1945. Finding the Greenglasses out for the evening,

Gold then *sought a hotel* in which to spend the night. He was *unable to get a hotel room but did find space for sleeping* in the hallway of a rooming house.
He did however, obtain a room at the Hilton Hotel in Albuquerque, and registered there on Sunday morning, June 3, 1945. [Emphasis added.]

The above emphasized phrases are *not* in the court record; they are Pollack's inventions. In our chapter "All Is Not Gold," the actual testimony can be seen:

[*Gold*]: I stayed that night [Saturday]—I finally managed to obtain a room in a hallway of a rooming house and then *on Sunday morning* I registered at the Hotel Hilton.
Q. Now, did you register under your own name?
A. Yes, I did. [Emphasis added.]

Why does Pollack alter the record? There is a subtle purpose here. By presenting Gold as desperate to find a hotel room and his being forced to sleep on a cot or even on a pad on the floor that night, he is trying to explain away our charge that the alleged registration at the Hilton the very next morning in Gold's *own name* was needless and dangerous. Be-

* In a 1975-released FBI memo of July 22, 1950, containing wartime letters written by Ruth Greenglass to David, we find detailed descriptions of *her* difficulties, not only in obtaining a "next to impossible" coach seat from Chicago to Albuquerque, but also during her return trip on the *same California Limited* which was *10 hours late*. (See *Addenda* to Chapter 16.)

cause, as shown in our analysis, if Gold was the veteran spy he claims to have been, then:

1. He knew he must pick up the data from Greenglass early that same Sunday morning and hurry to catch the "Chief" leaving at 9 A.M.—the *only* fast train which would make connections in Chicago for his rendezvous in New York.

2. He knew any delay was dangerous since he was carrying on his person "hot" material (the folder containing atomic secrets received from Dr. Fuchs the previous day in Santa Fe, and the envelope of Russian money, $500 in cash, to pay to Greenglass).

3. He knew that Albuquerque, nearest large city to the Los Alamos Atomic Project, was crawling with CID (Counter-Intelligence) agents disguised as taxi drivers, bellhops, and hotel clerks, all on the alert for any suspicious stranger—and that a highly trained spy does not make himself conspicuous.

4. He knew from his instructions that Greenglass would have the information ready and that, with the visit to pick up this additional hot material, he must leave Albuquerque as quickly as possible.

5. He knew, most importantly, his own strict rule (as he testified at the Rosenberg trial) never to use his own name or true residence.

And yet, in spite of all this and much more, he registers at the Hotel Hilton very early Sunday morning, at a time when the hotel lobby would be almost empty and he would be most conspicuous—a stranger with a wrinkled suit and no baggage. Would a trained spy, as Gold describes himself, take all these unnecessary risks and, to cap it all, register with his own name and Philadelphia address? Little wonder that Pollack admits:

The writer of this memorandum [Pollack] was *anxious* to know why Gold registered at the hotel when he was planning to see the Greenglasses that day and leave for the East on the same day. [Emphasis added.]

One can well understand this anxiety. Although, fully aware of the above reasons why Gold should not have registered (especially in his own name), we see

17

that Pollack carefully refrains from mentioning them. In any event, with his visit to Gold in his cell on July 10, 1957, we now find the *only* reasons ever given by *any* government official to explain Gold's alleged registration at the Hotel Hilton. Here is the first one as Pollack reports it without a blush:

Gold explained that the reason he registered was because he had had no opportunity to wash up at the rooming house so he wanted a hotel room.

Now we see why Pollack invented that "space for sleeping in the hallway." We are supposed to believe there was no available bathroom for Gold to "wash up." Rooming houses in cities as large as Albuquerque are licensed and must have sufficient bathroom facilities. Besides, it was very early on Sunday morning, when most of the roomers would still be fast asleep. Moreover, Gold must have had some breakfast, and almost every coffee shop has a washroom which he could have used without running any risk or signing a registration card.

Evidently, Gold's explanation was too wild to allay Pollack's anxiety (it might not "wash"), and so we are given another reason even wilder:

Furthermore, he [Gold] had hoped to obtain flight reservations from Albuquerque East, in which case he would have spent another night in Albuquerque and he wanted to be sure he would have a hotel room if he had to do so. This seems to be a fairly reasonable explanation. . . .

Seems to be . . . *fairly* reasonable! Why is Pollack so cautious, so reluctant to give unqualified support? Because he knows from the 1956 Senate testimony that Gold was "short of funds" and therefore "didn't fly." Why then, in 1957, should he buy Gold's hope of obtaining "flight reservations from Albuquerque East"? Cause enough for Pollack's uneasiness, but here is more. Why should Gold register using his own name—like a criminal leaving his visiting card at the scene of the crime? (*Note: This question has never been answered in any way by any government official or by anyone defending the Government's case!*) And why should a spy do this *before* he was certain of the flight reservations? The same wartime priorities existed in Albuquerque as in Chicago and with far fewer planes available. Suppose Gold failed to secure a seat the next day? Now the needless and dangerous risk-taking would be compounded. The risk of an extra day in and around the hotel, carrying not only Dr. Fuchs' atomic secrets but also those Greenglass had given him. The risk at the airport where Gold, checking in without baggage and then boarding the plane, would have to pass the closest scrutiny by an under-cover agent suspicious of any strange civilian. The risk that he might be "bumped" and have to wait all night in the airport—a most conspicuous figure. According to Hoover and other sources, "a fat, little man . . . short and chubby . . . mousey . . . swarthy . . . anxious eyes . . . a peculiar slouch . . ."

Every airport, bus and railroad station, according to General Leslie Groves, in charge of the Manhattan Project, was closely watched. Colonel Landsdale, a government witness at the Rosenberg trial, testified, "We took extraordinary measures. . . . We placed undercover agents in all of the surrounding towns."

All of these facts, of course, are avoided by Pollack in this sorry attempt to lay a foundation for Gold's alleged plane trip to Washington. In trying to cover up the hole of the hotel card, he hopes, at the same time, to patch the timetable hole. Actually, these two holes, like many of the moon's craters, are one within the other. The timetable proves that Gold, the "super-spy," would not have registered under any of the given circumstances—while the hotel card, illogically bearing Gold's own name, gives further support to the timetable as "a provable perjury."

Perhaps the best answer to the question why Gold (acting as he allegedly did) was never apprehended in June, 1945, in New Mexico is simply that the little man was never there! And this is precisely what Pollack is forced to deal with as we return to the interrupted portion of the report, where Pollack asks:

This seems to be a fairly reasonable explanation, but what does Wexley say about this?

Here is our reply, which Pollack selected from this book:

. . . It may be stated that there was absolutely no logical reason for Gold to register except the one we have indicated, namely, that the prosecution had no documentary evidence to corroborate Gold's claims, and that it felt it necessary to produce a hotel registration card in order to prove his presence in Albuquerque.

And here is Pollack's disparaging comment: . . . In other words the prosecution, the Department of Justice and the United States Attorney in New York, fabricated this item of evidence, a most absurd and fantastic claim.

Well, here we are—thrown back to the Unthinkable. Here is the knee-jerk response of a loyal member of the team of 1957. One simply did not question the authenticity of Harry Gold as a bona fide spy. The Government said this hotel card was 22-carat gold and that was it.

•

Concerning Pollack's hair-trigger readiness to defend the team, let us turn to his chapter on "The Conduct of the Prosecuting Attorney" which begins with a misquoted statement from this book:

Wexley criticizes the conduct of U.S. Attorney Saypol and contends that he was "a single mastermind, villainously plotting each and every step . . ." (W. 871).

First, the passage from which this excerpt is derived is not on "(W. 871)," but on page 211 in the original edition. Here, it is, with no possible doubt about its meaning:

In our study of modern frame-up we have *decried* the role of a single master-mind, villainously plotting each and every step. . . . *If it were so,* we pointed out, perhaps the frame-up would be more logically constructed or less anarchic. [Emphasis added.]

Thus, an entirely *opposite* meaning is given, but before examining the purpose for the deception, let us solve the mystery of the page reference, "(W. 871)." At first, I had thought it only a printer's typo. Then I remembered the review of this book appearing in the *New York University Law Review* of April, 1956, from which Pollack quotes extensively, omitting, to be sure, its favorable comments.* And it was here that I found the mysterious page reference. For on page 871 of the Law Review is the same excerpt carelessly torn out of context. Thus Pollack, apparently at a loss as to how to defend Saypol, extracts his distortion *not* from this book, but from another distorted excerpt appearing elsewhere. In short, documentation, not only based on *heresay*, but, as the FBI might put it, from "an unreliable source."

However, it is not what Pollack does, but why he does it that makes this sordid effort significant. It is because he is resolved to keep the creaking structure of the Government's case intact no matter what. Indeed, this was the true meaning behind his precise instructions: "to make a thorough study of the Wexley book and to prepare an appropriate reply thereto." And, apparently, what had struck home was the main thrust of our "Anatomy of Frame-up," which, contrary to Pollack's efforts to falsify it, states plainly:

No one single official, not even the prosecutor-in-chief, will risk being the mastermind. . . . Each participant is perfectly aware of the dangers involved should the frame-up be exposed. . . . And it may very well be that those on its periphery, merely acting on instructions, are completely ignorant of the significance of their particular part.

How closely this parallels the Watergate disclosures. Like Pollack, wasn't it John Dean who was ordered to prepare the cover-up memorandum, the "appropriate reply," to all the flap then appearing in the *Washington Post?* Didn't we see each participant stoutly denying responsibility or claiming to have acted on instructions? Indeed, there were those who were honestly ignorant of their involvement and ruefully con-

---

* For further references to Pollack's misuse of this Law Review, see *Addenda* to Chapters 14 and 15.

fessed to having succumbed to the prevailing slogan at that point in time: "If you want to get along, go along."

•

As we gaze up on a clear night, we know that against the starry background of our Galaxy there are several instrumented spacecraft traveling toward the distant planets hundreds of millions of miles from Earth. Others, in earth orbit, are observing the distant suns as well as our own. Indeed, massive space laboratories such as Salyut and Skylab have not only been manned by Soviet and American crews, but they have begun to work closely together. We live in the Space Age.

In 1951, much of what is commonplace today was unimaginable save by science-fiction writers and theoretical physicists. And yet, it was on the basis of testimony concerning the theft of information about a "sky-platform project" by Julius Rosenberg in 1947 that Judge Kaufman found part of his rationale to sentence him and his wife to death.

While we have dealt with this aspect of the case in this book, it was before the Space Age had begun. It is only recently (and with the aid of the Pollack report) that I have discovered documentary proof of the fraudulent nature of this testimony.

To turn to the court record dealing with the death sentences, it would appear that Kaufman was faced with a dilemma in imposing the unprecedented supreme penalty. Even assuming that the Rosenbergs were guilty of conveying the atomic-bomb information to the Russians, the act was supposedly committed during the war years when the Soviet Union was our principle ally. No enemy had been aided or abetted. The crime had not been "to the injury of the United States." Nothing even approaching the crime of treason. How then could Kaufman justify putting to death two American civilians in peacetime for an act which he himself had described as an idealistic one?

The solution was the "postwar evidence" elicited by Roy Cohn from David Greenglass. During conversations held "in privacy" with Julius in 1947, the latter had "told" him of espionage crimes committed *after*

22

World War II, including the stealing of "information about the sky platform." Thus, with testimony uncorroborated by any witness and unsupported by any evidence, Judge Kaufman was provided his rationale. As he put it, the Rosenbergs' activities did not

. . . cease in 1945, but that there was evidence right on down, even during a period when it was then apparent to everybody that we were now dealing with a hostile nation. . . .

And, if during World War II, their act had been motivated by a desire to share the atom-bomb secret with an ally in the common struggle to defeat Hitler, now they had no excuse:

The nature of Russian terrorism is now [in 1951] self-evident. Idealism as a rationale dissolves. . . . If this is your excuse, the error of your ways—must now be obvious.

Asked by Cohn to explain the "sky-platform project," Greenglass replied that Julius had described it as

. . . some large vessel which would be suspended at a point of no gravity between the moon and the earth, and as a satellite, it would spin around the earth.

Even with this primitive description of a space station, in the political atmosphere of 1951, the effect on the jury was deadly. If the theft of our atom-bomb secret was horrendous, how much more so this sky platform? In that year, intercontinental missiles (ICBM's) were years off in the future. While our long-range planes could drop atomic bombs on Soviet cities, the enemy had no such capability. Now, however, with the plans of our sky platform stolen, there loomed the nightmare of Soviet space stations laden with nuclear cargoes to be dropped on us at will from an invulnerable height "between the moon and the earth"!

How could any of the jurors know that no such sky platform *project* had any reality in 1947, the time of the alleged espionage? Or that it would not approach reality for *two decades* after the trial. Not until the Titan and Centaur rockets were developed to provide enough thrust could our first space station, Skylab, be placed in orbit in late 1972. Moreover, the modern computer, without which no space station could function, was still in an embryonic stage in 1947. In other words, while scientists everywhere knew that artificial satellites had become theoretically possible, no technology existed in 1947 to make such a project realistic. Thus the so-called sky platform project was nothing but a deliberate shocker designed to heighten the importance of the "postwar evidence."

Indeed, in his report, Pollack finds "the sky platform project" vital enough to devote a special section to it. In another section dealing with "*Julius Rosenberg's* postwar espionage" he refers to it as "a government project." [Emphasis added.] We will soon come to the significance of this emphasis, but first a few questions regarding Kaufman and his claims to having searched his conscience for an entire sleepless week before passing sentence.

During this week, according to the New York *Times* of April 6, 1951, Kaufman went "several times . . . to his synagogue seeking spiritual guidance." The questions are these: If there was no prior understanding between Saypol and Kaufman concerning the required postwar evidence, what was his reaction to the startling allegation about the theft of the sky-platform project? Would there not have been an inward gasp, if not in alarm, then in sheer wonder? Instead of seeking spiritual guidance from on high, should he not have called into his chambers Messrs. Saypol and Cohn and asked: Were there really any secret plans to construct such a sky platform? Had Saypol checked with government experts concerning the validity of the testimony? Would he not have said, "Look, gentlemen, if these defendants are to be executed on evidence of espionage taking place *after* the war, then I must be sure that this space project was a viable one and that the stolen information would be of significant value to an enemy."

Evidently, however, impatience to impose the death sentences was overriding. It was enough that the jury had believed the sky platform testimony and, considering all the other evidence presented at the trial,

24

there was no need to concern himself further. He had enough now to satisfy his conscience.

Returning to that section on the sky platform in the Pollack report, we find the admission that only

. . . theoretically basic research was actually started on such a project at the time Julius was supposed to have talked about it. The project, of course, was secret. (See page 59 of FBI report of March 14, 1951, by James P. Lee, Sec. 5 of Departmental files.)

Theoretical research. In other words, scientists inquiring if such a project was at all feasible at some distant date in the future. And the curious phrasing: "At the time Julius was *supposed* to have talked about it." Apparently, ten years later, Pollack, in 1957, with the beep-beep of Sputnik orbiting the earth every hour, had become somewhat doubtful about the truth of Greenglass' testimony. At any rate, in still another reference to the "sky platform project," Pollack assisted me with a definite clue, namely that

According to an FBI report dated October 10, 1950 . . . the Rand Corporation of California had already performed some research work on it, the results of which were contained in a secret report entitled "Satellite Vehicle Program."

Hence, in the summer of 1975, some twenty-eight years after Julius "was supposed to have" told Greenglass about his theft of the project, I asked Rand if I might see their "Satellite Vehicle Program." My request was courteously granted. In addition to a 332-page copy of a full report prepared in 1946, I was given a more recent article inspired by our 1969 landing on the Moon. Somewhat spoofingly, the article is presented as a "curiosity" piece in the Rand Annual Report of 1969 with the nostalgic title "World Circling Spaceship" and with the following introduction:

The visit, on July 20, 1969, of American astronauts to our nearest planetary neighbor prompted us to look back at some of the early Rand literature on extraterrestrial excursions.

What follows are excerpts from [the] *Preliminary Design of and Experimental World-Circling Spaceship,* issued by Rand on May 2, 1946.

In other words, Man had just walked on the moon and Rand, in its Annual Report, is suggesting what tremendous technological achievements had taken place in the twenty-three years since 1946. How primitive was "the state of the art" in that year is shown in this excerpt from the full report:

In making the decision as to whether or not to undertake construction of such a craft now, it is not inappropriate to view our present situation as similar to that in airplanes prior to the flight of the Wright brothers.

Thus the so-called sky-platform project, far from being anything viable or realistic, was only crystalgazing into the future:

Though the crystal ball is cloudy . . . the most fascinating aspect of successfully launching a satellite would be the pulse quickening stimulation it would give to considerations of interplanetary travel. Whose imagination is not fired by the possibility of . . . traveling to the Moon, to Venus and Mars?
Such thoughts when put on paper now seem like idle fancy. . . . Who would be so bold as to say that this might not come within our time?

Thus we have the answers to the questions Judge Kaufman should have asked before ordering the executions of the Rosenbergs. Nothing resembling the picture of a sky platform from which the enemy could rain death upon us, but only a *proposal* regarding the "possibility" of making a "first step" toward space exploration.
So that, even if we concede that Julius was guilty of having stolen the "Preliminary Design of an Experimental World-Circling Spaceship," and that this act can be defined technically as postwar espionage, there remains the disturbing question: If Judge Kaufman had no moral justification for sending the Rosenbergs to their deaths for atomic espionage committed when the U.S.S.R. was our ally, was there not much less reason to do so on this so-called postwar evidence so minimal that it is scarcely comparable?

Since he could have easily obtained the above information from the prosecution long before the imposition of the sentences on April 5, 1951, *i.e.*, from the FBI reports of October 10, 1950, and March 14, 1951, his claims about seeking spiritual guidance can only be regarded as pious cant. Moreover, as we shall now see, he had agreed to impose the death sentences many weeks *before* the trial had begun!

•

It will be recalled that we drew special attention to Pollack's phrase: "Julius Rosenberg's postwar espionage." Thus Ethel's name was omitted because there is not a word of testimony in the record which shows her to be involved in any crime *after* the war. Why, then, did Kaufman find her equally deserving of death as Julius, the alleged spy-master of a nationwide spy ring? The reasons he gave were that she had encouraged Julius and that since she was two years older she should have known better. Only in the political climate of the fifties could such hollow reasons have been accepted so uncritically.

As demonstrated in this book, the prosecution's determination to "break" Julius continued from the summer of 1950, when he and Ethel were jailed, right up to the time of trial in March, 1951. And the more he resisted, the more "evidence" was extracted from the self-entrapped prosecution witnesses, Elitcher and Greenglass, to make a stronger case. In the Pollack report, we find another indignant protest concerning this step-by-step pressure:

For example, he [Wexley] charges that when Saypol became convinced by the end of 1950 that the Rosenbergs would not break he pressured Elitcher into weaving more and more of the conspiracy. . . .

Earlier in the report, Pollack quotes extensively from the Epilogue in this book, wherein Julius, being led into the death chamber, sees the U.S. marshal waiting with an open telephone line to the Attorney General's office in Washington for the last-minute confession which would save his and Ethel's lives. And here Pollack becomes particularly upset, not with the *fact* that

27

such a macabre deal had been offered, but with the statement that Julius refused "to keep the ball rolling . . . to supply the insatiable demand" for "more and more names."

And now, fuming at such blasphemy ("the viciousness of Wexley's motivation"), Pollack can only find refuge in the euphemism used so frequently by Joe McCarthy: "Does this not sound familiar as Communist leftwing language?"

The reason, of course, that Pollack preferred to avoid any head-on clash was that he *knew* the Government's "torture rack" policy had been formulated officially in a twenty-eight-page document describing a secret meeting in Washington, D.C., on February 8, 1951, almost a month *before* the Rosenberg trial. This document, together with others recently released, also reveals that Judge Kaufman was drawn into the plan on the day before this meeting and, with this disclosure, we have the true reason for his sentencing of Ethel Rosenberg to death.

The high-level meeting had been arranged by the Department of Justice, with Saypol's chief assistant, Myles J. Lane, appearing before the Joint Congressional Committee on Atomic Energy and the Atomic Energy Commission headed by Gordon Dean, to discuss the legal technicalities involved in Greenglass' forthcoming testimony about the atom-bomb secret he allegedly gave to Julius Rosenberg. The problem facing the prosecution, as Lane presented it, was this:

MR. LANE: We feel that . . . the only thing that will break this man Rosenberg is the prospect of a death penalty or getting the chair, plus that if we can convict his wife, too, and give her a stiff sentence of 25 to 30 years, that combination may serve to make this fellow disgorge and give us the information on these other individuals.

THE CHAIRMAN [Sen. McMahon of the Joint Committee]: In other words . . . what you want to do is have Greenglass divulge some now-secret information on the chance that the death penalty would then result to Rosenberg.

MR. LANE: Yes. . . .

MR. DEAN [Chairman of the AEC]: Mr. Lane feels that if you don't prove in this case that he transmitted something very vital as of 1945, as distinguished from simply the population figures of Los Alamos and the names of some scientists there, you certainly couldn't impose a death penalty on the man.

For a full analysis of this document, there is the excellent article by David Gelman in *Newsday*, May 25, 1975, in which he comments on the extraordinary attitude of these prestigious officials, elected and appointed, in discussing the necessity of the death sentence before the evidence had been presented in open court and "as if the verdict itself were a foregone conclusion."

Indeed, it is fair to say that the document is a remarkable reflection of the political mores of the fifties. For not only were these officials indifferent to the presumption of innocence, but such was their readiness to prejudge that the question never entered their minds: What if the Rosenbergs were not guilty—how then could they "disgorge" unknown information concerning unknown individuals?

Lest it be thought this tendency to prejudge dissidents was confined only to government officials, it should be stated that it was shared by the vast majority of the American people. The same bias prevailed everywhere, in the universities, in trade unions, in churches of every denomination, in office and shop, in much of the media and, most visibly, in the nation's capital. Every day, investigative committees were badgering suspected Communists, "fellow-travelers and sympathizers." Unless they would "cooperate" by naming others—old friends, former acquaintances, fellow workers, and even relatives—their "repentance" could not be trusted. At stake were their jobs, their careers, their standing in the community, and, of course, friends and relatives too frightened to phone, visit or invite them. In a word, *fear*. And whether it was the fear of what one's neighbor might think if one voiced any unorthodox opinion or the fear of being hauled in as a traitor should the war in Korea erupt into World War III, the thinking of Judge Kaufman in his sentencing speech was hardly regarded as anything abnormal:

We have evidence of your treachery all around us every day—for the civilian defense activities throughout the nation are aimed at preparing us for an atom bomb attack.

With this picture in mind, let us return to that decisive meeting in Washington for some additional excerpts:

THE CHAIRMAN: Mr. Lane, what kind of fellow is Rosenberg, a tough egg?

MR. LANE: Rosenberg, I would say he is a tough sort of an individual.

REP. COLE: Is Greenglass ready to tell everything . . . . Even that which would involve his sister?

MR. LANE: Yes, but. . . . That is one point where he is reluctant, but he doesn't tell us too much about that, but Greenglass' wife will also testify.

The case is not too strong against Mrs. Rosenberg. But . . . I think it is very important that she be convicted, too, and given a stiff sentence.

MR. DEAN: Defense counsel is a professional Commie, isn't he?

MR. LANE: Emanuel Bloch . . . defended some of the people appearing before the Committees on the Hill . . . he has a sort of interest in lots of people who are Communists. He is one, and . . . there are two of them—defending Sobell. . . .

SENATOR BRICKER: Where did Rosenberg's family come from?

MR. LANE: Russia.

REP. ELSTON: Since counsel [Bloch] has some Communist ties or at least is suspected of it, they [the Russians] already have the information.

MR. DEAN: . . . It looks as though Rosenberg is the king pin of a very large ring, and if there is any way of breaking him by having the shadow of a death penalty over him, we want to do it.

SEN. BRICKER: You mean before the trial?

MR. DEAN: After the trial.

SEN. BRICKER: After the sentence has been imposed, you are dealing with him on the basis of his life.

MR. DEAN: He is a tough man and may not break, but his wife is in this too, and faces a 25 or 30 year sentence, and I think he might talk. . . .

SEN. HICKENLOOPER: . . . I hope that the Commission and the Department of Justice can . . . introduce fully sufficient evidence to hook this fellow with the most severe penalty you can give.

REP. COLE: . . . How much of a penalty [will] Greenglass get?

MR. LANE: He hasn't been sentenced yet. . . .

REP. COLE: He doesn't know where he stands today?

MR. LANE: That is right.

SEN. BRICKER: What is the limit of the penalty that can be imposed upon him?

MR. LANE: Death, the same as the others.

SEN. BRICKER: What judge has been assigned?

MR. LANE: No judge has been assigned. We hope to get the strongest judge assigned.

In a profound sense, what do we find here? Not one of them voices the slightest concern about the propriety of using the electric chair as a device "to hook this fellow" Rosenberg. Not one of them blinks an eye at the thought of giving a woman a twenty-five or thirty-year sentence so that this "tough egg" of a husband might be made to "talk." They learn that "the case is not too strong" against Ethel, that her brother has not told "too much," but they are assured he has not yet been sentenced and they get the drift. With that threatened penalty of death hanging over him and his wife, "who will also testify," there is little need to spell it out. They understand.

We hear the distant voices of the fifties. Even Emanuel Bloch, who, with his "Communist ties," has already conveyed to the enemy whatever atomic secrets Julius had confided in him. In other words, the defendant's attorney not only knows his client is guilty but he is a spy himself!

And where did Rosenberg's family come from? Russia. The rest is unsaid. They understand. And finally, it is hoped that the strongest judge will be assigned and that, too, is understood. One with a strong enough stomach to do whatever is required, *i.e.,* "a hanging judge."

Actually, as confirmed by an entry in the late Gordon Dean's diary accompanying the above document, such a candidate had already been selected by the Justice Department. Needless to say, he was Irving R. Kaufman. As for the device of using the death sentence to break Julius, this had been discussed with him, and his agreement "to impose it if the evidence warrants" had been obtained by the Assistant Attorney General, James B. McInerny, who had been working closely with Saypol during this period. It was on February 7, 1951, the day before the meeting, that Chairman Dean of the AEC had learned about it from McInerny and made the entry. Apparently, he and Lane were withholding the name until Kaufman would be officially assigned.

Before we leave this meeting which, with its viewpoint so reminiscent of the Inquisition, may be described by some future historian as a gathering of buzzards, let us not omit this statement dealing with the alleged postwar evidence:

MR. LANE: . . . Also Rosenberg had received information someplace in the Government about this air platform. I never heard of it, and I thought that was something out of Jules Verne, but I understand it was actually a project which the Government contemplated where they were going to fly rockets for 3000 or 4000 miles in the air, have them remain stationary for a time—it may never have worked out, but they had the theory that when the earth rotated on its axis, the things would be activated and float down and hit certain spots.

Here, with this wild description echoing the science fiction appearing in the late forties in magazines such as *Amazing Stories* and *Popular Science* (Greenglass' favorite reading), we see that the prosecution (Roy Cohn, in this instance) must have carefully rehearsed Greenglass for fully six weeks before he testified at the trial in order not to make it sound like "something out of Jules Verne."

Which brings us back to Judge Kaufman and the true reason for the death sentences. First, with regard to Julius, the lie is given to any serious consideration by Kaufman of the postwar evidence since the primary goal agreed on *before* the trial was to apply the utmost pressure ("the prospect of . . . getting the chair") to force his confession concerning the "spy ring." As for Ethel, despite Lane's admission that "the case is not too strong against" her, Kaufman asserts his role as Chief Inquisitor. Not content with "the stiff sentence of 25 to 30 years" for Ethel, which Saypol's spokesman had proposed as *sufficient* to bring Julius to the breaking point (the view shared without dissent at the meeting), Kaufman increases it to the maximum penalty of death. In short, the quintessence of modern torture is to be applied. Sooner or later, Kaufman was certain it would prove effective. With his wife and the mother of his two young children isolated in a death cell, Julius, equally isolated, was bound to break, confess his guilt and "disgorge."

Disgorge? Immediately following his description of the "air platform," Lane stresses that it is Julius who is the "key to the whole picture. . . . If we can really break him . . . he will open the gates . . . which will lead to a lot of other individuals." Thus, it is imperative to note that only Julius is the key, only *he* can open the mysterious gates. *Not* Ethel. So that, even if we believe her guilty of those illegal acts when the U.S.S.R. was our ally, here is supportive evidence from the prosecution itself that she was not equally deserving of death and that Kaufman's fatuous reasons given at her sentencing were only to mask the real one—to use her as a device for torture.

As for the alleged spy-ring, we know that in those two years before the executions, while Kaufman waited for his moment of triumph, the FBI made every effort to establish proof that such a ring did indeed exist. But they came up with nothing. With all of its thousands of agents alerted throughout the country, and with every suspect thoroughly investigated, not one of those "other individuals" was ever produced. And today, over two decades later, there is still nothing. The myth of the Rosenberg spy-ring has vanished together with all the other myths conjured up during the Hoover-Nixon-McCarthy Era.*

By way of a final comment on Kaufman, we find in the Pollack report that they worked closely together in the Department of Justice in 1947 and that, as Pollack indicates, Kaufman's fairness and total lack of prejudice during the trial can be vouched for "personally." Also, in the report, are Pollack's acknowledgments of appreciation to Myles Lane and James Kilsheimer (assistants to Saypol), but he points with special pride to the praise received from

Judge Irving R. Kaufman . . . when he complimented me on my contribution to the Bill Davidson article in *Look* magazine, October 29, 1957 issue.†

Thus, we see Kaufman, four years after the executions, giving his approval to the Government's ploy of using the *Look* article to cover up the "smoking gun" in Gold's Senate testimony of 1956. It would seem appropriate here to apply the question pressed during the Watergate inquiry: "What did Judge Kaufman know, and when did he know it?"

•

* See cover story, "The Truth About Hoover," *Time*, December 22, 1975.
† According to a recent disclosure from Justice Department files, it appears that Kaufman had written a previous letter marked "Personal" to U.S. Attorney General Herbert Brownell, dated October 15, 1957. Here, excerpted, is the gist of Kaufman's letter:

That he has "just finished reading . . . the October 29th issue of *Look* magazine dealing with the Rosenberg case [which] makes mention of the fact that . . . you directed your Internal Security Division to prepare a full report on the case." That it has "come as a great relief to [him] to know that you have undertaken the difficult task of exposing these accusations for what they are. . . ." And that the "article in *Look* indicates that Benjamin Pollack has indeed done a very thorough and scholarly job."

The letter concludes, "I hasten to commend you for undertaking this task" and for showing your "contempt for falsehood and a reverence for the truth."

And so we come full circle to Harry Gold, the weak link in the Government's alleged chain of evidence which, despite all efforts to repair it, lies broken. Indeed, a most unique effort to keep the chain intact has been made by the famous trial attorney, Louis Nizer, in his book about the Rosenberg case, *The Implosion Conspiracy*.*

However, instead of dealing with any of the gaping holes which we have disclosed, unlike the Justice Department, "he does not even admit to their existence," according to a prominent review of the Nizer book in *The New York Times* of February 11, 1973. In this review, Mr. Nizer is charged with avoiding the "controversial evidence" by simply dismissing it out of hand and calling it "the analytical syndrome." Thus, while Mr. Nizer asserts that his book will show not whether the Rosenbergs were guilty, but whether "there was sufficient evidence warranting the jury . . . to decide that the Rosenbergs were guilty," its basic thrust amounts to an apologia for the Government's case.

Of special interest here is his effort to preserve the image of Gold as an authentic spy by ignoring many of the inconsistencies and contradictions presented in the original edition of this book.

In his introduction, it is worth noting Nizer's claims concerning his conscientious research and utter neutrality:

My objective was to know . . . every book I could find for or against the verdict . . . every newspaper reference. . . . I let my thorough research carry me where it would. . . .

. . . I came up determined to present the facts . . . precisely as they were, not (to) . . . lean to one side or the other. . . . I wanted to suffer the confusion of neutrality.

Included in Nizer's "thorough research" was the original edition of this book, which, he states in his "Acknowledgments," was "helpful" to him. And while it is true that he has helped himself liberally to many portions which have suited his purposes, he has omitted

* Louis Nizer, *The Implosion Conspiracy*, Doubleday, New York, 1973.

or downplayed most of the important disclosures inimical to the Government's case.

For example, in Nizer's book, there is quoted from Gold's testimony that he "always used a false name." And yet, only three pages later, we find Nizer referring to the record and stating with apparent indifference, that Gold "registered at the Hotel Hilton in his own name." Since this contradiction is so patently clear one would expect that Nizer would probe deeper into Gold's claims, and deal somehow with our conclusion that the Hilton card *had* to be an "FBI-inspired forgery."

In his critique of the Rosenberg defense, although Nizer does suggest certain weak areas in Gold's testimony where he might have been tripped up in cross-examination, nowhere in his book is the all-important and glaring contradiction surrounding the Hilton card, or the liklihood of its being a forgery, given the slightest attention.

As for Nizer's claims "to present the facts precisely," let us examine a single passage in his chapter on Gold in which there are no less than *three* instances wherein we see the very opposite. But first, here are his fervent assurances of good faith given his reader in his introduction:

Writing about a trial. . . . There is no place for fiction or even imaginative reconstruction. That is the path to a counterfeit presentation. Authenticity is the key.

Very well, let us begin with Gold's actual testimony as quoted in this book from the record, to compare it with Nizer's doctored passage. Here, again, is the most crucial area in the case—Gold's alleged trip to New Mexico. Supposedly, he is being instructed by his Soviet superior, Yakovlev, to memorize Greenglass' address and the all-important "Recognition signal" connecting Julius Rosenberg to the alleged conspiracy.

[GOLD]: Yakovlev then gave me a sheet of paper; it was onionskin paper, and on it was typed the following: First, the name "Greenglass," just "Greenglass." Then a number "High Street"; all that I can recall about the number is that the last figure—it was a low number and the last figure, the second figure was "0" and the last figure was either 5, 7 or 9; and then underneath that was "Albuquerque, New Mexico."

The last thing that was on the paper was "Recognition signal. I come from Julius."

In our chapter, "All Is Not Gold," the reader will see our detailed analysis of the obvious "play-acting" contained in this testimony. By contrast here is Mr. Nizer's version of the above testimony:

YAKOVLEV (Took an onionskin paper out of his breast pocket. On it was typed: "Greenglass 259 North High Street." Underneath were the words "I come from Julius").

This is the contact and address. The recognition signal is "I come from Julius."

To begin with, Nizer's innocent reader believes he has been given Gold's verbatim testimony and thus is prevented from putting it to an objective test. Impressed and even awed by Nizer's reputation, he has put his full trust in Nizer's assurances. In any event, let us now examine the Nizer version point by point:

1. Concerning Gold's artful pretense about forgetting the exact address, Nizer—as a veteran lawyer—knows full well that this item must have been gone over countless times with the FBI, the prosecution, and Greenglass in the pretrial conferences mentioned repeatedly in the record. Yet he simply omits all of Gold's histrionic folderol and puts down the address as though Gold had remembered it. However, instead of the correct number, 209, Nizer gives it as "259."

In short, by omitting Gold's exact testimony concerning the address, so damaging to Gold's credibility, and by not rebutting our analysis on this point, Nizer weakens the credibility of his own interpretation.

2. Next, we see that Nizer has arbitrarily stricken the words, "Albuquerque, New Mexico" from "underneath" the address. Why, we asked in our analysis of Gold's testimony, would a KGB spy (Yakovlev) carry on his person such "damning evidence"? What if Yakovlev were arrested before or during this alleged meeting? Why would he write

down so precisely "Albuquerque," the closely guarded city so near to the Los Alamos Atomic Project? Thus, in Nizer's version, we find this item so damaging to Gold's image as an authentic spy (as well as to Yakovlev's), simply omitted.

3. Finally, and possibly most important in this particular analysis, we questioned with amazement whether a KGB spy would put in writing such *actual words* as "Recognition signal"! In the event of sudden arrest and search, this phrase alone would mean disaster. Why would not Yakovlev simply give Gold these incriminating instructions orally, we asked, especially, since as Gold testified, everything was to be memorized anyway?

So here again, we find Nizer altering Gold's testimony to comply with our analysis. Here we find Nizer not only *omitting* the "Recognition signal" from Yakovlev's *written* instruction, but having it told to Gold *orally*.

Actually, by striving to retain the image of Gold as a bona fide spy, Nizer, in effect, *endorses* our finding that Gold *is* the weak link breaking the Government's chain of evidence.

According to *The New York Times* book review mentioned earlier, Nizer's attitude toward Communism, at the time of the Rosenberg's arrests, was outspokenly hostile. Perhaps, in this sample of his handling of the Gold testimony, we have an invaluable lens through which we can better see the political thinking of the government officials involved in the pretrial stages of the Rosenberg-Sobell case, and their pre-disposition to convict. How much this thinking, conditioned by the moral code of the fifties at the height of McCarthyism, influenced the judgment not only of these officials of the FBI and the prosecution, but also of the Rosenberg jury, will be dealt with in the ensuing chapters.

●

In a recent biography of J. Edgar Hoover, *The Director*,* we are told that the secret of his success

* Ovid Demaris, *The Director,* Harper's Magazine Press, New York, 1975.

had been "zealotry and bigotry." And that "Richard M. Nixon, Roy Cohn and the late Senator Joseph McCarthy" would not have had "such dazzling careers without the Director's often surreptitious help." To these names, one may safely add that of Irving R. Kaufman, who, as far back as 1947, was an "idolator of Hoover," according to an article in *New Times* of May 16, 1975.

In 1972, when Nizer was writing approvingly of the conduct of Judge Kaufman, whom, together with Saypol, he still counts "among his oldest professional colleagues," it was a propitious time to "extol" the justice and fair play given to the Rosenbergs. Early in May, Nixon had eulogized Hoover at a state funeral for having "personified integrity, honor, principle . . . and patriotism. We can pay him no greater tribute than to live these virtues."

The nation, of course, did not know as yet about Hoover's vendetta against Martin Luther King aimed at linking Communism with King's civil-rights movement. Anonymous letters had been written by FBI agents warning King to commit suicide, threatening him with disclosure of tape-recordings of sexual escapades with "female plants." Nor was it known that Hoover would order his agents to *rewrite* reports on other citizens marked for harassment. And certainly we were unaware that on June 23, in the basement of the White House, that fateful tape with Nixon's orders to Haldeman to "play it tough" was being recorded—the tape containing the "smoking gun."

Not until 1975 did the illegal acts committed by our intelligence agencies over the past three decades come to be aired by a Congressional investigating committee. One may rightly draw a direct line between the climate of the fifties with the Rosenbergs as sacrificial victims of the Korean War, and that of the sixties, with the "wasted" victims of the Vietnam War.

In the analysis of the CIA-Mafia assassination plots reported by the Senate Intelligence Committee, we find that these "occurred in a Cold War atmosphere" with "perceptions" that we faced "a monolithic enemy in

Communism." * And that, although this was an "un-justified" assumption, it was this "attitude" which "helps explain" why our highest government officials participated so readily in these and other criminal activities.

"The picture which emerges" from the Senate report is that "explicit authorization was unnecessary." That officials acted "according to their judgment" as to what might be "an acceptable course of action." That all those who participated "appeared to believe they were advancing the best interests of their country" and could proceed without troubling their superiors. And, whether the illegal acts were committed by CIA or FBI agents, the consensus of the report shows that "the political atmosphere" was the most important factor.

When this book was first written over twenty years ago, all these intriguing euphemisms were not in our glossary. Nevertheless, the attitudes and prejudicial conduct of Hoover, Kaufman, Saypol, Lane, Cohn, and the FBI officials in handling the Rosenberg case were plainly visible. Then, as we wrote more bluntly, it was "the political atmosphere which generates, and at the same time cloaks, the frame-up." In 1975, we learned that the plotting fell within "the parameters of permissible action." In 1955, we wrote that such was the "dominant political ideology . . . that no matter what is done to a political dissident charged with being a Communist, it is moral, justified and patriotic" and with some officials, even considered "an act of faith."

Thus, as indicated at the start of this essay, we return to the Now and Then, to what is thinkable today and what was unthinkable in the fifties. As the reader will see in the chapters which follow, the now-familiar pattern of "permissible activity" was in its most virulent state at the time of the Rosenberg tragedy. And that even with our naïve phraseology and the facts then available, we were not far from the mark. What we are witnessing now is merely new wine bursting old bottles.

* See New York *Times,* November 21, 1975.

PROLOGUE

June 19, 1953

> "God offers to every mind its choice between Truth and Repose. Take which you please—you can never have both."
>
> —*Emerson*

There was a great unease throughout America that night following the execution of the Rosenbergs. No one could estimate how many were gratified, how many indifferent, and how many felt a terrible thing had been done. But there could be no question that a vast number of people experienced the most profound disquiet. Even though they were assured that the "A-spies" had been justly sentenced, two perplexing questions continued to gnaw at mind and heart:

If the Rosenbergs were really guilty, if no doubt existed that they had received their full measure of justice, then why had the conscience of the world been so deeply aroused? And if the Rosenbergs were truly innocent, why had they been put to death?

One could not airily dismiss as Communist propagandists men like Dr. Harold Urey, the Nobel Prize physicist, or James W. Wolfe, Chief Justice of the Utah Supreme Court. Such men could not be brushed aside as dupes, nor could one ignore the revelation made by Justice Hugo Black that the United States Supreme Court "had never reviewed this trial record and therefore never affirmed the fairness of this trial."

Why, then, did so many Americans continue to say that the Rosenbergs had been accorded all due process of law? Why had the Supreme Court been convened into extraordinary session with such desperate haste to dispose of a case which Justice Frankfurter considered so vital that he declared "the magnitude of the issue called for the most prolonged consideration"?

Thus the two initial questions produced many more: Was it really an issue of guilt or innocence? Had the trial really been a fair one? Were the Rosenbergs justly executed or were they the political victims of the "Cold War" and the convenient scapegoats of the

42

Korean War? Were their deaths to be a symbolic warning to terrify and silence all liberals and dissenters?

Perhaps one did not quite dare to test these questions except among trusted friends, yet one could not help thinking: What had our country gained in shocking the sensibilities, in alienating the respect of great nations? And how was it that the fate of these two obscure people had such a tremendous "global effect"? What were these "grave doubts" which disturbed so many millions abroad and at home? Who were these Greenglasses and how had they come to involve and destroy their own kin? And who were this strange Dr. Fuchs and this even stranger Harry Gold? Had it been a frame-up similar to so many others perpetrated in periods of national hysteria? If so, why was it so difficult to discern the familiar symptoms? Were any of them recognizable in the Rosenberg case? Could one get to the underlying facts and arrive at the truth? What was the truth? Where, and when, and how did it all start?

PART ONE

The Events Preceding the Trial

January–December, 1950

"Doubts are more cruel than the worst of truths."

—*Molière*

1 THE ANATOMY OF FRAME-UP

> "Falsehood flies and truth comes limping
> after it. ..."
>
> —Jonathan Swift

The history of man's inhumanity to man provides all too many examples of the device of frame-up, particularly in times of stress and tension. Perhaps the instance most universally deplored is that regarding the false testimony brought against Jesus when he was accused of "blasphemy" and "perverting the people." [1]

It was not the first time, and it was to happen again and again. In Spain there was the dread Inquisition. All over Europe the stench of burning human flesh arose from the pyres of heretics condemned to death on false testimony. In France there was the frame-up of Captain Dreyfus, designed to conceal the ineptitude of the military and the betrayal of the Republic into the hands of the monarchists.

In the United States the frame-up of union leaders became the stock device to retain child labor, the twelve-hour day, and the antistrike injunction.

In Chicago there was the Haymarket Square frame-up, the result of a police-provoked riot. A Grand Jury swiftly indicted the city's leading voices of labor, Albert Parsons and seven others. Despite their protestations of innocence, four of the eight were hanged. In later years Governor John Altgeld became famous for his exposure of the frame-up and his freeing of the two surviving victims. [2]

Just before America entered World War I, there was the frame-up of Tom Mooney, later officially exposed as "One of the dirtiest jobs ever put over. ... A contemptible piece of work." Such was the statement of the sentencing judge, Franklin A. Griffin. "When I look back upon the trial now, it seems to me that we must have been slightly crazed by the hysteria of the time. . . ." [8]

Each celebrated case of frame-up can be said to be a touchstone to its own particular period of history. The framing of blacks on trumped-up charges is no novelty. Its most notable example was the Scottsboro case in the depression years of the early thirties. That of Sacco and Vanzetti follows the classic pattern. It came soon after the convulsive events of World War I and the Russian revolution, and was integrally bound up with the notorious Palmer raids of the 1920s. The late Justice Felix Frankfurter, then a Harvard law professor, instantly recognized its political nature: "They were convicted by the atmosphere and not by the evidence." [4]

Such, then, is the briefest summary of the history of frame-up. In one form or another, it is a technique as old as human society. Hence, there arise the plaguing questions: Why is it so difficult to recognize clearly at the time it is taking place—before it is too late— that a frame-up is in progress? And why does it ordinarily take so many years for people to become undeceived?

First, there is the political atmosphere which generates, and at the same time cloaks, the frame-up. Since it usually occurs in the midst of, before, or after a war, the public becomes easy prey to patrioteering and official endorsement. Fear of the external enemy is whipped up by the creation of an internal "enemy," and the hunt for so-called saboteurs, spies, and traitors becomes daily fare.

Coupled with this is the fact that in such an atmosphere, those in control of the great media of propaganda are in sympathy with these objectives. The result is disastrous to any detached reasoning. The paralysis of intimidation and self-intimidation, the reluctance to stick one's neck out, the dread of becoming identified with the *verboten* ideas of the victim, and the threat of social ostracism and economic ruin all operate toward the concealment of the frame-up.

Second, even when the frame-up becomes finally revealed, most people are simply unwilling to believe that officials can be so wicked as to perpetrate or condone such outrages. In periods of national insecurity there is an almost childlike need to retain faith in those whom we have entrusted with high office.

Third, and most important, is the inability of people to accept the *reality* of frame-up. The moral, civilized mind simply cannot conceive of witnesses so depraved that they will provide false testimony, or that prosecutors will encourage them to do so.[5]

The common tendency is to view the charge of frame-up as too pat an explanation. Government officials just could not be that evil; it simply could not be that cut and dried. Would prosecuting officials risk their careers, or be so conscienceless as to scheme up a frame against a totally innocent person? It is too difficult to believe.

And rightly so! Because the technique of modern frame-up is not pat, and certainly cannot be explained in terms of black and white. Quite the contrary. The structure is exceedingly complex and made up of many interlocking parts, and all of these must be studied in all their multiple shadings:

Tentative and reluctant half-lies: At first the prospective accusing witness will not state flatly that the defendant conspired to commit espionage, but will put it on a basis that there existed a desire to aid the Soviet Union as an ally. As the various stages of interrogation proceed, what may have been partial or full truth develops into half-hearted perjury. On the stand, the witness avoids mentioning any actual act of espionage, but says reluctantly "We discussed this matter of espionage" or "this espionage business."

Coincidences and tenuous circumstantial evidence: These are "blown up" to provide links in the chain of guilt. The defendant, for example, owns a 35-mm. camera, as do millions of other Americans. At the trial this becomes circumstantial evidence that he used it to photograph stolen secret plans, even though no one ever saw him steal them or photograph them.

Half-truths and full truths: There is a deceptive

ring of truth when innocent incidents are connected to acts of conspiracy. Normal visits and conversations between friends and relatives are described in fine detail. However, they are then extended into conspiratorial acts by the addition of testimony that these visits or conversations were arranged for the purpose of delivery of secrets.

Since such inculpating conversations take place *only* between the witness and the accused, it is quite impossible to produce contradicting witnesses. In a politically charged atmosphere, the jury is inclined to accept the word of the witness appearing on behalf of the Government.

Elaboration and embroidery: Here, too, there is a basis of full truth and innocent incidents, but a careful insertion is made here and there so that the incident appears conspiratorial. The accusing witness tells of an incident when he conversed with the defendant and a third party. However, we are told it was *after* the third party left that the defendant related certain conspiratorial acts. Since the third party cannot refute what happened in his absence, the defendant cannot disprove the incident. In fact, when he admits that the third party was present during the initial part of the incident, credibility is given to the accusation.

Nuances, insinuations, and innuendos: The prosecutor asks the accusing witness: Did he ever see the defendant steal secret documents in his brief case from a defense plant? The witness replies that while he did not actually see such stealing, he did notice the defendant taking his briefcase to work each day. The jury's imagination completes the picture of the insinuated criminal act, even though no such act was described.

The technique of the carefully dropped hint or suggestion: The prospective witness is told about a name, a place, a date, or a certain incident. Does he know anything about it? Doesn't he remember it? No? Well, think about it—maybe it will come to mind.

Months go by. Finally the witness is aware that the FBI agent or prosecutor who is questioning him considers the name or incident important for the Government's case. When it is finally "remembered," the witness is almost certain that his recollection is accurate. If, on cross-examination, he is asked to explain why he failed to remember the name or incident originally, he merely replies that he forgot it and that it came to his mind later. This is also known as "belated memory."

"Piling it on," or the process of adding to the "story": While the accusing witness is being briefed and rehearsed for the trial, his testimony is gradually built up. If he is under arrest himself, he is disposed to please his interrogators. In each succeeding conference he adds new items. Some, when first mentioned, are encouraged and developed in subsequent conferences. Some are the result of the witness' own compulsion to make "a better story."

Prolonged and exhaustive interrogations: In the Rosenberg case this process was politely called "painstaking digging and digging and digging." During this process the prospective witness, terrified lest he be prosecuted for other crimes, is induced or pressured into a number of such statements, each of which serves to entrap him more deeply.

Self-entrapment: By agreeing to testify to conspiring with the accused, the prospective witness automatically creates of himself an accomplice, and thereby makes himself vulnerable to much more serious prosecution.

In the Rosenberg case the prosecution's first witness, Max Elitcher, feared arrest for perjury committed in connection with a false loyalty oath. By testifying against Morton Sobell, he also involved himself as an accomplice in the crime of conspiracy to commit espionage. As a result, an indictment for this "confessed" espionage hangs over his head for the rest of his life, since in a capital offense the statute of limitations does not apply. The same holds true for Ruth Greenglass, who, in exchange for supporting her husband's "confession," went scot-free.

The providing of "motive" and "intent": These are obtained by having the accusing witness remember political discussions, some of which may be honestly recalled, whereas others are "tailored" to make the crime fit the charges. For example, the accusing witness is briefed on the following: Did not the accused discuss the advantages of socialism over capitalism? Was there any preference indicated? How did the accused feel about the opening of the Second Front on D-Day? In this way a picture is gradually painted of the accused's readiness as a "dedicated Communist" to aid the Soviet Union even in espionage—and the prosecution has successfully established "motive."

And so, with these elements (separate and overlapping) as well as many more which will be later illustrated, the frame-up gradually takes shape. Where the puzzle needs another interlocking part, another insertion is furnished. Finally a judicious amount of color and intrigue is applied to liven up the picture, and frequently these additions, too, are based on truth. For example, David Greenglass had a poor handwriting. Therefore his secret reports had to be typed up. Ethel Rosenberg had a portable typewriter. Therefore, at the trial, it is she who "struck the keys, blow by blow, against her own country in the interests of the Soviets." Later we will see that it is unexplained why Greenglass' reports, given to Harry Gold, remained untyped despite the fact that Greenglass' wife, Ruth, was a professional typist.

In an over-all sense the modern frame-up does *not* consist of 100 percent fabrication, but, on the contrary, the various forms of perjury are well interwoven with actuality and truth. It is precisely for this reason that the uninformed public becomes deceived into accepting *all* of it as truth.

Actual collusion, or the core of the frame-up: At one point or another actual collusion becomes a necessity in the preparation of evidence and exhibits. Generally, where the core of the prosecution's case lies, there one can detect deliberate fabrication. The heart of the Government's case against the Rosenbergs lay in David Greenglass' claims that he delivered sketches of atomic secrets to Julius Rosenberg and Harry Gold. Since this testimony was totally uncorroborated by any independent witness, the prosecution had Greenglass duplicate "copies" of these alleged sketches, later introduced as the Government's most important exhibits. Greenglass swore that he had prepared these "copies" from memory and with no assistance of any kind.

It will be shown by official records that Greenglass and Gold were lodged together for many months on the "eleventh floor" of the Tombs (the New York City prison), where they had complete freedom to confer because of the dormitory arrangement. As we shall see later, there is reason to believe that means were provided for Greenglass to copy the sketches from books and drawings, and receive instructions and coaching from Gold. Only thus was it possible for Greenglass, an ordinary machinist without the slightest scientific education, to have prepared these sketches.

It should be noted that it was none other than Roy M. Cohn who was the prosecutor in full charge of Greenglass' testimony. In view of the charges made in open court by Harvey Matusow concerning his false testimony fabricated at the instigation of Roy Cohn, perhaps it is not difficult to believe in this crucial aspect of the frame-up.[6]

Important also in the technique of frame-up is that the coercion exerted upon each witness is not performed by any one person nor is it ordered by a single mastermind. It is exerted by a variety of persons as well as by the political atmospheric pressure. Today, it is no longer the glaring light, the circle of snarling detectives and the rubber hose, but rather the polite and friendly interrogation during which the tactic of the repetitive suggestion is the dominant feature. ("Didn't Julius Rosenberg tell you this and this . . . ? Try to remember. . . . It'll come back to you—you'll remember.")

Personal resentments and long-accumulated hostility toward the accused are also exploited, as well as the conscience-easing rationale that the defendant need only do likewise to save himself.

Apropos of this, there is the attitude of prosecuting officials, whose careers and thinking are an integral part of the dominant political ideology, and who, as a rule, are dedicated to the proposition that no matter what is done to a political dissident, it is moral, justified, and patriotic.

What must ever be borne in mind is the overpowering political atmosphere. Riding high on the wave of successful prosecutions, our modern inquisitors become overconfident, arrogant, and contemptuous of the public's intelligence. No one can possibly challenge them, for in doing so one would be challenging the hostile sentiment of the entire nation. But the result is that "holes" are overlooked and serious blunders are made; and even when they are finally repaired they display signs of hasty and clumsy patchwork.

In the chapters to follow it will be seen that the prosecution's case in the Rosenberg trial record is riddled with discrepancies, contradictions, and sheer improbabilities, betraying methods and procedures that were for the most part makeshift, off-the-cuff, and frequently the result of spur-of-the-moment "brainstorms."

(This was amply illustrated at the 1954 Army-McCarthy hearings, wherein the junior Senator's chief henchmen, led by Roy Cohn, produced a doctored photograph of Secretary Stevens as well as a so-called secret FBI summary of the "subversive" personnel at Fort Monmouth.)

This classic weakness is to be found in all modern frame-ups. No one single official, not even the prosecutor-in-chief, will risk being the mastermind and take the full responsibility to get the "story" straight in every detail. Each participant is perfectly aware of the dangers involved should the frame-up be exposed. Indeed, it is rare that an official will admit, even to himself, that he is involved in anything as heinous as a deliberate frame-up. And it may very well be that those on its periphery, merely acting on instructions, are completely ignorant of the significance of their particular part.

And it is precisely because there are so many participants, all working in different offices, interrogating, rehearsing, or coaching different witnesses, that the completed frame-up presents such a crazy-quilt appearance. But, at the same time, this very hodge-podge workmanship proves to be its Achilles' heel. In other words, too many cooks have spoiled the broth. And it is for this reason more than any other that it always proves vulnerable and eventually becomes exposed. Nevertheless, its very chaotic nature serves to confound and confuse, making it difficult even to know where to begin.

Therefore, in the Rosenberg case, though it may be an arduous process, one is constrained to take first things first and begin with the genesis of the Atomic Age—the shocking massacre of Hiroshima.

NOTES AND REFERENCES

1. "He stirs up the people, teaching throughout all Judea. . . ." Luke XXIII:5.
2. Harry Barnard, *Eagle Forgotten*, Bobbs-Merrill, New York, 1935.
3. Lillian Symes, "Our American Dreyfus Case," (California v. Mooney, et al.) *Harper's Magazine*, May, 1931.
4. Felix Frankfurter, *The Case of Sacco and Vanzetti*, Academic Reprints, Stanford, Calif., 1954.
5. A most notable example is that of the "honest cattleman," Frank Oxman, the chief witness against Tom Mooney, who testified to having been in San Francisco at the time of the crime. Later it was proven that Oxman was in a town some four hours distant from San Francisco by train! Lillian Symes, *op. cit.*
6. See Harvey Matusow, *False Witness*, Cameron & Kahn, New York, 1955.

The technique of dropping suggestions to government witnesses has been amply demonstrated by the admissions of a former FBI agent, Richard Brennan, on television in February, 1974. In an interview televised for a PBS documentary, Brennan was asked to describe his interrogations of Harry Gold regarding his alleged "recognition signal" wherein he had used the phrase: "I came from Julius." It was this crucial point in Gold's testimony which connected Julius Rosenberg with the alleged Jello-box arrangement described by David Greenglass.

At first, as Brennan replied, Gold had "used the expression 'Benny sent me.' " However, as the conferences continued, Brennan asked, "Could it have been 'Julie sent me' or 'Julius sent me'?" Whereupon, Gold, according to Brennan, "immediately brightened up" and eagerly responded: " 'Yes, that is it. It wasn't Benny, it was Julius sent me.' "

And when the former FBI agent was asked if this was not the same as providing Gold with the name of Julius, Brennan shrugged with a smile of casual indifference: "Oh, we didn't plant that idea in Gold's mind. . . . it was given to him as a suggestion."

(See the book based on the Public Broadcasting System documentary written by Alvin H. Goldstein, *The Unquiet Death of Julius and Ethel Rosenberg,* Laurence Hill, New York, 1975.)

•

At the conclusion of the Pollack report, there is this blanket rebuttal to our anatomy of frame-up: "The basic argument of Wexley . . . is preposterous." With this initial show of indignation, Pollack goes on to ask how anyone can believe that the principal prosecution witnesses

. . . all independently made up stories that just happened to coincide in detail; that dozens of FBI men and Government officials collaborated in faking evidence and testimony to support this invention . . . ?

First, as I showed throughout the book, the stories were not fabricated "independently." On the contrary, there was not only "actual collusion," but there were all the rehearsals during which the prosecution and FBI encouraged elaboration. Second, as the book amply demonstrates, the "stories" do not just happen to "coincide in detail." They reveal important contradictions. Third, as stated, "No one single official" will risk taking "the full responsibility to get the 'story' straight in every detail. . . . [or] admit, even to himself," that he is involved in "a deliberate frame-up."

In short, Pollack's protestations are merely a cop-out for what he is unable to refute and (understandably), unwilling to admit, even to himself.

2 A MAN CALLED FUCHS

I

> "On August 6, 1945, a split atom sent waves of destruction circling out over Hiroshima —an explosion whose implications still batter against the institutions of our time."
>
> —"The Rosenberg Case,"
> *Columbia Law Review,* February, 1954

With these portentous words, the *Columbia Law Review* begins its sober "reflections" on the Rosenberg case, which it designates as "the outstanding 'political' trial of this generation."

In each of his appeals to the higher courts, Emanuel Bloch, the attorney for the Rosenbergs, laid emphasis on the political events leading up to their arrests. To recapitulate these events: The years that followed World War II witnessed a rapid deterioration of relations between the U.S. and the U.S.S.R. The Hiroshima atom bomb had raised the spectre of mass annihilation by the most devastating weapon ever devised. Until its discovery, the American people had felt blithely secure from any serious air attack such as had reduced Europe to rubble. Now, however, there was the sudden realization that an atomic attack might very well kill twenty to thirty million people overnight.

It was a terrifying prospect, not quite dispelled by the illusion that the United States possessed the monopoly of the "secret." For the stark truth was that there was no secret at all! In its 1949 report, the Joint Congressional Committee on Atomic Energy endeavored to clear up the "confusion" surrounding "the nature of atomic secrets":

There existed for instance, an unfortunate notion that one marvelous "formula" explains how to make bombs and that it belonged exclusively to the United States. . . .
. . . The Soviet Union, for its part, possesses some of the world's most gifted scientists . . . whose understanding of the fundamental physics behind the bomb only the unrealistic were prone to underestimate. . . .

In September of 1945, Secretary Henry L. Stimson urged President Truman that unless we shared our atomic information with our allies, and particularly with the Soviet Union, unless we ceased the wearing of "this weapon ostentatiously on our hip, their suspicions and their distrust of our purposes and motives will increase."

The chief lesson I have learned in a long life is that the only way you can make a man trustworthy is to trust him; and the surest way to make him untrustworthy is to distrust him and show your distrust.[1]

And although our leading physicists pleaded for the banning of the weapon and for mankind to share its knowledge of the new source of energy, the "war psychosis" prevailed and the most profitable arms race of all history commenced.

To allay the undercurrent of disquiet, the semi-official propaganda ran that the Russians could not possibly master the "know-how" of the atom bomb in less than twenty, ten, five, or two years. But by that time, it was declared, we would be so far ahead with our stockpile of bigger and better A-bombs that the Russians could never catch up.

Lulled, therefore, into the delusion of invulnerability, the shattering impact of President Truman's announcement in September of 1949 that an atomic explosion had taken place in the Soviet Union produced nationwide consternation bordering on hysteria.

All through the tension created by the Cold War, the Democratic and Republican Parties had vied with each other about the hobgoblin of domestic Communism. Reckless charges of coddling spies and traitors had become the favorite scare headline.

To the Truman Administration, therefore, was presented a number of pressing problems: How to counter the Republican charges that it had sold out China to the Reds—that it had always been "soft on Communists"? How to explain away the false sense of security its military pundits had beguiled us with? How to account for the fact that the Russians had suddenly duplicated our multi-billion-dollar atomic effort, when they were supposed to be a nation of ignorant peasants incapable of even the "know-how" of repairing their rusting tractors?

One answer was found, and, *mirabile dictu*, it solved everything: The Russians stole the secret of the atom bomb from us and it was the American Communists who had done the dirty deed for them!

With the sensational arrest of Dr. Klaus Fuchs in England in the early months of 1950, the first step toward finding a suitable "Red" scapegoat was taken. For not only was his so-called confession that of a repentant Communist, but there was his claim that he had had an American accomplice while he had been part of the Los Alamos Atomic Project.

And so we come to the first link in the chain of events which led to the deaths of the Rosenbergs— the person of Dr. Klaus Fuchs.

II

"There are also some other crimes which I have committed, other than the ones with which I am charged . . . They are not crimes in the eyes of the law." [2]

In most newspapers, following the executions of the Rosenbergs, brief histories of the case appeared. Always there was the familiar sequence: First, a man called Fuchs, then Harry Gold, then the Greenglasses, and finally the Rosenbergs.

When, however, one examines the actual facts, the apparently cohesive sequence becomes a house of cards. Touch any part, and it all begins to shake. For example, we have been told that Fuchs definitely *named* Gold as his chief courier. Yet the official facts disclose that Fuchs never named anyone—Gold or anyone else. He could not even describe Gold or identify his photographs. Indeed, he identified the photos of an engineer whom J. Edgar Hoover has referred to as "James Davidson," and who was completely cleared of any suspicion.

We have also been told of a great manhunt conducted by the FBI and how from Fuchs the trail of conspiracy led them to Gold. Yet the truth is that no such manhunt ever took place save in the publicity releases of the FBI.

The "confession" of Klaus Fuchs was first revealed at his hearing at Bow Street Court, London, one week after his arrest. At the trial itself in Old Bailey, less than three weeks later, we learn that "there was no jury and no evidence beyond that offered at the prior Bow Street proceedings." [8] As part of his confession, Dr. Fuchs had offered this rather novel diagnosis:

I used my Marxian philosophy to conceal my thoughts in two separate compartments. . . . Looking back on it now, the best way is to call it a controlled schizophrenia.

Psychiatrists point out that this is utter nonsense, that there is no such thing as "controlled schizophrenia." The schizophrenic "does not with one part of his mind *know* and the other part *do*."

It is on the foundation of his being a fanatical Communist that Fuchs' role as a spy rests. When the Attorney General, Sir Hartley Shawcross, opened the trial, this point was emphasized:

The prisoner is a Communist, and that is at once the explanation and indeed the tragedy of this case. . . . The true adherents of Communism, indoctrinated with the Communist belief, must become traitors to their own country. . . .

59

Official declarations disclose that British Military Intelligence (M.I. 5) and Scotland Yard made the most exacting investigations of Fuchs throughout his seventeen years in England. There was never the slightest evidence of Communist Party membership or even association. In 1946, M.I. 5 placed him under secret surveillance for five full months. Not only was he found entirely above suspicion but he was given such a clean bill of political health that eventually he was promoted to Deputy Chief Scientific Officer at the Harwell Atomic Energy Research Establishment. And yet, despite these facts, there is the following claim by Dr. Fuchs:

When I learned about the purpose of the work [atomic research] I decided to inform Russia and I established contact through another member of the Communist Party.
Since that time I have had continuous contacts with persons completely *unknown* to me except that they would give information to the Russians. [Emphasis added.]

What support, if any, really exists of the claim that Fuchs was a Communist? The Nazi Gestapo! This astounding disclosure was made by Prime Minister Clement Attlee in the House of Commons only five days after Fuchs' trial:

Not long after this man came into this country—that was in 1933—it was said that he was a Communist. The source of that information was the Gestapo.
. . . When the matter was looked into there was *no support* for it whatever. And from that time onward there was *no support*. [Emphasis added.]

The Gestapo's accusation was made in 1934, one year after Fuchs arrived in England as a "refugee" from Nazi Germany. He was then twenty-three years old and had enrolled at the University of Bristol to complete his studies in mathematical physics, when the Chief Constable of that city received the report from the Nazi Consul there. It stated that Fuchs had been a member of the German Communist Party while a student in Kiel.

It will be recalled that it was a common practice

for the Gestapo to plant its agents in Belgium, Holland, France, and Norway as "anti-Fascist refugees." Some were given Communist credentials; some even claimed to be "escapees" from Nazi concentration camps.

Little wonder, then, that M.I. 5, suspicious of a Gestapo ruse, shipped Fuchs off to a Canadian internment camp the instant the Nazis invaded the Low Countries in 1940. And, at this point, we find another startling fact: that he was segregated from genuine anti-Nazi refugees and placed in "a camp of pronounced Nazis." [4]

Now Dr. Fuchs' enigmatic speech at the close of his trial starts to take on meaning. His "other crimes" may well have consisted of promises to undertake espionage in behalf of Nazi intelligence which allowed him to leave Germany. One tends to overlook the fact that the galvanizing force behind our original effort to produce the atomic bomb was the fear that Hitler was making rapid progress in the same direction. According to the Joint Report:

. . . British Military Intelligence was receiving reports of an extensive German plan to build a new weapon, an atom bomb, which would be decisive in the war.

In occupied Norway, secret underground agents reported construction of strange heavy-water plants, where hundreds of German scientists had been put on special duty. . . .

At the same time, a meeting was called in London to lay plans for an answer to German atomic research.

Even if we accept as true that the other crimes to which Fuchs alludes were "not crimes in the eyes of the law," the explanation of this bit of mystification could be: (1) That as a young German scientist Fuchs had agreed to keep abreast of British research in physics and to furnish information to agents of the Gestapo; (2) that soon after his arrival in England the Gestapo sought to cloak him as a Communist; and (3) that Fuchs, having had a change of heart, either refused to furnish the desired information, or delivered deceptive and worthless material, or kept stalling the Gestapo with promises.

At the trial of the Rosenbergs, the authenticity of Gold as the American confederate of Fuchs was never contested by the defense nor doubted by the jury. The FBI had officially announced it, Gold himself had confessed it, therefore it was accepted as God's own truth. And yet the foundation of Gold's testimony against the Rosenbergs, the story of his alleged two meetings with Fuchs in Santa Fe, had not the slightest corroboration as far as Dr. Fuchs was concerned!

These two Santa Fe meetings, supposed to have taken place on June 2 and September 19, 1945, were the two most important meetings in their relationship. In a signed article by J. Edgar Hoover in *Reader's Digest*, we are told that it was at the June 2 meeting that "Fuchs gave Gold a packet of vital information," and that on September 19 there took place "the final transfer of atomic-bomb information—data on the complete process." [5]

One would logically assume, therefore, that these two crucial transfers of atomic secrets in Santa Fe would be the very ones Dr. Fuchs should have recalled most vividly, just as Gold had. Certainly, if Fuchs had described them as minutely to M.I. 5 as Gold did to the FBI and the Rosenberg jury, some mention of them would have been included in his indictment. However, when we search that document, what do we find? Here are the only locations of Fuchs' offenses as officially charged:

(1) In Birmingham, England, in 1943; (2) in New York City between December 31, 1943, and August 1, 1944; (3) in Boston, Mass., in February, 1945; and (4) in Berkshire, England, in 1947.

As is seen, there is no mention of any meeting in Santa Fe, not on June 2 or on September 19. This "hole" in Gold's testimony goes to the very heart of the Rosenberg case. According to Gold's story, it was after he had picked up an envelope of atomic secrets from Dr. Fuchs in Santa Fe on June 2 that he proceeded to nearby Albuquerque to do likewise with David Greenglass on June 3. And since this basic difference between Gold's testimony and Fuchs' indictment was unknown to the Rosenberg jurors, they very naturally assumed that if Gold were telling the truth about his espionage with Dr. Fuchs in Santa Fe, then he was also telling the truth about his espionage with David Greenglass in Albuquerque.

Not only is there no corroboration from Fuchs that he ever met Harry Gold in Santa Fe, but there are the most serious doubts that he ever met him anywhere!

For the simple truth is that Fuchs proved completely unable to describe or identify Gold until compelled to do so *after* Gold's voluntary "confession"! In Mr. Hoover's official version of the Fuchs case, we are told that two FBI agents visited the prisoner to obtain a description of the Soviet courier with whom he had dealt during his stay in the United States. Here is the Joint Report on the result: "Fuchs was able neither to give the FBI Gold's name nor to furnish an accurate description."

In Mr. Hoover's *Digest* article we are told also that an attempt was made by the FBI agents to have Dr. Fuchs identify his American courier more accurately:

What did the man look like? Well, he was from 40 to 45 years of age, possibly five feet ten inches tall, broad build, round face, most likely a first generation American. A description which might fit millions of men!

Although Mr. Hoover readily acknowledges the vagueness of this description, let us compare it with that of Gold. In Fuchs' description, his courier was a man of broad build, 5 feet 10 inches tall. But Harry Gold, according to Mr. Hoover's article, is a "little, five-foot six-inch" man! According to Fuchs, the courier was 40 to 45 years old. But in the period 1944-45, when Fuchs is supposed to have met with Gold, the latter was only 34 or 35 years old!

It would seem logical, if Fuchs had really met with Gold on so many occasions, that he should remember someone of his own age, since he was exactly 34 himself in 1945. One would also think that he would remember that Gold was two inches *shorter* than himself, not taller!

In his *Digest* article Hoover describes Gold as "short and chubby . . . small and chunky . . . round face and curly hair."

Is it conceivable, if Gold were Dr. Fuchs' only confederate in the United States, that the scientist would not have retained a most memorable impression of a face and figure so striking?

Not only is he unable to describe Gold correctly but, according to the Joint Report, even when the FBI showed him various photos of Gold, he still could not "recall having seen the individual pictured." In fact, we learn that Dr. Fuchs identified a totally different person! Here is Mr. Hoover regarding this development: "Dr. Fuchs rejected all [photos] except one—a picture of the man we call James Davidson."

Incidentally, there is also Hoover's statement that Fuchs' sister, residing in the United States, also believed that the so-called "James Davidson" might have been the visitor to her home during the period her brother had lived with her.[6]

Thus far, we have seen that Dr. Fuchs was totally unable to oblige the FBI. No name, no accurate description, no recognition of Gold's photographs—and, to make matters even worse, his insistence that his courier had been an entirely different person! How, then, did Fuchs finally come to identify Gold? Unfortunately, there exists no official account, that is, one certified by a British official. Hence we are forced to turn to Hoover's account in the *Reader's Digest,* the gist of which is:

1. That on May 15, 1950, the FBI began a seven-day period of interviews with Harry Gold, during which Gold firmly denied knowing Dr. Fuchs.

2. That "much earlier" they had made a secret motion picture film of Gold and had flown it to England to be viewed by Fuchs.

3. That sometime following the first day of Gold's questioning, he had allowed the FBI to make an-

other motion picture of himself, and that this too had been flown to England for Fuchs' inspection.

4. That on May 22, or the seventh day that Gold was "interviewed," the FBI finally decided to search his home, and that they found in his room a certain "museum" map of Santa Fe. And that it was the discovery of this map which "unmanned" Gold and caused him to break down and confess.

5. That "quite by coincidence," less than one hour *after* Gold's confession, a cable was received from the FBI agents in London stating that Fuchs had at last identified Gold (tentatively, as it turns out) from the first motion picture.

6. And finally, that "two days later," additional word came from the FBI agents that Dr. Fuchs, having seen the second motion picture, was now "positive" that Gold was indeed "his American partner."

What is abundantly clear is that Mr. Hoover gave the harried Fuchs precious little choice. For, when we turn to the newspapers, we see that the FBI chief was too impatient even to wait the two days for Dr. Fuchs' "positive" identification. On the night of May 23, only a few minutes before Gold's "whirlwind" arraignment, there was issued an official pronunciamento from the Washington office of the FBI. Here is the New York *Times* of May 24, 1950:

PHILADELPHIAN SEIZED AS SPY
ON BASIS OF DATA FROM FUCHS
FBI Questioning of Atom Expert
in British Prison Brings About Arrest

. . . The Government had announced in Washington (in a joint statement made by J. Edgar Hoover and Attorney General McGrath) that Gold had been arrested on espionage charges *based on information supplied by Dr. Fuchs."* [Emphasis added.]

Thus, we see about as palpable a piece of sleight of hand as ever was practiced. What actually happened was that Mr. Hoover simply forced Dr. Fuchs' hand by the "fait accompli" of announcing to the world that Gold had been arrested on the basis of Dr. Fuchs' questioning. But Gold was *not* arrested on "information supplied by Dr. Fuchs," because according to Hoover's own words the information was not only so vague as to "fit millions of men," but it was completely inaccurate!

By way of a final comment on the FBI's questioning of Fuchs, it must be noted that it took place *without* a proper independent witness present. No representative of the British Attorney General's office was present. No newspaperman; no one representing Fuchs as counsel; no one from British Military Intelligence or Scotland Yard—no one but the harassed prisoner, the two FBI agents, and a "prison officer"! How do we know this fact? By the House of Commons' records of a parliamentary debate which took place on May 11 and 18, 1950.

These official records reveal that Members of Parliament were greatly disturbed when they learned of the FBI request to interrogate Fuchs in his cell. Some M.P.'s demanded that "there be present responsible British scientists." Others proposed that "M.I. 5 and Scotland Yard" were sufficiently "capable of interviewing this man and getting from him, if he is prepared to volunteer it, the information which the Americans are seeking."

On the eighteenth of May, the House of Commons' records show clearly, the FBI agents in England had not as yet interviewed the prisoner:

"Mr. Ede: A British officer will be present if this interview takes place, and it will be conducted according to British practice."

And so we see that the very first time the FBI could have possibly questioned Fuchs as to his courier's description was sometime *later* than May 18, or at least three days after Gold's interrogation had begun in Philadelphia! But we have been told about a nationwide "manhunt" which Hoover claims took many months, involving each of the fifty-two field offices of the FBI.

In his *Digest* article he describes the combing of thousands of chemical firms, the final narrowing down of "1,500 possibilities" to the "one suspect [who] was beginning to stand out"—Harry Gold. And then, after "heartbreaking setbacks," there is described the closing-in period of May 15–22.

And yet we have just seen by the House of Commons' records that on the fifteenth of May the FBI detectives had *not yet* talked to Dr. Fuchs; indeed, could not have talked to him until three or four days later. How then was it possible for them to obtain any information, even inaccurate information, about Gold? How was the FBI able to conduct a nationwide manhunt "in the spring of 1950" for a person whose description they did not obtain until the beginning of summer? The answer, of course, is simply that there wasn't any such manhunt, and that Hoover's description of it is pure fiction.

What actually happened in the cell of Dr. Fuchs during his interviews with the FBI we cannot know, since there exists no British official confirmation of Mr. Hoover's account. It may be that the wearied prisoner finally resigned himself to the acceptance of Harry Gold with total indifference. In truth, it could not have been of great concern to him at this stage (almost three months after his trial) which person was selected to play the role of his "American partner." [7]

Admittedly, it is not feasible to explore all the possibilities. But the one avenue we have been able to explore in part—the alleged relationship between Dr. Fuchs and Harry Gold—reveals so many contradictions, "holes," and discrepancies that it is impossible to believe that there existed any such relationship.

In the chapter on Gold, what must be already apparent will become increasingly clear, namely: That it was Harry Gold with his phenomenal talents who contributed most of the illusion of his authenticity as Fuchs' mysterious American partner.

NOTES AND REFERENCES

1. Henry L. Stimson and McGeorge Bundy, *On Active Service,* Harper, New York, 1947.
2. Final statement by Dr. Fuchs at his "trial." See p. 35, Joint Congressional Committee Report of 1951 on "Soviet Atomic Espionage," hereafter referred to as the "Joint Report."
3. Excerpts from the testimony at Fuch's trial and the House of Commons minutes are from the Joint Report.
4. Alan Moorehead, *The Traitors,* Scribner's, New York, 1952.
5. J. Edgar Hoover, "The Crime of the Century," *Reader's Digest,* May, 1951.
6. This sister was also unable to describe Gold, even though Hoover tells us that she recalled three visits, one of them an extended luncheon.
7. With one-third of his fourteen-year sentence off for good behavior, Dr. Fuchs was released on July 1, 1959.

ADDENDA

Concerning the factual evidence showing that Dr. Fuchs never actually identified Gold as his American accomplice and had only agreed to do so *after* J. Edgar Hoover had announced Gold's "confession" and arrest, this has been confirmed by Marshall Perlin, the attorney, long associated with the Rosenberg-Sobell appeals. In an interview with Fuchs in early 1959, shortly before his release from prison, and in the presence of a British M.P., our scenario of Fuchs' weary and resigned acceptance of Gold as a *fait accompli* is closely paralleled by what really took place. Mr. Perlin's account of this interview was shown on the PBS television documentary mentioned earlier. As reported by Mr. Perlin, Dr. Fuchs had explained during the interview:

I never identified Gold. Gold insisted he was the courier, and I finally said [to the FBI], "If he wants to be the guy, let him be the guy." [See the New York *Times*, February 14, 1974.]

•

Among the investigative reports released from the FBI files, there is now disclosed another possible motive behind Dr. Fuchs' puzzling voluntary confession. The following is from one of these reports as described in the New York *Times* of December 4, 1975:

Dr. Rudolph Peierls, head of the British mission to Los Alamos, expressed doubt that a confessed spy-scientist, Klaus Fuchs, ever transmitted information on atomic research to the Soviet Union and said that in his opinion Dr. Fuchs "surrendered himself and created the story of his espionage activities" in 1950 to induce declassification of the secrets.

This opinion, stated in early 1950, would tend to explain not only Dr. Fuchs' strange surrender and even surprised reaction to his prosecution, but also his steadfast denials that Harry Gold had been his American accomplice.

3 "THE NECESSARY LINK"

I

> "The impostors . . . frequently belong in this category [psychopathic behavior disorders]. . . . The variety and complexity of these frauds and deceptions are determined only by the imagination of man and the gullibility of the public at large."[1]

If ever a case history is required to illustrate the above, psychiatrists need but examine the various lives of Harry Gold, real and fancied, as revealed by the court records, by the material disclosed at his sentencing, by the account written by J. Edgar Hoover, and by this writer's personal investigations.[2]

In his summation to the Rosenberg jury, the prosecutor emphasized the importance of Gold to the Government's case:

Harry Gold, who furnished the absolute corroboration of the testimony of the Greenglasses, forged the necessary link in the chain that points indisputably to the guilt of the Rosenbergs.

It is with the object of testing this "necessary link" that we examine the personality of Gold before appraising the worth of his corroboration. For by the time of the Rosenberg trial, Gold had become so unquestioningly accepted as the American partner of Dr. Fuchs that the pivotal issue of whether this was truth or fiction never came up.

No one on the Rosenberg jury could dream that Gold's role as a Soviet spy might be a self-assumed one. Certainly no juror suspected it to be simply a product of his phenomenal imagination and pathological needs, since not one of the pertaining facts was ever disclosed to them.

It is, therefore, essential to turn to Gold's childhood and to the realities he found so intolerable to see how his needs led him inevitably to the role of an impostor and a pseudologist of first rank—or, in common parlance, a pathologic liar.

II

"Here, one finds persons getting from their environment by fraud and deception those elements of security, love, affection, and the materials for self-esteem which are lacking in real life." [8]

In the year 1910 there lived in Berne, Switzerland, a Russian couple named Samuel and Cecilia Golodnitsky. In that year, a first son was born to them, whom they named Heinrich. In 1914 they immigrated to the United States, shortened their name to Gold and Americanized little Heinrich as Harry. The father was a cabinet-maker and in his search for work dragged his family from city to city until finally they settled down in a slum area of Philadelphia.

If it was a bitter struggle for the parents, it was much worse for their uprooted son. The new kid on the block was not merely a foreigner with an accent to ridicule; he was Jewish to boot and therefore doubly despised. Shy and small for his age, he was scornfully called "Goldie," a nickname for a girl. The result was an overdependency on his mother and an equally neurotic overprotection on her part toward him. When another son, Joseph, was born, the event caused more than the normal rivalry. Unlike Harry, who was in ill health much of the time, Joseph turned out to be a sturdy boy and easily held his own in the streets.

Furthermore, he possessed an advantage that was insurmountable. He was American-born and never burdened with the sense of inferiority that was to remain with Harry throughout his life.

Here then was this forlorn creature—"very mild and quite a little introverted," as his high school principal recalls him—never able to deal with others on any basis of equality. In his teens, we find him retreating into "a monastic life, a prodigious reader, refraining from normal boyhood activities."

Concerned that Harry might fall into the trade of his father, Mrs. Gold was relieved when he obtained a position at the Pennsylvania Sugar Company. Proudly, the eighteen-year-old youth told his mother that he was a laboratory assistant; however, it was "really a janitor's job." Yet it offered promise, since his ambition was to become a "brilliant scientist" in the field of chemistry.

For the next ten years of his life there is recorded the most abnormal application of work and study toward this end. Doggedly going to school at night, he was so diligent that it was common practice for him to work twelve and fourteen hours a day, seven days a week.

Certainly the genesis of this excessive drive must

have been a need to compensate for his sense of inferiority by achievement, as well as to prove himself worthy of his mother's hopes. Until her death she remained the focal center of his life. At the time of his arrest he was a bachelor of forty, still grieving over her death three years earlier. Even in his twenties "he had no sweethearts, no girl friends, went to no dances or parties." Although there exists no known evidence of overt homosexuality, there does seem to have been a man in his life, one "Tom Black," who played, as we shall see, a most dominant role in his various phantasies.

When Gold was twenty-eight he still lacked his longed-for degree in chemistry. He had made attempts to enroll at "some 10 or 12 technical schools" but most of "his credits were not in shape." Finally he managed to find a school which would admit him. It was the small Catholic college of Xavier in Cincinnati. The two years he spent there were possibly the happiest in his life, since it was the first time he experienced some self-esteem.

From Father Frederick Miller, this writer learned that Gold was treated with unusual respect by classmates and faculty. Since he was much older than the other undergraduates and had the experience of laboratory work, it was natural for him to be considered more a member of the faculty than a student.

Oddly enough, Gold possessed an additional distinction; he was a Jew. As such he was conspicuous among the 600 Catholic boys, but the fact that he had dared choose this particular college helped spare him from the anti-Semitism he might have met with elsewhere.

In 1940 he received his B.S.; he was then thirty years of age. When he was re-employed by the Pennsylvania Sugar Company, however, his hard-won diploma yielded him no greater reward than a $50-per-week job. This salary remained the same throughout the next five years.

So from 1940 on, Gold led his humdrum bachelor existence, living placidly at home with his parents until the war broke out. Perhaps more important than anything else would have been the uniform of a G.I.

and the opportunity to prove his Americanism and masculinity. Not only were these denied him but his inferiority feelings on both scores were further increased. Whereas he was rejected as 4-F because of hypertension (high blood pressure), his brother Joseph was accepted and served bravely throughout the war, earning three Bronze Stars in the South Pacific.

For some five years following his return from Xavier, Gold had done odd jobs for a chemical engineer in New York City named Abraham Brothman, using the laboratory facilities of the sugar plant surreptitiously. Evidently worried that Brothman might be indiscreet and that his unauthorized use of the laboratory might get back to his Philadelphia employers, he gave his name as "Frank Kessler." And since it was necessary to give Brothman some address, he gave that of a "friend," who, of course, was himself.

Early in 1946 Pennsylvania Sugar sold its holdings and Gold was forced to find a position elsewhere. By this time Brothman had his own laboratory and invited Gold to work in New York City at double his previous salary. Since it was no longer necessary to continue as "Frank Kessler," Gold lamely admitted the pseudonym and explained the reason he had used it. But there remained another obstacle, for though the thirty-six-year-old bachelor was eager to start on his new job, his mother exerted her domination over him to this extraordinary extent:

Celia Gold was inconsolable when Harry told of his impending move to New York. Promises that he would come home to Philadelphia every single week-end failed to dry her tears. . . . Harry Gold got so upset over his mother's plaints that he postponed going to work in New York until June, 1946, four whole months after he accepted Brothman's offer.[4]

In May, 1947, after Gold had been working for Brothman for about a year, the two were questioned by the FBI concerning their past relations with one Jacob Golos, who had been suspected of espionage activities previous to his death in 1943. Denying any knowledge of such activities, Brothman stated that

Golos had come to him as a representative of Amtorg, the official Soviet purchasing agency in the United States, with the idea of buying rights to a mixing apparatus Brothman had invented and had offered for sale through a trade journal.

When the agents questioned Gold separately, he told them he had first met Golos through another chemist and that Golos had asked him to make some laboratory checks on Brothman's mixing apparatus. One month later Brothman and Gold were requested to appear before the Grand Jury, and evidently their testimony was found satisfactory since they were excused.

All during these six years, Gold's relationship with Brothman had been on a warm level. Gold admired his employer for his superior scientific training, and Brothman appreciated Gold's readiness for hard work. Eventually, he promised Gold a share in the business.

However, in September, 1947, Gold's mother died, and from that time on he became increasingly hostile toward Brothman. He blamed himself so bitterly for his mother's death that he often considered suicide. As he defined his feelings later: If he had not allowed himself to be seduced by Brothman away from his mother she might have lived many more years. Moreover Brothman's blandishments had proved illusory whenever the firm had run into financial difficulties. As Gold expressed it: "When there was no money, I was a partner. When there was money, I became an employee."

Recriminations followed, sharpened by Gold's demands for $4,000 back pay. In June, 1948, Gold was threatening suit and his employer was accusing him of stealing laboratory equipment.

In September, Gold obtained a $70-per-week position in the laboratory of the Philadelphia General Hospital. He kept this hospital job for the next three years until May 22, 1950, on which day he placed himself, as he claims, "in voluntary custody" with the FBI after having "confessed" to being the Soviet courier for Dr. Klaus Fuchs.

•

Such, then, in substance, was the real life of Harry Gold as distinguished from his fancied life. In short, here was a lonely creature in full manhood with a crying need for personal relationships, for close human contact and love. With no wife, no children, no home of his own, he had not even the compensation of the brilliant career he had so desperately longed for. Save for his mother, no meaningful relationship had ever existed for him. And, not being devoid of human emotions, such a barren existence had proved quite impossible.

We know that his private life was one of almost complete withdrawal, and that he tried to answer the problem of his inner tensions with an excess of work, exhausting himself to a point where he had no physical energy left to give to anything but dreams and phantasies. What shape and form these assumed might remain in the realm of conjecture, but fortunately there is the court record describing them in utmost detail. And it is here that we will see almost clinically "the realistic acting out of the phantasy."

III

Some six months after Gold's arrest, Abraham Brothman was tried on charges that he had conspired with Gold to impede the 1947 Grand Jury's investigation of espionage. This trial took place in November, 1950. The presiding judge was Irving R. Kaufman, who four months later was to preside over the Rosenberg trial. The prosecutor was U.S. Attorney Irving H. Saypol, who at this time was preparing his case against the Rosenbergs. Saypol's chief assistant at both trials was Roy M. Cohn. The Government's star witnesses were Harry Gold and Elizabeth Bentley, both major witnesses at the Rosenberg trial.

There were other striking features about the Brothman trial which give strong basis for the belief that it was to a great extent a "try-out" for the big A-bomb spy "show" to take place in March, 1951.

For four and one-half days of the one-week trial,

Harry Gold was on the witness stand, and it is from his own testimony that we have the astounding tale of his romances, courtship, honeymoon, marriage, children, separation, and divorce as recounted to Brothman, to fellow employees, friends, and acquaintances over a period of six years. Here, culled from the Brothman trial record, are the highlights as Gold had told them "in intimate detail":

While riding in a trolley car one day in Philadelphia, he had met and fallen in love with a beautiful girl named Helen who had "one brown eye and one blue eye." He had tried to court her, but a wealthy rival named Frank had won out.

However, through Helen he had met another Philadelphia girl named Sarah, "a young, gawky, long-legged girl" who worked as a model in Gimbels and in time "developed into a comely, good-looking, young lady."

While courting Sarah, Gold had learned of another "suitor"—an "underworld character . . . with a reputation for conscripting girls for brothels." "In order to save her" from this sinister fate, Gold was spurred into marriage. After some postponements, the two lovers were finally wed and enjoyed their honeymoon in Atlantic City.

In 1935, Gold's "wife" gave birth to twins, a girl and boy named Essie and David. Soon after, Gold purchased a house "for his wife and family."

As the twins grew older, Gold would tell of their growing up, of their progress in school, how little Essie broke her leg while playing, and how the boy David had developed polio but had fortunately recovered.

When in 1945 Brothman had first suggested to Gold that he work full time in New York, Gold had declined, giving as his reason that "his wife would not like to be transplanted" from the suburb of Philadelphia where they had bought their new home. In fact, whenever he had to leave home on business, Sarah had "resented" his absences. Eventually this caused a serious "rift" between Gold and his wife, since she had started to have an affair with an "elderly, rich real estate broker."

When this situation had resulted in his home being "broken up," Gold would sadly tell friends that he went home on weekends to secretly watch his children "playing in the park," and that he "looked at them from afar," unable to bear the pain of visiting them in his formerly happy home.

In addition to this tragedy of his "family life," Gold had also told of "the death of [his] brother while in service for his country." In 1945 he had tearfully described how his brother had "died overseas" while completing a parachute jump in Hollandia, New Guinea. Later, he had gone on to tell that his parents in their grief had sought to replace their hero son, Joseph, by "taking into the family like a son" a cousin, also named Joe.

Toward the conclusion of Gold's direct testimony, we find the following admission:

Contrary to that story . . . I actually had no wife and two twin children. . . . I was a bachelor and had always been one. . . .

Sometime before I came to work for Abe [Brothman] I had told him that my brother had been killed in action in the South Pacific, and [after the FBI visit of May, 1947] I told Abe that this was not so, that my brother was still alive.

Thus, each and every detail of the above incidents was shown to have been fictitious from start to finish! In short, Gold had created a completely mythical life, never having paid court to any Helen, never having married any Sarah, never having had a wedding or a honeymoon or children or anything remotely resembling the family and circumstances he had described so elaborately for so many years.

It does appear, however, that he did base his phantasies on two actual women named Helen and Sarah, both of whom, of course, remained entirely unaware of their participation in Gold's imaginary romances. But what is especially revealing is how, at the Brothman trial, Gold confuses his imaginary wife with his mother or, rather, substitutes one for the other:

Q. Did you not say as a result of your being away from home in 1942 and 1943 that Sarah resented your absences—your wife, Sarah?

A. Actually, it was my mother.

And concerning the purchase of the home in the suburbs and his "wife's" refusal to be transplanted to New York:

That was partly false but it was based on truth. My mother and I had purchased a home and I didn't want to be transplanted to New York.

But even so, the actual facts were different, for it was his father together with his brother who had really purchased the house.

This tendency to substitute himself for his father and brother reached its height with his wishful "killing" of at least one rival, his brother Joseph. Apparently Gold was so guilt-stricken that he had to invent the story of his parents' replacement of their lost son with a cousin of the same name, *which incident was also a fabrication.*

At the Brothman trial, Gold had a glib explanation for all this fabulous deception. It was that he had been assigned to contact Brothman not by Jacob Golos but by a Soviet superior named "Sam," and that it was "Sam" who had instructed him to present himself as a family man so that he would appear less "unstable." [5]

The absurdity of the explanation is exposed by its irrationality: Why should the spy-master "Sam" endanger his entire operation by instructing his agent to play a complicated fictitious role in addition to his espionage tasks—a role requiring a daily continuity of lies told to numerous people, and a role so easily exposed by the slightest happenstance?

Moreover there was the direct challenge put to Gold by Brothman's attorney as follows: If it was true that he and Brothman had been brother spies "working toward a common end," why was it necessary for Gold to continue the fiction? Why didn't he simply tell Brothman the real reason for the pretense, just as he had once explained the practical reason for using the name Frank Kessler? In reply to this point, Gold furnished this excuse:

I had become so tangled up in this web of lies that it was easier to continue telling an occasional one than to try and straighten the whole hideous mess out.

But then he adds, in awe of his own prowess: "It is a wonder that steam didn't come out of my ears at times."

Comment might be made on Gold's penchant for pulp-fiction phraseology. Apparently a goodly portion of his reading consisted of mystery stories, detective thrillers, and spy tales. Here, from the Brothman trial record, is some of the purple prose he seems to have absorbed:

I knew that once the FBI began to probe into the hideous snarl that was my life, once they pulled one thread, the whole horrible skein would become untangled. . . .

From his subsequent testimony at the Rosenberg trial, here is this morsel concerning one of his "Soviet superiors":

He was tall, about 6 feet 2, had blond hair, and a very determined feature. He walked with a catlike stride almost on the balls of his feet. . . . [R. 842] [6]

Returning to the standard definition given by psychiatry to "pseudologia phantastica," or the pathology of abnormal lying:

The lies are seemingly phantasy wish-fulfillments, not unlike the more or less normal phantasies of children which grow by a two-fold process of elaboration and by the continuous addition of material in the effort to continue the appearance of veracity. [7]

All through Gold's alleged spy career, there is the acting out of his phantasies as a compensation for his barren emotional life. In his choice of spy pseudonyms, we see that he utilizes his own father's name, Samuel, to give it to another Russian-born person who becomes his alleged superior, that is, "Sam." In other words, a direct substitute for his parent, who must have pestered his bachelor son to get married, settle down, and have children. Incidentally, according to Gold's testimony it was this "Sam" who assigned him to his original espionage meeting with Dr. Fuchs.

Examining Gold's pseudonyms, it is significant that they were the names of actual persons whom he secretly envied. For example, his rival, the wealthy "Frank," really did marry the beautiful "Helen." Thus one of the pseudonyms Gold assumed while posing as a happily married man was that of "Frank Kessler." Again in his testimony at the Brothman trial, we find there was an actual Martin who married the "Sarah" whom Gold imagined to be his wife.

To restate it: The two real women, Helen and Sarah, featured so prominently in Gold's *imaginary* love life, actually married two men, Frank and Martin, whose names figured with equal prominence in Gold's imaginary spy life.

In short, one has every justification to conclude that there was no more a Soviet superior called Sam than there was a wife called Sarah or a pair of twins called Essie and David.

The ease with which Gold could juggle these names, as well as various real incidents, from one imaginary life to another demonstrates that there was no possible way to distinguish between them, *i.e.*, between his phantasy love life and his professed espionage life. Both were so interwoven—as Gold admits in speaking of being enmeshed in a tangled skein—that no line can be drawn between what he admits is pure fiction and what he claims is so-help-me-God truth.

At the trial of Brothman, Judge Irving Kaufman showed that he was clearly aware of Gold's special talents when he addressed Brothman's attorney impatiently:

The Court: . . . The witness [Gold] said he concocted these things from beginning to end. Are you going to take each and every detail he concocted?

How, then, was it possible for Judge Kaufman to extract or pin down the truth in Gold's testimony at any one point? If he was aware that Gold was capable of concocting a mythical family life *from beginning to end,* how could he know that Gold's espionage life was not also a complete concoction?

Gold was a major witness in the Rosenberg trial, yet what the reader knows at this point concerning Gold's astonishing facility to invent and spin any yarn in the minutest detail was totally *unknown* to the Rosenberg jury! Let this be clear—the two men at the Rosenberg trial who were in full possession of this highly significant information were the same two who had served as prosecutor and presiding judge at the Brothman trial—namely, U.S. Attorney Saypol and Judge Kaufman.

And let it be stated that it was largely on the basis of Gold's supporting testimony against the Rosenbergs, which Saypol declared was "the necessary link" in the chain of their guilt, that their conviction was obtained and their sentence of death imposed.

It was the testimony, as Saypol and Kaufman both knew, of a self-admitted pathologic impostor whose only means of gratifying a lifetime of starved emotional needs was in the acting out of a spy career based on nothing more than his "phantasy wish-fulfillments."

IV

In 1947, according to Mr. Hoover, the FBI was well aware of the potential value of Gold as an "accomplished deceiver," because its investigation of him had "developed some highly useful information." Exactly what went on between Gold and the FBI until they were ready to produce him as the "American confederate" of Dr. Fuchs we have no way of knowing. But we can examine how his talents were utilized to fabricate a spy biography, and we can ask whether or not this new fabrication contained any more truth than the others.

What is the FBI explanation of how Gold became a spy for the Russians? At the outset we learn that the "Tom Black" earlier referred to was the mysterious gentleman most responsible for Gold's downfall. Here is how Hoover describes him in the *Reader's Digest:*

. . . A singular character in Jersey City whom we shall call Troy Niles. . . .

Niles [Black] was an eccentric individual who liked to coil a pet black snake around his neck and who pitched marbles to a crow that was trained to catch them in flight.

If we are to believe Mr. Hoover, it was this grotesque "Communist" who first "captivated" Gold back in 1932. "By precise and insidious techniques," Gold was soon "softened up" for his spy career. These techniques consisted of his being taken to Greenwich Village "gab-fests composed of Communists, parlor pinks, leftist intelligentsia, and people of that sort."

But while Gold was apparently impressed with Black's charming of crows and snakes, here is his opinion of Communists in his testimony at the Brothman trial: "I didn't like them. . . . I thought they were a lot of wacked-up Bohemians." And here is his attorney's statement at his sentencing:

Let the record in this case show . . . that Harry Gold has never been a Communist and he is not a Communist now, nor was he in those younger days.

If, according to Hoover, all adherents to Communism are potential spies and if, as we have seen, Gold was hostile to Communism, then how does one account for his motivations? Did he do it for money? The record shows that Gold never asked for or received any financial reward. But evidently some explanation was thought necessary. At the Brothman trial these were the two astonishing reasons which Gold offered:

The Witness: The first was a debt of gratitude to Black because of the fact that he had gotten me a job in the worst years of the depression. . . . We were a family with a fierce sort of pride and we would have hated to go on relief. . . . Black saved us from that.

. . . The second reason was that I got Black off my neck about joining the Communist party. I didn't want to. I didn't like them.

Thus we are asked to believe that because of a temporary job, Gold's "gratitude" to Black was so overwhelming that he became a spy for a government he despised!

However, it is his second reason that staggers the mind. Here his motive is not gratitude but simply a means to stop Black from pestering him!

In his article, Hoover, avoiding any mention of Gold's feeble motivations, advances his own rather mystical interpretation, that because Gold's parents had been born in Russia, the word "Russia" or "the sound of it had an odd appeal" for Gold and that "the name vaguely stirred" him.

Having asked why Gold became a Soviet spy, let us also ask why the Soviet spy-masters were so eager to obtain his services and so ready to trust him with their most precious contact, Dr. Fuchs.

It seems strange, in the face of Gold's unconcealed political hostility, that they would take such grave risks. We are told that their meetings with him were conducted in true cloak-and-dagger style, starting with one "Paul Smith" to whom Black introduced him in 1935 and with whom he took a walk, which is described by Mr. Hoover as "a favorite technique of Red agents."

Following Smith, there came a succession of other Soviet superiors: "Steve Swartz," described as "a virtual giant, about six feet two inches and weighing approximately 220 pounds. . . ." [8] Then came another Russian, "Fred," who taught Gold the secrets of spy technique:

. . . How to determine whether he was being followed: stop and tie a shoe-lace or walk up a deserted side street. And if Gold had a piece of paper he wanted to destroy, tear the paper into very small pieces and drop each piece into a separate block.[9]

As for the vital secrets the KGB obtained from Gold, we learn from Hoover that Gold's espionage included the "data on lanolin" (commonly used for hair pomades), "a soap-making technique . . . and industrial solvents of the type used in varnishes and lacquer." [10]

During these same years there were more than

"1,540 scientific institutes and laboratories in the Soviet Union," employing thousands of skilled chemists and engineers in addition to British, American, French, Swedish, and German technicians of every category.[11] To make any further comment would be to dignify an absurdity.

A great deal of Gold's testimony is concerned with his alleged espionage meetings with Brothman for the transmission of the results of another of his experiments. This one had to do with synthetic rubber. But here, too, we find in *Nation's Business* of September, 1953, that the U.S.S.R. was far more advanced than we in this field, not only in 1943, the time of the alleged espionage, but as early as 1930:

A decade before we embarked upon our synthetic rubber program, the USSR was producing it in quantity with potato alcohol or limestone as key ingredients.

Having thus weighed the value of the "secrets" which Gold claims to have delivered to the Russians, let us now test the credibility of his relations with them. Suppose we glance at the record of his spy career, as disclosed by his own attorney previous to his sentencing:

He [Gold] began feeding these people in New York, these Soviet agents—fictitious names, any number of them, and would report to them on what he was doing with these fictitious names. . . .
. . . He again resorted to fiction in that he made up trips to Dayton which he never took—and he did that in order to keep these men off his back. . . .

Just as he had admitted concocting a mythical wife and children, Gold now admits the fabrication of a host of recruits, reports of fictional meetings with them and imaginary trips to see them!

If he could make up trips to Dayton, could he not also make up trips to Santa Fe for his alleged meetings with Dr. Fuchs? If he could be so glib with Soviet agents about any number of fictitious names and invented meetings, could he not also be glib with FBI agents about any number of invented meetings with Fuchs, Greenglass, and Yakovlev?

How can anyone such as a Judge Kaufman state with positive assurance: Here Gold is lying and here he is not?

Even if we grant every word about Gold's espionage to be gospel truth, Mr. Hoover could scarcely support the theory that the Russians were interested merely in securing endless lists of fictitious names! He cannot on the one hand say there exists an efficient Russian spy network and on the other hand show it to be as gullible as Gold would have us believe.

Is it likely that the KGB would have delegated to this untrustworthy and unwilling person *the most important* assignment of all recorded espionage? Why not someone whose espionage achievements included something more than soap and varnish formulae and a list of nonexistent recruits?

V

Soon after the FBI announced the capture of Gold, a general press release was broadcast that the feat had been accomplished because of one thoughtless mistake:

TRICK QUESTION LED TO SPY CONFESSION
Gold Was Trapped by Denial He Ever Had Been
Out West—Evidence Refuted Him

The evidence was supposedly a certain map of Santa Fe found in Gold's room by the FBI. Here is Hoover's article:

Like a casual tourist he [Gold] entered a museum [in Santa Fe] and obtained a city map. Now he would not have to ask questions to the Castillo Street Bridge —he aimed at leaving not the slightest clue. Little did he suspect that the day would come when he would wish he had never picked up that map.

Now five years later, Mr. Hoover relates, after the week of useless questioning by the FBI, Gold himself suggested a search of his room, and the following occurred:

Suddenly, an agent dredged up from behind a bookcase a yellow folder marked "Santa Fe, the Capitol City." . . .

Silently, Gold was shown the folder. A startled gleam flashed through his eyes, his mouth fell open and he seemed momentarily to freeze.

The map he had obtained in the Santa Fe Museum so that he could find the way to the bridge without asking questions!

Following this denouement, Mr. Hoover goes on to tell that Gold, realizing he was trapped, "abruptly blurted out: 'I . . . I am the man to whom Klaus Fuchs gave his information.' "

Now let us turn to Gold's sentencing. Here is the version offered by his attorney:

That in late December of 1944, Dr. Fuchs had met with Gold in Cambridge, and that it was *there* that they had arranged their Santa Fe rendezvous for June 2, 1945, and it was *there* that

. . . *Fuchs gave to Gold a map of Sante Fe, where he [Gold] had never been, marked with the place of the rendezvous.* [Emphasis added.]

Why, then, are we given this fanciful story by Mr. Hoover that Gold had obtained the map in the museum, *when the court record states so clearly that Gold had received the map from Dr. Fuchs in Cambridge?* [12]

But there is still the implied claim that it was brought all the way from New Mexico to Philadelphia, only to be tossed thoughtlessly on the bookcase in Gold's bedroom.

One might be willing to accept such carelessness if Hoover had not built up Gold as so cautious that he would not even risk asking a passer-by a simple street direction.[13]

In addition, we were told that Gold had been "groomed" by his spy-masters on methods of destroying incriminating papers. And yet the one and only piece of paper which could possibly connect him with Dr. Fuchs is the one Gold fails to destroy!

Further: that Gold's "confession," given after seven days of questioning, had resulted from the discovery of the "museum" map. According to Mr. Hoover's version, this was the end of the "long, painstaking quest." Finally, the FBI had trapped the most "wanted person" in the United States: "In all the history of the FBI there never was a more important problem than this one."

Hence, one would normally expect that trained FBI detectives, with appetites whetted, would immediately make a thorough search of the rest of Gold's house for other incriminating documents. But what happens on May 22, the day of Gold's "confession"? Do they make their thorough search on that day? Not at all. A routine search? Not even that. When do they make their search?

According to the Brothman trial record, not until June 3, *thirteen days later!* Moreover, we find that this search was divided into two parts, since another search was conducted on June 6, an additional three days later.

First, according to FBI detective Fred Birkby, he searched the living room, but found nothing. Then he descended to the basement, and it was there that he found "a large wooden box, approximately three feet square filled with papers and blueprints":

[Birkby]: There was similar material in a closet approximately four feet across and running from the floor to the ceiling.

In this closet, conveniently enough, there was the most damaging evidence against Gold's former employer, Abraham Brothman. In a red folder marked "A.B.'s stuff," there turned out to be a certain "small white card" containing the details of Gold's first espionage rendezvous with Brothman, allegedly prearranged *nine years earlier* by their mutual Soviet superior "Sam." It should be added that all these damning details happened to be in Gold's own handwriting, and that he made no effort to destroy this card in all the nine years since he had written it! [14]

First, we see that according to Gold's testimony there was "a huge amount of material." In other words, if the FBI detectives had merely gone down into the basement with Gold on May 22, the evidence would have stared them in the face.

Next, that there was more than sufficient time for this distinctive red, initialed folder to be "planted," either during the seven days of questioning when Gold had been *free to go home every night,* or during the two and one-half weeks after his "confession."

Third, that there was a period of two weeks for the "making of a case" against Brothman *before* the folder was found. Fourth, the suspicious interval between June 3 and 6.

Pursuing another line of inquiry, let us examine the incredible claim that Gold had preserved the "small white card" for nine years. But, in his testimony at the Brothman trial, it is disclosed that the FBI had searched his house as far back as May of 1947, *three years before his arrest.* Thus the question arises: Since this "small white card" existed in 1947, why didn't the FBI discover it *then,* instead of three years later?

And now comes the "built-in" excuse, with Gold attempting to explain away the FBI's failure to find "A.B.'s stuff" at that time. How? Gold simply testifies that the 1947 search was but a "cursory search." But even in a cursory search, how could the highly trained FBI overlook a three-foot-square crate and a closet, bulging not only with "incriminating" blueprints, but with the conspicuously marked folder bearing Abraham Brothman's *initials?*

Why, after so narrow an escape in 1947, didn't Gold make an effort to destroy these incriminating documents? Indeed, why, when he read the frightening news of Dr. Fuchs' confession in early February, 1950, did he still make no effort to destroy this evidence of espionage? And finally, why, more than three months later, during those seven days of questioning in mid-May, with every opportunity to do so, did he still take no measures to protect himself?

By way of a reply, it is not at all surprising that one of the FBI men involved in this so-called search aptly referred to Gold's hoard of documents with the tongue-in-cheek comment that it was akin to "Fibber Mc-Gee's closet."

A word of explanation about these "incriminating"

blueprints. It will be recalled that many were produced at Brothman's trial as "evidence" of espionage despite the fact that they were merely "flow-sheets" describing soap-making, lanolin, anaesthetics, and varnish techniques. In fact, Gold admitted that one set of "espionage" blueprints described Brothman's invention of a process "for the preparation of shortening materials from vegetable oils, such as Crisco and Spry"!

Another invention of Brothman's had been the well known "Aerosol" fly-spray container.

Let us accept as true that Gold, a routine chemist's assistant, who had admired Brothman professionally, had saved a copy of almost every blueprint Brothman had ever given him for laboratory checking. To him they were prized research experiments worth keeping for future reference. Very well, but now we come to another example of how a full truth is easily twisted into something else, for at the Brothman trial these stacks of harmless blueprints were presented by Saypol as Government Exhibits 11 to 19 inclusive, and the "small white card" became Government Exhibit 10—magically transforming a fly-spray and a shortening formula into Soviet espionage!

Why was no search made of Gold's home all during the week of his questioning, nor during the two weeks following his alleged "confession"?

In line with our anatomy of frame-up, suggestions had to be made in such a way that no one actually would tell Gold what to say or do, but would merely indicate what the needs were. (Did he happen to have anything in his house that might help prove he had met Brothman on instructions from a Soviet superior? Perhaps among all those blueprints he might have forgotten something—just as he had forgotten about the Santa Fe map?)

There is much to be said about this "small white card," which became the prosecution's *only* concrete evidence of Gold's espionage connections with his Soviet superior "Sam," and was *the deciding factor* in the conviction of Brothman. At the Rosenberg trial, we will see how Saypol produces still another white card (the Hotel Hilton registration card), this one purporting to be the *only* concrete evidence that Gold had ever visited Albuquerque. And this card too will be seen to have all the suspicious earmarks of convenient prearrangement.

VI

> "The pathologic liar lies for the satisfaction and perhaps urge of lying, with insufficient objective. As the lies are elaborated, it is questionable how clearly the patient himself can distinguish between truth or falsehood." [15]

Reviewing briefly the official version of the story of Harry Gold, one is taken aback by the sheer impudence of the fabrication. From the description of Gold which failed to describe him, to the manhunt which never took place, from the apocryphal museum map which never trapped him, to the two vital Santa Fe meetings which are absent in the Fuchs indictment, from the Communist indoctrination of Gold who was never indoctrinated, to all the claptrap about Tom Black with his charmed snake and marble-catching crow, it is such a hodgepodge of incredibility that one can attribute its wide acceptance only to the Hitlerian axiom: "The bigger the lie, the more it will be believed."

As in everything else, when one is given an unreasonable explanation of a certain set of facts, one is forced to search for a reasonable one.

What were the actual circumstances and motivations behind Gold's confession vis-à-vis the requirements and objectives of the FBI? We do not know all the answers. What took place between Harry Gold and the FBI was behind closed doors and involved a period of many years. But we do know from our study of the political setting that the time was ripe for the creation of an internal "enemy." Not only did Gold (as brought out by Hoover: "Golodnitsky") meet with the usual requirements of a foreign-sounding name coupled with Jewish parents of Russian birth, but he could also be given the impressive title of "biochemist."

90

There was only one drawback about Gold from the viewpoint of J. Edgar Hoover. He was not a member of the Communist Party. But that problem could be solved by having him testify that he had been "indoctrinated" in Communism by Tom Black.

That Gold could be relied upon to supply such "dressing" convincingly, the FBI had not the slightest doubt. With Gold's amazing record of his mythical private lives, he had been tried and tested for years. With such a witness appearing first against Brothman and then against Rosenberg, there need never be any concern. With his fertile imagination he could be relied upon to meet any contingency arising in cross-examination. Not only could he resist successfully any attempt to shake him, but he could even confound his questioner with an unexpected outpouring of phantasied detail. Most important, Gold seemed to believe his phantasies almost as promptly as he invented them— and not merely during the time he was describing them, but in a permanent sense. Hence, he could be depended on with each court appearance to achieve "with more and more assurance . . . the appearance of veracity." [16]

VII

In our anatomy of frame-up, we have indicated that there are various methods used to secure perjured testimony from prospective government witnesses. It is nothing unusual in police practice to secure gossip, tips, and "state's evidence" from persons who have committed crimes of one sort or another. Indeed, our police chiefs cry out that they are forced to rely on stool-pigeon assistance in most of their crime detection. But since these stool pigeons are motivated by fear of prosecution, their normal inclination is to do everything possible to oblige the police. Very often they become imbued with the psychology of the "cop" or "dick," and become known as "police-sucks." The expression graphically describes that type of fawning, obsequious creature whom detectives have at their beck and call for whatever purpose is required.

In his chapter on the psychology of the informer, Whittaker Chambers describes the political type, with first-hand knowledge, as a person who invariably becomes a "creature" of the police. "When they whistle, he fetches a soiled bone of information." [17]

And while we cannot say with certainty that Harry Gold was such a "creature" before his arrest in 1950, we do know this: Mr. Hoover's heralded manhunt for him in that year is so much stuff and nonsense. Not only is it completely contradicted by official records, but there was not the slightest need to hunt Gold! The FBI already had him in its pocket, so to speak, at least since May of 1947, when they had interrogated him and searched his house.

With the arrest of Dr. Fuchs in February, 1950, all they had to do was to look in their "Central Subversive Files" under the possible heading: "Suspected of Soviet Espionage—New York Area—Harry Gold and Abraham Brothman."

And there, in less than five minutes, they could have seen the cross-reference to Gold's dossier containing Elizabeth Bentley's charges against Brothman as well as "the highly useful information" Mr. Hoover has written about so tantalizingly.

What exactly was this information, what were the true motivations behind Gold's confession, and what were the inducements, the pressures, promises, or rewards—are questions impossible to answer with any certainty. It may be that Gold was actually an *agent provocateur* or a volunteer counterspy all along. It may be that the FBI's "highly useful information" included some crime involving some abnormal deviation.

On the other hand, with what we know about Gold psychologically from his own admission, it was not necessary for him to have committed any actual crime; he could very well have had a compulsion for punishment *other* than for the crime he confessed.

In the field of psychiatry, the pathology is well known. The would-be confessant is so tormented by some secret sin or misdeed (real or fancied) which he dares not admit—sometimes not even to himself—that his compulsion to confess and his need to be punished are overpowering.[18]

In view of Gold's constant striving to emulate Dr. Fuchs, it is interesting to weigh the possibility that he was inspired to imitate Fuchs' compulsion for atonement and thus expiate for some "other crimes" of his own. Judging from Gold's "killing" of his brother, there could well have been some *unmentionable* crime committed in his vivid phantasies—one that had caused such an accumulation of guilt and inner tension over the years that it was impossible for him to wipe it out unless he received punishment for an invented, substitute crime.

We know that Gold, in proclaiming himself as the "American partner" of Dr. Fuchs, played his new role with as much conviction as he had played the broken-hearted husband of "Sarah," and the noble, sacrificing father watching his twins from afar. According to *Life* of June 12, 1950, Gold always had an inordinate ambition to become "a great scientist, so great that everyone in the world would know him. . . ." The extent to which he attempted to pattern himself after Dr. Fuchs can be seen in this comparison between parts of the former's confession and Gold's statements at the Brothman trial:

Dr. Fuchs: I used my Marxian philosophy to conceal my thoughts in two separate compartments. One side was the man I wanted to be. . . . I knew the other compartment would step in if I reached the danger point.

Harry Gold: When I went on a mission for the Soviet Union, I used a one-track mind . . . I forgot work, family, everything. When I returned, I just turned the switch and I used a one-track mind in regard to my work.

Thus, Gold achieves closer identification with Dr. Fuchs. Not only does he become his "partner" in the transmission of the most important scientific secret in world history, but he, too, becomes a "controlled schizophrenic."

In essence, this much is certain—that when Harry Gold was ready to step forward to the center of the world stage and be accepted on equal terms with Dr. Fuchs, no gratification could have meant more to him. His phantasy spy life had become much more gratifying than his real prosaic and barren life could ever be.

VIII

Perhaps no aspect of the anatomy of frame-up is more interesting, and of necessity more complex, than self-entrapment. It is a separate jigsaw puzzle contained within the larger one, and therefore has its own bits and pieces which must be reassembled. It is not a simple matter to reconstruct, for involved are not only the individual's changing attitudes during the various stages of entrapment, but there is the very intricate machinery of the law, which, of course, constitutes the trap.

It is also necessary to point out that since we have access only to the available facts, the picture must remain incomplete. In addition, one is hampered by separate and conflicting hypotheses, each of which leads to a different line of inquiry, and therefore a different picture, although there may be overlapping. For example, if one pursues the hypothesis that Gold was partly induced and partly pressured by the threat of exposing some minor criminal conduct in his past, (e.g., an overt homosexual act), his expectation of punishment would be quite realistic, because such a situation would presuppose some kind of a "deal."

On the other hand, if we pursue the hypothesis that the pathologic Gold—operating under a compulsion to expiate some secret and/or phantasied crime—actually sought and welcomed punishment, then the reality of his sentence, in terms of actual years of imprisonment, would scarcely concern him.

However, since the avenue of psychological exploration is virtually endless and the boundaries between one hypothesis and another are impossible to determine, it is entirely feasible that Gold's decision to play the role of Dr. Fuchs' partner had more than one motivation.

In other words, he may have wanted to be punished, but not too severely. At the same time, with his boundless confidence that he could match wits with the FBI, he could have involved himself little by little by his own glib tongue. Then again, considering his suddenly released and over-inflated ego, compensating for a lifetime of inferiority, he may have been oblivious to any thought of punishment at all at the time of his arrest, which he describes as "voluntary custody." But, whatever the case may be, let us examine some of the possibilities.

In the first place, we know that the delicate matter of Gold's sentencing was postponed for an *unprecedented* period of time—almost seven months after his arrest on May 23, 1950.[19] Since Gold pleaded guilty on July 20, 1950, this delay had only one purpose, namely, the "making of a case" against Brothman, whose trial was to take place in November. In other words, only *after* Gold had "delivered the goods" at that trial did he come up for sentencing on December 7, 1950.

Needless to say, testimony under such circumstances is regarded as suspect and unreliable. Since the witness, giving accomplice testimony, has not yet been sentenced, he has every motive to "pile it on" in the hope that his sentence will be lighter. And because the incentive for lying is recognized to be so great, in many such cases the courts seek to minimize the danger, either by giving the accomplice a guarantee of freedom, or by imposing sentence prior to his testimony.

There can be little doubt that by the time Gold took the stand to relate his espionage exploits with Brothman, he had already passed through many stages of self-entrapment. In preparing the case against Brothman, the FBI and the prosecution (Saypol, Lane, Cohn, et al.) had to go over the story innumerable times with Gold, and one can be sure that all of it was taken down in sworn statements, each one of which involved him a little deeper. Thus, by the time the Brothman trial was over, whatever illusions Gold may have entertained, or whatever promises had been made, there was no turning back.

Concerning Gold's possible illusions in the early

stages of his "voluntary custody," it is not unlikely that he was persuaded to believe that he would receive light punishment. He had every justification to believe he would be treated as lightly as Greenglass, who had not only been promised a "deal" of one or two years, but the possibility of a suspended sentence.[20]

In addition, Gold was aware that other self-confessed "spies" had been treated most generously. There was Whittaker Chambers, the self-confessed espionage courier between Alger Hiss and the Russians. Not only had he not been prosecuted, but in scores of editorials throughout the country he was being eulogized as a great American patriot. There was Elizabeth Bentley, by her own description the "Red Spy Queen" and top courier for the Kremlin. Instead of being punished, she was now a well-paid lecturer for patriotic organizations, receiving considerable royalties for her published memoirs and articles. And there was, of course, Ruth Greenglass, his so-called co-conspirator, who, despite her admitted crimes, was not even to be indicted!

From official records, we know how benevolently Gold was treated during the six-month period before his sentencing. In later pages we will see how he was "lodged," not in a prison cell, but in the eleventh-floor dormitory of the Tombs, otherwise known as "Singers' Heaven." Here he could loll about almost without supervision, enjoying special privileges. Here, as we will see charged, he became the representative of the prosecution and the FBI in the matter of coaching his bunkmate, Greenglass, on the mysteries of the atom bomb "secrets" about which the latter was to testify. Frequent conferences with him were held in the offices of the FBI and the United States Attorney for the preparation of his testimony at the trials of Brothman and the Rosenbergs. In addition, there were a number of trips made to Philadelphia to confer with his prestigious attorney, John D. M. Hamilton, the former Chairman of the Republican National Committee! (Concerning this curious legal representation awarded to Gold, we will have more to say later.)

Hence, it is not difficult to see how this one-time "nonentity"—as he was described in *Life*—working for years "at a succession of dreary jobs," must have felt exhilarated with his sudden sense of importance.

On the witness stand during the Brothman trial as the Government's star witness, Gold enjoyed the public limelight with huge relish as well as the opportunity to present himself as a "scientist." Indeed, as he indulged himself in lengthy descriptions of the Aerosol "bomb" and the chemical processes involved in the manufacture of vegetable shortenings, his audience was enormously impressed with his scientific knowledge—except, of course, his former employer, Brothman.

IX

From the moment Gold consented to become the springboard for the FBI's case against the Rosenbergs, he was in a bargaining position where he could insist upon being treated with the importance he craved. According to the Brothman record, we find that he had demanded these "three conditions" at the time of his arraignment before Judge McGranery in Philadelphia:

The Witness [Gold]: They were conditions which I stipulated for myself. I was the only one that could meet them. Here were the three conditions:

First, I said that the lawyer appointed must permit me to talk to the FBI. Secondly, he must have no Communist or leftwing tinges whatever, and in conducting whatever mitigating circumstances there are for my defense, he must not put on a circus or show. The third point was that I must be permitted to plead guilty.

Regarding these three conditions, one can only approach them gingerly. Taking his first and last demands together—that he *must be permitted* to talk to the FBI, and that he *must be permitted* to plead guilty—they would seem to point to the following interpretation: that Gold was not too confident he could carry through the hoax should the *wrong* attorney be appointed. For example, a conscientious attorney might insist that Gold repudiate his confession, decline to confer further with the FBI, and demand a real show of evidence at a public trial.

Such advice would be nothing less than catastrophic. For, in the face of a repudiated confession, how could the Government *prove* that Gold was indeed Fuchs' "partner"? In view of the difficulties the FBI already had had with Dr. Fuchs, it was highly questionable what he might do at a public trial of Gold, whether he testified in person or by deposition. What if he again insisted that his courier had been the fictitious "James Davidson"?

Thus the meaning of the second condition also becomes clarified. Without the stipulation forbidding a left-wing lawyer, Judge McGranery might have appointed one with a "tinge." And such a lawyer might very well expose the hoax in open court, or enough of it to set the press agog and thus bring about the very "circus" Gold and the FBI were so determined to avoid. With the appointment of the former Chairman of the Republican National Committee, all such dangers were insured against and, as we shall soon see, Mr. Hamilton proved to be a Gibraltar of reliability.

It was in the official records relating to Harry Gold at the Federal Courthouse in Philadelphia that we found the gaping "hole" in Mr. Hoover's tale of the "museum" map. But this is not all, for the record further discloses that the veteran politician James P. McGranery, the sentencing judge (later to be appointed United States Attorney General), smelled something rotten in the much delayed sentencing of Gold, and showed a determination to keep his robes clean.

When we turn to Gold's plea of guilty on July 20, 1950, we find the cautious McGranery warning the government prosecutor, Mr. Gleeson, that he will have to specify *exactly* what crimes Gold had committed. Here is Mr. Gleeson's response:

In view of the plea of guilty, the Government will not wish to present *any evidence* with respect to the commission of the crime, because I think your Honor can very well understand that there is certain information we do not want made public since the man has entered his plea.

The same information, of course, if he pleaded not guilty, we would probably have to make public at a trial, but in view of the fact that he had entered a guilty plea, it may very well be that the Government does not wish to make public certain things that it has learned, for security reasons. [Emphasis added.]

The evasiveness of the answer is clear; the "security reasons" would have to be *made public* if Gold had not been so obliging, had insisted on a trial. But Judge McGranery remains politely insistent:

The Court: Certainly, that may be, but I will require enough evidence to satisfy me beyond any doubt as to the crimes charged and for imposition of sentence.

Mr. Gleeson: We will try. . . . It is difficult to determine. . . . It is only evidence, after all, to satisfy your Honor in determining the question of sentence. We will do the best we can.

If anything reveals the extent of the farce, it is what followed. For here is the defense counsel, springing to the prosecutor's aid!

Mr. Hamilton: I would be perfectly willing on behalf of the defendant, to accept *any statement* of the crime that he [Mr. Gleeson] might make, *without* supporting evidence. [Emphasis added.]

It is in these same records, in a colloquy between the judge and T. Scott Miller, representing the FBI, that we find the lie given to Mr. Hoover's fanciful account of the tracking down of Harry Gold. We recall being told how Fuchs cooperated with the Federal Bureau—how he gave the age and height of his courier—how Gold's photos were flown to Fuchs—how movies were flown for further study—and, finally, "positive assurance." And yet, here is Judge McGranery telling us that not a solitary word of this is true:

The Court: I think it is important for me to say there has been some view that has gone abroad that this case probably was first exposed by Fuchs. This is not true. This matter was uncovered by the Federal Bureau and Fuchs, as a matter of fact, as I understand it, *had never cooperated in any way, shape or form until after the arrest of Harry Gold.* Am I correct in that?

Mr. Miller: I think the statement is, Your Honor, that the identification of Harry Gold's picture was not made until after Gold signed a confession.

The Court: The point that I make is that Fuchs had *never* cooperated with the Federal Bureau. I am told that by both the Attorney General and *Mr. Hoover.*

Mr. Miller: *That is correct.* [Emphasis added.]

And so we discover not only that Fuchs had never given the FBI a description of Gold "in any way, shape or form," but also that Hoover told Judge McGranery one thing and the American public another!

•

Two days before Gold's sentence was imposed, the Government brought to Judge McGranery's attention the recommendation of Attorney General McGrath that Gold's sentence be limited to twenty-five years. While this might sound severe enough, actually it meant Gold would be eligible for parole in eight years and four months.

In any event, there appeared to be no objection by Gold or his attorney, Mr. Hamilton. But not so the overcautious McGranery as he weighed the matter for the next two days. For he knew that he was soon to replace McGrath and be appointed Attorney General himself by President Truman. Thus, on December 9, when he imposed sentence, he added an extra five years, bringing it up to the maximum of thirty. By doing so, he was obviously avoiding any future charge of having rubber-stamped a fraud.

(*Note:* By this date also, the death sentence for Julius Rosenberg had become the strategic aim of the Justice Department. Thus the maximum sentence for

100

Gold served two purposes. First, it would counteract the comparatively light sentence of fourteen years which Dr. Fuchs had received in England, and second, it would lay a foundation for the death penalty designed for Julius.)

Perhaps the biggest day of Gold's life was at his sentencing. For two and a half hours he had listened raptly to Mr. Hamilton extolling his virtues. Then, as sentence was about to be passed, Gold rose with a prepared speech. It sounded like the banquet address of a retiring faithful employee thanking all the Company's executives.

I have received the most scrupulously fair trial [21] and treatment that could be described and this has been not only in this court, but has been the case with the FBI, with the other agencies of the Justice Department and at the various prisons where I have been lodged both here and in New York. . . . There is a puny inadequacy about any words telling how deep and horrible is my remorse.

•

In our effort to comprehend the workings of a mind such as Gold's, and especially his passivity vis-à-vis his punishment, we come upon a most revealing statement made by his attorney at the time of his sentencing: "Harry Gold had a fatalistic attitude. He has always had a peculiar fatalistic attitude."

With this key, one can open the door to Gold's attitude as he resigned himself to paying the price for the tremendous gratification he received in hoaxing the entire world, in seeing his name in headlines and his every quoted word accepted as truth.

What is the worst aspect of imprisonment to the normal person? Primarily, he is deprived of contact with those he cherishes: wife, children, parents, and friends. But for Gold, who did not possess such relationships, there was not the slightest deprivation. There had been only his mother, but she had died three years before. With his lifelong tendency to withdraw from the real world emotionally, we can venture that it was all the same to him wherever he happened to live, whether in prison or outside.

In fact, in a deeper sense, prison for Gold represented almost a sanctuary, a retreat. Since his chief pleasures were to indulge in phantasies, he simply took them along with him. And working in the prison hospital laboratory afforded him as much self-esteem as he had ever received in the obscurity of the Philadelphia General Hospital, and perhaps more. For his work was not merely welcomed by the shorthanded prison hospital staff, but also he was looked upon as a famous man with an aura of world importance.

It is a known fact among penologists that many inmates find their surroundings preferable to the world outside. With no care or anxieties, Gold found much more serenity within his safe, monastic surroundings than in the hazardous tension-ridden world without.[22]

At the very conclusion of Mr. Hoover's "case history" on Harry Gold in the *Reader's Digest,* we are told that the Soviets "had honored him with an Order of the Red Star," and that "one of the privileges of the award was free trolley rides in the city of Moscow!"

Nowhere in Gold's testimony is there any mention of any "Order of the Red Star"; nowhere in the Brothman trial, nor in the Rosenberg trial, nor anywhere else in official records! It is to be found only alongside such theatrics as the museum map and the pet snake and trained crow of Tom Black.

As previously stated, it is not our task or responsibility to expose Gold's real relations with the Federal Bureau. Nor is it to deny that espionage exists. All great powers have always conducted espionage and always will, as long as military general staffs are employed to counteract each other's military plans. Our purpose is simply to show that the FBI and the prosecuting officials have failed to produce in Gold an acceptable and convincing picture of a Soviet spy, one capable of being believed beyond all reasonable doubt —and one on whose *credibility* two human beings should have been put to death.

In later chapters we will take up the phenomenon of Harry Gold again. Thus far we have studied him from the viewpoint of his credibility before his entrance into the Rosenberg case. Later, we will examine his value as the prosecution's "necessary link." And since this link is claimed to be directly connected with that of the Greenglasses, let us now turn to them.

NOTES AND REFERENCES

1. Strecher, Ebaugh, and Ewalt, *Practical Clinical Psychiatry*, 7th ed., Blakiston, New York, 1951.
2. The trial record of the Brothman case (U.S. v. Brothman, et at.) is available at the U.S. Courthouse, Foley Square, N.Y.C. Gold's presentencing records are available at the U.S. Courthouse in Philadelphia. See "The Making of a Spy," *Life*, June 12, 1950; and the New York *Times*, May 24, 1950. Personal investigations were made in New York City, Philadelphia, Cincinnati, Albuquerque, and Santa Fe.
3. Strecher, et al., *op. cit.*
4. Oliver Pilat, *The Atom Spies*, Putnam, New York, 1952.
5. In the opinion of psychologists with whom this writer conferred, this explanation reveals how unstable Gold appeared to himself and how desperately he longed to be taken for a virile married man who could produce twins. And yet, it was because of his inability to enjoy a normal relationship, even in phantasy, that he surrendered both wife and children to "the elderly, rich real estate broker."
6. Quotations from the Rosenberg trial record will hereafter be noted in the text thus: R. 842, *i.e.*, Record, p. 842.
7. Strecher, et al., *op. cit.* See also Alfred P. Noyes, *Modern Clinical Psychiatry*, Saunders, Philadelphia, 1951.
8. The reader will recall that the blond cat-man mentioned earlier was also "6 feet 2." One cannot help wonder at the KGB's selection of such "giants" for their secret agents. In all standard spy operations, emphasis is given to selecting the most inconspicuous persons.
9. Hoover, *op. cit. Note:* Certainly, no example of a spy behaving more suspiciously could be furnished: Gold leaving a trail of torn bits of paper behind him!

10. From the record of Gold's sentencing, we learn that these so-called secrets were nothing more than commercial processes known to all countries for decades.

11. *Nation's Business*, September, 1953. See also article in *Newsweek*, "Red Science," March 1, 1954.

12. The date of Gold's sentencing was December 9, 1950; Mr. Hoover's article appeared five months later in May, 1951. Hence, Mr. Hoover was aware of Gold's statement that he had received the map from Fuchs. (See *This Week* magazine article by Hoover, "What Was the FBI's Toughest Case?" in which the fiction is continued as late as February 20, 1955.)

13. As a matter of curiosity, this writer asked several persons in Santa Fe, including two police officers: "Where is the Catillo Street Bridge?" Despite his showing sufficient furtiveness, there was not even a backward glance. Most of the passers-by gave wrong directions.

14. Thus, again, we are asked to believe that a spy "groomed" to destroy dangerous documents carefully retains the very evidence that will put him in jail!

15. Strecher, et al., *op. cit.*

16. Gold was not cross-examined at the Rosenberg trial. For a discussion of Mr. Bloch's reasons, see section v, Chapter 16.

17. Whittaker Chambers, *Witness*, Random House, New York, 1952, pp. 454–456.

18. Dr. Theodore Reik has written a definitive article on this phenomenon, called "Geständniszwang und Strafbedürfnis" (The Urge to Confess and the Need for Punishment).

19. Although the sentencing judge (McGranery) granted repeated requests for delay of sentence, he cautiously dissociated himself from possible trouble by this statement: "I know of no case on record where sentence has been deferred for so long a time."

20. It will be shown through the officially acknowledged memos of Greenglass' attorney, O. John Rogge, that such a "deal" had been made.

21. It is a matter of record that Gold never received a trial in any sense of the word.

22. Gold was released from prison in May, 1966. On Aug. 28, 1972, Gold died in Philadelphia at the age of sixty.

Casting further light on our psychiatric investigation of Gold, the New York *Times* of December 6, 1975, had this headline:

Harry Gold Held Neurotic in FBI-Rosenberg Files

Disclosed in this account is a summary of an official psychiatric report made on Gold in August, 1950, by Dr. Samuel Leopold, director of the Neuropsychiatric Division of the Philadelphia Municipal Court:

The report indicated that Gold has above-normal mentality. He is not insane but shows a neurotic personality characterized by extreme orderliness and compulsions. He has poor relationship to the world, dominated by resentful ideas and with immature psychosexual development.

Thus the summary—which includes such findings as "exaggerated ego," "repressed hostility," and a "fanatic drive" which "made him totally oblivious of everything" —would seem to confirm each and every point in our analysis of Gold's psychopathic personality.

What is both tragic and outrageous in these disclosures, coming to light after a quarter of a century, is that this FBI-puppet and mentally sick person was knowingly utilized by J. Edgar Hoover, Saypol, and Kaufman as the "necessary link" to obtain the convictions of the Rosenbergs.

In an article on the Op-Ed page of the New York *Times* of June 19, 1974, this view is supported by Allen G. Schwartz, a former assistant district attorney in New York and a member of the Committee on Criminal Courts, Law and Procedure of the Association of the Bar of the City of New York.

4 A SPECK OF URANIUM

I

Early in the cross-examination of David Greenglass, he was asked by the defense counsel, Emanuel Bloch, about his feelings toward his sister, Ethel Rosenberg:

Q. Do you bear affection for your sister Ethel?
A. I do.
Q. And you realize the possible death penalty, in the event that Ethel is convicted by this jury, do you not?
A. I do.
Q. And you bear affection for her?
A. I do.
Q. This moment?
A. At this moment. [R. 558–559]

Perhaps nowhere in the trial was there anything as horrendous as this moment. For almost two court days Greenglass had been testifying against his sister with the realization that his every word might be another nail in her coffin. And yet here was this claim that he bore affection for her at that very moment.

All through his testimony, if there were the slightest truth to his claim, one would recognize some evidence of sympathy. No matter how desperate to save himself, he would have sought in some way to mitigate his sister's part in the crime by adding, "Yes, but she didn't realize it was wrong, didn't think of it really as a crime, because we were allies of Russia . . ."

On the contrary, this modern Cain pours out his damning testimony quite gratuitously, revealing at every moment his anxiety to insure his promised reward—his wife's immunity and the "pat on the back" of a three-year sentence for himself, as his attorney's speech in the record discloses.

II

On the Lower East Side of New York, at 64 Sheriff Street, there is a dismal slum tenement. Alongside its entrance was the small store once occupied by Barnet Greenglass, an immigrant from Russia. Here he eked out an existence repairing sewing machines for the sweatshops of the ghetto.

Up a flight of creaking wooden stairs above a dark, dank hallway was his cold-water flat, the toilet off in the hall to be shared with other tenants. In 1922 his wife, Tessie, gave birth to a fourth child, David. The oldest son, Samuel, was fifteen at the time, then came sister Ethel, who was seven, and brother Bernard, aged five. While the mother helped tend the store downstairs, the task of caring for the baby brother fell to the little girl.

After finishing public school, David attended a trade school to learn to be an auto mechanic. When he was sixteen he tried to get into a handball tournament at the local community center as a member of either the Yipsels (Young People's Socialist League) or the YCL (Young Communist League).

During this period, around 1938, many youths on the East Side joined one group or another to be in the social swim for dances, parties, and sports. Thus it was that when young Greenglass joined the YCL handball team, he unknowingly entered the FBI's "Central Subversive File Checks."

Only a block or so away, on Rivington Street, lived a girl named Ruth Printz, some two years younger than David. Her immigrant parents owned a small cotton-goods store behind which the family lived. When Ruth was sixteen, she went to work as a typist at $8 per week. As the saying goes, David and Ruth were "serious" about each other, even though he was only eighteen and earning very little at the time. Anxious to have her future husband amount to something more than an ordinary mechanic, Ruth encouraged him to enroll at Brooklyn Polytechnic High School.

His sister, Ethel, had recently married a young graduate engineer from City College named Julius Rosenberg, and there was no reason why David shouldn't try to be one, too. But whether it was the streak of hard luck which David always felt himself "jinxed" with or lack of aptitude, in his very first semester he failed all of the eight technical courses.

On their wedding day, November 29, 1942, David was twenty and his bride eighteen. They found a cold-water tenement flat at a rental of $18 per month. Only four months later he was drafted into the Army, classified as an automotive machinist, and assigned to a motor pool in Pomona, California, and eventually reassigned to the student machine shop of an installation at Los Alamos, New Mexico.

In November, 1944, Ruth made a five-day visit to David in Albuquerque to celebrate their second wedding anniversary and to explore possibilities for an apartment and a job. Two months later, Ruth set up housekeeping in Albuquerque in a one-room kitchenette apartment.

In March, 1946, when David had received his discharge and the couple had returned to New York, Ruth found a flat in another cold-water tenement just across the street from her father's store.

Anticipating David's return to civilian life, his mother had arranged a partnership for him in a small war-surplus business formed by Julius and her other son, Bernard. In that same year, 1946, Ruth gave birth to a baby boy named Stephen. The partnership scarcely paid expenses, and the business was reorganized to do machine work, with David in charge of production, but the new effort fared just as badly.

In 1947 the partnership was reorganized again with a new and "silent" partner, one Mr. Schein, who invested $15,000 to match the others' assets. But fortune still eluded them, and as the business kept foundering, Julius and David began to find increasing fault with each other. It started with mild bickering, but soon there was such heated quarreling that by

1949 their relations had approached an open family feud.

Ruth would complain that while David did most of the hard work Julius, the so-called idea man and sales chief, just "handed out orders instead of obtaining any." In turn, Julius objected that David's machine work was frequently faulty and this caused numerous rejects, resulting in loss of customers.

As business continued to decline, the feuding increased. David would take long lunch hours at his flat. Frequently Ruth would keep him at home to mind the child while she went shopping. On such occasions she would scornfully tell him he was a fool to hurry back and sent him on errands.

Not a little of this was sheer spite, for Ruth had always been intensely jealous of David's "wonderful" sister Ethel. Particularly, she envied Ethel's modern apartment with its steam heat and resented that her own child had to play in a filthy back alley while Ethel's children had a "fancy" playground.[1] Whereas she had to lug parcels up three flights of stairs Ethel could step into an elevator and just press a button. On the East Side, to describe someone's social standing in the most awesome terms it was enough to say the lucky one lived in a house which had an elevator.

In her heart, too, Ruth had always resented the invidious comparisons made by members of the family between Julius and David. Ethel had married a college graduate, "a big engineer," whereas all David amounted to was "just a machinist." So bitter had the feud become that at the time of David's arrest, Ruth had not visited the Rosenbergs for almost eighteen months. It reached its height one day when David had answered Julius' objections to his "goofing off on the job" with an outright threat to "knock his block off."

In August, 1949, David quit trying to be a businessman and took a job with the Arma Corporation in Brooklyn. Bernard, burdened with a wife dying of Hodgkin's disease and a two-year-old daughter, also left. Julius, however, decided to carry on the remnants of the business, but enmity still remained, for Julius had to make a down payment to Mr. Schein of $1,000 on a settlement of $5,500, and therefore had nothing left to pay Bernard or David.

Knowing that Julius had cashed in his last Defense Savings Bond and was living on borrowed money from his relatives, Bernard agreed to wait. But David and Ruth demanded immediate payment. When in May, 1950, only a few weeks before David's arrest, Julius asked for a transfer of stock, Ruth refused unless he first signed a number of promissory notes. Since these would have obligated him to pay off the debt in monthly installments, Julius replied that he could not possibly meet such a series of notes. This incident served to intensify the feud—so much so that even after Julius' arrest, Ruth instructed her attorney to institute suit for the $1,000 still unpaid.[2]

III

Earlier that same year, the nervous strain of the Greenglasses had been heightened by two serious incidents. In February, a few days after the arrest of Dr. Fuchs, an FBI man had appeared at their flat to question David about a "specimen of uranium" he was suspected of having stolen from Los Alamos.

In addition David had engaged in considerable black-market activities in Albuquerque, selling precision tools and other stolen Army materials. There is no way of knowing what took place between the Greenglasses and the FBI following this February inquiry, but it is known that the Greenglasses felt themselves to be "the object of persecution" by the FBI. It is also known that David had actually stolen such "a sample of uranium," and that, terrified by the FBI visit coming so close upon the arrest of the "Communist" spy, Fuchs, and by the emphasis placed upon his youthful YCL membership, "he had thrown this uranium into the East River."[3]

On top of this suspicion and the threat of imprisonment on several counts for his Army thefts, an almost-fatal accident occurred. On February 14, Ruth was almost burned to death when her nightgown

110

caught fire at the gas stove. David managed to extinguish the flames, but Ruth was burned so badly she had to be rushed to the hospital for emergency blood transfusions.

At this time she was six months pregnant and was forced to leave her three-year-old boy in the care of relatives for two months until her return home in mid-April. Life had become a rat race for the Greenglasses. Heavy with child in her ninth month, her burns still not healed, Ruth tried to keep up with the housework as well as with David's tensions.

On May 16, Ruth was taken to the maternity hospital to give birth to a daughter, Barbara. No sooner had she returned to tend her newborn infant than she developed a serious infection from her burns. High fever resulted and again she had to be rushed to the hospital. Unable to afford a nurse, David took a leave of absence from work in order to care for the children, and once again their income was cut off.

And so it was, at the height of all this stress and strain, after years of worsening poverty and embittered family relations, after the harassment by the FBI and the ordeal of Ruth's festering burns, that final disaster struck on June 15, 1950. Although the next day's headlines reported him as "seized," the prosaic truth is that when David Greenglass wearily answered the FBI's knock on his door at 2 o'clock that afternoon he was found preparing a milk formula for his baby.

IV

Such, then, were the raw materials which the FBI presented to the prosecution on the day of Greenglass' arrest, confident that they were malleable enough to be successfully forged into the necessary "chain of evidence."

Their chief weapon, of course, was the universally accepted courier of Dr. Fuchs, the imperturbable Harry Gold. It was a foregone conclusion that any story he fabricated linking Greenglass with himself

111

and the Soviet Consulate would be believed by any jury. Greenglass' YCL membership and theft of the uranium sample constituted both "motive" and an overt act. The next link lay in the fact that his brother-in-law, Julius Rosenberg, formerly an engineer with the Signal Corps, had been dismissed on charges of membership in the Communist Party. The "chain" was designed, therefore, to link Gold to Greenglass, Greenglass to Rosenberg, Rosenberg to the Communist Party, the party to the Soviet spy-masters, and the spy-masters back to Gold. Hence the first step was to break down Greenglass and get him to "cooperate" and agree to involve his brother-in-law, if necessary by passing the blame to him.

According to the Government's announcements regarding the so-called confession of Greenglass, it was all very simple and happened overnight. Greenglass had been "seized," confronted with Gold's charges, and "after several hours" of obduracy, had decided to make amends by giving a voluntary and full confession to the FBI that very first night. According to the popular conception broadcast by the newspapers, it was on this first night that Greenglass had confessed the dominant role of his sister and brother-in-law in the espionage conspiracy.

Actually, however, the facts disclose that it took almost a full month for Greenglass' "story" to be developed sufficiently to make the arrest of Julius Rosenberg. During this time, pressure had to be exerted to make Greenglass stick to the story and continue its elaboration. It took almost another month before he agreed to involve his sister. And, following Ethel's arrest, it required more than six months of additional pressure to keep David in line and to build up his story for the trial. Indeed, by the device of holding up his sentence until *after* the trial, it can be said the process totaled a period of almost ten months.

Let us see what happened that first crucial month after David opened the door on June 15. To begin with, why did four agents of the FBI come on that particular day? Had a warrant of arrest been sworn out on the basis of Gold's charges? No. Were these four agents in possession of a proper search warrant? No. Did they find any evidence of guilt? No.

A curious situation: Although the FBI has supposedly learned all about Gold's atomic espionage with Greenglass *three weeks* earlier, they now send four detectives empowered with nothing more than their badges. And more curious, we find Greenglass so amenable that he allows himself to be questioned a total of twelve hours without once exercising his right to telephone an attorney. When does he finally decide he needs an attorney? Only after he permits himself to be taken down to FBI headquarters, and only after he has signed his confession at 2 o'clock in the morning. Only then does he telephone his brother-in-law, Louis Abel, to go to the law offices of O. John Rogge and engage him as counsel.

Now, if we assume that Greenglass was really guilty and confessed everything that night, these questions arise: In the first place, why did Greenglass need to confess at all? There was only Gold's word against his and not a single witness or a shred of supporting evidence that Greenglass had committed any espionage. To be sure, there had been the FBI inquiry back in February concerning the stolen "specimen of uranium," but this had no necessary connection with espionage or with Gold.

In fact, nowhere in the record does the prosecutor or Gold ever mention this matter of the uranium. Hence, what becomes clear is that the very nucleus of Greenglass' fear—his theft of the uranium—is significantly absent in the Government's case.

In the second place, still assuming Greenglass and the Rosenbergs were guilty as charged, why was it necessary for David to drag in Ethel? One may concede that Greenglass was in a state of panic and that it took very little pressure on him to shift the blame to his disliked brother-in-law. But why his sister, someone he loved dearly? Even if Ethel had been involved in the conspiracy, the stark fact remains that no one *knew* about it save the Greenglasses and the Rosenbergs. Why then should David unnecessarily expose her to arrest, imprisonment, and possibly the electric chair?

113

If all this inconceivable "cooperation" really took place, then why weren't the Rosenbergs arrested that very same night? Why was a full month allowed to pass before Julius' arrest and why almost two months before Ethel's arrest? Surely, with the Rosenbergs learning from the next day's newspapers of David's confession, they would realize their danger and be quick to destroy whatever evidence might still be present in their apartment.

Forewarned, and aware that the FBI would keep them under strict surveillance, the Rosenbergs could scarcely be expected to make any rash blunders such as attempting to flee the country with or without their two children, or stupidly involving their superiors by frantic telephone calls or midnight visits. For what reason, then, were they permitted their liberty for so long a time if Greenglass voluntarily made his full confession that first night, as the Government insists and as he later testified?

The reason is quite plain. Whatever testimony David swore to at the trial was carefully worked out in the weeks that followed, in conferences between Gold and Greenglass, Greenglass and Roy Cohn, Ruth Greenglass and the FBI together with Saypol and his staff, and, of course, Mr. O. John Rogge.

Perhaps it is best to introduce Mr. Rogge at this point. Once known as a liberal during World War II, he had turned into a violent anti-Communist with the development of the Cold War.[4]

There has never been any explanation why Greenglass happened to select Rogge as his counsel. Later, we will see that another government witness, the terrified Max Elitcher, also happened to engage Mr. Rogge as counsel, and that this choice is explained away as a mere "coincidence."

In the light of Rogge's subsequent "arrangement" with Saypol and the FBI, there is every reason to believe that on or before June 15 his name was suggested to Greenglass as the "right kind" of lawyer to obtain; one who had excellent contacts with the Justice Department and one whom the Federal Bureau might best get along with.

Certainly, this would explain Greenglass' extraordinary compliance on the day of his arrest without a warrant. Everything that happened that day indicates there must have been several previous visits of the FBI to persuade him to "confess" more than his uranium theft. In Greenglass' testimony, he himself reveals why he finally took the line of least resistance on June 15. He wanted to see just "what the Government was going to do"; he wanted to find out just "what they wanted me to put in the statement."

Having seen and found out, having allowed himself to become entrapped into signing a first statement, his fright became so great that he hastened to telephone Louis Abel at the hour of 2 A.M. After this, he fell into a deep sleep of exhaustion on a cot in one of the offices of the FBI's suite. On the next morning, June 16, one of Rogge's partners, Herbert Fabricant, arrived to confer with him. Later in the afternoon, Greenglass had a brief talk with Rogge himself. Then he was taken down to be arraigned.

And here we see, in the court record, that Rogge "protested his innocence" vehemently, even asking for the light bail of only $5,000. Saypol insisted on a bail bond of $100,000. This served as a double purpose: First, it increased the importance of Greenglass as a dangerous atom-spy. Second, it further terrified Greenglass and his wife into accepting the hopelessness of their predicament.

It is through Saypol's description of this arraignment that the lie is given to the Government's claim that Greenglass furnished a full confession that first night:

[Saypol]: When David Greenglass was arrested . . . I remember well how at his arraignment . . . Mr. Rogge protested his innocence. Through Ruth Greenglass, his wife, came the subsequent recantation of the facts by both of them. [R. 1623]

Let us see how this "recantation" was induced. According to Saypol, it was "penitence, contriteness, [and] remorse" that spurred the Greenglasses toward confessing their guilt and the disclosure of the Rosenbergs' complicity. But the facts tell a quite different story—one of steadily applied and carefully timed coercion. On the morning of June 17, 1950, the New York *Times* reported,

The espionage complaint against Greenglass was signed in Albuquerque, New Mexico. Commissioner McDonald set Friday [June 23] for a removal hearing.

Thus the impression given the public was twofold: First, that Greenglass had been arrested on the basis of a complaint *originating* in the district of the alleged crime, and second, that he would be swiftly *removed* to New Mexico, there to answer for his crime.

However, the fact is that the New Mexico authorities knew nothing about Greenglass' alleged crime, nor had they issued a complaint until the Department of Justice in Washington so ordered. This is plainly reported in the Albuquerque *Tribune* of June 16, which states that the U.S. Attorney in Albuquerque received a long-distance call from the Chief of the United States Criminal Division, during which Greenglass' "alleged violations" were outlined and the request was made that a complaint be filed against him in Albuquerque.

It is further reported in the same newspaper that the U.S. Attorney in Albuquerque then communicated with Saypol, stating that if "Greenglass indicates willingness to have his case transferred to the New York District," New Mexico would be "agreeable." "Otherwise . . . the defendant should be removed to this district for prosecution."

It is not at all difficult to reconstruct the coercive maneuver: After having been pressured into signing a dictated statement of his guilt in the early hours of June 16, Greenglass reneged and had Rogge protest his innocence at the arraignment that afternoon. Now the problem was to get him to stick to the FBI statement, plead guilty, and sign additional statements. Whereupon the threat of shipping him off to New Mexico was conceived. To make this threat realistic, New York requested Washington to order the filing of the Albuquerque complaint. Thus Greenglass was faced with this choice: On the one hand, if he would cooperate (show "willingness") in New York, then jurisdiction would be transferred to that city. On the other hand ("otherwise"), if he refused, then he would be removed to face the hostility of a New Mexico court.

How powerful was this pressure is attested by Ruth Greenglass. In a confidential file memo, the following was recorded by Mr. R. H. Goldman, an associate of Rogge, concerning their interview with her three days after her husband's arrest:

OJR [O. John Rogge] and I visited Mrs. Greenglass at her home, 285 Rivington St., New York, at 4:00 p.m. Sunday, June 18, 1950. She was in bed as she had just returned from the hospital. . . .
She feels that New Mexico is a very bad place to try the case since the citizens did not like GI's, because of the big boom and then the big slack, because of the anti-semitism and because the local citizens all feel bitter about the wives of the GI's taking jobs there.[5]

On June 23, the removal hearing of Greenglass "was adjourned until July 13 *at the request of the Government*." (Emphasis added.) Mr. Saypol's stated reason for the delay was that he needed "an additional week to gather evidence to present to the Grand Jury."

When we consider that Greenglass' self-admitted espionage rests on *no other evidence* than the testimony of Ruth, Gold, and himself, it becomes apparent that Saypol's three-week delay was to maintain and increase the pressure.

In the next two days, however, a new element was added. On June 25 came this menacing news:

WAR IS DECLARED BY NORTH KOREA
Communist Regime Attacks South Republic . . .
U. S. Holding Soviet Responsible . . .

It is hardly necessary to dwell on the panic of the Greenglasses at this moment of history, nor on the reactions of the politically astute Mr. Rogge. This was no time to protest the innocence of a former YCL member accused by the atom-spy, Harry Gold.[6] As for Irving H. Saypol, the Korean news presaged the "inevitable" all-out war with the Soviet Union, and it was open season on all "potential traitors and 5th Column-ists." [7]

On July 6, the day of the Santa Fe Grand Jury meeting, the Albuquerque *Tribune* contained these ominous headlines:

YANKS IN GENERAL RETREAT; PYONG TAEK LOST

LOCAL SPY DRAMA OPENS IN SANTA FE; QUICK REPORT SEEN

The choice given Greenglass was unmistakably clear:

Greenglass would be brought to New Mexico for trial if he is indicted *unless he pleads guilty*. [Emphasis added.]

On the next day, July 7, the Albuquerque *Tribune* hinted at the swift "justice" Greenglass might expect in New Mexico:

. . . The former Y.C.L. member was indicted yesterday. The Grand Jury took only two hours to reach a decision. . . .
Court officials said that the Grand Jury's action would not affect a "removal hearing" scheduled in New York next Thursday [July 13]. . . .

But the Greenglasses and Rogge did not dare wait for the "removal hearing" of July 13. Now with the Korean War in full blast and the forbidding news from New Mexico, Rogge surrenders his client completely. Indeed, the *Tribune* report of July 12 shows that he hastened to surrender one day *before* the deadline:

The hearing before U. S. Commissioner Edward W. McDonald had been scheduled for tomorrow.
The adjournment was granted at the request of O. J. Rogge, counsel for the 28-year-old Brooklyn-born defendant.

This, then, was one of the principal pressures exerted against the Greenglasses. It was not unlike the practice of Southern prosecutors who obtain "confessions" from black "suspects" by threatening to turn them over to the tender mercies of hostile deputies.

Perhaps the oldest and most effective form of police

coercion lies in the use of terrifying object lessons. It is what we see happening to other victims that strikes home. Such an object lesson was provided Greenglass on the very day of his arrest with front-page headlines that another spy contact of Harry Gold had been "seized" in upstate New York on charges of "having given Mr. Gold a sample of a secret explosive" back in the year 1943. He was a chemist by the name of Alfred Dean Slack residing in Syracuse, and it was announced that he had "admitted" his espionage with Gold.

One can be reasonably certain that the event reported so sensationally must have had a considerable effect on Greenglass' temporary submission that night as well as throughout the various stages leading to his final submission.

At every stage in Slack's arrest there was studied deception. His admission of guilt stemmed only from the FBI; his denials received scant attention and were buried away in back pages. At his arraignment, according to the New York *Times* of June 16 and 18, 1950, he told reporters:

This mistake will be eventually explained. . . . I am not now and never was a member of the Communist Party and never will be.

Asked if he knew Harry Gold, he said, "I don't recall ever knowing anybody by that name."

So powerful, however, was the force of official dictum, that only one day after it had printed the admission of guilt as an FBI *announcement*, the New York *Times* stated erroneously on June 17:

On Thursday, the FBI seized Alfred Dean Slack, 44-year-old Syracuse chemist. *He admitted* giving samples of a secret high explosive to Gold. [Emphasis added.]

In addition, Slack's alleged espionage with Gold was tied in directly with that of Greenglass in the same article:

This [Greenglass'] was the third arrest in the Russian spy ring investigation since Fuchs talked to FBI agents in London. The first was that of Gold.

Here, then, was another victim of Gold's accusations *also* being held under $100,000 bail, *also* being charged with "wartime spying" carrying a penalty of death, and *also* being "removed" to a distant and potentially hostile state, namely Tennessee. On June 21 Slack was taken there in chains by three armed U.S. deputy marshals.[8]

On June 23, the New York *Times* reported that Slack had arrived in Knoxville to be "taken before a Grand Jury." On July 6, there was the *Times* account about his wife and two children, aged four and two, apparently stranded, since "the family income was cut off by the arrest."

In the meantime, the frantic wife had rushed to Tennessee to aid her husband. And here one must try to see the full picture. Each couple became object lessons to the other, mutual victims of the unsupported accusation of Harry Gold. In Tennessee the Slacks could conclude that Greenglass had made a "deal" to prevent his removal to New Mexico; and in New York the Greenglasses could deduce that Slack had "admitted" his guilt from the very beginning.[9]

In support of this time-worn police method of playing off one victim against another, there is this revealing point made by New York *Post* reporter Oliver Pilat in his book:

Paraphrased fragments of a confession by Slack . . . *confirmed* Gold's story and set the stage for future prosecutions. The outcome of this particular prosecution [Slack's] really carried *a private message to others exposed by Gold:* If you tell what you know, and thereby help to unroll the net further, you may receive as much leniency as can be arranged through the courts; otherwise, you will get the legal limit.[10] [Emphasis added.]

To recapitulate the various pressures that led the Greenglasses to "cooperate" that first month, they can be summed up as follows:

1. The pressure which the prosecution had in Harry Gold, ready to make and elaborate any accusation required of him.

2. The example of Slack, whose reported ad-

mission of Gold's charges made Greenglass realize the futility of further resistance.

3. The fact of Greenglass' YCL membership coupled with Julius' dismissal as a Communist Party member, which became, with the outbreak of the Korean War, accepted proof of "motive" to serve the Kremlin.

4. The threat of prosecution on charges of espionage concerning the stolen uranium sample. Here, Greenglass must have feared that he would be accused of turning over the uranium to the Soviet Union via Harry Gold.[11]

5. The additional threat to expose Greenglass' Army thefts and black marketing, which would not only lay a foundation for his lack of patriotism, but serve to further inflame a New Mexico jury.

6. The tightening vise of the threatened removal to face trial in New Mexico, so dreaded by the Greenglasses, as revealed in Ruth's confidences to Rogge.

7. And finally, the pressure created by their own attorney, O. John Rogge, who, as will be shown by his own file memos, was accused by the defense of negotiating a "deal" with the prosecution.

V

> [Judge Kaufman]: I must say, Mr. Rogge . . . a lawyer plays a vital part in clarifying in a witness's or defendant's mind the proper thinking. . . .
> —*Proceedings re sentence of David Greenglass (Record, p. 1629)*

In the record of the Rosenbergs' final appeal, there is contained the "newly discovered evidence" proving beyond question that the Greenglasses were "liars and perjurers." Documentary evidence was furnished in the form of Rogge's confidential file memos, previously mentioned. These memos were officially acknowledged as authentic.[12]

In Chapter 6 we will show that Rogge promised

the Greenglasses that neither of them was to be indicted, and that each would "merely be named as a co-conspirator." Later, when this "deal" was threatened with exposure, there was the promise that David would receive a very light sentence—possibly even a suspended sentence, otherwise termed by Rogge as a "pat on the back."

It was by means of such promises that the Greenglasses were entrapped deeper and deeper. When we consider the enormous tensions they were under at the time of David's arrest, it is doubtful that Rogge had much difficulty in preparing them for "the proper thinking."

To illustrate, let us examine the memo concerning Ruth Greenglass' confidential interview with Rogge following her husband's arrest. It concludes with these remarks:

> OJR pointed out that if Dave was innocent he should talk; that if not it would be advisable not to talk but to let the Government prove its case.
> The third course was that of cooperation. That was also discussed at length.

At the outset, we see that Rogge and Ruth Greenglass are concerned *not* with the question of guilt or innocence, but rather with what course of action to take in reply to the New Mexico complaint. In other words, should the Greenglasses insist on their innocence, plead guilty, or cooperate with the Government—and what to do in each instance?

The phrase "he should talk" meant that David would make public the entire story of the FBI's coercion. This would include not only the FBI's intimidation of recent weeks, but also the harassment that began in February regarding his theft of the uranium sample.[13] That this harassment was the key to David's compliance is evident from Ruth's disclosures in this same memo:

> Shortly before their accident [Ruth's burns in February] the FBI asked if they had a specimen of uranium in the house. . . .

And in the paragraph preceding the above, the following is divulged:

She would not have allowed her husband to bring anything home after Hiroshima had disclosed what the project was. She intended to raise a family and did not want that kind of material around.

Immediately following the discussion of the uranium, the memo shows that the Greenglasses were considering public support:

People in the neighborhood want to raise a petition . . . keep flocking to the house to offer support and advice. . . . The Jewish *Daily Forward,* which is certainly not a leftist newspaper, is very excited about the antisemitic issue and has offered a lawyer.

Thus a stand of innocence by the Greenglasses would include acceptance of this support, repudiation of David's signed confession, and the exposure of the coercion. In other words, fighting the Government's charges all the way down the line.

In the second instance, what was meant was to admit the theft of the uranium. In this event, his defense would be that the stealing of the uranium souvenir did not constitute espionage. "Let the Government prove its case" meant let it prove not only Gold's charges, but that the uranium was stolen for purposes of espionage.

In the third instance, we come to the euphemism "cooperation." And while taking this course would avoid removal to New Mexico and even spare David the risk of standing trial (which was the initial "deal" between Rogge and Saypol), it would necessitate the elaboration of the conspiracy to include Julius Rosenberg. And so, as we return to the memo, we find that "cooperation" leads directly to the last chilling sentence in the memo:

There was a long discussion about JR. [Emphasis added.]

The initials stand for Julius Rosenberg. This was the very ending of the Rogge memorandum. It was dated June 19, 1950. Exactly three years later, this "long discussion" led to the ending of Ethel and Julius Rosenberg's lives.

In our analysis of the trial of the Rosenbergs, we will see that David Greenglass concealed the important fact that he was interrogated by the FBI in February, 1950, concerning the theft of uranium from Los Alamos. This fact is confirmed by Rogge's conference with Ruth. In addition, we know from David's brother Bernard that the uranium was stolen by Greenglass.[14]

Therefore, if Greenglass were really a member of the alleged Rosenberg spy ring, the uranium would have had to be stolen in connection with Julius. But the record shows *no such* connection. Hence one is forced to ask: Why did Greenglass and the prosecution conceal the fact of his uranium theft? There can be only one answer: As the nub of the pressure exerted upon Greenglass, it *had* to be concealed in order to mask the entire frame-up against the Rosenbergs.

In a further effort to conceal the frame-up, it was the testimony of the Greenglasses that they had not been coerced in any way, and that they had told the FBI the full truth at the very outset because of remorse and a patriotic desire to make amends. But our inquiry demonstrates that their testimony was obtained through coercive measures, applied over a period of months during which the Greenglasses were entrapped by their anxiety to obtain immunity.

In our analysis thus far, we have focused our attention not on the trial testimony of the Greenglasses, but on the pressures to procure that testimony in the first period following David's arrest. But, simultaneous with those pressures, there was also the effort made to intimidate Julius Rosenberg; in fact, on the very next morning following David's submission.

1. These attitudes of Ruth Greenglass were related to this writer by neighbors and former friends on the Lower East Side.
2. In the light of the subsequent Greenglass testimony that they had received $5,000 of "Russian money" from the Rosenbergs for "flight," it would seem that the $5,000 was too imaginary for Ruth to forget the *real* $1,000 which Julius owed David.
3. These facts concerning the theft and disposal of the uranium, suppressed by the prosecution during the trial, were later revealed by the confidential memos of O. John Rogge, the Greenglass attorney, as well as by an affidavit of Bernard Greenglass.
4. There is a most revealing chapter on Mr. Rogge's willingness to serve the interests of the FBI in the book *In Battle for Peace* by W. E. B. Du Bois with the heading: "Oh! John Rogge." (Masses & Mainstream, New York, 1952.)
5. Rogge file memo dated June 19, 1950. (See Appendix 3.)
6. On the day after Greenglass' arrest, there was this legend under his front-page photo in the Albuquerque *Tribune:*

GREENGLASS FORMER MEMBER OF YOUNG COMMUNIST LEAGUE

In the New York *Times,* Greenglass' "Red" past had been emphasized in the opening sentence of its front-page story: "A 28-year-old former Young Communist League member. . . ."
7. Saypol was chosen by *Time* as "the nation's No. 1 legal hunter of top Communists." (July 23, 1951.)
8. According to reporter Oliver Pilat, Slack "was treated with noticeable severity as long as he pretended innocence." (See p. 265, Oliver Pilat, *The Atom Spies,* Putnam, New York, 1952.)
9. Slack was never tried before a jury. As the result of persuasion by his court-appointed attorney to "cooperate" and the pressure by the FBI during the three-month period before his indictment, Slack pleaded guilty in exchange for a "deal."

This "deal" was to have been a ten-year sentence with promise of quick parole. (New York *Times,* September 19, 1950.) When, however, Slack was given a fifteen-year term, he charged in his appeal that "a Government prosecutor, Mr. Meek, told him . . . he would be paroled after a few years if he pleaded guilty, and accepted a ten-year term." (New York *Times,* June 20, 1952.)

10. Pilat, *op. cit.,* p. 266. It should be noted in further proof of the existence of this particular form of pressure that Pilat's relationship to Saypol was that of confidential public-relations expert. This fact is exposed plainly in another confidential memo of Rogge, dated August 23, 1950. (See Appendix 5.)

11. In this regard, it is significant that the FBI announcement about Slack also emphasized secret samples of explosives delivered to Russia via Gold. (New York *Times,* June 20, 1950.)

12. Transcript of Appeal, October Term, 1953.

13. It is in this same memo that Ruth tells Rogge about the FBI's intimidation tactics. (See Appendix 3.)

14. An affidavit to this effect, sworn and signed by Bernard Greenglass on May 31, 1953, is contained in the record of the final appeal. (See Appendix 6.)

ADDENDA

Concerning the "sample of uranium" which David Greenglass stole from the Los Alamos Atomic Project, this fact is further confirmed by the disclosures from the FBI files as reported in the New York *Times* of December 4, 1975:

Mr. Greenglass admitted about the same time, March 23, 1953, that he had stolen a two- or three-ounce hemisphere of uranium-238 from the Los Alamos bomb laboratory, and action he denied in a 1950 interrogation.

His wife, Ruth, said he had kept it in "an old sock" as a souvenir. Mr. Greenglass said he threw it into the East River after his first denial of the theft.

It it noteworthy that Greenglass made this admission some three months prior to the executions of the Rosenbergs. According to the report, he also had his attorney,

O. John Rogge, send a letter to President Eisenhower urging that the Rosenbergs' death sentences be commuted with these tormented words:

If these two die, I shall live the rest of my life with a very dark shadow on my conscience.

In the light of these disclosures coming at the same time, it is possible that the entrapped Greenglass was desperately trying to reveal that the entire case against himself and the Rosenbergs had been built on his theft of this "hemisphere of uranium-238" which, together with the political climate, provided the basis for his long harassment by the FBI, the relentless pressure of the prosecution, and his gradual agreement to implicate the Rosenbergs in exchange for the promise of a suspended sentence and his wife's freedom.

Confirming the "arrangement" which the Greenglasses' lawyer, O. John Rogge, had made with the prosecution, here is his recent recollection of it:

"That Ruth would be left out of the indictment and she was. And that David would have a sentence of no more than three to five years. But when it came to judgment day, the judge wrapped himself in the flag, went overboard, and began with death penalties." (See Goldstein, *op. cit.*)

In the PBS television interview with Mr. Rogge, the latter stated that, with respect to this arrangement, he had been "double-crossed."

5 "NEVER SEND TO KNOW . . ."

I

> ". . . Any man's death diminishes me, Because I am involved in Mankinde; And therefore never send to know for whom the bell tolls; It tolls for thee."
>
> —John Donne

It was shortly after eight in the morning. It was a Friday, the sixteenth of June, 1950. A car with three men drew up before a large apartment development on the Lower East Side of New York known as Knickerbocker Village. They entered one of the buildings, numbered 10 Monroe Street, and examined the panel of letter boxes for the name of Rosenberg. Finding it, they stepped into the elevator and pressed the button. . . .

In his undershirt, shaving before the bathroom mirror, Julius Rosenberg listened to the children's chatter as their mother strove to ready them for school.[1] The two boys shared the bedroom. In the living room, a studio couch served as a bed for the parents. The kitchen was the third room. The apartment was so small Julius could easily hear the percolator bubbling.

They had stayed up late worrying about David. They had wondered how much the FBI would try to make out of a twenty-two-year-old GI's impulse to take home a souvenir sample of the mysterious metal that had gone into the atomic bomb.

They knew that back in February the FBI had come to question David. They had guessed it was about those things he had stolen from the Army. From what Ruth had once told them, they had always supposed that the thefts had been confined to tools, parts, and gasoline. This had been a widespread practice in Army camps during the war. But subsequently David had divulged that it was much more serious than black marketing; that he had been questioned about having taken a sample of uranium from Los Alamos. Evidently, following Dr. Fuchs' arrest, the FBI was trying to tie up David's adolescent membership in the YCL with the stolen uranium. In the present political climate anything was possible. . . .

There was a knock on the door. His face still lathered, Julius crossed to open it. Three men stood in the hall. One said, politely, "We are from the FBI—we would like to talk to you."[2]

It was David they wanted to talk about, and from their manner it appeared he was still in custody. As Ethel hastened to put the room in order, one of the detectives suggested it might be more convenient if Julius accompanied them to their office.

It was only a few minutes' drive to the Federal

Building on Foley Square. The elevator carried them swiftly up to the tower, where the FBI maintained its offices high above the courtrooms below.

One of the agents, Norton, took his place at the desk with pad and pencil. Another, called Harrington, sat at the side of the desk. The third agent pulled up a chair a little behind Julius and the questioning commenced. It had, as its main direction, his previous business relations with his brother-in-law. However, they also wanted to know about his own background, his schooling and his work. . . .

II

In the testimony of Julius Rosenberg at his trial, there is considerable biographical material.[3] In addition, there are autobiographical references contained in his published letters as well as the research made by Virginia Gardner.[4] Finally, there are the personal interviews this writer has had with friends of the Rosenbergs, their attorneys, and members of the family. From all these sources, we are able to assemble the following account of the life of Julius Rosenberg.

•

I was born of orthodox parents and raised in the slum tenements of the lower East Side.

In the year 1902, Harry Rosenberg arrived in Ellis Island, a young steerage immigrant from Czarist Russia. He readily found work as an apprentice in the great sweatshop garment industry of New York. When he was twenty, he fell in love with a round-cheeked girl of seventeen, named Sophie Cohen, also of Russian parentage, who worked in a shirt factory. A year or so later they were married, and eventually they were blessed with five children. The youngest, a boy born on May 12, 1918, was named Julius.

When Julius was three years old the family lived on the top floor of a five-story tenement on Broome

Street. In winter, with the melting snows, the roof leaked so badly that icicles formed from the ceiling drip.

"We were so poor," one of Julius' sisters recalls, "my mother would hardboil an egg so that she could divide it among us all." In the early twenties, strikes were frequent in the garment industry, and it was "quite a pull to make ends meet" for the Rosenbergs. "There was no bread in the house finally, and no milk," tells Julius' mother. "I had to leave Julie and stand in line, a long line, where the union was giving out milk. . . ."

At Hebrew School . . . I absorbed quite naturally the culture of my people, their struggle for freedom. . . .

When Julius was enrolled at Public School 88, he also entered the Downtown Talmud Torah. Here he studied Hebrew and Biblical philosophy, and was graduated with highest honors. Yet he was not altogether the Bible student; on the streets of the East Side Julius proved no more saintly than any other kid on the block. "When some boy would pick a fight, my Julie would fight him," his mother conceded, "but he'd never tell who the other boy was. So I stopped asking."

While attending Seward High, Julius had been elected vice-president of the Young Men's Synagogue Organization. On Sundays the fifteen-year-old vice-president earned pocket money by peddling penny candy. Sometimes, he recalled, "the profit went from a low of forty cents up to eighty cents for a good day."

It was 1933, the year of farm foreclosures, bread-lines, and "Hoovervilles." It was the year when Hitler came to power and when Hermann Goering had his Storm Troopers set fire to the Reichstag, but cast the "blame upon the Communists," as the first step toward "proscribing all political parties." And in 1933, in San Quentin Penitentiary, a trade unionist was serving the sixteenth year of a life sentence.

One day I stopped to listen to a speaker at a street corner meeting. . . . His topic was to win freedom for Tom Mooney, labor leader who was imprisoned on a frame-up.

Some six years later, after twenty-two years of imprisonment, a "full and unconditional pardon" was granted by Governor Culbert Olsen, stating unequivocally: "Thomas J. Mooney is wholly innocent . . . his conviction was based wholly on perjured testimony presented by representatives of the State of California."

At school, I took a very active part in the campaign to free the Scottsboro Boys. . . .

In the year 1933, another frame-up came to national attention. It was that of the nine Negro boys sentenced to death in Scottsboro, Alabama. Their conviction, too, had been based on perjured testimony, most of it from a self-admitted prostitute. But in those years there had been a different climate of public opinion, and the United States Supreme Court reflected it by ordering the state of Alabama to grant new trials.

By 1934, when Julius entered the College of the City of New York to study engineering, Mussolini had commenced his armed attacks on Ethiopia. Then came the Nazi occupation of the Rhineland, then the war upon Spain and the Japanese onslaught on China; soon to follow were Austria and Czechoslovakia.

In American colleges, the American Student Union was one of the few organizations that spoke out against the coming world blood bath. Some fifteen years later, at Julius' trial, activity in this organization constituted "premature anti-Fascism" and was offered as further proof of his inclination toward "treasonable activities."

At eighteen, Julius was a tall, good-looking boy. It was Christmas week of 1936, and he was invited to a party on the East Side. One of the girls there sang the famous aria "One Fine Day" from *Madame Butterfly* She was a petite girl with soft, dark brown hair, a shy smile, and a most expressive face, one which Julius' mother would describe as a "malach's ponim"—the face of an angel.

Her name was Ethel Greenglass, and, although she was two years his senior, he felt himself a good deal older and more experienced. He was very proud when she later confided that he was actually her first "boy friend."

On June 18, 1939, Julius and Ethel became man and wife in an orthodox ceremony. The young husband, graduated from college only four months before, had obtained a temporary job as a tool designer. And while Ethel continued her work as a secretary, they made their home in a bedroom of a Brooklyn apartment belonging to friends.

In the interim Julius had passed his government examination as Junior Engineer, his work consisting of the inspection of electronic equipment manufactured for the Signal Corps.

By 1942, when he had been promoted to Assistant Engineer at a salary of $50 per week, the Rosenbergs felt affluent enough to apply for an apartment in the new housing development on Monroe Street. It was only three rooms, but they considered it a palace compared to anything they had had before. From a friendly couple moving to California, they borrowed the essentials: a bed, a maple table, and a bookcase. There was an advertisement in the *Knickerbocker News* of a second-hand piano for sale at $25, and Ethel made the purchase.

In the year 1943, their first son was born and named Michael Allan. Ever since Pearl Harbor, Ethel had served as a Civil Defense worker. With her first baby, however, there was little time for more than her housework. Frequently Julius, as Civil Service Chairman of his union, would stay up late working over grievance appeals. Sometimes a neighbor would drop in and ask them to contribute to the Joint Anti-Fascist Refugee Committee, then aiding the forgotten victims of Franco; they were asked to circulate a coin-collection can labeled "Save a Spanish Republican Child." Ethel contributed a dollar and kept the little can on an open shelf as a hint to their friends to do likewise.[5]

In the autumn of 1944, Ethel became bedridden for many months. It was due to a weak back from which she had suffered since childhood. During this period, Ethel had a woman come in to help.

It was in February, 1945, that Julius was brought up on FBI charges before the Signal Corps "that he was a member of the Communist Party." In reply, Julius denied in a written statement that he was or had ever been a member of the Communist Party.[6]

Despite this denial, Julius was dismissed without a hearing and was forced to look for another job. He found one at the Emerson Radio Company at a salary of $70 a week.

Early in 1946, Julius' father died. A year later, when a second son was born, he was named Robert Harry "in beloved memory." Recalling his family life while in the death house, Julius wrote to his wife:

Do you remember the procession when it came time for the little one to be put to bed? You led the way holding his feet, I held his shoulders and Michael marched in the middle with his brother's back resting on his head. It was loads of fun. . . .

In the spring of 1946, Julius left Emerson Radio, to enter a partnership with his brothers-in-law, Bernard and David Greenglass, the latter recently discharged from the Army. Twice the failing business was reorganized, and, as has been recounted, after 1949 the Greenglass brothers left Julius to carry on alone.

With his absentee partner, Mr. Schein, Julius had negotiated for the transfer of stock. It took his last Savings Bond, plus scraped-up loans from his family, to make the $1,000 down payment, and he still had to pay off the $4,500 balance to Mr. Schein in installments of $160 per month.

As for the $1,000 he had agreed to pay David for his share of stock, it seemed to Julius that the Greenglasses, as relatives, ought to be less demanding; certainly they shouldn't be plaguing him for promissory notes which they knew very well he could not pay until business improved.

> "Somewhere in the long ago I had a normal
> life with a sweet wife and two fine children
> and now all is gone and we are facing
> death. . . ."

Following these highlights of his background, the FBI men questioned Julius about David Greenglass when he had been home on furlough. Didn't he have a talk with David on or about January 5, 1945? Yes, he could remember inviting the Greenglasses for dinner, but that was more than five years ago; what exact day he could not recall. More of this line of questioning, when suddenly one of the detectives tossed at him: "Do you know that your brother-in-law said you told him to supply information for Russia?"

Julius stared at them incredulously, then replied, "He'd have to be out of his mind to say things like that. Will you bring him here and let him tell me that to my face?"

There was no attorney Julius knew particularly well, but recalling the one who represented his union, he stated that he wished to call his lawyer, Mr. Victor Rabinowitz.

The request was ignored; instead they used such delaying tactics as "Have a smoke? Have a piece of gum? Would you like something to eat?" Then again the question: "Did you ask David Greenglass to turn over information for the Russians?"

"No!" Julius retorted. "I did nothing of the sort!"

Didn't he take David along with him one night in January of 1945 to meet a certain man who wanted to ask David certain data on the A-bomb? No, he did not! He never knew any such man and there had never been any such meeting! Finally acceding to Julius' demand for counsel, Norton put in the call to Mr. Rabinowitz' office.

"They say his partner is there—"

Taking the phone, Julius introduced himself and explained that he was being questioned by the FBI. The lawyer came directly to the point:

"Are you under arrest?"

"I don't know."

"Ask if you are under arrest."

Julius turned. "Am I under arrest?"

"No," Norton said.

"He says, 'No,' " Julius relayed.

"Well then, just pick yourself up and come down to our office."

Whereupon Julius rose, said good-bye, and walked to the door. None of the detectives tried to stop him.

It was a little after 3 o'clock when Julius descended the granite steps of the Federal Building and passed a newsstand. He stopped short. There, staring at him from the front page, was a photo of David Greenglass and the FBI's official announcement of his arrest—as an atomic spy!

Along with the story about David's YCL membership was the ominous phrase: "Greenglass, if convicted, faces a maximum penalty of death."

At the office of his union attorneys, Julius was advised to secure counsel with wider experience in civil liberties cases. The name recommended was Emanuel H. Bloch.

IV

At his apartment that evening, Emanuel Bloch was entertaining some friends. When the call came from Julius, he suggested that they meet at the subway station a short distance from Bloch's apartment. They recognized each other from their self-descriptions: Julius' glasses, mustache, and gray suit; and the older man's iron-gray hair.

Emanuel Bloch's first impression of Julius was that of "a rather soft, sweet, intellectual sort of fellow," and his first reaction to what had happened that day was that it would be "just another routine" Fifth Amendment case. It seemed to him, in view of Julius' past harassment by the FBI (their accusations to the

Signal Corps that he had been a Party member), that they were now endeavoring to involve him more seriously. It was possible he might be summoned before a Grand Jury and questioned about Greenglass' alleged espionage or YCL membership. If he were to deny his own Communist Party membership and/or espionage, they could then charge him with perjury, and in the present atmosphere conviction was more than possible. Thus, there was only left his Fifth Amendment privilege.

In short, Mr. Bloch thought Julius was "in the same boat with hundreds of other people" these days, and there was only one course open to him if he should be summoned: to simply take his stand on his constitutional rights no matter what was made of it. Above all, not to worry about it.

Thanking the lawyer, and adding half-jokingly that he could not afford to take time to worry since he had a wife and two children to support, Julius shook hands with Mr. Bloch and went home.[7]

And so it was, on that night of June 16, 1950, that Emanuel Bloch became the attorney for Julius Rosenberg, and a short while later, for his wife, Ethel. And for the next three years thereafter, he was destined to do little else. In fact, it was his destiny to give his very life in the effort to save theirs.[8]

V

At no time perhaps is the nature of frame-up more apparent than during this initial period when the government officials were endeavoring to "make" their case against the Rosenbergs. It was perforce a hectic period, for the prosecution not only found it necessary to work out the main elements of the Greenglass story, but also the proper pressures to get the Greenglasses to elaborate on it. For example, when the FBI questioned Julius on June 16, the undisputed record shows that the man he was supposed to have taken David to meet was just a "man." Only at the trial did this "man" blossom forth as a "Russian."

Examining further this early period, we see by the very illogic of the Government's moves the creaking machinery of the frame-up, for example, the FBI's premature interrogation of Julius and his unexplained release.

It is not difficult to reconstruct the FBI's thinking when they came to get Julius at 8:30 A.M., only six hours after David had signed their statement and had fallen into his sleep of exhaustion. They were hopeful that the engineer whom they had gotten fired as a Communist from the Signal Corps would also prove tractable; that he, too, would make some statement that could be used against him. They knew all about his business difficulties with David. Everything about their questioning has the overtone of inciting Julius against his brother-in-law, playing one against the other. Since they had already obtained some results with David (and it is quite possible that David's inclusion of Julius in the conspiracy stemmed from exactly such tactics, that is, hints that Julius had implicated David), they were hopeful that they could achieve similar results with Julius.

Returning to the Government's claim that Greenglass had confessed his full story on June 15, one can test its reliability by simply asking: Why were Julius and Ethel Rosenberg not arrested on June 16? Why was Julius released that afternoon if Greenglass had "told the truth about their conspiracy" the night before? And one might add, why was he released if Harry Gold had really made a "true confession" three weeks earlier on May 22?

For, after all, what was the keystone that held together the testimony of Gold and Greenglass at the trial? It was the famous Jello-box recognition device. This was Greenglass' testimony: that the Rosenbergs had arranged this device by tearing the side of a Jello box into two halves. That Julius had given him one half to match that produced by his courier. And that the eventual courier proved to be Harry Gold.

As for Gold, this was his testimony: that he had not only received his half of the Jello box from the Soviet Vice Consul, Yakovlev, but also that he had been instructed to tell Greenglass that he had been sent by "Julius."

Therefore, if we are to believe the Government's case, the FBI had before them on June 16 the confessions of the two recipients of the two halves of the Jello-box—in other words, they had with these two links the *completed* chain pointing "indisputably to the guilt of the Rosenbergs."

Why, then, if the Government was truly in possession of this completed chain of evidence, was Julius not arrested for an entire month? And why was Ethel not arrested for almost two months?

It was also Greenglass' testimony that he had told the FBI on June 15 all about the principal crime he had committed, that is, the turning over to the Rosenbergs of the cross-section and the twelve-page description of the Nagasaki atom bomb. That Ethel had typed it up; that the Rosenbergs had told him how they microfilmed it on a "hollowed-out" console table, and that they had received wristwatches as gifts from the Russians as well as a citation.

Why, if the FBI knew on June 16 that they had in Julius a most important atomic spy, was there not a search made immediately for all this incriminating evidence instead of on the night of his arrest one month later?

By every rule of logic and precaution, they should have arrested the Rosenbergs forthwith and made as thorough a search of their apartment as they did of the Greenglass apartment. But the truth is they had no case *as yet* against the Rosenbergs on June 16. As for the accusations conveyed to Julius on that day, these were not accusations which had originated with David Greenglass, but with the FBI! And not only did the FBI agents know they were false, but there was also the fear that Greenglass would fail to substantiate them, because this is what happened on that morning of June 16:

At 8:30 o'clock, when the FBI men went to pick up Julius, the compliant Greenglass was still asleep in an adjoining office in the FBI suite. By noon he was awake and conferring with his lawyer protesting his *innocence*. We know this from the undisputed file memos of Rogge, and also from the latter's disclosures at Greenglass' sentencing. Hence, even at the moment the detectives, Norton and Harrington, were telling Julius about David's "accusations" in one office, Greenglass, in another office, was repudiating his confession. That it had been virtually dictated to him is evident from the opening paragraph of his statement given his attorney the next day:

I stated [in the statement signed for the FBI on June 15] that I met Gold in N.M. at 209 N. High St., my place. *They told me* that I had told him to come back later because I didn't have it [the information] ready. *I didn't remember this but I allowed it in the statement.*[9] [Emphasis added.]

To sum up, the prosecution could not arrest Julius on June 16 on the basis of the Jello-box story, for the simple reason that it had not yet been fabricated by Gold. The latter's recognition signal, "I came from Julius," was still to be invented. Ethel's typing had not yet been added to the "story." Nor had it yet been determined just what atomic secrets Greenglass was to have "stolen." The Nagasaki atom bomb was still to be "piled on" the Russian console table. And as for the table itself, that item had not yet been "hollowed out" for the microfilming.

In short, the FBI had to proceed by the usual one-by-one method. First, Saypol had to insure a plea of guilt by Greenglass. Second, the prisoner had to be made to burn his bridges, or entrap himself further by elaborating his initial statement into such a self-incriminating series of statements that he could not possibly repudiate them. Not until the prosecution had made these necessary steps could they proceed with the arrest of Julius. But, to make these steps, pressure on Greenglass had to be intensified. And, as we have seen, it was for this reason that the removal proceedings were instituted and kept going up to the point of Greenglass' submission on July 12.

Indeed, it is highly probable that had it not been for the outbreak of the Korean War on June 25, Saypol might not have succeeded as well as he did. But, even so, the prosecution could not afford to tarnish its case with the disclosure that the testimony of the Green-glasses had been procured by intimidation and the "deal" arranged through Rogge.

That is why Cohn carefully rehearsed the Green-glasses and why they insisted they had cooperated from the start, presenting themselves as "repenting individuals" eagerly "coming forward and helping the Government." And it was precisely because Saypol was burdened with this shaky framework that he could offer, in explanation of Julius' month of liberty, only the specious excuse that the FBI wanted to keep him under surveillance.

Thus we come to another important piece of the jigsaw puzzle, one that frequently appears in the technique of frame-ups: the "built-in justification." Why, according to Saypol, did the FBI fail to arrest Julius Rosenberg or search his apartment? Because the FBI wanted to see if he would make an attempt to escape or contact his "superiors." To expose the absurdity of this we need only to turn to Saypol's summation on this point. For here he accuses Julius, during this month of liberty, of: ". . . trying to keep two steps ahead of the FBI; financing flight of other members of the ring and making his own plans to flee."

First, if the FBI *knew* that Julius was a dangerous spy, why would they allow him to keep "two steps ahead" of them, and how could he possibly "finance the flight" of other spies and arrange his own escape without their knowledge? Second, there exists not one scrap of evidence, and not one word of testimony to support this charge made by Saypol.

In the third place, common sense demands: Why would the FBI first warn him so explicitly and then place him under surveillance? Surely, the proper course should have been the most secret surveillance on a twenty-four-hour schedule. Certainly, one cannot expect to trap an experienced spy-master by alerting him in advance! And, *after* such an alert, one cannot expect a seasoned spy to carelessly pick up the telephone and call his co-conspirators for aid, or absentmindedly lead the FBI directly to his "superiors" in their inner sanctum! Furthermore, since the FBI had so sensationally released the news of Gold's and Greenglass' arrests, it was hardly necessary for Julius to alert his "superiors"!

Thus, no matter how one views it, the only valid explanation for Julius' liberty between June 16 and July 17 is that the prosecution needed this period to terrorize the Greenglasses and, with the aid of Ruth, to get David to add to his first statement all those others revealed at the trial. And it is most significant that it was exactly five days after the Greenglass capitulation regarding the final removal hearing that Julius was arrested, on the seventeenth of July.[10]

VI

They came at night this time at about 8:30. It was bedtime for the two little boys when there came the knock on the door. Standing in the hallway were *twelve* of them! [11] Recognizing Norton and Harrington, Julius asked them in. Before he realized it, all the rest swarmed inside. Ethel was trying to shoo the youngsters into their room when she stopped short. There was a sudden movement near Julius, a flash of metal and the clink of handcuffs snapping fast.

While Julius stood handcuffed to two of them, the others began the search. When Julius asked whether they had a search warrant, he was told that his permitting them to enter constituted a waiver. The two little boys stood frozen, wide-eyed; it was like the "Lone Ranger" on the radio, being captured by a bunch of bandits. Two of the detectives pushed past Ethel and went into the children's bedroom, where they searched the closet and the small chest of drawers.

In the kitchen one detective saw a coin-collection can on the shelf. As he showed it to his companion, the latter nodded to take it along. One FBI man took a bundle of family snapshots. Another, inspecting the living-room closet, came out with a box camera which Julius had won as a prize when he was fourteen years old. Still another took some books from their shelves

141

to the console table to sort out those of political content.[12]

It was all happening so fast—so many men crowded into the tiny apartment—that Ethel felt herself almost a bystander. As though in a daze, she followed them about with the children at her heels—when suddenly, she realized that Julius was no longer there.

She ran out into the hallway, but the whine of the descending elevator told her it was too late. She started back to look up Mr. Bloch's telephone number . . .

VII

Fortunately, as Emanuel Bloch related the events to this writer, he was at home when the call came from Ethel Rosenberg. He told her he would hurry down to the Federal Building at once, but that the arraignment might not take place for an hour or two. In an case, suppose she called him at his apartment about midnight. In the meantime, try to calm down— no sense becoming hysterical—it certainly wouldn't help her husband or the children. Ethel promised . . .

Hanging up, his ear caught the 9 P.M. news broadcast which his wife was listening to in the adjoining room. It was a special announcement from Washington made jointly by Attorney General J. Howard McGrath and FBI Director J. Edgar Hoover: Today, the FBI had seized one Julius Rosenberg "as another important link in the Soviet espionage apparatus." According to Mr. Hoover, Rosenberg had recruited his brother-in-law, David Greenglass, to steal "atomic data," and for some years had made himself "available to Soviet espionage agents" so that he could do "the work he was fated for. . . ."

It was instantly clear to Bloch that the announcement had been released to the wire services to synchronize with the arrest taking place only a few minutes before.

When he arrived at the U.S. Courthouse, he saw additional evidence of the "timing." Reporters and photographers had been stationed on the steps so that they might photograph Julius' arrival in handcuffs. Usually there would be only a U.S. Commissioner available for such late arraignments. This time, it turned out to be Federal Judge John F. X. McGohey, who swiftly set the bail at $100,000. It was, of course, a prohibitive one, therefore tantamount to no bail at all. Mr. Bloch tried his utmost to point this out, but it was useless.[13]

Later, in describing the arraignment to Ethel, he had been hesitant to mention this staggering sum. He could readily imagine the shock of the arrest—trying to quiet the children, trying to explain what they could not possibly understand. Indeed, most of it was beyond her own understanding. Only last Saturday she had gone to her mother's house to inquire about her brother—how they were treating him in prison and whether it was possible for her to visit him. And Ruth had been there. . . .

At first, Ruth had told her in the strongest terms that David was "not guilty" and that they were going "to fight this case." But then, when Ethel had offered to borrow money from relatives to aid David's defense and had embraced her sister-in-law to kiss her, the latter had "remained rigid" in her arms. Then, after an abrupt good-bye uttered very "coldly," Ruth had suddenly "turned on her heel and left."

It had been at this point, as Mr. Bloch reviewed his reactions, that the thought had struck him that Ruth might very well be the Lady Macbeth in this unfolding drama; that it was she, more than David, who might be responsible for what had happened to Julius. He had had a gnawing suspicion of this when Rogge had hurried to beat the deadline of the removal hearing on July 12. That was the previous Wednesday. By Saturday (July 16), therefore, when Ruth was telling Ethel that she intended to fight the case, she had already concluded the "deal" to sacrifice Julius.

Little wonder then that Ethel's impulse to help had met with that icy rigidity. In his mind's eye, Mr. Bloch had seen the entire tragedy of Macbeth dominated by his ruthless wife: How Lady Macbeth conceived the brutal plot against Duncan's life; how she forced her vacillating husband to carry it out; and how, when he was unable to complete the bloody task, she herself finished the awful work . . .

That night he had found it difficult to sleep. The more he had thought of Ruth's cold-blooded deception, the more convinced he had become that it was she who had encouraged David to involve Julius.

There was one element, however, that had never entered his mind that night: that this drama of one family pitted against another would take on the classic pattern of Greek tragedy, and that Ethel, too, would soon be forced into the role of a protagonist together with her husband.

NOTES AND REFERENCES

1. The younger one, Robert, aged three, attended a nursery school. Michael, aged seven, attended public school.
2. The details of Julius' interrogation by the FBI on June 16, 1950, will be found in his direct examination; Record, pp. 1137–1141. See also cross-examination, pp. 1202–1203, 1222–1223, 1225–1228.
3. Record, pp. 1051–1060, 1293–1299, 1302, 1305–1307.
4. *Death House Letters of Ethel and Julius Rosenberg*, Jero Publishing Co., New York, 1953; Virginia Gardner, *The Rosenberg Story*, Masses & Mainstream, New York, 1954.
5. During the trial, this coin-collection became Government Exhibit 27, introduced as "documentary evidence" to prove the Rosenbergs' inclination for espionage. (Record, pp. 1176–1177.)
6. Record, p. 1185.
7. In an interview with Mr. Bloch, this writer asked the attorney: "Then you had not the slightest idea how far off you were that night?" Mr. Bloch's reply was: "My God, no!"
8. Emanuel Bloch died of a heart attack on January 30, 1954, at the age of fifty-two, some seven months following the execution of the Rosenbergs. (New York *Times*, January 31, 1954.)

9. This three-page handwritten statement of Greenglass to Rogge, officially acknowledged, became a crucial part of the "newly discovered evidence" in the final appeal. (See Appendix 2.)

10. According to the Record, it was within this five-day period that Ruth Greenglass, accompanied by Rogge, signed a *prepared* statement at the Federal Building. In other words, it was within this precise period that the first of the prosecution-Rogge-Greenglass "deals" was agreed upon. (Record, pp. 742–745.)

11. New York *Times,* July 18, 1950.

12. Since the console table had not yet become a "gift from the Russians," and since its underside had not yet been "hollowed out" by the Greenglasses, it remained ignored by the FBI. In a later chapter, we will discuss the prosecution's failure to produce the console table.

13. In 1950, $100,000 bail would be equivalent to at least $500,000 in 1977. Thus, under Article VIII of the Bill of Rights, clearly "excessive." Later, with Ethel's bail also set at $100,000, the equivalent total would be $1 million!

ADDENDA

Concerning the Rosenberg sons, Michael, 34, is now an assistant professor of economics at a New England college. Robert, 30, teaches anthropology at the same college. After their parents' deaths, both boys were adopted by Anne and Abel Meeropol. In 1973, they helped found the National Committee to Reopen the Rosenberg Case. In 1975, under the Freedom of Information Act, they obtained the release of some 30,000 pages from the FBI files dealing with the case. They have written sensitively about their youth as well as their belief in their parents' innocence in an excellent and stimulating book, *We Are Your Sons,* by Robert and Michael Meeropol, Houghton Mifflin, Boston, 1975; reprinted in paperback by Ballantine Books, New York, 1976.

•

As an example of the questionable accuracy and pre-judicial slanting in many of the FBI memos, there is that of September 12, 1950, telling of an interview with Samuel Greenglass (the oldest brother of David) in which he is reported as having said that between 1932 and 1935 "both Julius Rosenberg and Ethel Rosenberg became violent Communists, and since that time have maintained that nothing is more important than the Communist cause." (See New York *Times*, December 4, 1975.)

However, in 1932, Julius was only a fourteen-year-old high-school boy and *not* until 1936, when he was eighteen, had he met Ethel.

6 "A TENDENCY TO HYSTERIA"

I

> "And the Lord said unto Cain, 'Where is Abel thy brother?' And he said, 'I know not: Am I my brother's keeper?' "

Thus is recorded the first subterfuge made by the first murderer in written history, a lie made even to his God. For millennia, the name of Cain has been a curse, not so much because of the unnatural crime but rather because of the utter lack of remorse. Only one concern does Cain show—the extent of his punishment: It "is greater than I can bear . . . every one that findeth me shall slay me."

And while their sins differ, in that Cain killed in jealous rage whereas Greenglass killed to save himself, there is the same deadening of conscience. On the witness stand and thereafter, for more than eight hundred days and nights, until that final night when his sister was strapped into the electric chair, he held fast to his rationale: She doesn't have to die—if she chooses to die, the responsibility is hers, not mine, not mine . . .

•

Did Greenglass realize during the period before Julius' arrest that he would be required to include his sister in the "conspiracy"? It is extremely doubtful. It was hardly necessary for the prosecution to alarm him with such a premature demand. With Julius behind bars, Ethel would soon come to accept the course of cooperation just as Ruth had. Certainly the prosecution knew the serious predicament Ethel was left in. In a letter she sent Julius shortly after his arrest, she writes desperately, "How long can I wait to pay bills?"

It was precisely what the prosecution had counted on to bring the Rosenbergs to heel. Not only was Ethel faced with her daily housework and caring for two small children—but she was suddenly forced to take over the operation of the machine shop. With Julius' arrest, creditors lost no time in demanding immediate payment.

In addition, there was the emotional strain in a woman whose brother and husband were both behind bars. Finally, there was the traumatic shock upon the children. Three-year-old Robby was reliving the nightmare of the arrest with fits of trembling and whimpering. Seven-year-old Michael gave Ethel no rest: Why couldn't he visit his father? Why had Uncle David been arrested? Why had the detectives torn apart the house . . . ?

As for friends and relatives, Ethel was virtually cut off from any contact. The very immensity of the charge produced a paralyzing fear in everyone who had ever known the Rosenbergs. They, too, might be suspected of involvement in the "spy ring." [1]

As for her mother (Tessie Greenglass), when Ethel had called upon her for help, not once had she responded; not even to mind the children. It was her mother's stubborn opinion that David was in trouble mostly because of Julius' and Ethel's "Communistic" ideas.

What was particularly galling was the extent of the rapport between her mother and Ruth, now her mortal enemy. In subsequent talks with Mr. Bloch, Ethel would discuss almost obsessively this unholy alliance between Tessie and Ruth. She saw their basic personalities as astonishingly similar. Both women were egocentric; both calloused by poverty and struggle. The jungle existence on the Lower East Side frequently dehumanized people. Some emerged unscathed, others became warped. Some became sensitive and compassionate. Others became embittered and let their suffering harden into a self-protective armor.

During these conversations with her lawyer, Ethel would also discuss the psychological reasons for her brother's now-open hatred of Julius. David had been about fourteen when she had met Julius, and had not taken too well to her first boy friend. She remembered the testy remarks he had often made about the typing she did for Julius and their staying up so late . . .

II

It was a very cold winter the year Ethel Greenglass met Julius Rosenberg, and the two would sit close to the kitchen stove to keep warm. With his long legs outstretched beneath the stove, Julius would write his college reports while Ethel typed them up neatly. One winter, she told him, it had been so cold in her house that when her girl friends dropped over they would thaw out their feet by placing them inside the oven.[2]

Sometimes in her room Ethel would play the piano and sing for Julius songs like "Ciribiribin," and show that she could hit high C.[3] But when she returned from the hallway below after kissing Julius good night she would meet with David's dark look.

It had never occurred to her that her teen-aged brother might be secretly jealous, had resented those good-night kisses and whatever else he imagined took place between the young lovers. Now she wondered whether it was this repressed rivalry or guilt that was the underlying cause for all those difficult years in Julius' and David's partnership.[4] It would not be surprising, since she had been the only girl among three boys; and toward David there had been a special maternal attachment as her "baby brother."

As for the relations between her mother and David,

she remembered that her mother had always dominated him. And perhaps this explained the present alliance of Ruth and Tessie, especially since David's arrest. They had been rather close before, when her mother had lent David the money to invest in the shop. However, since his arrest the relationship had become quite thick. It seemed as though Ruth, having become physically husbandless, was conscious of the restored balance of power. Now the older woman could more equitably share and protect her son's interests.

III

Exactly two weeks after Julius' arrest, Ethel was subpoenaed to appear before the Grand Jury on the seventh of August. As Mr. Bloch reasoned, it was unlikely that the prosecution expected her to testify against her own husband. Therefore, the intention was to trap her into making some damaging statement against David. Thus, the only safeguard was in the Fifth Amendment.

At the Grand Jury hearing, the questioning was conducted by Myles J. Lane, chief assistant to Saypol.[5] It was all very polite at first, but then Lane inquired pointblank: "Did you ever sign a Communist Party nominating petition for elective office?"

Her reply was straightforward: "I did sign a Communist Party petition."

Nine years earlier, in 1941, some 50,000 American citizens had signed this nominating petition to put the New York City Councilman Peter Cacchione on the ballot, but her reply, no doubt, in the viewpoint of the Grand Jury, made her immediately an unrepentant member of the Communist "international conspiracy." Thus she was damned if she answered and damned if she didn't. For, had she refused to answer on constitutional grounds, she would have been equally condemned as a "Fifth Amendment Communist."

And now, as Lane moved from the question of political heresy to an invitation to legal suicide, there was only one refuge—to exercise her privilege of the

Fifth Amendment. But this suited Lane perfectly: "Did you ever hear David Greenglass discuss his work in connection with the atom bomb and nuclear fission?"

"I decline to answer. . . ."

"Have you ever met Harry Gold?"

"I decline to answer. . . ."

How malicious this question was can be judged by the fact that Gold never claimed to have met Julius or Ethel Rosenberg. And while Ethel and Mr. Bloch were aware of the tactic when she later reported the gist of the hearing, what they did not realize was that her taking of the Fifth Amendment was later to become inferential evidence of her guilt.

IV

It is well to note the mounting war hysteria during that early August of 1950, because there can be little doubt that the prosecution relied heavily on the effect it would have on the compliance of the Rosenbergs. On August 6, the day before Ethel's questioning, there were these headlines:

ATOM BOMB SHELTERS FOR CITY
AT COST OF $450,000,000 URGED

SEARCH OF BATORY [the Polish motorship] YIELDS
NO [atomic] BOMB—SHIP DETAINED
4 HOURS IN BAY

On August 9, in the New York *Times*, there was this unique grouping of headlines reporting President Truman's most recent message to Congress:

[Truman] WARNS AGAINST HYSTERIA

DEMANDS REGISTRATION OF ANY TRAINED
AS SPIES

On the next day, many prominent liberals hastened to prove themselves "clean" in a full-page advertisement in the New York *Times* of August 10:

. . . From now on, let us make no mistake about it:

the war is on, the chips are down. Those among us who defend Russia or Communism are enemies of freedom and traitors to the United Nations and the United States. American soldiers are dying . . . every man's house will be in a target area before this [Korean war] ends. . . .

And so we come to August 11, the day Ethel Rosenberg was again summoned before the Grand Jury, but, as we shall see, not for further questioning. By this date the prosecution had waited patiently for Julius to cry "Enough!" For, in the three weeks since his arrest, his business was almost ruined. Ethel informed her husband that they had been cut off "from any more credit." "The accountant will be in next week. I'll be in the shop tomorrow early and will make calls to various accounts and try to get them to pay up."

The problem of the children was steadily increasing. For Julius, helpless behind bars, it was tormenting to hear that the shock of his arrest might leave the boys with permanent psychological scars. He begged her to forget the shop entirely. Better to sell the machinery now at a fraction of its value than to be utterly stranded later.

From the prosecution's point of view, it must have seemed that it required only one more blow to shatter the Rosenbergs' morale completely. It proceeded swiftly. On the morning of her second appearance before the Grand Jury, Ethel was again faced with the task of finding a neighbor to take care of the children. Fortunately, a woman in the same building volunteered to mind them, stating, "I'm not such a hero—but if I have to be afraid of my own shadow, then what kind of America will I give my kids?"

The second Grand Jury hearing turned out to be a repetition of the first; virtually the same questions and answers. It was 1:15 P.M. when Ethel left the Federal Building. Suddenly two men were at her side. One of them said, "You'll have to come with us—you're under arrest." They had no warrant; they said they didn't require one. Then they took her right back into the same building and up to the FBI suite on the twenty-ninth floor.

She was permitted to call her attorney. Since Emanuel Bloch was out of town his secretary quickly got in touch with his elderly father and law partner, Alexander Bloch. She was also permitted to telephone her neighbor to explain what was keeping her. Then Ethel asked to speak to Michael. She had no idea how to break the news to the boy. There was no sense lying; he would hear it on the radio soon enough.

"Michael, do you remember what happened to Daddy—?"

It was as far as she got; the boy instantly guessed and there was a "long agonized scream" of utter despair. For the next three years, whether tossing in restless sleep in her cell in the Women's House of Detention or pacing her death cell in Sing Sing, Ethel Rosenberg was to hear again and again that despairing scream of her first-born.

The arraignment took place that afternoon before Commissioner Edward W. McDonald. As Mr. Lane presented the complaint, Ethel heard that she was

accused of assisting her husband, Julius, 32, and others, in recruiting her brother, David Greenglass, 28, to obtain . . . secret information concerning the atomic bomb for the Soviet Union.[6]

On the question of bail, Alexander Bloch requested that she be paroled "in his custody until Monday so that she could make arrangements for her children." Stating that "he would not entertain any parole suggestion," Commissioner McDonald set Ethel's bail at $100,000. A few moments later she was whisked off to the Greenwich Avenue prison where she was to remain for the next eight months. At a press interview following the arraignment, Lane stated:

There is ample evidence that Mrs. Rosenberg and her husband have been affiliated with Communist activities for a long period of time. . . . If the crime with which she is charged had not occurred, perhaps we would not have the present situation in Korea.

It was, of course, "conviction by public opinion," since it placed upon the Rosenbergs the full responsibility for the Korean war. Indeed, when Judge Kaufman enlarged upon this theme in his sentencing speech, he added to their guilt not only the 50,000 casualties of the Korean war but also the *inevitable* deaths of all those millions of Americans whose lives would be destroyed in World War III. Suffice it to say that there is not a single recognized expert of military or foreign affairs who has ever endorsed this fantastic charge.

V

In our anatomy of frame-up, we touched upon the prevailing attitudes of officialdom toward people believed to be unrepentant Communists. Whether it be a Judge Kaufman finding a rationale in the 1950's to impose the death sentences upon the Rosenbergs or a Judge Thayer finding one in the 1920's to justify the executions of Sacco and Vanzetti, never do those in authority question their own motives or see themselves as evil. Always it is their victims who are evil, who must be destroyed.

What did it matter to Judge Kaufman that Brothman had not committed any espionage? Wasn't he nevertheless a potential spy? Hadn't he admitted that he had been a member of the Young Communist League while a student at Columbia University? And when Brothman's attorney pleaded with Kaufman not to confuse the case with the current "spy investigations," there was this impatient interruption:

[Kaufman]: It is merely a question of degree. . . . All leading to the same net result, though.

Similarly, the prosecuting official assumes the role of crusader for the Free World. And it is in the light of this so-called higher morality that we examine the conduct of the prosecution in its effort to obtain from the Rosenbergs a "confession" that the American Communist Party was nothing more than an espionage branch of the international Soviet spy network. That this was the entire crux of the Rosenberg case is indicated quite explicitly in the *Columbia Law Review*'s reference to it as "the outstanding 'political' trial of this generation."

A few minutes after the sentencing of the Rosenbergs, this post-mortem exchange took place between Judge Irving Kaufman and O. John Rogge:

The Court: I know it required a great deal of courage [of Greenglass]. . . .

Mr. Rogge: It is the toughest I have ever been in, Judge.

The Court: A brother testifying against his sister. I suppose that he did a lot of soul-searching and came to the conclusion that [what] he was doing is bigger than his relationship with his sister. [R. 1618]

Such then is the rationale offered by Judge Kaufman to explain the most tormenting question in all this tragedy: How did a brother bring himself to send his own sister to the electric chair? Because even if Ethel had been guilty, such an act is still beyond comprehension. The record shows that outside of David's testimony (supported *only* by Ruth) there existed not a scrap of evidence against her! It was not as if the FBI had dug up a substantial amount of evidence against a man's sister and then the man, unable to hold out, had reluctantly confessed to her part in the conspiracy. To repeat, no such evidence (circumstantial or otherwise) is contained in the record or anywhere else.

In short, we are asked to believe that Greenglass testified against his sister all on his own—voluntarily and gratuitously. And, according to Kaufman's sanctimonious explanation, he did it only because he had searched his soul and found within it something bigger than his love for his sister.

And what was that big something? According to Kaufman, it was his reawakened sense of patriotic duty. Another test of the spuriousness of Kaufman's rationale is simply to ask: "If Greenglass really implicated Ethel in the conspiracy on June 15 (which was his testimony), why wasn't she arrested together with Julius on July 17?" Surely that one-month period gave the FBI enough time to obtain the full story. In fact the record shows that Ruth's signed statement of mid-July was the *only one* she gave. In his sentencing speech, Kaufman described Ethel as a "full-fledged partner in this crime." We have seen that Ethel was considered so dangerous a criminal that when she was arrested she was placed under the same bail of $100,000 as Julius. Hence one must ask, if she was so dangerous on August 11, was she not equally dangerous on July 17?

There is only the logical answer: David's testimony was "tailored" to fit the Kaufman rationale of patriotic "courage" so that the truth of the Greenglass "deal" would be concealed. It was the prosecution pursuing its one-by-one tactic. Having pressured David into accusing Julius, they now had him trapped sufficiently by his series of statements to force him to involve Ethel.[7]

When we search for the key to this self-entrapment we find it in the first indictment, dated August 17, 1950. It is significant to study its interpretation in the New York *Times* of August 18, 1950:

Named as co-conspirators, but *not as defendants* [were] Harry Gold, David Greenglass, and his wife Ruth. . . . Mr. Irving H. Saypol said, "The Grand Jury had directed that she not be prosecuted." Thus, it was indicated that she was cooperative in the investigation and might turn Government witness.[8] [Emphasis added.]

What does this mean? Simply that as a reward for their "cooperation," both David and Ruth had been promised they would go scot-free! Concerning Ruth's immunity, as the *Times* has just shown us, there was little difficulty. As for David, as we shall soon see, the deal had been made that if he would plead guilty to the Santa Fe indictment in New York, he would receive his "pat on the back" and a "suspended sentence." It is a measure of the naïveté of the Greenglasses that they could believe such a flagrant bargain would not be protested. Of course it was, as soon as Emanuel Bloch found an opportunity to do so.

On August 23, when Ethel and Julius appeared before Judge T. Hoyt Davis to plead "not guilty" to the indictment, Mr. Bloch flatly charged the prosecution with having made a "deal" with the Greenglasses in exchange for their agreement to be Government witnesses. Proof? The Greenglasses had not been indicted as defendants despite their admitted crimes as atomic spies.

Let us now turn to the interoffice memo written by R. H. Goldman to O. John Rogge on August 21 concerning David's promised reward:

I spoke to Ruth Greenglass this morning. She is feeling better and so is Dave apparently about the fact that they were not named as defendants. . . . Now she feels the thing is moving smoothly. . . . She feels that Dave may not get a *suspended sentence* and is worried about the kind of treatment he will get [while in prison].

I was able to reassure him through Ruth. . . . I told her that we were happy to say that few of our clients went to jail. . . . I further assured her that Saypol would not permit any mistreatment. [Emphasis added.]

So far so good for the Greenglasses. Everything was "moving smoothly"—and, at the very worst, if David should serve a nominal term of a year or so, Saypol would look out for him. One can therefore visualize the consternation which must have followed Bloch's courtroom exposure of the "deal" two days later. Here is the memo of August 23, as Goldman dispatches an anxious communiqué to his chief, O. John Rogge, that same afternoon:

Lane, the Assistant U. S. Attorney, called me at 1:00 o'clock and told me something important had come up. . . .
. . . From the fact that Greenglass was not indicted but merely named as co-conspirator in the New York indictment, it looked to Bloch as if the Government had made a deal with you as Greenglass' attorney. Lane felt that we would now have to consider the question of whether it was OK that Greenglass be indicted here in a superseding indictment and not merely named as a co-conspirator. He would then be a defendant and be tried here in New York but would testify against the others [the Rosenbergs].

The New Mexico District Attorney, acting on instructions from the Attorney General's office, with whom

Lane had been in touch, would agree to such a procedure. . . .

. . . But Lane said something should be done on this before September 6th and reiterated again it was to our advantage not to take any chance of getting before a judge in New Mexico, clearly indicating that he felt that in a small state like New Mexico they might well prefer to give a good stiff sentence (of course, he added he did not want to sell us on anything, and so forth).

There was no indication that Ruth is to be indicted. . . .

. . . I think it best not to discuss this with Ruth until you return as she might get somewhat excited about it and at any rate we don't have to do anything before September 6th.[9]

.To sum up, these were the terms of the "deal" made partly before and partly after Ethel's arrest:
1. Ruth Greenglass was not to be indicted.
2. All threats of trial before a hostile jury, and of "a good stiff sentence" in New Mexico were to be withdrawn.
3. David "would now have to consider" becoming a defendant in the Rosenberg trial.

In looking back, there can be little question that the prosecution pursued its policy of coercion with every possible means. On the one hand there was its continuing pressure against the Greenglasses in the event the Rosenbergs held out. On the other hand, with Ethel's arrest, there was still the hope that trial could be avoided by Julius consenting to plead guilty. To be sure, the political atmosphere almost guaranteed a conviction; however, anything could happen during trial. It needed only one soft-hearted juror to upset the applecart. It was a risk any veteran prosecutor would seek to avoid if he could attain the same ends without trial.

And Saypol was not only such a veteran prosecutor but he was also the United States Attorney for the most important Federal District in the country, the famous Southern New York.[10] Both he and his chief assistant, Myles Lane, were ambitious for promotion.

With the arrest of Ethel they knew they had some six or seven months to pressure her and Julius into making a confession. They could bargain with one with threats against the other—by asking Ethel, for example: "You want to save him? Talk!" (And vice versa.) And if until now Julius had given no sign of willingness to cooperate, then his wife, wild with anxiety for her stranded children, might be the deciding factor. But even if she should hold out, there was still a good chance that Julius, unable to bear her sufferings, would finally break and say, "Okay, I'm guilty but my wife is innocent."

The tactics of producing self-entrapment are many and varied. We know from David's confidential statement to Rogge that, in his initial efforts to appease the FBI, he committed the blunder of involving his own wife in the "conspiracy." And since there was a geographical problem involved (when David was in New Mexico in 1944, Julius was in New York), it was necessary for Greenglass to agree to the detail that Ruth had been used as a messenger by Julius during her anniversary trip. That David was wary of the danger of this detail is evidenced by the caution indicated in his statement:

I made sure to tell the FBI that she [Ruth] was transmitting this info from my brother-in-law Julius and was not her own idea. . . . Also, I definitely placed my wife out of the room at the time of Gold's visit.[11]

Interviewed the next day by Rogge, it is little wonder that Ruth, enraged at her husband's stupidity, disclosed the following facts about his character:

As to her husband, she stated that he had a *"tendency to hysteria."* At other times he would become delirious and once when he had the grippe he ran nude through the hallway, shrieking of "elephants," "Lead Pants."
She had known him since she was ten years old. *She said that he would say things were so even if they were not.* He talked of suicide as if he were a character in the movies but she didn't think he would do it.[12] [Emphasis added.]

Nevertheless, despite his hopes that the Rosenbergs would also entrap themselves, Saypol had to reckon with every contingency. In the event of a court battle, it was essential to have Ethel accused as a spy together with her husband. For if she remained free of all blame, she would also be free to testify.

How far-fetched it would appear if the Greenglasses swore they had numerous conspiratorial meetings at the Rosenberg apartment but were forced to admit that Ethel knew nothing about them! How could Julius be presented as the big-time spy-master, the recipient of the console table, citations, and wristwatches from the Russians, the entertainer of recruits in expensive restaurants and night clubs, the accomplished microfilm photographer—with his own innocent wife stoutly testifying that none of this intensive activity could possibly have taken place over a period of years without her knowledge?

In addition, if Ethel remained a free woman, she would also be free to aid her husband's defense. She could confer with him and his attorney regularly, assisting in all the complex preparations for trial. In the event of Julius' conviction, she might appeal to the public for financial aid. Indeed, as a spirited and devoted wife, she might succeed in arousing considerable popular support.

Finally, if Ethel were to remain blameless, there would be lost to the prosecution the tremendous psychological advantage of placing a brother on the stand to accuse his sister. This was, in itself, so powerful a factor that it obviated the necessity for providing corroborative evidence. (And, as the record shows, there was absolutely none with regard to the charges against Ethel.)

In contrast, by arresting Ethel and keeping her in prison under prohibitive bail, every advantage accrued to the prosecution. With the husband in one prison and the wife in another, their only means of conferring would be through censored letters or whatever alternate visits their attorney might manage. Under such demoralizing conditions and with the trial at least seven months off, it was not unreasonable to expect disintegration of morale.

It should be added that this course of coercion continued after the trial, when Ethel was transferred to the death house at Sing Sing *alone*. The maneuver was commented upon bitterly by Ethel in a letter to her attorney:

> They expect me to break under the strain because I am a woman. They think that in the Death House I will be haunted by images, alone, and without Julius, I'll collapse.

VI

In closing this chapter, it is appropriate to ask, what *in essence* was the Government's case against the Rosenbergs? At the trial itself, we will see that it depended chiefly on the testimony of the Greenglasses. Here is the opinion of the Court of Appeals:

> Doubtless, if that testimony were disregarded, the conviction could not stand. [R. 1648]

Hence, it was simply the word of two people declaring that two other people were spies, and testifying to certain conspiratorial conversations which *no other person* had ever heard or witnessed. Throughout the entire trial, as we shall see, no substantiation of the Greenglass testimony with regard to the Rosenbergs was ever produced by the Government.

From the very start of the case, Saypol realized the need for additional witnesses. In an effort to find them, his assistant, Roy Cohn, and the FBI combed through a list of Julius Rosenberg's former CCNY classmates. Particular emphasis was directed toward those who were or had been employed by government agencies, and who had falsely signed non-Communist applications under oath. With such persons subject to perjury prosecution, there was a realistic basis that they could be induced to "cooperate."

One such prospective and compliant witness was found, a former engineer for the Navy's Bureau of Ordnance, named Max Elitcher. When he had worked in Washington, he had been a member of a Communist Party branch. Furthermore, having signed a non-Communist oath for the Navy back in 1947, he was living in a state of fear that he would be arrested any day and jailed for perjury.

At the trial, although Max Elitcher's testimony was *completely* unrelated to and uncorroborative of the Greenglass testimony, its great value to the prosecution was the impression it gave the jury that Julius Rosenberg was the spy-master of a veritable ring of espionage agents. For Elitcher not only included himself as one of Julius' espionage contacts, but also included his best friend, Morton Sobell.

And it is with the case of Sobell that we shall now concern ourselves. Just as we have seen how Greenglass was coerced into a series of perjuries involving his sister, so we shall see how Elitcher came to involve his best friend by a similar process after Sobell had refused to bear false witness against the Rosenbergs.

In this regard, it is appropriate to refer to a colloquy between Saypol and Kaufman, which came about as the result of a persistent defense inquiry into the suspicious nature of Elitcher's series of statements made to the FBI. During this colloquy, there was this significant admission made by Saypol:

Initially, nobody knows whether an individual is a prospective witness or a prospective defendant. [R. 435]

Applying this to Sobell, we shall see how the prosecution stopped at nothing to make of him an accusing witness against the Rosenbergs—not even at a brutal assault and an illegal act of kidnapping. For, in the course of the FBI's investigations, it had been discovered that Sobell was on a trip to Mexico with his family. This trip was eventually turned into "flight" and "consciousness of guilt." And as for the kidnapping, which was carried out in clear violation of the laws of the United States and Mexico, this was eventually turned into a "deportation."

NOTES AND REFERENCES

1. FBI detectives had interrogated some of Ethel's former high-school chums. One had some snap-

shots the girls had taken. Learning of FBI visits to other friends, she hurriedly burned them. (Virginia Gardner, *The Rosenberg Story*, Masses & Mainstream, New York, 1954.)

2. Ibid.; many of the details regarding Ethel's girl-hood were compiled by Virginia Gardner from inter-views with former friends.

3. Despite her mother's opposition, Ethel had bought an old piano to practice her singing. Evidently her voice had genuine quality, for she became the youngest member of the Schola Cantorum at the Metropolitan. (Record, pp. 1305–1306.)

4. According to David's testimony, there were "quarrels of every type . . . arguments over personality . . . . . . over money . . . the way the shop was run . . . the way the outside was run." (Record, p. 664.)

5. These excerpts are derived from Ethel's cross-exam-ination at the trial. (Record, pp. 1344–1398.)

6. New York *Times*, August 12, 1950.

7. ". . . I signed statements, plenty of statements." (Testimony of David Greenglass, Record, pp. 602, 604.)

8. In the record, Saypol states that it was *he* who di-rected that Ruth "not be prosecuted." (Record, pp. 1623–1624.)

9. See Appendix 5.

10. Before his appointment as United States Attorney, Saypol had been Chief Assistant in the same district from 1945 to 1949. (See *Addenda*.)

11. In their trial testimony, the Greenglasses were forced to "restage" the scene *with Ruth present during Gold's visit*, obviously in order to bear witness. *Note:* Here is another example of our anatomy of frame-up: First, there is the full truth that Ruth went to Albuquerque innocently in November, 1944; then David embroiders it with a tentative lie; finally, at the trial, it is elaborated into out-and-out perjury. (For Greenglass' full memo to Rogge, see Appendix 2.)

12. From Rogge's file memo of June 19, 1950 (see Ap-pendix 3). This is the same memo that ends with: "There was a long discussion about JR."

ADDENDA

Concerning the question of why David testified against his sister Ethel, our analysis of his step-by-step coercion is now partially confirmed by the transcript of an interview related by the Criminal Division of the Department of Justice. As reported by the Washington *Post* of December 6, 1975, the following "exchange" took place on August 1 or 2, 1950, seven months before the trial, between David Greenglass and Myles J. Lane (Chief Assistant U.S. Attorney) regarding the alleged meetings with the Rosenbergs in 1944 and 1945:

Q. Was Ethel present in any of these occasions?
A. Never.
Q. Did Ethel talk to you about it?
A. Never spoke about it to me and that's a fact. Aside from trying to protect my sister, believe me that's a fact.

Since it was at these two crucial meetings involving the alleged recruitment of David and Ruth Greenglass and the subsequent delivery of atomic secrets to the Rosenbergs, it is clear that Greenglass' testimony at the trial was the result of the many admitted conferences with the FBI and the prosecution attorneys. (See also New York *Times* of November 22 and December 14, 1975.)

Saypol's reward for the convictions of the Rosenbergs in 1951 came promptly in the same year with his nomination (and assured election) to the highest judicial position in New York as a Justice on the State Supreme Court. After his first term of fourteen years, he was re-elected for a similar term. (See *Addenda* to Chapter 20 regarding his indictment by a special Grand Jury in May, 1976, on charges of bribery, perjury and corruption.)

Concerning Myles Lane, his chief assistant, he too, was rewarded with speedy promotion to U.S. Attorney to replace Saypol, and subsequently was appointed to the Appellate Division of the New York State Supreme Court.

7 "WHEN IT RAINS IT POURS"

> "In the last five years the use of the word panic in the public press has increased by 1,447 per cent. . . ." [1]

The afternoon of June 22, 1950, was a pleasant day in suburban Long Island, and vacation was in the air. Skipping along the street, one little girl of ten joyfully waved good-by to her playmates. She had an odd name, Sydney Sobell. In her house her mother, Helen, was folding away things to take along for her year-old baby brother, Mark. Upstairs her father, Morton Sobell, was packing their suitcases.

Since 1948 the Sobells had been dreaming of a vacation in Mexico, but for some time now it had grown to something more.

They had finally come to grips with a long-standing anxiety. As an electronics engineer with Reeves Instrument Company in 1947, Morton Sobell had signed an affidavit swearing that he was not and never had been a member of the Communist Party. Since he needed the job and his past membership seemed far away, he had signed readily. In addition, his wife Helen, also employed by Reeves, had signed a false non-Communist affidavit. Thus, both had committed perjury, and Sobell, recently assigned to military work at Reeves, had become fearful that at any moment he might be investigated by the FBI and find himself convicted with a sentence of five years. [2]

Some of his friends had already been visited by FBI agents. There had been the usual polite inquiries about other friends' politics. What papers did they read—any magazines like *The Nation* or the *New Republic*? What sort of people did they associate with? What organizations did they belong to?

One had to be blind not to recognize the signs of

the gathering storm. Certainly the Cold War was getting hotter, and there were rumors of concentration camps to be filled with "Reds" in the event of war. In the schools, children were being dog-tagged and terrorized with air-raid drills against atom-bomb attacks. Snooping and informing were becoming a patriotic duty. Everywhere was tension, insecurity and distrust.

About a week earlier, the headlines had announced the arrest of a former Army sergeant named David Greenglass, accused of stealing the atomic bomb for the Soviet Union. To Morton Sobell it was more fuel for the fires of an inevitable World War III. He had no idea that the ex-GI was the brother-in-law of his college friend, Julius Rosenberg. This trip to Mexico, if nothing else, would be a welcome respite from the oppressive atmosphere.

(The atmosphere was aptly described by Justice William O. Douglas as "The Black Silence of Fear" in an article written for the New York *Times* of February 13, 1952: "Fear has mounted—fear of losing one's job, fear of being investigated, fear of being pilloried. This fear has . . . driven many thoughtful people to despair.")

For Morton and Helen Sobell, it wasn't so much despair, but rather the feeling of "having had it." Mexico was close, living inexpensive, one didn't even need passports. One simply called the airline for reservations. By summer's end, if there were any promise of restored sanity at home, they could always come back.

II

After picking up his tourist visas at the Mexican Consulate, Sobell went to the American Airlines office to pay for his round-trip tickets. He was advised to register the serial numbers of his cameras to avoid duty charges on the return trip. When, therefore, the plane stopped at Dallas, he had them "checked and identified" at the U.S. Customs there.

From the moment the Sobells arrived in Mexico

City they welcomed the reduced tempo. Here was no threat of war; in fact, an abhorrence of anything connected with it. It was the third most populous city in the Western Hemisphere, yet there was so little nervous tension that the city could boast only one psychoanalyst, and he catered primarily to Americans.

Looking for a suitable apartment, Sobell found one on the Calle Octava de Cordoba at a reasonable rent. On the way back to tell his wife about it, he passed a newsstand with the air edition of the New York *Times*. The large headlines of June 25 announced:

WAR IS DECLARED BY NORTH KOREA

In the days that followed the headlines grew increasingly alarming. With the full commitment of MacArthur's armed forces, the threat of an atomic Armageddon appeared close at hand.

As yet they hadn't written home, but since his hunches about the possibility of war had been proved so right, why not continue to be prudent? Just before leaving he had told his old friend Bill Danziger that he was flying down to Mexico and had promised to write. Dashing off a brief note, he asked him to mail some enclosed messages to his family. For the sender's name, he decided to use a pseudonym: "Morty Sowell." He had thought of it impulsively and with some amusement. It meant he was getting along *so well*.

Since the prosecution laid special emphasis on such pseudonyms as evidence of guilt, this is an appropriate place to comment that it is inconceivable that such would be the conduct of a trained spy following *prearranged instructions* as was repeatedly charged. First, it is not the practice of spies to use their own initials. If the FBI were going to intercept his letters, it would be just as dangerous to use "Morty Sowell" as to use "Morty Sobell." Moreover, if he were trying to conceal his whereabouts, why would he put his correct address on the envelope? Finally, throughout his stay in Mexico City, Sobell resided there under his *own name*.

Sobell's silly behavior was typical of many frightened

166

Americans in the period of 1950, who considered themselves "refugees" and made half-hearted attempts to inquire about political asylum abroad.

Concerning Danziger, there was an additional Sobell letter, sent to him with the pseudonym "Morty Levitov"—his wife's maiden name! Again, a trained spy would know that the FBI was capable of ascertaining that Helen Sobell was previously Helen Levitov. And again, why was it necessary to put the sender's name on the envelope? Above all, would a spy fleeing for his life be so foolish as to begin corresponding with relatives certain to be questioned?

III

A few days after the Sobells had moved into their apartment, their neighbor from across the hall dropped in to introduce himself. His name was Manuel de los Rios, and he owned an interior-decorating shop.

Learning that Rios was a refugee from Franco Spain, Sobell warmed up to him and invited him to dinner. The conversation drifted to the world situation and the blindness of the West in permitting Hitler and Mussolini to destroy the Spanish Republic. Was that tragic lesson completely forgotten? What could have been the "graveyard of fascism" had led to World War II. Was it Korea now that was to lead to World War III? In an all-out conflict, it was hardly likely that the long arm of Washington would not place a heavy hand of control over the whole of Mexico. If so, Rios pointed out, all anti-Fascist refugees might find it necessary to leave the country. Sobell agreed.

Again, if Sobell had received prearranged spy instructions, would he be so blissfully trusting? It was common knowledge that many of the Spanish refugees residing in Mexico were secret Franco agents planted to spy on the rest for the Falangista. Others, threatened with deportation by the DFS (Direccion Federal de Seguridad—Mexican Secret Police), had become informers. Their reports were cheerfully relayed to the FBI in exchange for generous payments or reciprocal favors. It is not at all unlikely (Rios was later produced as a prosecution witness) that the moment Sobell moved into the apartment opposite, Rios immediately reported the fact to the DFS, and/or that he was promptly instructed to keep Sobell under surveillance. According to the Mexican newspaper *La Prensa* of August 20, 1950, "There was not a single moment in which Sobell was not followed by agents of the DFS."

Putting two and two together, one must ask why, if Sobell arrived in Mexico legally as an American tourist and resided there with wife and children under his own name, would the DFS keep him under such strict surveillance? There can be only one answer: that the FBI and the DFS were in close collaboration, and that the sole purpose of this surveillance was a waiting game to see how many missteps and indiscretions Sobell might make—*not as a spy, but as a panic-stricken political refugee.*

Also, if Sobell was a fleeing spy, why would he be so reckless as to overlook the possibility of surveillance? If by this time Elitcher had exposed Sobell as a member of the Rosenberg spy ring (which is his testimony), why didn't the FBI order his immediate arrest? The obvious answer is that the FBI was operating on the basis that Sobell—as one of Julius' classmates, as a radar specialist, as an outspoken "leftist," and as one who was unwittingly supplying them with "suspicious" conduct in Mexico—presented splendid material for a prospective witness against the Rosenbergs.

IV

The shock came on a Tuesday, when Sobell picked up the air edition of the New York *Times* of July 18:

FOURTH AMERICAN HELD AS ATOM SPY

The Federal Bureau of Investigation today arrested Julius Rosenberg, 32 years old, a New Yorker, on charges of spying for Russia. . . .

168

"Atom Spy"! "Hand-cuffed"! "$100,000 bail"! It was just too fantastic. It could only be that the charge "was calculated to intimidate and silence political dissent in the United States." Now, any thought of returning to the United States was out of the question. For what? To be questioned about Julius' political background? To face charges of perjury for that non-Communist affidavit? It was at this point that Morton Sobell became obsessed with the idea that "A dictatorship was taking over the country!" Almost in a state of panic, the notion to leave for South America or Europe took on definite shape. Rios and he discussed the advisability of going to Vera Cruz to inquire about transportation abroad by whatever means.

Here again, according to Rios' testimony at the trial, Sobell showed an extraordinary faith in a stranger. Since such conduct would be incredible in a spy, one can view Sobell only as an amateur refugee seeking advice from one who had more experience.

Exploring the possibility that Rios was acting in the role of an agent provocateur for the DFS, this instance should be mentioned: When Sobell was about to leave for Vera Cruz, Rios suggested that if Señor Sobell wished to write to Señora Sobell, that the letters be addressed to himself. Sobell thanked him gratefully. However, the precaution was not only an invitation to more suspicion, but it did not even make good sense. For if Helen Sobell's mail was being watched, then by all logic the surveillance should also include Morton's quixotic attempts to leave Mexico.

V

As one approaches the port of Vera Cruz by bus from Mexico City, one abruptly leaves the temperate highlands to enter a steaming coastal area. But instead of the busy harbor which Sobell expected, there was only a sleepy waterfront with a couple of rusty freighters and tankers rocking lazily at anchor. There was also an expanse of sandy beach which looked inviting. At the Hotel Diligencias, Sobell reserved a room with the largest fan available. As he took up the pen to register, again he yielded to an impulsive choice of name, an association with the seashore: "Morris Sand."

During the next days, he made inquiries at the steamship offices, but very few passenger vessels docked at the port, and even freighters were rare and infrequent. Advised to try at the port of Tampico, he reserved a plane ticket for the coming Sunday, still using the name "M. Sand." In the meantime, Sobell had decided to order a pair of prescription sunglasses in an optical shop. In this instance, too, he used the name "M. Sand."

On July 30, Sobell flew to Tampico, where he checked in at a hotel using the name "Marvin Salt"— evidently another association with the sea. After a useless three days in Tampico, Sobel flew directly back to Mexico City on August 2. His plane ticket was reserved in the name of "Morton Salt." (*Note:* In the trial record, this is misspelled as "Solt.")

According to the Government's case, it was the use of these five pseudonyms together with Sobell's inquiries for passage that proved he was following an "elaborate prearranged scheme to flee the country of [his] birth."

It is vital, therefore, to put the Government's charges under scrutiny by asking: Was Sobell's conduct consistent with that of a spy following a prearranged scheme to escape to the Soviet Union—or was it rather that of a former Communist, who, in a moment of panic, sought political asylum, paralleling the behavior of all those refugees who fled from countries overrun by Hitler?

Let us test the conduct of Sobell in this three-day period in Tampico. What does this so-called spy do as he goes about inquiring for illegal ship passage? Does he assume one pseudonym and stick to it consistently? No. Not only does he arrive at the Tampico airfield as "M. Sand," then register at the Hotel Tampico as "Marvin Salt," but, within a day or so, reserves plane passage at the same airlines office using a third name, "Morton Salt." In other words, we are asked to believe that a trained spy would use three different names within a period of three days in the same confined locality!

On the other hand, the picture of Sobell as one of many floundering victims of a hysterical time—governed solely by impulses—is not unreasonable. If Sobell had had but a fraction of the espionage experience he is credited with, surely it would have occurred to him that, if any FBI or DFS "tails" were trailing him, they could easily do so whether he signed himself "Sand" or "Salt."

As the prime example of a man playing impulsively, even with some wry amusement, the role of a political refugee, we see that when he chooses his final pseudonym, he resorts not only to his given name, but combines it lugubriously into that famous trademark known to millions: MORTON SALT ("When it rains it pours") or, as he may have ruefully regarded his seriocomic behavior at the time: "It never rains but it pours!"

Whatever one may think of Sobell's romanticism and pathetic floundering, there were hundreds of political heretics and dissidents who behaved similarly during this period. This writer can attest that he saw at first hand in Mexico City numerous such examples. It was during a business trip made only eight months after Sobell's arrest, and the following incidents were typical.

In 1950-51, several writers from Hollywood had taken up residence in Mexico City. Some were seeking opportunities in the Mexican film industry. Some could no longer "take it" in the tension-ridden atmosphere of Hollywood, where blacklists had become the order of the day. In addition, there was the fear of war and of long-threatened mass arrests. Finally, it was cheaper to live in Mexico. One of these self-styled refugees who had become a "fugitive" from the Un-American Activities Committee greeted this writer with: "Welcome, fellow Sudeten-American!"

Two other friends, one a movie director and the other a screen writer, were at this time "ducking" subpoenas issued by the "Committee." When this writer finally located them, the director was living "incognito" at the Hotel L. As for the screen writer, he had moved from hotel to hotel, registering under so many names that he was quite confused which one he had used at which hotel!

When they learned that this writer intended to stay at the Hotel Reforma under his own name, both men professed solicitous alarm. Its reputation was such that it was referred to as the "Hotel Informer."

Subsequently, this writer had occasion to meet the "Walter Winchell" of Mexico City, a Mexican gossip columnist who reported about visiting American celebrities, not only in his column, but also in his daily meetings with agents of the FBI. Quite blandly, he asked this writer, "Have you yet seen your Hollywood friends hiding out over at the Hotel L?"

Whereupon, when this writer discreetly asked which friends he meant, he laughingly named them, adding about the screen writer: "He's using so many phony names, he doesn't know who he is any more!"

Some weeks later the harried screen writer, faced with dwindling funds, ruined career, and the feeling of being driven from pillar to post, decided to "cooperate" and flew to Washington with an anti-Communist statement designed to satisfy the "Committee."

During this trip to Mexico this writer also had occasion to meet a distinguished American physicist who had driven down with wife and child from the Midwest in a veritable panic. He was terribly anxious about the threatened mass arrests following the Supreme Court's upholding of the Smith Act. Although he himself was of old American stock, his wife happened to be of Russian birth, and both had been outspoken liberals quite left of center. However, after a two-week stay, he confided to this writer he was sick of behaving like a hunted refugee, that America was his country as much as it was McCarthy's, and he was damned if he was going to let anyone push him around. He and his family left for home the next day.

VI

On the evening of his return from Tampico, Sobell lighted his pipe after dinner and said to his wife, "Helen, we're going back home." The wild-goose chase had brought him to his senses; he must have been "punchy," and the whole idea of expatriating themselves was "a stupid thing . . . inept and pointless."

They had read recently of men like Adrian Scott and Ring Lardner, Jr., two of the "Hollywood Ten," cited for contempt for refusing to name other Communists. These men could have remained safely abroad employed by film studios in England, but chose to return to face imprisonment rather than desert the principle they had originally upheld—the freedom of association guaranteed by the First Amendment.

In the next two weeks, after the Sobells had secured the vaccinations required for their return to the United States, they decided to relax. The rent at the apartment was paid through August, and their daughter did not have to return to school until after Labor Day. They visited the usual tourist spots in and around Mexico City. There was the warm mingling with the Sunday crowds at Chapultepec Park and the Palace of Maximilian with its mute evidence of the monarch's efforts to conquer Mexico—his ornately carved royal carriage. And nearby, in sharp contrast, was that of the Indian, Juarez—the flimsy, black shay from which he rallied his people to the decisive victory at Querétaro. It was a further inspiration to return, Helen Sobell thought at the time.

In the meantime, back in New York, the prosecution and the FBI had already set the wheels in motion for Sobell's kidnapping. In later pages we will see that Saypol himself made a special trip to Mexico City, obviously to arrange with members of the Mexican Secret Police the timing and details of this illegal seizure.

On August 3, Saypol had an FBI agent in New York City named Rex I. Shroder swear out a complaint for the arrest of Sobell as a spy and co-conspirator of Julius Rosenberg. This warrant, of course, was kept secret until after Sobell was kidnapped two weeks later. Furthermore, we shall see that not only did it fail to contain any specified overt act of espionage, but that Saypol ordered this warrant at least *two months* before submitting any evidence of Sobell's alleged crime to the Grand Jury. Let it be stated plainly that the official records prove indisputably that the prosecution had not a shred of evidence against Sobell when it arranged its brutal assault upon him. It operated on the basis of a two-way strategy: If it was possible to terrorize Sobell into becoming a witness against the Rosenbergs, it did not need any evidence. And if Sobell refused to "cooperate," there was plenty of time to pressure Elitcher into providing enough evidence to obtain an indictment.

Before continuing with Sobell's kidnapping, a brief comment is in order on his alleged conduct as a carefully instructed spy seeking to save himself by flight. On August 12, the sensational news of Ethel Rosenberg's arrest would have made him realize that his own days were numbered. Despite this clear warning which, as a "spy," he must have read with alarm, he made not the slightest effort to carry out the "carefully planned pattern" of escape instructions supposedly given by Julius Rosenberg.

One would imagine that a Communist spy, upon seeing his co-conspirators arrested one by one, would seek refuge with one of the many thousands of local Communists in the vast working-class section of Mexico City. However, not only did Sobell remain at his apartment, but all during the eight weeks he was in Mexico he carried on his person no less that eight identification cards bearing the name "Morton Sobell"! Among these were his Social Security card, his driver's license, his birth certificate, and his membership card in the New York Academy of Sciences.

Is it conceivable that a spy anxious to conceal his identity would dare, or have any reason, to carry such material in flight? On the other hand, an innocent man, seeking political freedom and employment in another country, would take along exactly such proofs of identity.

According to the Government's case, Greenglass' flight instructions included contact with the Soviet Embassy in Mexico City, which would offer him immediate assistance, forged passports, and airplane passage abroad. This was supposed to be the "pattern" of escape also given to Sobell. And yet, despite surveillance (officially acknowledged in the Pollack report), there was no indication that Sobell made any attempt to contact the Soviet Embassy.

In sum, we are asked to accept the improbability that he was completely indifferent to capture and that for five days and nights he just waited in his apartment like a sitting duck to be "kidnapped" by the FBI through local hirelings.

VII

> "On Wednesday, August 16, 1950, at about 8:00 P.M., we had just finished our dinner in our apartment in Mexico City . . . and while my wife and I were lingering over our coffee. . . ." [3]

In the bedroom upstairs, the baby was sound asleep, and it was especially nice having their coffee by candlelight. A few minutes before, when the electric lights had gone out, Sydney had exclaimed "Here we go again," since it was an almost daily occurrence in Mexico City. Just as Helen was pouring their second cups of coffee, there was a knock on the door. Then suddenly—"three men burst into the room with drawn guns and bodies poised for shooting."

In the candlelight it had every aspect of a grade-B movie; the more so when the leader accused Sobell of being one "Johnny Jones" who "robbed a bank in Acapulco in the sum of $15,000"!

Then, as the lights went on, it became all too real. They pushed him roughly onto the sofa and "one of the men showed a piece of metal in his hand and said they were police. They were dressed in civilian clothes." A moment later a fourth man entered and demanded to see what was in the bedroom upstairs. Helen ran ahead to assure him there was only the baby, but was stopped by her husband's outcry. As she turned, she saw him being dragged to the door.

Helen frantically raced after them. A taxi was at the curb. It was raining; a light drizzle. Still struggling, Sobell cried out "Call the police!"—but one of the men raised his gun and brought down the butt of it on his head. As Helen tried to reach his side, one of the assailants grabbed her arms. (Later, she remembered, "I bit his thumb and he howled—then forced me down on the wet pavement.")

In the taxi, Sobell made an effort to rise, but the men beat him "over the head" until he lost consciousness. When he came to, the cab was in front of a nondescript government building, and he was ordered to get up.

In the interim, the man holding Helen had managed to find another cab to follow the other. Inside the building, she was hurried along the corridor where her husband was seated under guard. He was minus his glasses and his face was badly bruised. As they hustled her into a small room bearing the sign "Homicide," she heard him call to her, "Take it easy." His guard quickly silenced him with a slap across the face.

•

It was still dark. All Helen could see from the fast-traveling car was that they were driving through the suburbs. Soon they were on the open highway. Just ahead was the other black sedan containing the four men guarding her husband. In the car, with her and the children, rode three more. All seemed to be Mexicans.

Someone had been thoughtful enough to bring an armful of diapers and coats from their apartment. These had been dumped on the back seat. After an hour or so, when the morning light appeared at her right, she figured they must be traveling north. That was as much as she knew. . . .

The places they stopped at were little fly-infested

"cantinas" on the outskirts of small adobe villages. They would hand Helen a punctured can of milk for the baby and a couple of cheese sandwiches. And so it went all that day, mile after mile. They drove very fast, seventy and eighty miles per hour. Until the sun set, the heat was almost unbearable. At about 2 o'clock in the morning, August 18, they arrived at Nuevo Laredo. Just across the Rio Grande was Laredo, Texas.

When we reached the bridge . . . the boundary between the United States and Mexico, our car was flagged. . . . A man entered with a badge in his hand and stated he was a United States agent and he remained in the car.

The man was the FBI detective, Rex Shroder, who had obtained the warrant on August 3. Shroder directed the driver to stop at the United States Customs, where Sobell's baggage was deposited. In the meantime, the second car had stopped on the Mexican side of the bridge to transfer Helen and the children to another car. She arrived at the U.S. Customs only a moment or two after Sobell was led into the nearby Immigration Office. She asked about her husband but it was suggested that she check into a hotel with the children and try to see him in the morning.

Inside the Immigration Office an inspector named James S. Huggins sat at his desk filling out a card. Flanking Sobell were Shroder and some other FBI men. The card was entitled, "A Manifest, Port of Laredo, Texas." On it were already typed Sobell's name and some pertaining data. Inquiring about Sobell's place of birth, Huggins wrote in by pen: "New York City." Then, looking up, he asked, "Ever been in the United States?"

After they had handcuffed Sobell and led him off to the Laredo jail, Huggins picked up the "manifest" and carefully wrote on "the bottom of the face of the card": *"DEPORTED FROM MEXICO"*

According to Huggins' testimony at the trial, he admitted having no authority to make this damaging notation and that he *knew* that Sobell had not been deported, officially or otherwise. Nevertheless, Judge Kaufman permitted this "spurious" notation to be admitted into evidence. And since the jury knew nothing whatsoever about the kidnapping, it assumed that Sobell had been arrested, extradited and deported from Mexico in complete accordance with the law.[4]

•

In his cell next morning, Sobell showed Helen the copy of the complaint which they had just given him. Appended to the statute charging him with conspiracy to commit espionage, there were these five "overt acts" which she read with amazement:

1. In January, 1946, the defendant Sobell had a conversation with Julius Rosenberg at the Southern District of New York.
2. In June, 1946 [same wording as above].
3. In February, 1947 [same].
4. In July, 1947 [same].
5. In May, 1948 [same]. [R. 26]

VIII

In New York, looking for a suitable attorney, Helen found Edward Kuntz, who was later joined by an associate, Harold M. Phillips. In the meantime, the FBI and the prosecution had done everything to destroy all presumption of innocence. The following are fair examples of Sobell's "conviction by newspaper":

FLEEING RADAR EXPERT NABBED AS ATOM SPY

In Washington, FBI Director Hoover said Sobell fled the U. S. in June to avoid arrest *the day after* the arrest of David Greenglass. . . .[5] [Emphasis added.]

We have seen that Greenglass was arrested on June 16 and that Sobell's departure for Mexico was not "the day after," but almost a week later. And if, as the prosecution claims, Rosenberg warned Greenglass to flee as early as February, it is inconceivable that he would not have taken similar precautions with Sobell. Further, the Department of Justice was aware that

Sobell did not behave as a fleeing spy, since we have Saypol's admission that he knew exactly from what airline Sobell had purchased his tickets—and that these tickets were purchased in Sobell's *own name!* Here is Saypol's admission made during Sobell's sentencing:

. . . From my own experience in Mexico City where a witness from the airlines told me that this defendant and his wife had cashed in the return portions of their tickets. . . . [R. 1598]

In addition, Saypol knew that Sobell had openly applied for visas at the Mexican Consulate. During his trip to Mexico, Saypol doubtlessly checked these visas with the Mexican immigration authorities, and no evidence was produced that the Sobells had entered Mexico in any illegal way.

As for the publicity that Sobell was an "atom spy," not only did the FBI lack any evidence connecting Sobell with atomic espionage, but Judge Kaufman was forced to acknowledge at Sobell's sentencing:

. . . the evidence in the case did not point to any activity on your part in connection with the atom bomb project. [R. 1620]

It is also significant in this discussion of trial by newspaper to see how the press helped create a *fact* out of fiction. Here is the New York *Times* of August 19, concerning Sobell's arrest:

ENGINEER IS SEIZED AT LAREDO
AS SPY FOR RUSSIAN RING

Deported by Mexico, to Which He Is Believed to Have Gone to Get Passage to Soviet.

The suspect, Morton Sobell . . . was picked up at the border by FBI agents as he was being *deported from Mexico.* [Emphasis added.]

All of this was featured prominently on the front page, but no official action regarding Sobell's deportation ever took place before any constituted authority in Mexico or in the United States.

In a later chapter it will be proved by photostats of official documents which this writer obtained that the

Mexican government was in complete ignorance of the so-called deportation.

In short, Morton Sobell was *not* deported from Mexico except in the instructions, overt or covert, made to Huggins to write that notation on that card of "Manifest." Why was this done? So that that damaging card could be *admitted into evidence* as proof that Sobell had no intention of returning to the United States voluntarily! Here is the prosecution's statement on the importance of this card:

Had it not been for that evidence the jury might have inferred that Sobell returned to the United States voluntarily (perhaps from a vacation in Mexico) and that he had always intended to do so.[6]

In actuality, the only evidence Saypol had at the time of Sobell's kidnapping was the information from the FBI that Julius Rosenberg had been his classmate, and that over a period of some two years *after the war,* the two friends had five conversations together in the Southern District of New York!

IX

In concluding this examination of the prosecution's disregard for the law, there arise these pertinent questions: Why did the FBI arrange to have Sobell spirited away in the middle of the night? Why didn't the men who seized Sobell bring him before the proper authorities? Or allow him to communicate with the American Embassy? Why was it all done so brutally? Was this initial showing of the naked fist designed to terrorize Sobell into becoming a compliant government witness?

As indicated earlier, there were two parts to the Government's case against Sobell—his alleged flight and the uncorroborated testimony of Max Elitcher. How vital was this testimony is clear from the warning Judge Kaufman was required to give the jury:

If you do not believe the testimony of Max Elitcher as

it pertains to Sobell, then you must acquit the defendant Sobell. [R. 1560]

Before we take up this testimony, let us first see how Max Elitcher, who had been Morton Sobell's boyhood schoolmate, college chum, and best friend—indeed, the best man at his wedding—came to send him to a living death of over eighteen years in prison, with five of them served in Alcatraz.

NOTES AND REFERENCES

1. From an article entitled "Panic!" Collier's, September 21, 1953.
2. For Sobell's reasons for his trip to Mexico, and his kidnapping there, see his affidavit of October 8, 1953, presented to the U.S. Court of Appeals. See also his book, *On Doing Time*, Scribner's, New York, 1974 —an absorbing account of his long ordeal.
3. From the affidavit of Sobell presented April 5, 1951, in "Arrest of Judgment." (Record, pp. 1590–1593.) *Note:* Further details of the kidnapping were related to this writer by Mrs. Sobell.
4. Since Sobell was advised by his counsel not to testify on the grounds that the Government had failed to prove its case, *i.e.*, that he had in fact conspired to commit espionage, the exposure of the kidnapping became part of the record only during the proceedings of his sentencing; in other words, *after* the verdict.
   The decision of Sobell's counsel may have been a grave error as we review it with the advantage of hindsight. However, at the time of trial, it was felt that any such sharp attack on the FBI would be resented by the jury and would therefore react unfavorably on their verdict. (See Chapter 25, Note 6 for further discussion of the question of Sobell not taking the stand.)
5. New York *Daily News*, August 19, 1950; New York *Post*, August 18, 1950.
6. Transcript of Record, No. 687, U.S. Supreme Court, October Term, 1952.

Concerning the pressure from the FBI "to induce [Sobell] to give up his protestation of innocence," FBI documents now disclose "repeated but unsuccessful" efforts to turn him into a prosecution witness. These efforts included the use of "a confidential prison informant" who reported that Sobell could be persuaded "to cooperate" with the Government but was being prevented by the "influence" of his wife, Helen. (See New York *Times,* December 6, 1975.)

For further comment of Sobell's choice of pseudonyms, see Addenda to Chapter 23.

8 MY INFORMER FRIEND

I

"The informer is different, particularly the ex-Communist informer. He risks little. He sits in security and uses his special knowledge to destroy others . . . . because he once lived within their confidence, in a shared faith . . . feeling their pleasures and griefs, sitting in their houses, eating at their tables, accepting their kindnesses. . . . If he had not done these things, he would have no use as an informer."[1]

They first met at Stuyvesant High as boys in their teens. Morton, about a year older than Max, was born on April 11, 1917. Both were native New Yorkers, both children of immigrant parents, both from more or less the same environments.

In 1934, when Sobell entered the School of Engineering at CCNY, Elitcher followed suit. In their class, Morton formed other friendships, one with a boy named Julius Rosenberg. To Max, the latter remained only a casual acquaintance. It had always been difficult for Max to make friends. Throughout college, his testimony discloses, he maintained "almost no social relations" with the members of his class.[2]

In 1938, both were appointed junior engineers with the Navy's Bureau of Ordnance in Washington, where they decided to share an apartment. After about three years, Sobell realized he needed more study in the field of electronics, and decided to try for his Master's degree at the University of Michigan. Only a few months later, the United States entered World War II. On February 25, 1942, we find him registered with the National Roster of Scientific and Specialized Personnel of the War Manpower Commission as No. 8-27 194.

Throughout the war years, Sobell worked at the Schenectady plant of General Electric, designing radar apparatus. In the meantime, he had fallen in love with a girl in Washington whom he had been courting by correspondence. Her name was Helen Levitov, a petite brunette with dark eyes and given much to writing poetry. She had graduated from Wilson Teachers College in Washington and worked for the Bureau of Standards.

In the intervening years, Elitcher had married a girl with a similar name: Helene. In March, 1945, Max was asked by Morton to be best man at his wedding. For the next two years the Sobells lived in Schenectady. In 1947 Sobell received an offer to work at the Reeves Instrument Corporation in New York City. Early in 1948 they bought a house out in Flushing, Long Island, at a cost of $13,500, having put up their savings of $4,500 as a down payment.

•

Back in Washington, Elitcher also wanted a change, but for different reasons. In 1947, to retain his job with the Navy, Elitcher signed a non-Communist loyalty oath and with it committed perjury. In that same year, as Elitcher later testified, he became "fearful" of arrest. In 1948 Elitcher learned that the FBI had questioned his mother in New York and, with the political climate worsening, his fears became so great that even his psychiatrist could not assuage them. The following is from his cross-examination:

Q. You were scared to death at that time, were you not?
A. [Elitcher]: Yes.
Q. You have been scared to death ever since, have you not?
A. Yes. [R. 361]

Having decided to leave Washington, Elitcher sounded out Sobell about prospects at Reeves. Assured that he would be promptly employed, he took a two-week vacation in July and drove to New York to spend it with the Sobells while he and his wife looked about for a permanent home. While driving up from Washington, Elitcher "found a suspicion taking shape in his mind" that he was being followed by some cars which he presumed contained FBI agents.

On arrival, when Elitcher mentioned the possibility of surveillance, Sobell was rather upset. If it were true, Elitcher should not have come to the home of a friend with a Communist background, especially one who had also signed a perjurious affidavit. To make a test, the two men drove around the area for some twenty minutes. Since there were no signs of anyone following, they laughed it off and thought no more about it.

It was this visit which became the basis for the celebrated cloak-and-dagger automobile ride to a rendezvous with Julius Rosenberg, the most damaging portion of Elitcher's testimony. When we come to its analysis we will see another instance of how a friend's hospitality was elaborated into an act of conspiracy.

In October, 1948, Elitcher started work at Reeves and, soon after, purchased a house just around the corner from that of the Sobells. The two houses had their rear yards abutting. Each morning the friends rode to work together "in a sort of car pool," using each other's car alternately.

As a passing comment, it seems unlikely that Sobell and Elitcher, if they were members of the same spy ring, would have entered into so close a relationship at this time, considering their fears of FBI exposure of their false affidavits. Also, that Julius Rosenberg, their "superior," would not have voiced the strongest objections.

•

In June, 1949, Helen Sobell gave birth to a son, Mark. A few months later the Elitchers had their second child, a boy named Anthony.

Thereafter, the two couples found themselves gradually drifting apart. The rift widened with the changing political climate. Whenever the Sobells mentioned it, the Elitchers would react uncomfortably. By 1950, the two couples had become just polite neighbors. Indeed, from mutual friends, the Sobells heard speculations that Max may have gone to the FBI to give them the names of former "comrades," thereby hoping to stave off prosecution on his perjured oath. Morton simply could not believe this and condemned such rumors as contributing to the atmosphere of suspicion.

Nonetheless, toward the end of June, when he told Max he was leaving for Mexico, he simply mentioned they were going on vacation. To offer his political reasons for going would lead only to a fruitless argument.

Reviewing the relationship as a whole, one cannot help thinking that there were other grounds why Sobell refrained from confiding in Elitcher at this time: that he was just too proud to display his own fears to the friend he had so often criticized for that very weakness.

II

> ". . . Because he [the informer] has that use, the police protect him. He is their creature. When they whistle, he fetches a soiled bone of information."

In reconstructing the jigsaw puzzle of the frame-up, the case of Max Elitcher almost parallels that of David Greenglass. In both cases, a minor crime had been committed having nothing to do with espionage. In both cases, fear of arrest and prosecution gave the FBI pliable material to work on. In both cases, deals were made in exchange for perjured testimony. In both cases the step-by-step technique of self-entrapment was applied by pressuring the witness to sign a series of statements, each one a little more incriminating. And finally, in both cases the witnesses concealed the true facts concerning these deals and statements, and testified falsely that they had told the entire truth promptly and voluntarily.

In our later analysis of Elitcher's trial testimony, the full extent of his perjuries will be exposed, but at this point we will concentrate on the above parallels, beginning with the following claim:

[Elitcher]: . . . From the *first time* that I was approached by the FBI I decided to tell *the whole complete story*.[3] [Emphasis added.]

According to the prosecution, this first time was on July 20, 1950, three days after Julius Rosenberg's arrest. At noon on that day, two FBI detectives visited him at Reeves, and requested him to accompany them to FBI headquarters. There, after a "short talk," it is Elitcher's claim that he "freely" admitted his part in the conspiracy and that for the next three hours he filled in the details. Further, that he made his confession without advice of an attorney, and that he only engaged Rogge as his lawyer one week later.

Following this initial discussion "confined mostly to Rosenberg," the detectives drove Elitcher out to his house, where the interrogation continued for another eight hours. "About midnight," after an "exhaustive statement" had been prepared by the detectives, it was read to him point by point. This statement (No. 1) "took more than an' hour" to read.

On the next day, July 21, Elitcher testified that the FBI detectives came again to Reeves and that after a "full discussion" about Sobell's part in the conspiracy he signed a second statement (No. 2). During this interrogation, he states, he was asked by one of the detectives about Elizabeth Bentley, and his reply had been that he knew *nothing* about her.

Some seven months later, however, he signed a third statement (No. 3), in which he provided "additional information." It was during the interrogation preceding this statement that he "brought up the name of Bentley" as well as the incident in which he had heard this name from Sobell who had heard it from Rosenberg.

Now let us turn back to July 20, which Elitcher insists was the first time he had met with the FBI.

Q. [Bloch]: And when was the first time that you spoke to the FBI?

A. [Elitcher]: In—it was July of 1950.

It should be stated, that as cross-examination proceeded, Elitcher became increasingly nervous, especially when the defense commenced to probe into the matter of Bentley, and why it had taken him seven months to remember the highly important incident in which her name had been talked about by Rosenberg and Sobell.

Unable to explain how he had omitted this incident on the twentieth and twenty-first of July, Elitcher became rattled. And suddenly, as Bloch flung at him a series of questions, the entire tissue of lies concerning his *concealed* meetings with the FBI, the prosecution, and Rogge *before* July 20 became exposed:

Q. All right. When did you make that first statement?

A. [Elitcher]: The first time I was called down here [to the Federal Building].

Q. When did you make your second statement?

A. The next day.

Q. When did you make your third statement?

A. Quite a bit later. Some months later.

Q. You made that first statement *after* you had consulted a lawyer, is that right?

A. That is correct.

Q. *After* you had already retained a lawyer?

A. Yes

Q. And *after* you had been interrogated a number of times by FBI agents and members of the prosecuting staff, is that right?

A. Yes. [R. 339; emphasis added.]

And so we see that his previous testimony claiming that he had told the FBI (because of conscience and patriotism) the complete truth on July 20—in his first interview—is here revealed as a fabrication. And when we study that portion smacking of collusion and rehearsed instructions, it becomes almost certain that he was initially interrogated by the FBI in *June,* possibly a month *before* Rosenberg's arrest.

Q. Now, when you were interrogated by the FBI for the first time, as you say, in *June,* 1950, did that fear of prosecution persist in your mind?
A. Yes, I *realized* what the implications might be. [Emphasis added.]

In short, while Elitcher may finally have succumbed by July 20, and signed Statement No. 1 on that date, actually it was the result of a *number* of interviews held during the latter half of June. In other words, commencing about the same time Julius was questioned on June 16—and certainly not much later than June 22, the date Sobell departed for Mexico.

To sum up, these are the reasons why the prosecution pushed up the date of Elitcher's first interview from some time in June to July 20:

1. Because if he were to tell the truth to the jury that he had signed Statement No. 1 *after* he "had been interrogated a number of times," then its entire value as a voluntary confession would have been completely destroyed.

2. Because if he had truthfully revealed that he "had consulted" with Rogge for weeks *prior* to his signing of Statement No.1, there was the risk of the defense probing into the deal Rogge had made with the prosecution.

Certainly, it would have appeared suspicious to the jury to hear that Rogge had advised Elitcher not only to submit to a twelve-hour interrogation but to sign a confession of guilt (Statement No. 1) without so much as telephoning his counsel!

While we are on the subject of these concealed relations with Rogge, let us examine how Elitcher came to employ him, *i.e.,* the *same* attorney representing the Greenglasses. Here is the record as Mr. Block asks Elitcher pointblank:

Q. Who recommended you to Mr. Rogge's office?
A. No one.

And here is Elitcher's slip as he wearies under further cross-examination:

The Witness: Well, we (my wife was with me) went down to Mr. Rogge's firm *with our recommendation.* [Emphasis added.]

Thus Elitcher, as we see, did come to Rogge's office with a *recommendation.* If it was from a source other than the FBI or the prosecution, why does he try to conceal it by stating "no one" recommended him? The answer is obvious: The jury must not know of the close bond existing among the FBI, the prosecution, and Rogge.

On this question of who recommended Rogge to Elitcher, let us not forget that it was this "unholy three"—Elitcher and the Greenglasses—who provided the convicting testimony against Sobell and the Rosenbergs. And if further comment be needed, surely it is found in Elitcher's own testimony:

They [Rogge, etc.] told us then that they were employed by Mr. Greenglass, which was a great surprise to us.

III

"... For what is the day's work of the police is the ex–Communist's necessity. They may choose what they will or will not do. He has no choice. He has surrendered his choice."

We will recall that Statement No. 2 was alleged to have been based on a "full discussion about Sobell" and that what Elitcher had told the FBI on those two

189

days—July 20 and 21—was "substantially the same story" he was telling on the witness stand.

Now we have seen by Elitcher's own admissions [4] that his discussions with the FBI and the prosecution actually commenced about a month before July 20. Therefore, if it is true that Elitcher was determined to tell "the whole truth" the *first time* he was approached by the FBI, then Saypol should have known all about Sobell's guilt almost as soon as the latter had arrived in Mexico on June 23.

Why, then, would Saypol delay ordering a warrant for Sobell's arrest until August 3? And more important, why did he not have Sobell indicted together with the Rosenbergs on August 17?

Faced with these contradictions, Saypol resorted to the familiar device of the "built-in justification" in an effort to explain that Elitcher's confession had been on the installment plan:

Q. [Saypol]: There came a time in the development of the case by the Government agencies that you continued your conferences and you supplied additional information?

A. [Elitcher]: Yes.

Here, then, in Saypol's best effort to bolster the credibility of his *only* witness against Sobell, is a clear admission of the step-by-step process which took place between the early summer of 1950 and the early spring of 1951. It was simply that Elitcher had slavishly fetched what was wanted of him, soiled bone by soiled bone. By the logic of his entrapped position, he was made to understand that if he didn't agree to become a witness against the Rosenbergs and Sobell, he would find himself a co-defendant with them.

In another of Rogge's file memos, dated March 19, 1951, we see that shortly after Elitcher had testified, Rogge requested of Assistant Attorney General McInerny that his client be rewarded, not only with permanent immunity, but FBI security clearance for future employment:

He [Elitcher] has never been named as a defendant or

as a co-conspirator *in any prosecution* and it is reasonable to assume *he never will be*. [Emphasis added.]

IV

> ". . . To that extent, though he be free in every other way, the informer is a slave. He is no longer a man."

When one studies the line-by-line testimony of Max Elitcher, one is struck by the frequency with which he unintentionally reveals the truth. It should be noted that Elitcher had been under a psychiatrist's care for two years. According to his own testimony, he had been a neurotic all his life.[5] In his years in Washington, this was manifested by the hoarding of an excessive number of shirts and suits. Unless he was able to choose a different shirt and suit each day, he found it difficult to go to work.

Some additional light is thrown on Elitcher's mental state at the time of his first two FBI statements. In that same month of July, he paid his *last visit* to his psychiatrist. This point seemed sufficiently significant to this writer to consult with some outstanding psychiatrists. The consensus was this:

First, that Elitcher found it beyond his capacity to admit to his doctor his intention to testify falsely in order to save himself from imprisonment for perjury. As for attempting to conceal this from his physician, that would be absurd, for the very essence of analytical treatment is to air honestly all of one's anxieties.

Second, if he did admit his perfidy, it is most probable that his psychiatrist informed him that under such circumstances he could no longer treat him. However, it is safe to venture that he must have been instructed by the FBI and/or Rogge to be extremely careful what he confided to his analyst, since a physician is not ethically bound to silence where a crime has been committed.

And third, that Elitcher had resolved his conflict

by himself. Right after Julius' arrest on July 17, he could have entertained the rationale that Rosenberg had decided to "play ball." [6] Later, he could also rationalize that Sobell would surely do the same. Thus he could assure himself that he was not *really* doing them any irreparable harm. And having reached this or some such solution, and having taken the road of confession with the FBI, he no longer needed the psychiatrist's couch.

The following excerpts are from an article by J. Edgar Hoover entitled "Breaking the Communist Spell," in which he gives counsel and comfort to the ex-Communist informer about to "break the bonds which have enslaved his mind":

We of the FBI have known and talked with many who were going through this painful process of decision.

. . . He [the ex-Communist] may feel a sense of loyalty to those persons who, like himself, entered the Communist movement with certain ideals. They, like him, refused to accept passively the injustices and prejudices of their society.

. . . On the other hand the ex-Communist . . . has come to realize that the Communist conspiracy stands for the social evils he deplored. If this conspiracy is successful . . . he and his friends and their children will be the tragic victims of the evils they erroneously thought they were fighting.

. . . So now the ex-Communist faces this question: Is he actually "protecting" his former associates by withholding the information he possesses? Or is he not in reality endangering them, as well as his family, himself and his society? . . . Where lies his higher loyalty—?

. . . At the FBI, we have assured them [the ex-Communists] that all revelations will be regarded as confidential until they are willing—as they will be if their repentance is sincere—to use their knowledge as testimony in trials or loyalty hearings.[7]

"On that road of the informer it is always night."

In his attempt to bolster the credibility of Elitcher, Saypol also exposed the fact that there was no evidence against Sobell at the time of his arrest on August 18. At his appearance before the Grand Jury on August 14, Elitcher was examined by Lane. Considering all the previous conferences in addition to Elitcher's full discussion about Sobell on July 21, one must assume this examination was done thoroughly. And yet, when the Grand Jury returned its indictment (No. 1) of August 17 against the Rosenbergs, we find:

. . . And with divers other persons presently to the Grand Jury *unknown*. [Emphasis added.]

Not until the indictment of October 10 (No. 2), do we find Sobell named as a co-conspirator of the Rosenbergs. By that date, finally, Saypol had decided to name him as a defendant. Now we have seen that it took over two months to indict Sobell despite Elitcher's "full discussion" about him on July 21. Why, when Saypol, on August 18, said to the press "that Sobell had many dealings with Rosenberg in the conspiracy to supply Russia with atomic secrets," did he not also say it to the Grand Jury? According to the record, there was *only one source* from which he could have had this knowledge, and that was Elitcher. If so, why did Lane fail to have Elitcher repeat this information to the Grand Jury on August 14?

So we see by the calendar of events that there were no possible grounds for the Mexican assault on Sobell and his subsequent incarceration *other than his so-called flight*. Evidently, the five "conversations" between Sobell and Rosenberg were not considered sufficient to bring to the attention of the Grand Jury on August 14.

And rightly so. Because these were supposed to be espionage conversations taking place between two spies. Obviously, they were not overheard by anyone. How, then, did Shroder *know* that these conversations involved espionage? Certainly, the conversing conspirators never confided in him.

It should also be noted that not only was none of these five "overt acts" ever proved to have taken place, *but not one of them was even mentioned at the trial.* In fact, for a period of six months and three weeks after his arrest, the only way Sobell was "informed of the nature and cause of the accusation" was by the dreary repetition of these five "conversations."

If anything illustrates the political climate of 1950, it is this mind-boggling situation. For on such outrageous grounds any friend of any suspected man could be arrested—one's neighbor, cousin, fellow worker —anyone who could be said to have conversed with the accused!

It would appear that Saypol went on the assumption that the more outrageous "Justice" appeared to Sobell, the more disheartened he would become and the more ready to cooperate. To be sure, Saypol was equally sanguine about the Rosenbergs' inevitable submission. And even though they had shown no signs of yielding thus far, there was still a good chance they might. After all, Saypol knew he had his pair of aces back to back in the Greenglasses. However, to really "make a case," how much better it would be if he could also add to his aces a pair of jacks, with Elitcher and Sobell confirming each other. And perhaps, very soon now, he would draw still a third jack in the person of William Perl, and thereby hold a full house!

In any event, Sobell would soon realize the deck was stacked against him. He was already convicted by newspaper as an atom spy "nabbed" while fleeing the United States. He was helpless behind bars under $100,000 bail. The next step was more subtle:

Let him remain there in total ignorance and let him torture himself with the unknown, together with the Rosenbergs. Let them keep pacing their cells day after day, each interminable day an agony of longing— husband for wife and wife for husband—longing for each other's touch, for the caress of their children, for fun and laughter, for sun and fresh air. And let the summer of 1950 pass, and the autumn and the winter too if necessary, and let them keep pacing their cells—still plagued by the unknown—all three in their three different prisons contained within a single square mile on the lower end of the island of Manhattan.

NOTES AND REFERENCES

1. This epigraph and others to follow are from Whittaker Chambers' *Witness,* Random House, New York, 1952, pp. 454–456.
2. Record, pp. 264–265. (See Record for additional personal material regarding Elitcher; direct testimony: pp. 197–263; cross-examination: 264–394.)
3. Record, p. 295. Regarding Elitcher's testimony about his FBI interrogations, see cross-examination beginning on p. 269.
4. Unfortunately, these vital admissions were overlooked by the defense and were neither used for further cross-examination nor as a point to emphasize in summation. In discussing this oversight with one of Sobell's present attorneys, the latter agreed that it was a serious one, but offered in explanation that in the heat of court battle such oversights frequently occur.

   It was, however, the duty and responsibility of Judge Kaufman to see the importance of these admissions. Before he imposed his thirty-year sentence on Sobell—and by law he could base that sentence *only* on Elitcher's testimony—he had an entire week to study the court record, certainly enough time to grasp the full significance of Elitcher's rehearsed perjuries.
5. For Elitcher's description of his psychiatric treatment, see Record, pp. 380–381.
6. At the trial, Elitcher stated that he had followed closely the newspaper accounts of Rosenberg's arrest. It is reasonably certain, in the terrified frame of mind he was in, that these accounts gave him the impression Rosenberg was also "cooperating," and had even decided to "confess" to something. For example, in

the New York *Post* report of Julius' arrest (July 18, 1950), it appeared as though it were a clear admission of guilt: "The FBI quoted Rosenberg as saying, 'I wanted to do something to directly help Russia.'"

7. *This Week,* November 1, 1953.

ADDENDA

In the New York *Times* of November 24, 1975, there was this headline: "U.S. Withheld Evidence in 1951 Rosenberg Case." Among the released government files, the *Times* relates, was a letter written by Saypol to Attorney General MacGrath on September 11, 1950, saying that

the evidence in the proposed case against Morton Sobell, standing by itself, is not very strong.

What this means, of course, is that he has not yet succeeded in "breaking" Sobell. In any event, according to Saypol's further admission in this letter, Sobell was sentenced to thirty years on evidence consisting "*solely* of the testimony of one Max Elitcher and the fact that Sobell *apparently* fled the country *after* Rosenberg's arrest." [Emphasis added.]

In short, he was sentenced solely on the uncorroborated testimony of an admitted perjurer given immunity from prosecution. As for Sobell having left for Mexico to seek political asylum, not only does Saypol describe this as an apparent flight, but he misstates the "fact" by stating that it was *after* Rosenberg's arrest. As the record shows, Sobell flew to Mexico on June 22, 1950, almost a month *before* Julius' arrest on July 17, 1950.

9 "THE ELEVENTH FLOOR"

I

> ". . . It is three paces wide, four paces long, and seven feet high. A fine wire mesh forms the ceiling. An electric bulb struggles in vain to send its puny light through the accumulated dust. . . ." [1]

A man is thrown into jail, then a month later his wife, and then a friend. In every city, screaming headlines about the "Atom Spies." In blind agreement, tens of millions of Americans nod their heads gravely. Editorials appear about "Termites and Treason," and again, nodding heads.

Some eight months later, the trial. Reporters describe how the wife wears a "pink blouse," how the husband wears a "smudge-sized mustache" and how the friend has "sallow features." But beyond this they are ciphers. Of what happened to that man, wife, and friend during those hundreds of days and nights waiting in their cells, not a word. To most of the public, they have become but faceless symbols of the "enemy" within.

•

They were permitted only one letter each week, but it seemed to Ethel that whenever she became most depressed, a letter from Julius would arrive just in time. The tedium was helped also by the daily hour of exercise up on the roof, playing "games of catch." Always, however, there was the long night, and she would toss restlessly on her cot with thoughts of her "shattered home."

Some nights her cellmate would wake to hear Ethel's moaning from the cot below. It was another nightmare, Ethel explained, with "that scream again" over the telephone on the day of her arrest.

Some days, during the exercise period on the roof of the grim structure with its four-hundred-odd women prisoners, Ethel and her cellmate would stand on tiptoe on the benches along the wire-fenced edge. There they would catch a glimpse of the busy corner of Eighth Street and Sixth Avenue with "all those free people." Then Ethel would look westward in an effort to see "the flag on top of the West Street jail," hoping that Julius, too, at this moment, might be looking eastward toward the Women's House of Detention.

II

It was the first of October, and Julius had taken to crossing off the days on a calendar. Two months and two weeks had passed since his arrest, but he knew as little as he did then what evidence the prosecution intended to offer at the trial. Today Mr. Bloch was giving up their apartment; it was only $51 a month, but there was simply no money. Neither was there any for Mr. Bloch's fee or legal expenses. One of his sisters had already sold their furniture to the junkman and had received less than $100 for the lot. His machine shop had long been liquidated. Up in the Bronx, somewhere in a shelter home, overcrowded and understaffed, were his two boys, reportedly in need of psychological care.

When Julius had first learned about his mother-in-law's attitude to the children, he had been shocked. The Greenglass family had always been dominated by the matriarchal Tessie, but for some unknown reason Ethel had retained an almost neurotic allegiance toward her. She called this her "family ties," and would continue to torment herself with the anguish of her mother's rejection.

•

Even as a little girl, Ethel had plagued herself about her mother's antagonism. In her adult years she began to understand what was wrong, but still kept striving for her mother's love. When she had been in high school, her mother had resented her interest in the arts. This was unusual, since immigrant parents generally "thirsted for education" for their children. Perhaps her mother would not have minded it so much in one of the boys, but in a daughter she found it unseemly. Perhaps, also, because her daughter happened to be the favorite of her husband. When Ethel began to save for the purchase of a second-hand piano, her mother had tried to discourage her: If God had meant them to have a piano, He would have provided for it. It was almost as though she resented Ethel's talents as emphasizing her own spiritual barrenness.

In any event, Ethel's self-imposed burden of obligation was so heavy that it weighed her down even after her mother's monstrous demand when finally she came to visit her daughter in prison. Almost immediately after their embrace her mother began to belabor her: "What are you doing to Davy? You have it in your power to save Davy!"

Realizing what her mother was implying, Ethel wanted to scream: "What is Davy doing to us?" But she remained frozen; in effect, her mother was asking her to confirm her brother's accusations!

She sank down into a chair as her mother continued to rail at her for defying those in power. In the old country, when the Cossacks had started pogroms, a good Jewish daughter and her man hid themselves until the fury was spent. The foolhardy ones who tried to fight back were crippled and slaughtered. If during the rampage a Jew chanced to be trapped, the wise one would give the hoodlums all the wine and schnapps in the house, hoping to get them into a stupor. He would even let them pull his beard and dance for them —anything to ward off catastrophe—anything . . . !

There was nothing Ethel could reply; she just sat there in dull misery waiting for the matron to call time. When she reported this incident to Mr. Bloch some days later, she still appeared like a stricken person.[2]

III

At first Helen Sobell had wondered why they had chosen the New York City Tombs for Morton, instead of the Federal prison. Later it became evident. The pressure to turn Sobell into a government witness had already begun in that steaming cell back in Laredo, when the FBI agents had suggested, "Look, why be a patsy? Make it easy for yourself. Why don't you co-operate?"

The "breaking process" on Sobell in the Tombs assumed various methods. Certain prisoners would be assigned to make friends with him. After a while, there would be the furtive question: "Are you the kind of guy who can be told something important?" Then they would tell him what they had overheard in the Warden's office: . . . Sobell wasn't going to be given an inch; it was going to be plenty tough on him unless he played ball and started "talking." Anything—any kind of a story. Just say Rosenberg tried to get him to spy, but that he had refused to go through with it. Or they would come with "grapevine" rumors about his wife's faithlessness. These would be followed by anonymous notes such as: "Is it true your wife is going to leave you? A friend."

From time to time one of the guards or a trusty would jokingly remark that special privileges were to be had up on the famous eleventh floor. The implied invitation was not lost upon Sobell. He had learned that both Gold and Greenglass were being quartered there in comparative comfort.

IV

> ". . . Saypol requested in referring to where he [Greenglass] is stationed . . . we simply mention the Tombs and not mention that it is the 11th floor." [3]

In our study of the anatomy of frame-up, emphasis has been made of the point that the various officials involved generally do not risk direct participation. There is a time when actual machination is essential. One time-tested method is to delegate responsibility to someone who is in no position to expose the fabrication, since he himself is entrapped by it.

Certainly there was much to be "remembered" and ironed out by Gold and Greenglass up there on "canary row," as the eleventh floor was called. There were the details of the Jello box to be worked out. There was the "Russian" console table, which, as we will show, could not possibly have been invented until after October, 1950. There was the Russian "citation" to be given to Julius (evidently inspired by Hoover's "Order of the Red Star" awarded to Gold). Above all, there was the necessity of having Greenglass study, copy, and memorize the scientific material he was to describe at the trial.

It goes without saying that when such an arrangement constitutes the crux of the frame-up, it is the one best concealed. However, long after the trial, during argument on a motion made before Judge Ryan for a new trial, Emanuel Bloch made the following charge:

. . . I say to the Court that if the records of the Tombs were subpoenaed, and the guards who were stationed at the eleventh floor came before the Court, you will find that books were brought in to Greenglass and that Gold was in consultation with others.[4]

Continuing the challenge, Mr. Bloch described the notorious "eleventh floor" as particularly conducive to the collusion:

Gold and Greenglass were lodged on the eleventh floor of the Tombs for many months prior to the trial. There are no separate cells on this floor, which is reserved for 'informers,' and they are permitted to fraternize without any molestation or restraint by the guards.

And here is Ryan taking judicial notice of the reasons why cooperating prisoners are lodged on this particular floor:

. . . It is a certain portion of the jail known . . . as the singing quarters.

And here is Mr. Lane's attempt to weaken the force of Bloch's charge:

The fact that Greenglass saw Harry Gold while the two were lodged in the same prison was *admitted by Greenglass at the trial*. [Emphasis added.]

During the argument which followed, Mr. Bloch continued with the specific charge that Gold and Greenglass had consulted together after scientific "books were brought in":

Mr. Lane makes no denial of my allegation that the prosecuting officials or the FBI aided in coaching of Greenglass.

In Bloch's challenge, Judge Ryan had before him a veritable powder keg. Apparently, however, he found an "out" in an affidavit signed by one of the FBI detectives who had originally "interviewed" Greenglass. This affidavit, submitted by the prosecution, reads in part:

Under no circumstances and at no time did I ever make available to Greenglass any books or scientific texts nor any other material pertaining in any way to atomic energy. To the best of my knowledge and belief, no other agent of the Federal Bureau of Investigation furnished any such material to Greenglass.[5]

What have we here? A cautiously formulated statement in which a certain FBI detective swears that he did not *personally* commit an illegal act, and that he does not know *personally* about such an illegal act having been committed by some other FBI agent. In short, as Mr. Bloch pointed out,

. . . There is no denial that *some other Government official,* either on the prosecuting staff or otherwise working for or with the FBI, did make available to Greenglass the coaching material, *or that he was otherwise coached.* [Emphasis added.]

What possible reason was there for Gold and Greenglass to be quartered together in the same prison? Up to the day of Julius' arrest on July 17, Greenglass had been held for a full month in the Federal Prison on

West Street. On or about July 18 he was transferred to the Tombs, a city prison. Immediately after Gold's plea of guilty in Philadelphia on July 20, he too was removed to the Tombs instead of to a prison in Pennsylvania. It is more than suspicious that, within a period of forty-eight hours, "the two were lodged in the same prison" dormitory and remained there together for the entire period before trial.

On the basis of the disclosures quoted above, one can readily visualize the activities of these two bunkmates lolling about in "Singers' Heaven" up to the moment they testified in March. For example . . .

Whenever the FBI came to escort Gold to their suite or to the offices of the prosecution, one can see him, briefcase in hand, striding out with a jaunty step of pride. One can see him returning with his briefcase crammed full of scientific books, making copious notes and sketches for Greenglass to study. And, as suggested by Mr. Bloch, the guards would deliver other scientific books with no comment as to who had sent them, and even ignorant of their content. One can see Gold, with infinite patience, describing to his protégé the implosion principle of the "High Explosive lens," and going over these portions of his future testimony again and again. And one can visualize Greenglass copying diagrams from Gold's notebook, their various parts marked "A," "B," "C," etc., and finally memorizing the primitively worded description:

"A" is the light source which projects a light through this tube "E". . . . Around the tube it is a cross-section of the high-explosive lens "C" and a detonator "B" showing where it is detonated. . . .[6]

Following each period of Gold's coaching, one can also imagine the quizzes Greenglass was put through by Roy Cohn. Under cross-examination, one detects the reason for Greenglass' evasiveness when he is asked how many times he was "brought down to [the] Federal Building."

[Greenglass]: I couldn't give you an estimate. . . . You got me. I really—I can't give an estimate of times on things like that.

V

In early October of 1950, Saypol was faced with this inventory in his case against the Rosenbergs: On the one hand he had Elitcher, the Greenglasses, and Gold. However, while Gold stood ready to support the Greenglass testimony, there was no one to corroborate Elitcher. Hence, an effort was made to find another CCNY classmate of Rosenberg who would prove equally tractable.

Such a "prospective witness" had been found by the FBI. His name was William Perl. Thus far, they had him before the Grand Jury three times, and upon the last occasion he had shown signs of becoming compliant.

Back on August 18, on his first appearance before the Grand Jury, Perl had denied being able to recall Rosenberg and Sobell after college days.[7] Saypol reckoned he had a charge of perjury to slap on Perl. Elitcher could swear that he knew Perl, not only as a friend of Rosenberg and Sobell, but as a member of the YCL.

Moreover the FBI dossier on Perl contained further information. First, Perl had done important research for the National Advisory Committee for Aeronautics, in Cleveland. Right now, he was teaching physics at Columbia University, but only a year ago he had applied for a post with the Atomic Energy Commission. Hence, if he could be linked to the Rosenberg "atomic spy ring," the case would be strengthened by having at least one physicist on a level with Dr. Klaus Fuchs. Second, there was enough on Perl to ruin his career and to have him harried before various investigating committees. For his dossier revealed that

. . . He had sworn falsely in a loyalty questionnaire of the National Advisory Committee for Aeronautics that he had been married in 1944 and divorced in 1946.

To be sure, the infraction was only a technicality. In those particular years Perl had been living "in sin" but had not wanted to risk losing the prospective job by mentioning it. However, in view of another false statement (one of omission) in the questionnaire, Saypol was sure he could bring considerable pressure to bear on Perl.

This latter sin could be made to look more sinister. When Perl had listed the places he had lived during the preceding ten years, he had failed to include a certain apartment in Greenwich Village which he had subleased from one Alfred Sarant, another friend of Julius Rosenberg!

Thus Perl's "guilt by association" could be compounded because Sarant had shared that apartment with one Joel Barr, another classmate of Rosenberg, and Barr had sailed for Europe early in 1948, which action could be construed as "flight." And finally, the FBI file revealed that Perl had not only denied ever being a Communist, but now appeared sufficiently anti-Communist to warrant belief that he would prove cooperative.

Although Perl, on August 18, had opened the door to a perjury prosecution, Saypol chose not to use the direct threat. It was best to let him stew a while. Later, if necessary, the pressure could be increased.

On September 11, this was done by hauling him again before the Grand Jury. Saypol had reason now to congratulate himself on his patience. Whereas on his first appearance Perl had sworn he did not "know" Rosenberg or Sobell after their college days, now he was softening up. He was beginning to have "a recollection" of the two youths he had known twelve to fifteen years earlier. Moreover, he was admitting fear that acknowledgment of any connection between himself and Communists would prevent him from pursuing his career as a physicist.

Now polite visits were paid Perl by FBI agents who "warned him" (as he later testified at his trial) that "Rosenberg and Sobell are going to fry."

Three weeks later, on October 4, Saypol tried again. Whereas previously Perl had denied that his relations with Sobell had continued "into the 40's," now he was admitting that they might have kept in touch for a while after graduation.

Saypol was content. Perl was still insistent he had

no knowledge about any espionage, but there were still many months until trial. . . .

VI

A few weeks after Sobell's indictment on October 10, his wife found a purchaser for their house and recovered almost all of their $4,500, but the money had to be used entirely for legal expenses.

When the Elitchers heard that the house was sold, they offered to buy some of the furnishings. Helen, unaware of Max's secret interviews with the prosecution, thought it was nice of them to help out this way, even though no cash was involved. They had suggested that she sell the washing machine which they owned in common, and that they would take out their half in furniture.

With the washing machine sold, Max dropped over to point out the various items he and his wife had chosen: the piano, the bookcases (Morton had built them himself), the baby folding gates, the garden chaise, a globe of the world, and some stepping stones bought for the back yard. Helen thought Max was striking quite a bargain, but was grateful that the piano would be owned by friends. Max said he was glad to do them the favor. Some days later, the Elitchers offered to buy two chairs for $5 and to hold the house key for the new owner.

That was the last time Helen saw the Elitchers until they appeared in court the following March. But even when they greeted her with a friendly smile out in the corridor just before trial started, she was still unaware that it was to be Max's testimony that was to send her husband to prison for thirty years.

VII

"With all due modesty, I feel free to refer to myself as somewhat experienced in prosecution."
—*U.S. Attorney Irving Saypol* [R. 1621]

In our study of modern frame-up we have decried the role, and shown as false the notion, of a single master-mind, villainously plotting each and every step, giving personal commands to each of his various lieutenants and generally manipulating all the various strings attached to his major puppets. If it were so, we pointed out, perhaps, the frame-up would be more logically constructed or less anarchic. Nevertheless, despite the many participants, there is, of necessity, a general coordinator—someone who undertakes responsibility for conducting the case.

Such, to be sure, was U.S. Attorney Saypol, honored by *Time* magazine as the nation's "Number One legal hunter of top Communists." Only forty-five years old, he was already nationally famous for his part in the conviction of Alger Hiss and the eleven Communist leaders. Later came the trials of Abraham Brothman and William Remington. The Rosenberg case was to be the apex of his career as a prosecutor.

Even if one studies him only through the pages of the record, one notices his lack of distinction. Examples of the bluster of the ambitious politico will be seen frequently. Here is an illustration of his penchant for tasteless punning as he interrupts the cross-examination of the photographer, Schneider:

Mr. Bloch: Now there are some Saturdays when you do a rather rushing business?

A. [Schneider]: Not a rushing business.

Mr. Saypol: Did you say "a Russian business" or "rushing business"?

The Court: Let's get on. Try to restrain your desire to be another Milton Berle.

•

On the thirteenth of November, 1950, Saypol made his opening statement in the Brothman trial. The political aspects can be judged by the New York *Times* report on the next day:

Mr. Saypol said that the jury would hear evidence of espionage for the Russian government and activities in behalf of the Communist Party.

As the trial began, it was established that Brothman had admitted belonging "briefly to the Young Communist League."

. . . Assistant U.S. Attorney Roy M. Cohn declared that the Government held that the affiliation of both defendants [Brothman and his former secretary] with the Communist Party was the motive for their acts.[8]

And so began the "try-out" for the big Rosenberg atom-spy spectacle scheduled to take place four months later. As was pointed out in Chapter 3, it was Judge Kaufman who presided at this trial, and Saypol and Cohn who were its producers.[9] With Gold and Elizabeth Bentley as its star performers, we will soon see that this analogy to show business is not inappropriate. To see how the Brothman trial was used to build up the "advance publicity" for the big show, these were some of the headlines in the New York *Times* during the trial:

DEALINGS WITH SPY ALLEGED AT TRIAL
. . . Official Washington Sources Say Brothman and Gold Try to Get Atomic Secrets

BROTHMAN A SPY, SAYS MISS BENTLEY

SOVIET GRATITUDE TO SPIES DEPICTED

ATOMIC SPY TELLS OF PERSUASION TO LIE TO U.S. GRAND JURY IN 1947

CHEMIST, WOMAN AIDE, GUILTY, ESPIONAGE JURY HERE FINDS

Atomic secrets—Soviet espionage! And yet, the record shows that no espionage whatsoever was charged.[10] As for the inflammatory issue of Communists as spies, we have already seen the Government's position advanced by Roy Cohn that "affiliation" alone was sufficient proof of motive. Thus, it was in the Brothman trial that the prosecution laid the foundation for the Rosenbergs' motivation.

One illustration of the spy-thriller type of testimony which Saypol rehearsed at the Brothman tryout is worth examination. In the chapter on Gold, we recall how the FBI found the folder so conveniently marked "A.B.'s stuff." And how, in this folder, so carefully retained by Gold for nine years, they came upon that certain "small white card."

It was with this card that Saypol was enabled to demonstrate (1) that Gold and Brothman were spies as far back as 1941, (2) that the two had common Soviet superiors, and (3) that this was the actual manner in which they had originally met—and not in the harmless manner which they had falsely explained to the Grand Jury in 1947.

Thus, this card was as important in connecting Brothman and Gold through their Russian superior, Semenov, as the Jello box was in connecting Gold and Greenglass through the Russian Vice Consul Anatoli Yakovlev. Here is how Saypol presented this:

First, he had Bentley testify that her lover, Golos, instructed her to arrange, "a new contact" for Brothman, and that on a certain evening Brothman was to drive to West 27th Street. Here is Bentley as she describes the instructions given to Gold:

. . . At the appointed hour, [Gold] the new contact [briefed by Semenov] would slide into the front right seat [of Brothman's car].

I then asked Mr. Brothman to give me the license number of his car so that license number could be turned over via Mr. Golos to the new contact.

Here one wonders why Gold could not have been simply told to meet Brothman in his office. Apparently, Miss Bentley must have decided that the tale sounded contrived, for she adds this explanation:

Mr. Brothman objected again. He said he did not understand why he had to meet people via that odd way. Why couldn't I or Mr. Golos do the introducing? I explained to him again that this was a decision of the Communist Party and that he must abide by it.

Here is something unique. Suddenly it is the American Communist Party which makes decisions about espionage, and not the Russian KGB. Continuing with Bentley's testimony, we find that Brothman "ended by agreeing" to a rendezvous with his new courier, Gold:

The new contact was to identify himself, not only by getting into the car, but by bringing greetings from me, or in other words, greetings from Helen, since that was the name I used at that time.[11]

Now our impresario, Saypol, has his other star performer, Gold, take the stage to describe the rendezvous:

[Gold]: . . . A car came along. I withdrew the card on which I had written the instructions . . . and checked the license number against that of the car. The man inside seemed startled but he became assured when I gave him the rest of the recognition signal as it was written on the card. I said, "I bring regards from Helen," and then I asked how was his wife.

And now Saypol, to bolster this testimony with something tangible, introduces the "small white card" as evidence "to corroborate" Gold's oral testimony.[12] Here is that portion of the card later read to the jury:

Mon 10 P.M.—N. 27 6 and 7 Ave License No. 2N9088 Abe—Give regards from Helen—and ask him about his wife Naomi and his baby girl.

One need not be trained in the legal profession to appraise the value of such corroboration, for the card was in Gold's own handwriting! It is, at best, Gold corroborating Gold. How, then, can it be admitted as *evidence?* And yet, despite defense objections, we find that Judge Kaufman does admit it as Government Exhibit 10. How? By the use of a rule known as "past recollection recorded." To be sure, Judge Kaufman was shrewd enough to cover himself against possible error by the following explanation:

. . . It is not admitted as an independent piece of cor-roborative evidence. . . . These items, therefore [con-tained on the card] . . . are really to fill in missing links in the witness's story that he cannot remember.

But this is fulfilling only the letter of the law. Its "force and effect" (ironically, Kaufman's own words) on the jury was complete; the damage had been done the defendants. Moreover, once it was in evidence, the card was carefully read to the jury, thus serving as a documentary corroboration of Gold's oral testimony—to wit, that he had been given these instructions by his Soviet superiors, that the meeting had taken place, and that the card had been discovered by the FBI in Gold's basement.

But why would Gold, a veteran spy, risk carrying on his person such precise information? Why would he write down the "recognition signal" about bringing regards from Helen? As Bentley herself admitted, why was Gold required to meet Brothman in this "odd way" at all?

Did it have to be done with all this intrigue, the checking of the number on the card against the license number on a dark street, and the pointless instructions about sliding into the front right seat? (Where else should he enter?) Why couldn't he simply ask, "Mr. Brothman?" and then introduce himself? But far and beyond this nonsense, *why would a seasoned spy retain such an incriminating card so tenaciously for nine years?*

Because a pattern had to be tried out for Bentley's "greetings," so that in the Rosenberg trial Julius' "greetings" could be sent to Greenglass in a similar manner. Because Saypol could not substantiate a ren-dezvous arranged by a simple telephone call from Gold to Brothman. Because Saypol needed that card in or-der to "nail" Brothman to the rendezvous. Because it was necessary to give some harmless, sporadic talks between Brothman and Gold—during which the latter was obtaining some odd jobs—an aura of espionage which would make the jury say: "Oo-oo-oo-oo!" And because future testimony about more cloak-and-dagger meetings between Gold and Yakovlev, between Gold

—and Fuchs, between Gold and Greenglass, had to be unquestioningly accepted in the coming Rosenberg trial.

In other words, because Gold primarily, and Bentley incidentally, had to be set up and accepted as top-flight Soviet spies in this, their first court trial before a jury! For, until the Brothman trial, Gold had been suspended in a state of legal limbo; he was without an officially accepted spy background. Worse—there had been not only the Grand Jury inquiry in 1947 which had *cleared* him, but the FBI search of his house which had proved nothing! And still worse—if anyone happened to touch the house of cards with which Fuchs' identification of Gold had been built, the entire shaky structure might suddenly collapse.

But now the conviction of Brothman had insured against that danger. Now Harry Gold had an elaborate background as a veteran spy since 1935. Now Gold's testimony had sent Brothman, a brother spy—who had refused to confess—to prison for a maximum term.

This was the acid test and Gold, before a Federal jury, had come through with flying colors. Gold had become as *officially* accepted as Dr. Fuchs' courier as he had been *publicly* accepted at the time of his arrest.

In addition, the try-out had established motive for espionage by simply "connecting" it up with Communist Party membership or even YCL membership in one's youth. In this respect the team of Saypol and Kaufman had smoothed out their routine, so that mere belief in, or former sympathy with, Communism could be introduced as motive. Now no holds were barred. Anything Saypol would introduce—Ethel's signature on a nominating petition, or Julius' college membership in the Steinmetz Club—Kaufman would permit into evidence.

Finally, there was achieved for the Department of Justice the pinning down of Gold to his own testimony. For there was a vast difference between a "voluntary" confession made to the FBI and sworn testimony before a jury at a public trial. And although Gold had pleaded guilty in July, the Government could not be sure how he might react to the stiff sentence scheduled to be passed on him in December. It had requested Judge McGranery to postpone sentence until *after* the Brothman trial for this vital reason: to get Gold to swear publicly to the main features of his espionage tale. If they had allowed him to be sentenced *before* the Brothman trial, there was the risk that he might suddenly balk at a long prison term. But by holding up sentence until *after* his elaborately detailed spy career was sworn to under oath, he would be hoist by his own petard.

Such, then, was the total significance of this seemingly minor case. Yet, with due regard to Saypol's abilities, others should also receive well-merited credit—namely, J. Edgar Hoover, Attorney General McGrath, and, to be sure, Judge Kaufman. Separately or together, there can be no question that these officials conferred on every aspect of the two cases involving the FBI's two prize puppets, Gold and Bentley.

It is noteworthy that in two classic frame-ups, the Sacco-Vanzetti case and the Mooney case, both main trials were preceded by such try-outs. In the Mooney case, there was the trial of Warren Billings just before that of Tom Mooney. In the Sacco-Vanzetti case, there was the trial of Vanzetti on a charge of robbery preceding the main trial, both presided over by the same judge and tried by the same prosecutor. Few legal scholars would deny that the strategy in these cases was to condition the public mind to the acceptance of guilt *in advance* of the main trials so that no presumption of innocence might benefit the defendants.

•

When the Brothman jury brought in their verdict of guilty, Judge Kaufman congratulated them and added this tribute to the FBI:

. . . It gives me great mental security . . . that we have an agency such as the FBI. . . . Their work is truly amazing, particularly their work on Mr Gold. It is just amazing.

No truer words were ever spoken, but the work Kaufman himself did on the Brothman jury with that "little white card" was no less amazing. On the weekend before Kaufman imposed sentences on Brothman and his secretary, Chinese troops had suddenly entered the war and MacArthur had been hurled back from the Yalu border "with large losses, trapping units of the 1st Marine Division and the 7th Infantry Division at Changjin Reservoir." It was the blackest Sunday in our military history.

On November 29, 1950, when Judge Kaufman imposed maximum sentences on Brothman and Miss Moskowitz, he was responding not to the charges against them, but to the scare headlines. Although he had instructed the jury that there was not the slightest evidence of espionage, he stated:

. . . I regret that the law under which these defendants are to be sentenced is so limited . . . for I consider their offenses in this case to be of such gross magnitude.

It was a portentous sign of what lay in store for the Rosenbergs and Sobell. Even more ominous was the headline in the New York *Times* on December 10, when Gold was sentenced in Philadelphia:

GOLD, ATOM SPY, GETS 30 YEAR MAXIMUM
FOR AIDING SPY RING

VIII

And so ended the year 1950: for the bewildered engineer, Brothman, who was tersely denied bail by Kaufman and hustled off in manacles to Atlanta penitentiary. For his shocked secretary, who was to meet Ethel Rosenberg in the Women's House of Detention while awaiting transfer to another prison.[13] For some ten thousand American youth, whose frozen corpses lay strewn over the wintry wastes of Northern Korea. And for the Rosenbergs and Sobell, who perceived in these sacrifices the magnification of their own possible fate, because they well understood the reason why all these Americans had died. It was for the essential reason that foreign soldiers had always died in Asia, no matter what other reasons might be advanced: to defend colonialism.

It was a year that, according to the New York *Times*, had opened "one of the most extraordinary chapters in United States political history." It had begun with fantastic charges against the State Department by an unknown senator, which, although exposed as a "fraud and a hoax," nevertheless intimidated the Democratic administration to such an extent that four years later it was forced to defend itself against charges of "Twenty Years of Treason." [14]

It was a year that marked a departure from everything we had ever cherished—the dignity and ultimate worth of the individual. It began with an Oklahoma judge depriving an American mother of her two children because of her opinion that we had no business entering the Korean War.[15] It ended with Americans condemning a presumably innocent man and wife *before* trial with epithets reminiscent of the Middle Ages: "They don't deserve a trial! Fry 'em! Sizzle 'em!"

It was a year that began with a wave of corroding suspicion, meanness, and violence, and it was a year that ended with the triumph of the informer—with each man coming to eye "his neighbor as a possible enemy," and where, as Judge Learned Hand pointed out:

. . . Non-conformity [becomes] a mark of disaffection; where denunciation takes the place of evidence; where orthodoxy chokes freedom of dissent. . . .[16]

To tell why and how all this extraordinary change came about is not the purpose of this book. But it is our purpose to tell the why and how of the Rosenberg case, "the most important political case of this generation." [17]

That part of an iceberg floating above the surface is but one-ninth of its mass. The remaining eight-ninths lie hidden beneath. We have tried to show some of this hidden mass, and now, as we approach the trial itself, we will see much more of it. We will see the "empty ritual" of justice, and perhaps the answer to that haunting question: Did the Rosenbergs and Sobell really have their "day in court"?

NOTES AND REFERENCES

1. From a letter of Julius Rosenberg describing his cell in the West Street jail, dated April 19, 1951.

2. About a year and a half later Tessie Greenglass visited her daughter again in the death house at Sing Sing and renewed this proposal. Ethel described it in a letter to her attorney, dated January 21, 1953:

   Dear Manny,
   This is to let you know that my mother was here on Monday . . . I am still in a state of stupefaction over its bold-faced immorality. . . . Our conversation follows. . . . Said she: "So what would have been so terrible if you had backed up his [Davy's] story?" I guess my mouth kind of fell open. ". . . Wait a minute, maybe I'm not getting you straight. Just what are you driving at?" She answered, "Yes, you get me straight; I mean even if it was a lie, you should have said it was true anyway! You think that way you would have been sent here? No, if you had agreed that what Davy said was so, even if it wasn't, you wouldn't have got this!"
   I protested . . . "But, Ma, would you have had me willingly commit perjury?"
   She shrugged her shoulders indifferently . . . "You wouldn't be here!"

3. From a Rogge file memo dated July 20, 1950. This memo describes a telephone call to Rogge from Saypol concerning Greenglass' transfer "to the Tombs Prison, 11th Floor." (See Appendix 3A.)

4. Transcript of Record submitted to Supreme Court, No. 687, p. 284.

5. *Ibid.*, pp. 146–148.

6. Excerpt from Greenglass' testimony describing one of the replicas he had prepared for the trial. (Record, p. 465.)

7. From an interview between Mr. Philip J. Wittenberg, William Perl's attorney, and this writer. (See also Eugene Daniel, "Guilty of What?" in *The Nation*, June 20, 1953.) *Note:* Quoted excerpts are from the Perl record of his long-delayed trial in May, 1953,

available at the U.S. Courthouse in Foley Square, New York City.

8. Brothman's co-defendant was his former secretary, Miriam Moskowitz. *Note:* It will be recalled that the charge was not espionage, but a conspiracy to obstruct justice in having lied to a Grand Jury in 1947 about their activities with Harry Gold. (Excerpts of testimony in this section, unless otherwise stated, are from the Brothman trial record, available at the U.S. Courthouse in Foley Square, New York City.)

9. In addition to Cohn, Saypol "was assisted by Thomas J. Donegan, Special Assistant to the Attorney General." (New York *Times,* November 23, 1950.) Other assistants, besides Cohn, Lane and Kilsheimer, were John M. Foley and James E. Brannigan.

10. Here are Kaufman's words to the jury: "There is no claim made in the indictment that Abraham Brothman engaged in espionage." (Brothman Record, pp. 1129–1130.)

11. Here the pattern is rehearsed for Ruth Greenglass' subsequent testimony about Julius' "greetings" to be carried to David via Gold.

12. Although in a Federal court accomplice testimony requires no corroboration, some twenty-one states have recognized this practice as archaic. California requires the "corroboration of two (independent) witnesses"; New York is another such state. This safer code is summed up by the *Columbia Law Review* as follows: "While an accomplice . . . is a competent witness if his own testimony is corroborated, he cannot corroborate the testimony of another accomplice." (See *Columbia Law Review,* p. 236.)

13. During this meeting, Ethel, in a feeling of sympathy toward Miriam Moskowitz, gave her a locket she wore, a tiny gold replica of the Ten Commandments. Two years later it was returned to Ethel in the death house through Mr. Bloch, and subsequently became her only legacy to her children.

14. See "McCarthy: A Chronology Since 1950," New York *Times,* February 28, 1954.

15. The Jean Field case in Oklahoma.

16. From a speech by Judge Learned Hand, New York *Times,* October 25, 1952.

17. *Columbia Law Review, op. cit.,* p. 219.

As reported in the New York *Times* on December 4, 1975, it appears that J. Edgar Hoover ordered the New York FBI office to provide him with "personality data" on the Rosenbergs. Here is a portion of the FBI agent's response to Hoover on May 18, 1951:

Rosenberg believes that he is brilliant both as an engineer and as an espionage agent and feels that he is a martyr to "the cause," resolving that he will not reveal his associates in espionage and relying on the advent of a "sovietized America" to free him.

Because this memo is so outlandish and reflective of FBI practice and attitude, it is worth examination. On its very face, it consists only of the subjective opinion of the FBI official supplying the Director with what he wants to hear, *i.e.*, the most prejudicial clichés of the McCarthy Era. For if Julius was the spy-master of a widespread ring as charged at the trial, why would he express or divulge such incriminating beliefs and bizarre hopes for deliverance when he and his wife were fighting for their lives by appealing to the higher courts on a stand of complete innocence?

The sheer absurdity and malevolence in this so-called data are particularly striking in the last sentence of the memo. For Julius, at the height of the McCarthy Era and the Korean War, to rely "on the advent of a 'sovietized America' to free him" from the death house, would be as far-fetched as relying on some little green men coming to rescue him in a flying saucer. One can only ascribe such mind-bending projections to the paranoic propaganda of a Communist takeover to which the obsessed Director of the FBI had contributed so much during his long reign in office.

Finally, if this is the FBI's *only* explanation for Julius' refusal to confess (his reliance on a "sovietized America") then why, when the "storming of the Bastille" failed to occur, did the Rosenbergs continue to maintain their innocence to the last? Unfortunately, no matter how irrational, the myth of the Rosenbergs as fanatics and martyrs has been swallowed whole by most of the American public.

PART TWO
The Empty Ritual

January–April, 1951

"It is error only and not truth that shrinks from inquiry."

—*Benjamin Franklin*

10 "THE INSOLENCE OF OFFICE"

I

> "The law's delay, the insolence of office. . . ."
>
> —*Hamlet*

In the two months preceding trial, world events moved swiftly. In Korea the continuing retreat of our troops further intensified the need for scapegoats at home. Perhaps at no time since the Soviet Union's first atomic explosion was the fear as great as it was in these early months of 1951. The nightmare of what we had done to Hiroshima and Nagasaki returned to us in the form of daily "fright" stories. For example, the New York *Journal-American* reports of January 8 and 9:

IF SOVIETS START WAR, ATOMIC BOMB ATTACK EXPECTED ON NEW YORK FIRST

Nobody will have to run if H-bombs start detonating. A big black cloud full of radio-active particles will get you even if . . . you happen to be browsing around the bottom of an abandoned lead mine.

Day after day such accounts continued to whip up tension. With one blast, 160,000 city dwellers would be annihilated. Atom bombs would be smuggled into our ports by Russian or Polish ships. With such alarums following hard upon the arrests of "Communist spies," it was a serious question whether any prospective juror could remain immune to the horror of gruesome death interwoven with the other three lines of propaganda: Communism as an international conspiracy; Communist spies high in government circles, like Alger Hiss; and A-bomb spies like the Rosenbergs. And as the trial drew nearer, there was the

widespread refrain: Only thing to do with such rats—
hunt 'em all down and shoot 'em! [1]

II

In the office of United States Attorney Saypol, there
were also various lines to be coordinated before trial.
One may better describe them as reins held in the
hands of Saypol's various drivers. Most important was
the team of Myles Lane and Roy Cohn handling Gold
and Greenglass up on the eleventh floor. Then the
team of James Kilsheimer and O. John Rogge groom-
ing Ruth Greenglass. As for Sobell, Perl, and Elitcher,
these three sets of reins Saypol delegated to himself.

Right at this moment, however, Sobell was proving
unruly. Not only had Indictment No. 2 failed to bring
anticipated results, but Sobell's attorneys had moved
to dismiss it "on the ground that the contents thereof
[were] vague and indefinite."

On the fifteenth of January, five months after the
kidnapping of Sobell, we find him still waiting in the
Tombs under $100,000 bail for "a scintilla of legal
proof to justify the finding of an indictment." Here is
the affidavit of that date by Mr. Phillips, attorney for
Sobell, still demanding a Bill of Particulars:

. . . Naturally, we must assume that the United States
Attorney realizes that the delay is injurious to the rights
of the defendant Sobell and it is, therefore, hoped that
any further delay will be avoided. [2]

And here is the bill finally submitted on January 24,
five weeks before trial:

Bill of Particulars Re Morton Sobell

1. The approximate date when the defendant Sobell
joined the alleged conspiracy is on or about June 15,
1944.

2. The Government still charges the defendant Sobell
with the commission of the overt acts [the five conversa-
tions] set forth in the complaint before the United States
Commissioner, sworn to on August 3, 1950.

In short, the only item of information given the defense was the altered "approximate date" Sobell was supposed to have joined the conspiracy, which in Shroder's complaint had been designated as "July of 1944." As for the dates of the alleged five conversations, it is significant to point out that they began in January of 1946, or *after* the war! Nevertheless, this wartime 1944 date was retained in the Bill of Particulars. Why? Because for a violation of the Espionage Act in peacetime, the maximum sentence could be only twenty years.

In time of war, however, the Act provides for a sentence up to thirty years or punishment by death. And thus, by the arbitrary insertion of an unsubstantiated wartime date, Saypol was enabled to threaten Sobell with the death penalty!

III

We have just seen in the Bill of Particulars that Sobell was supposed to have joined the conspiracy on June 15, 1944, which, if true, presents this curious conflict: On the one hand Julius is accused of recruiting Elitcher into the conspiracy on June 6, but on the other hand it is the latter's testimony that he accepted the spy proposal only because of Sobell's *prior presence* in the conspiracy. In other words, the logic of Elitcher's entry into the spy ring is completely destroyed by the date attributed to Sobell's entry!

The meaning of this is quite clear. As Saypol became convinced by the end of 1950 that Rosenberg would not break, he pressured Elitcher into weaving more and more of the "conspiracy." And when Saypol failed in coercing Sobell to become a government witness, Elitcher was further pressured. This is why Elitcher's final appearance before the Grand Jury comes as late as January, 1951—six months after his so-called telling of "the whole truth."

Returning to Saypol's third set of reins leading to William Perl, strong measures were taken to couple him with Elitcher in February, just a few weeks before trial:

In the winter of 1951, he [Perl] was summoned to a conference of FBI agents and government prosecutors.
Roy Cohn, then an assistant United States Attorney and now Senator McCarthy's assistant, said to him, "Confess or you will be indicted."
Perl replied: "I have nothing to confess. I would like to hear any charges against me in open court." [3]

Despite Perl's defiance, Saypol still refrained from indicting him on perjury charges, counting on the approaching date of the Rosenberg trial to effect a change. So confident was Saypol of Perl's inevitable submission that he announced him as a government witness notwithstanding his six months of consistent denials of any knowledge of espionage!

IV

There remained but one more chore for Saypol—to restore the prestige of Elizabeth Bentley, the ubiquitous "Red Spy Queen," prior to the Rosenberg trial.

Among the many Washington government workers she had named as members of a Communist spy ring was a Commerce Department employee, one William W. Remington. Denying the charges, Remington appealed to the Loyalty Review Board. And since Bentley had repeated her charges on an unprivileged radio program, Remington filed a libel suit against her.

In the course of the Loyalty Review Board's inquiry, not only was he cleared, but Bentley's reputation suffered a serious setback. Although she had been called as the only witness against Remington, evidently she was too apprehensive to appear before the Board. An explanation of why she "had been eluding process servers in Remington's libel suit" was reported in the press with the dry comment that she had suddenly "embraced Catholicism." [4]

Thus Saypol found himself with a prized witness whose reputation had been seriously tarnished by

Remington's victories. It was essential to restore her legitimacy in the most forceful way: by having Remington sent to prison on her testimony. Obtaining a perjury indictment against him presented no difficulty, since the foreman of the Grand Jury, one John Brunini, happened to be the "financial and literary collaborator of the chief prosecution witness, Elizabeth Bentley"! [5]

Even less difficulty was encountered at Remington's trial, which was presided over by Judge Gregory F. Noonan, a former law partner of Irving Kaufman. Needless to say, Remington was swiftly convicted. And although the verdict was subsequently reversed by the Appellate Court, which held "that the jury was not charged properly on what constitutes Communist Party membership," Saypol had vindicated his leading lady in time for the Rosenberg trial. [6]

V

It was the morning of March 5, 1951, the day before trial, and Julius Rosenberg was awaiting the arrival of Emanuel Bloch for a final conference. He had slept little that night—the 231st since his arrest. His mind was on the conference . . .

•

In the discussion with Mr. Bloch (as subsequently related to this writer), the most important question was whether or not Julius and Ethel were to use the Fifth Amendment. In previous talks, they had decided that standing on their constitutional rights was the only principled, and even honorable, position. Mr. Bloch now added that it was also the only practical one. Once they abandoned their Fifth Amendment protection and opened the area of questioning, Saypol would drag in every one of Julius' classmates. Some of these friends who, like Julius, had been members of the YCL at CCNY, would be hounded and ruined. [7]

There was, however, the viewpoint of his father

Alexander Bloch, to be considered: Since the prevailing public attitude was hostile toward anyone "hiding behind the Fifth Amendment," perhaps it would be best to come right out and frankly admit his student membership in the YCL. And since Julius' dismissal from the Signal Corps on FBI charges of membership in the Communist Party was bound to come up in any case, perhaps a stout admission of what was after all guaranteed under the First Amendment—the freedom of association and political beliefs—would forestall the prosecution's political onslaught and force it to stick to the evidence.

To which Julius replied that he had given this alternative considerable thought:

Okay, suppose I admit YCL membership, or even full party membership back in 1945, but insist it had nothing whatsoever to do with being a spy? The prosecution would then say that I had lied to the Signal Corps in my denials. And suppose I would try to explain that I had a family to support, that the denial was necessary to keep my job? Then they'd really clobber me—saying if I lied to save my job, certainly I'm lying now to save my life.

On the other hand, taking the opposite course—saying that I was never actually a card-carrying member, what good would it do? I could swear it on a stack of bibles a hundred times—it would be my word against the word of the FBI.

As Julius concluded, Bloch added that Saypol, moreover, would be sure to counter with the widely accepted theory that all Reds were trained to lie.[8]

Nodding, Julius mentioned Remington as an example, just convicted in January. Not only had he not taken the Fifth Amendment but had even tried to prove his "anti-Communist views." Or there was the case of Alger Hiss, vouched for by Justice Frankfurter, Dean Acheson, and Adlai Stevenson, also denying party membership. And what had happened to him . . . ?

During the conference, another important question had to be decided, that of asking friends and neighbors to testify as character witnesses. And on this, too, Julius and Ethel were in agreement that it would serve little purpose. For one thing, such character witnesses could swear only that they had known the Rosenbergs as a decent, moral, and hard-working couple. But Saypol would hardly trouble to contest this. In fact with the grotesque logic by which everything was stood on its head these days, their very virtues might be presented as a "front" behind which the "spy ring" operated.[9]

For another thing, suppose Saypol threw the question, "Do you know for a fact that your friends the Rosenbergs were *not* spies?" What could the friend reply but a feeble, "Well, I don't know—but I am sure they couldn't have been." And to this Saypol could retort, "If Alger Hiss was able to fool Dean Acheson, certainly the Rosenbergs could fool you!"

Finally, there was the danger that such friends would be asked about their own political beliefs and associations. How many could afford to risk perjury prosecution by truthful denials or contempt citations by refusal to name other friends? And again, if they took the privilege, would not their character endorsements be considered worthless as coming from "Fifth Amendment Communists"?

Unfortunately, it may be said with the advantage of hindsight, neither Julius nor Bloch had any concept of the lengths to which Saypol, Cohn, and Kaufman were prepared to go in their resolve to make of the Rosenbergs the ideological effigy of the dread specter of Communism.

(*Note:* The opinion of many lawyers with whom this writer has discussed this principled stand of the Rosenbergs was that while it was unrealistic and even naïve, it should have tended to convince the jury of their innocence. Because if one believes the prosecution's theory that Julius was truly the veteran spy, then one must assume that he knew that the "jig was up" as he faced exposure by his own relatives, the Greenglasses. If this was the case, it is inconceivable in the climate of 1951 that he would brand himself as a "Communist hiding behind the Fifth Amendment."

Since there was no direct proof offered by the Government that he was a member of the Communist Party, he could have forsaken his constitutional privilege, denied it, and risked a perjury charge in another prosecution with a maximum sentence of five years. And if he refused to inflict similar risks upon friends whom he might be called upon to name, then all he would have risked in this regard would have been a series of contempt penalties. It would seem reasonable therefore, that if he were a spy realizing he was on trial for his life he would gladly have accepted these comparatively minor risks. Instead, his stand on the Fifth Amendment appears to have been the very opposite of a man with any consciousness of guilt.)

VI

Early on the morning of March 6 there was an unusual bustle of activity on the fifth floor of the Women's House of Detention. The matrons, though they knew what it was all about, pretended ignorance. As soon as the cell block was opened, Ethel's fellow prisoners went from cell to cell collecting bits of clothing they had quietly prepared for her appearance in court that morning.

Each woman tried to muster what she could—here a bag, there a pair of stockings, a handkerchief, a veil, and even a pair of shoes. When Ethel stepped out into the corridor dressed in her make-shift outfit there were stifled groans. Ethel told them that it didn't matter all that much; with Julius' modest income she had never given serious thought to clothes. This didn't mean, however, she reminded them, that she had ever "lacked for anything in her marriage."[10]

•

When the prison van stopped in the yard of the West Street jail to pick up the prisoners to be taken to the courthouse that morning, the same thing happened as on previous occasions when Julius had to go along to appear on his various indictments. Now as before, the prisoners stayed back to allow Julius to enter the "pie-wagon" first. It was so that he might sit close to the steel mesh screen which separated the men from the women who would be picked up on the way to the courthouse.

Ethel's cellmate, Anna, had to appear that morning on a legal development in her own case and therefore could report firsthand what she witnessed in the prison van. She had always taken Ethel's story of a happy married life with Julius with a large grain of salt:

. . . I just couldn't believe that any marriage was all she said hers was, but after what I saw in that pie-wagon, jolting along to Foley Square, why, I know Romeo and Juliet weren't even in it.

. . . The women who were going to court that day had let Ethel take her seat. I sat down opposite her. It was dark in the van. . . . Then I happened to strike a match to light a cigarette. . . .

I didn't even wait to get a light. I blew it right out. . . . Julie and Ethel, kissing through that damned screen. . . . I didn't want that cigarette that bad.[11]

•

The two touched fingers through the wire mesh but remained silent, for they knew each other's thoughts. Would they get a fair trial? Would it be a jury of their peers? Would there be any jurors who would not look at them scornfully as Jews, and hatefully as Reds?

There was no way of foretelling. Also, they wondered about the judge. Would he be fair and impartial? Would he ignore the stigma of Communism and not allow himself to be swayed by the political atmosphere? They had heard that he was young and had children of his own. Surely this would tend to open his heart to them and to the plight of their children. Perhaps being Jewish himself would make him more understanding. But here too there was no foretelling. They knew little more than his name, Irving R. Kaufman. Indeed, they knew as little about this judge who was to decide their fate as any average American, which is to say, almost nothing.

1. In Vice-President Nixon's televised rendition of this refrain three years later, there was this word of caution:

   Some Red-hunters feel that Communists deserve to be shot like rats. Well, I'll agree; they're a bunch of rats, but just remember this. When you go out to shoot rats, you have to shoot straight, because when you shoot wildly, it not only means that the rats may get away more easily, you make it easier on the rat, but you might hit someone else who's trying to shoot rats, too. [*Time*, March 22, 1954.]

2. See Record, pp. 8–26 re Bill of Particulars.
3. Article previously cited in *The Nation*, June 20, 1953.
4. Located by a reporter of the New York *Daily News*, Bentley was found hiding "in a Catholic retreat . . . the newest of the ex-Communist recruits converted by Monsignor Fulton Sheen." (See article, "The Remington Loyalty Case," *New Republic*, February 28, 1949.)
   The libel suit was subsequently won by Remington. (See *I. F. Stone's Weekly*, November 30, 1953.)
5. This coincidence was brought to light in Remington's appeal to the Supreme Court. (New York *Post*, August 2, 1953; New York *Times*, December 25, 1953.)
6. This Court of Appeals reversal was on August 22, 1951, some five months after the Rosenberg conviction. However, on January 27, 1953, Remington was retried and convicted. He was sentenced to a three-year term in Federal prison. Late in 1954 he was murdered in prison.
7. Headline of October 7, 1953, in Los Angeles *Times:*

   FIRING OF FIVE MAY END IN PROBE
   RIVALING ROSENBERG SPY CASE

   This was the opening salvo of McCarthy's investigation of Fort Monmouth, since recognized as a "phony crusade." See survey made by New York *Times,* January 11–13, 1954, and its editorial conclusion that it "must leave any impartial reader with a sense of uneasiness, if not dismay."

8. In sentencing six Michigan Communists after a Smith Act trial, United States District Judge Frank A. Picard stated to the defendants:

There isn't any doubt in my mind, and there wasn't any doubt in the jury's mind, that there is nothing you wouldn't do—lie, cheat, or even worse—in order to obtain your objectives. [*U.S. News & World Report,* March 19, 1954.]

Note: With such a predetermined point of view as Judge Picard's, a sham was made of the very trial he presided over, since it automatically ruled out all defense testimony as perjurious and also denied the presumption of innocence.

9. In Judge Picard's sentencing speech previously quoted, he adds:

. . . There hasn't been a divorce among the whole six of you. None of you make any money on this. You're not mercenary so far as the FBI . . . have been able to learn and tell me. You have wives and children who are devoted, *but you have that quirk in your thinking. . . .*

You, Mr. Allan, are a rather likable person . . . but you have those ideas too, and *because you are such a likable person you are . . . dangerous. . . .* [Emphasis added.]

10. The record discloses that Ethel Rosenberg's wardrobe expense in all the ten years of her marriage totaled $300. This included the purchase of an $80 fur coat. (Record, pp. 1083–1084.)

11. Excerpts regarding Ethel's cellmates are from personal interviews by Virginia Gardner, *The Rosenberg Story,* Masses & Mainstream, New York, 1954.

ADDENDA

One of the more publicized FBI memos released in 1975 alleges that Julius, while imprisoned before and during the trial, had confessed his guilt to one Jerome Tartakow, an inmate in the same prison and an FBI informant. This memo, when carefully examined, falls into the same category as that dealing with J. Edgar Hoover's "personality data" on Julius, wherein he was expecting a "sovietized America" to free him. (See *Addenda*, Chapter 9.) It would appear that the FBI's recent release of the Tartakow memo was designed as a damaging blow to the sons of the Rosenbergs demanding the files.

In some of the press it was reported almost with elation as though to say: Well, you asked for it—what the FBI is hiding—and now you have it: Rosenberg's guilt as he "actually confessed" it to a fellow prisoner!

Other reporters, more discerning, brought out the details in the surrounding 1951 FBI memos which disclosed: That Tartakow had "a most unsavory record and might be trying to 'con' his way out of prison" where he had been serving a two-year term for interstate selling of stolen automobiles and hoped for an "early parole." That the FBI was urging such early parole as a reward for his "information regarding Rosenberg." That indictments against Tartakow involving narcotics possession and "receiving earnings from a prostitute" had been dismissed. And that the FBI itself described Tartakow as a "Confidential Informant T-1, of unknown reliability."

Hence, as implied in the New York *Times* account, Tartakow may have been an FBI "plant."

The account also poses the key question why Julius should have trusted Tartakow with such incriminating information. The *Times* states that no satisfactory answer is provided in the FBI memos.

Concerning Tartakow's motive, whether that of a "plant" or a voluntary stool-pigeon, the fact that he was seeking favors and received them is plainly evident.

On the other hand, what motive would Julius have, as a veteran spymaster then facing trial, for confiding in a stranger at a risk of putting his neck in the noose? Indeed, as an *experienced* spy, he would be especially suspicious about any inmate seeking to win his confidence.

It should be apparent from this sorry example how hollow have been the claims of Hoover and the prosecution that the FBI files contain "overwhelming" evidence of the Rosenbergs' guilt. If this "Tartakow" memo represents the best of such evidence the FBI can come up with amongst the 30,000 pages released in 1975, one may reasonably assume that much of what is still being withheld is equally worthless.

As indicated in the Author's Note, not even the Pollack report, ready to grasp at any straw to prove the guilt of the Rosenbergs, saw fit to mention this FBI memo so obviously tainted with the imprint of a "police-suck." (See article "Rosenbergs' Guilt Proven" by John D. Loften, Jr., Philadelphia *Inquirer*, November 29, 1975. See New York *Times*, December 8 and 14, 1975; also January 3 and 8, 1976.)

· For further comment on the FBI's questionable use of the Tartakow material to deceive the public, see *Addenda* in Chapter 24.

11 "POPE KAUFMAN"

I

> "A judge . . . is or comes to be the product of his environment, his education, his experience, and yes, his prejudices." [1]

In 1951, the year of the Rosenberg trial, Irving R. Kaufman, only forty years old, was still known as "the boy judge." He lived a sedate family life in his Park Avenue apartment and, as a devoted father, would take his three boys each Saturday to Yankee Stadium. On Sunday mornings the family attended the reformed Park Avenue Synagogue.

The foundations for what has been called Judge Kaufman's "whirlwind career" were laid in his undergraduate years at Fordham University, From the day he enrolled to the day he was graduated with highest honors, he had always "impressed the Catholic fathers who taught him." [2] They stared with amazement not only at this small boy of fifteen, an age when most lads were just in their second year of high school, but also at his record card, which indicated that he was Jewish. (He had been born in New York City on June 24, 1910, the son of Herman Kaufman, a manufacturer or tobacco humidors.) It was most unusual to find an adolescent Jewish boy choosing a Catholic college for his general education.

In the mid twenties, there was a considerable advantage in attending a college like Fordham in a city dominated by the Tammany machine. With the vast population of Jewish and Catholic voters in New York, choice political posts were parceled out more or less in proportion—so many to Jews, so many to Catholics and, of course, a reasonable few to Protestants. It is possible that some politically astute friend of the family had pointed out that the brilliant boy would double his chances for advancement by going to Fordham. (*Note:* In Tammany circles, the usual designation for such a person is a "Catholic Jew.")

Of young Kaufman's abilities as a student, including his readiness to conform, there can be little dispute. Even in his "difficult course in Christian Doctrine"—"when the final grades . . . were announced, the Murphys and O'Briens drew down 75's and 80's but Irving Kaufman rated 99, the highest in the class. Thereafter, his classmates took to calling him 'Pope Kaufman.' "

One aspect of this curious phenomenon was Kaufman's isolation from liberal student groups which existed in most American universities by the late twenties. It is certain, too, that he could not have remained entirely immune to the opposition of the Church to American radicalism. Unlike undergraduates in other colleges, he was also deprived of all those literary classics (from Voltaire and Rousseau to G. B. Shaw and Anatole France) forbidden by the Papal Index. To be sure, he was free to read them at home, but when one considers that he completed his four-year course in only three, it is doubtful that he had much leisure for extracurricular reading.

At the age of twenty, we see him graduated from Fordham Law School, not only as the top man in his class, but as "the youngest graduate in the law school's history." Following his admission to the bar in 1932, we find Kaufman's legal career and marital prospects beginning simultaneously in the office of the prominent New York attorney, Louis Rosenberg.[3] Here he was captivated by his boss' daughter who, according to a New York *Post* article, would often "traipse through the office to see her father." We are assured, however, that although Kaufman "knew immediately this was the girl he wanted to marry . . . he made no overt move lest somebody might think he was trying to get in with the boss."

Early in 1935, Kaufman was appointed Special Assistant to the United States Attorney in the Southern District of New York. In 1936, when he was promoted to Assistant United States Attorney, he and Helen Rosenberg were married. In 1940, Kaufman entered private practice with Gregory F. Noonan and Colonel Edward Eagan, chairman of the State Athletic Commission. Before Kaufman was thirty-five years old, he was netting more than $100,000 annually.

In 1947, Kaufman became Special Assistant to Attorney General Tom Clark. After some nine months at the Department of Justice in Washington, Kaufman returned to private practice in 1948. By this time he had reached a position of considerable power in the political machine headed by James A. Farley. His particular role was that of confidential coordinator of Federal patronage. Prospective appointees for positions with the United States Attorney and for the Federal bench in New York were channeled through Kaufman to Attorney General Clark for recommendation to the President. He had also become a friend of John Edgar Hoover whose political views toward dissidents he not only shared but zealously admired. There can be little doubt that this relationship (on a first-name basis) with the all-powerful "Director" contributed to Kaufman's political clout.

By 1949, having amassed a personal fortune, Kaufman was ready to recommend himself and his partner, Gregory F. Noonan, for the Federal judiciary, which he had always held was "the capstone of the legal profession." And so, on November 1, 1949, when

Kaufman was only thirty-nine, *both* partners were appointed Federal judges of the Southern District of New York. This simultaneous appointment, unprecedented, gives some idea of that political clout which Kaufman wielded.

II

> ". . . He [the judge] must not take on the role of a partisan; he must not enter the lists; he must not by his ardor induce the jury to join in a hue and cry against the accused. Prosecution and judgment are two quite separate functions in the administration of justice; they must not merge."[4]

Was Judge Kaufman the product of his environment and prejudices? Was he at all swayed by the prevalent hysteria? Did he tend to take on the role of a partisan against the accused, and did he merge the functions of judge and prosecutor?

There was at the Brothman tryout a passage later repeated almost verbatim at the Rosenberg trial. By comparing Kaufman's conduct during these passages in both trials, we can see the extent of his prejudice.

In the Brothman trial it occurred when Gold weakened his entire story of prewar espionage by admitting that numerous American engineers had been employed in the Soviet Union to build industrial plants. Here is the defense pinning Gold down to a further admission of the friendly relations between the U.S. and U.S.S.R.:

> Q. [Kleinman]: It was also during this period that you knew that Amtorg Agency was going out into the open markets and purchasing things like steel and rubber, chemicals, industrial equipment to ship to Russia. Isn't that so?
> A. [Gold]: That is correct.

Here, Kaufman, unwilling to permit so favorable a fact to the defense to remain in the jurors' minds, interjects:

The Court: Wasn't there a period there when Russia was an ally of Germany?

The Witness: There was. . . .

Mr. Saypol: May I state the dates since they are matters of common information?

The Court: Yes.

Mr. Saypol: The Soviet-Nazi Pact was in effect from August 24, 1939 until June 22, 1941.

So far, we see all three—judge, prosecutor, and self-proclaimed spy—in full accord that Russia and Germany had been "allies," which, of course, was a point designed to place Brothman in the enemy camp. But the defense counters:

Mr. Kleinman: Your Honor perhaps states Russia was an ally of Germany. I didn't quite get it.

The Court: That is the way I put the question.

Here, even when Kaufman is challenged, he shows no willingness to correct the distortion. That is the way he has put it and that is the way history has to be. However, Saypol, evidently concerned about possible reversal, hastens to correct Kaufman:

Mr. Saypol: There was some agreement, they were never allies.

The Court: I will accept your statement that they had a pact.[5]

It is indicative of Kaufman's rigidity that he just cannot bring himself to admit error. In this regard, he reflects the pattern of thinking which had become the stock formula for establishing "motive" for Communists accused of committing espionage. This formula was propounded by Whittaker Chambers in his mind-boggling rationale explaining his decision to expose Alger Hiss and others as "traitors" at the outbreak of World War II:

Specifically, I was afraid that, with the Communist-Nazi Pact, the Soviet Government and the American Communist Party would at once put their underground apparatuses at the service of the Nazis against the United

States. . . . To prevent that, I had . . . decided to become an informer.[6]

It is hardly necessary to point out that there has never been the slightest evidence to support this charge of American Communists aiding the Nazis. Far from being allies, Germany and Russia were literally at swords' points, according to the distinguished historian, Professor Frederick Schuman.

The constant misrepresentation of the Nazi-Soviet Pact as an "alliance" and the distortions of its meaning by . . . anti-Soviet publicists cannot alter this judgment among those concerned with facts rather than fancies.[7]

Now let us turn to the Rosenberg trial to see how the team of Kaufman and Saypol again used this formula of Russia and Germany as "allies" to prove treasonable intent. Saypol's first witness, Max Elitcher, was being questioned about Communist Party meetings at which Sobell was present.

Mr. Saypol: . . . I am going to prove the crime; I am trying to prove common association, common purpose.

However, Elitcher describes only harmless group discussions of "news events" and articles about "Marxist theory."

Finally Saypol loses patience. Nothing so far has been brought out involving any "intent," or any instructions to commit espionage. And so he resorts to the same political juggling act rehearsed at the Brothman tryout:

Q. [Saypol]: At this time do you recall what the situation was in respect to the Hitler-Stalin pact?
Mr. E. H. Bloch: Objected to as incompetent, irrelevant and immaterial to the issues in this case.
The Court: Overruled.
Mr. E. H. Bloch: Exception.
[Elitcher]: Well, at the time, the pact was in effect, I believe.
The Court: Will you fix the time? What year was this?

Q. [Saypol]: 1939 and 1940?
A. [Elitcher]: Yes sir. [R. 218, 226–228]

So far we see Kaufman resorting to the same routine as at the Brothman trial when he asks Elitcher to fix the time, but now comes something that makes one wonder which trial record one is reading, for Saypol repeats almost verbatim:

Mr. Saypol: I have the official date of the existence of that pact. I think it was August, 1939 to June, 1941.

Q. [Saypol]: Were any instructions issued by the chairman [to] . . . the members of the cell in so far as the attitude toward Russia was concerned in the light of the existence of the Hitler-Stalin pact?

Now, Elitcher "recalls" something that might be regarded as "instructions":

A. Well, the pact was in effect and support was to be obtained for the pact for the Soviet Union's position, and we were to talk with people and to get general support for the existence of the pact and its aims.

Q. [Saypol]: *In the course of that pact, of course, Russia was an ally of Hitler, isn't that so?* [Emphasis added.]

Here we see the roles reversed! Instead of Kaufman being the "feedman," it is Saypol, who only four months before had affirmed that the Soviet Union and Nazi Germany "were never allies." It matters not that Elitcher's so-called instructions have nothing whatsoever to do with espionage. "To talk with people," *five years before* the alleged conspiracy, scarcely constitutes "intent" to commit espionage!

At this point we see that the defense objected and Judge Kaufman, who only a few moments ago overruled Bloch and allowed Saypol carte blanche, suddenly retreats:

The Court: I sustain the objection. Well, the fact

238

is that there was a pact in existence between Germany and Russia at that time, is that correct?

The Witness [Elitcher]: That is correct.

Note that Kaufman manages to get in the same last lick he used at the Brothman trial. Whereupon Saypol is inspired to do likewise:

Mr. Saypol: That is no different from what I asked, if the Court please.

The Court: Well, he didn't like the way you had asked it. Is this a convenient place to pause? . . . Ladies and gentlemen, you may retire to the jury room. (Short recess.)

In the light of the Brothman record, the politically charged atmosphere in the Rosenberg trial is more clearly seen. Only four months before, we saw Kaufman introduce this precise technique to prejudice the jury against Brothman. Now again, not only does he encourage Saypol to repeat the maneuver, but dismisses the defense with the snide remark, "Well, he didn't like the way you had asked it." And, evidently to ward off protest, he hastily calls a strategic recess.

Such, then, was the judge who claimed to have given the Rosenbergs a fair and impartial trial—a judge who was as predisposed against them as was the infamous Judge Webster Thayer against Sacco and Vanzetti. A judge who only three years earlier had returned from Washington as a devoted disciple of J. Edgar Hoover, one so "indoctrinated" with the latter's obsession toward the "Communist menace" that, according to a former senior FBI official: "Hoover was like Jesus Christ to him."[8]

NOTES AND REFERENCES

1. From an article, "No Longer a Judge," by U.S. Federal Judge Delbert Metzger, United States District Court of

Hawaii from 1939 to 1952. (*The Nation,* July 18, 1953.)

2. This excerpt and others concerning Kaufman at Fordham are from an article, "Rosenberg Case; Judge Kaufman's Two Terrible Years," *Saturday Evening Post,* August 8, 1953.

3. Not related to Julius Rosenberg.

4. U.S. v. Marzano, 149 F. 2nd 923, 926. (See also Adler v. U.S., 182 F. 464; Frantz v. U.S., Gomila v. U.S.)

5. Brothman record, pp. 695–697.

6. Whittaker Chambers, *Witness,* Random House, New York, 1952, p. 453.

7. Frederick L. Schuman, *Soviet Politics at Home and Abroad,* Alfred A. Knopf, New York, 1946.

8. From an article, "Victims of a Desperate Age," by Daniel Yergin, *New Times,* May 16, 1975.

ADDENDA

In 1961, Kaufman was appointed to the U.S. Court of Appeals for the 2nd Circuit. In 1973, he was appointed Chief Judge of the above Court. (See New York *Times,* April 6, 1973.)

It may be noted that despite this prestigious position on the most important Circuit bench in the land, just under that of a justice on the U.S. Supreme Court, Kaufman has become increasingly uneasy about the "unfolding publicity" which threatens to reveal his true role in the convictions and deaths of the Rosenbergs. (See New York *Times,* January 9 and June 11, 1976.) For further comment on Kaufman's clandestine efforts to prevent a 1962 appeal by Sobell from reaching the Supreme Court, see *Addenda* to Chapter 25.

•

According to disclosures regarding "The Kaufman Papers," made to the press on June 10, 1976, an FBI memorandum demonstrates Kaufman's persistent efforts to use the highest officials of the FBI to suppress and deter any critical comments about the case, particularly those made in this book since publication. The FBI memo is dated July 3, 1956, apparently about a year after Kaufman had read this book.

The memo, addressed to Hoover's alter ego, Clyde Tolson, and written by Assistant FBI Director Louis Nichols, relates a call by Kaufman to advise [Hoover] about a new pamphlet on the case authored by a Nathan Glazier. The memo continues on a first name basis:

Irving stated he has read this pamphlet. It is an answer to the Wexley book and suggested that we might want to get several copies.

It is suggested the New York Office [FBI] be requested to secure a supply as they might be used to good advantage.

When we recall from "The Letter 'W'," Kaufman's subsequent 1957 letter to the Attorney General on the Pollack report and the *Look* article and align it with the other covert efforts Kaufman has made over the past two decades to see that his "conduct in the trial" is defended, we begin to see a picture of an obsessed, driven person—a sort of eager beaver busily calling and writing "Edgar" or his assistants, to do everything possible to sponsor favorable comment and to suppress all other.

Most recently, Kaufman has not only utilized the help of a colleague, the retired Federal judge, Simon Rifkind, to act as his spokesman by writing numerous articles, but, according to FBI documents, Kaufman has also used his high level connections to get Rifkind's articles printed and even widely distributed in reprints at public expense. Moreover, fearful of eventual exposure, whether as the result of an inquiry by the Congressional Committee on the Judiciary or even by possible impeachment, he has had Mr. Rifkind form an American Bar Association subcommittee "to counteract unwarranted criticism" of his conduct at the trial. (See New York *Times,* January 9, 1976. See also documented statement of January 28, 1976, by the New York Chapter of the National Lawyers Guild rebutting the claims of Mr. Rifkind quoted in the *Times* article cited above.)

12 "YOU ADD A COLUMN OF FIGURES . . ."

I

> ". . . The influence of the trial judge on the jury is necessarily . . . of great weight and jurors are ever watchful of the words that fall from him."
> — *Bollenbach v. U. S., 326 U. S. 607 (1946)*

It was exactly 10:30 A.M. and the bell of the nearby St. Andrew's Church had just struck the half-hour when the bailiff came through the judge's door. An instant later he was followed by the short, black-robed figure of Judge Kaufman, almost dwarfed by the high, wide bench.

All three defendants looked upon him for the first time. Certainly, he was young for a Federal judge. He was a little man, with brown eyes and black hair, and wearing glasses. There was a wide mouth with a somewhat petulant lower lip and heavy jaws which he kept champing. To Mr. Bloch, Julius stated that Kaufman looked like a cross between a rabbinical student and a buck sergeant.

About three hundred talesmen waited for the clerk to call out the names for the first panel of prospective jurors. Directly in front of the bench were the two legal tables, the one containing Saypol, Lane, Cohn, Kilsheimer, Foley, and Branigan for the prosecution; the other containing Emanuel Bloch together with his father, Alexander Bloch, representing the Rosenbergs, and Edward Kuntz with Harold Phillips, representing Sobell. Alongside their attorneys sat the Rosenbergs and Sobell. Down front were the packed reporters. Circulating among the crowded spectators in the rear were the marshals and court attendants. Despite the deceptive quiet, the atmosphere in the huge, dimly lighted courtroom was heavy and ominous.

One cannot help wondering what Judge Kaufman felt when he first looked down at the Rosenbergs. To the press, they appeared surprisingly calm. They were particularly struck with Ethel's tiny figure, her "soft and pleasant features." Julius was described simply as "tall, pale and bespectacled." Certainly, in Judge Kaufman, their name "Rosenberg" must have produced some sort of reaction. The coincidence that his principal in-laws on his wife's side were similarly named was unknown to the defense.[1]

II

> "Not a single jury member was Jewish, and this in the city of New York, which has a Jewish population amounting to one-third of the total population. Strange, or rather sinister, if you ask us."
> —*Indiana Jewish Chronicle, March 7, 1952*

All that day and half the next, the clerk spun the drum, calling out the names of the talesmen. As the first group of twelve took their places in the jury box, the Court outlined their duties:

> It is our purpose and object to secure a jury that has no feeling, no bias, no prejudice as to either side of this controversy. To put it another way, the minds of the jurors should be the same as a white sheet of paper with nothing on it. . . . It is just like adding a column of figures. You add a column of figures and you get a result.[2]

In present-day vernacular, there is an apt phrase to describe Judge Kaufman's conduct of the Rosenberg trial. It is called "going through the motions." It was also described by Judge Jerome Frank of the Court of Appeals when he weighed the value of Judge Kaufman's charge to the jury:

> It may be that such warnings are no more than an empty ritual without any practical effect on the jurors. [R. 1656]

All during Kaufman's instructions to the jury—to remember that the defendants were to be presumed innocent and stood before them "clothed with that presumption all through that trial"—there was not the slightest semblance of reality to these instructions. Not only did Kaufman know this, but he knew that the jurors were aware that he knew it and would be sure to take it all with tongue in cheek. Certainly he left them little room for doubt when they saw that no liberal-minded person, no person even remotely suspected of dissent and nonconformity, would remain among the chosen twelve. Which brings us to the questions:

How was it possible that "not a single jury member was Jewish" when more than thirty per cent of the population of New York City happens to be of that faith or ancestry? And since a goodly percentage of the talesmen were Jewish, how was it that all of those called up were eliminated?

To accomplish this end, Kaufman and Saypol made use of a device to screen out most of the "undesirable" talesmen by simply inducing self-censorship. This device was the lengthy list of 105 "subversive" organizations published by the Attorney General, which was read aloud to the jury. It ranged from the American League against War and Fascism down to the Veterans of the Abraham Lincoln Brigade, and included the American Jewish Labor Council, the Jewish Peoples Committee, and the School of Jewish Studies. After the list was read, Judge Kaufman asked:

Well now, the question is whether any juror has been a member of, contributed to or been associated with, or any member of his family, or close friend, with any of those organizations. . . .

It is important to recall the self-intimidation which existed during this period of war hysteria among all Americans; with the defendants being Jewish there is little doubt their average co-religionists felt especially sensitive to the danger of "guilt by association." Certainly the reading of this *verboten* list could not but make any prospective juror, Jew or Gentile, take pause. What if some friend or relative had once contributed to one of the organizations that had fought Hitler, Chiang Kai-shek, Franco, racial discrimination, or to an organization that had raised funds for civil rights and refugee relief?

Hence each Jewish talesman, keenly aware of the prevailing anti-Semitic charge that Jews and Communists were synonymous, felt sufficiently warned to eliminate himself. Why look for trouble in this "era of suspicion"? Why not simply bow out on grounds that were acceptable and did not entail "guilt by association"?

And so we find many such talesmen excused because of their sincerely stated opposition to capital punishment. As for those Jewish talesmen who felt themselves politically pure, we find them promptly eliminated either by Saypol's challenges or by Kaufman's. These were Edna Pincous, Esther Field, Rhea Kobus, and Morris Haber. In sharp contrast, a Mr. Louis Friedlander seemed to meet with no opposition from Saypol or Kaufman. The reason becomes apparent when we see that Mr. Friedlander was the vice-president of a company which had been "an agent for the Rubber Reserve Company during the war." And evidently, the defense, feeling that such a juror, so closely associated with government contracts, might not be as objective as he believed himself to be, decided to challenge him.

It should be pointed out that wage-earners were looked upon with open distrust by the prosecution whether they were Jewish or not. Here is the background of Mr. Albert Wallace:

The Court: Mr. Wallace, you are a longshore-man?
A. I am.
Q. For the United Fruit Company?
A. That's right.

A moment or two later we see the clerk calling out that the furrier, Morris Haber, and the longshore-man, Albert Wallace, were "excused by the Government." Why is it that Saypol and Kaufman were so determined to have an all-Gentile jury, save for a vice-president of a rubber company? There was simply too much at stake to risk a possible hung jury. One may safely venture that Kaufman and Saypol would have been overjoyed with the inclusion of the *right* kind of a Jew. For then the Government would have had yet another weapon to use in reply to possible charges of anti-Semitism.

But what if, despite all precautions, the *wrong* Jew were chosen? What if such a juror saw in the Rosenberg case an ominous parallel to the Nazi charge that all Jews were traitors? Suppose there were a split verdict with one Jew for acquittal and eleven Gentiles for conviction? Would this isolation not be equivalent to an admission of racism?

It may be contended that the Government had every right to screen out jurors suspected of latent prejudice in favor of the defendants. *But, on the other hand, it made certain to select a jury with the strongest prejudice against the defendants.*

For example, a Mr. William Baring-Gould stated that he had been previously employed by the Hearst newspapers, and that at the present time he was working for *Time* magazine. Whereupon, the defense requested that Kaufman ask Mr. Baring-Gould whether or not he subscribed to the editorial policy of *Time-Life* publications:

> The Court: . . . Editorial policy with respect to what?
>
> Mr. E. H. Bloch: With respect to foreign policy of the United States and the policy adopted by his employer generally in the field of international relations.
>
> The Court: You may consider that question put to you.
>
> [Mr. Baring-Gould]: In general, I believe I do.
>
> Mr. E. H. Bloch: I challenge for cause.
>
> The Court: Denied.
>
> Mr. E. H. Bloch: Exception.

Thus, unable to dismiss this prospective juror "for cause," the defense was forced to use up another of its peremptory challenges.

In contrast to Kaufman's approval of Mr. Baring-Gould, here is what happened to Donald S. Layman, who volunteered that he had once read *In Fact*, a liberal weekly, out of "curiosity" and only "occasionally."

> The Court: Do you feel that you could leave your mind open and decide this case based on the evidence and the evidence alone?
> Mr. Layman: Yes.

However, when Kaufman announced that he had excused Mr. Layman, the defense inquired:

> Mr. E. H. Bloch: May I direct an inquiry to the Court: Is that a peremptory challenge on the part of the Government?
> The Court: No, it is my challenge.
> The Clerk: Donald S. Layman is excused.

What must be understood is that the entire screening process *insured* the presence of jurors favorably disposed to the side of the Government by the simple method of asking each prospect to evaluate his own prejudices. Hence, those honestly aware of their bias eliminated themselves. Let us grant that those jurors who were finally selected were sincere in their self-evaluation. Yet, how many bigoted people do we know who will insist they are the soul of tolerance?

•

Somehow, despite the many called, only one woman passed through the fine sieve.[3] And since it was Saypol who challenged almost all of them, we may presume that he feared that women jurors might find it too difficult to bring in a conviction which could send to her death a young wife and mother of two children. Nevertheless, a woman was found, willing and capable of serving—Mrs. Lisette Dammas. Here is her background:

> [Mrs. Dammas]: . . . My son-in-law is in the

National Guard, that is all, and I have served on the Grand Jury, that is all.[4]

Further questioning disclosed that she had been employed as a switchboard operator, and that her husband was a dispatcher for the Interborough Rapid Transit Company. Shortly thereafter we find that although the Court advised both the prosecution and the defense that each had its last challenge coming up, both sides waived.

In discussing this point with Mr. Bloch, this writer learned that he and his associates were so relieved at finally seeing a woman in the jury box that they were willing to overlook her somewhat forbidding background. Had they used up their last challenge on her, the result might have been not only an out-and-out hostile juror, but an all-male jury.

One black, Mr. Emanuel Clarence Dean, also managed to make the final twelve, and here, too, the defense was so relieved to obtain one member of a minority race that it was willing to risk his establishment background:

The Court: Mr. Dean, what do you do?
A. I work for the Consolidated Edison Company.

If it should be asked why the prosecution did not exercise its last challenge against Mr. Dean, Saypol readily saw the advantage of having an employee of the Consolidated Edison Company.[5]

In any event, let us present the chosen twelve—those twelve who were so certain they were not biased, prejudiced, or influenced by anything they had ever read or heard against the alleged Communist atom spies and traitors. Here they are:

No. 1: (Foreman) Vincent J. Lebonitte. Residence: White Plains. A manager for an R. H. Macy branch in that suburb.

No. 2: Richard Booth. A caterer for a tennis club in Forest Hills, Long Island.

No. 3: Howard G. Becker. Residence: Mamaroneck, New York. An auditor for the Irving Trust Company for twenty-four years.

No. 4: James A. Gibbons. An accountant for the New York City Omnibus Company for twenty-eight years.

No. 5: Charles W. Christie. An auditor for the Tidewater Associated Oil Company, which had "contracts with the Government" to do war work.

No. 6: Harold H. Axley. A restaurant owner, previously employed as a civilian expert in the finance department of the Army from 1942 to 1946.

No. 7: Emanuel Clarence Dean. (Already mentioned.)

No. 8: Chauncey E. Miller. Residence: Scarsdale, New York. A secretary of the Board of Commissioners of Pilots, an agency of the State of New York for twenty years. A member of the American Legion.

No. 9: Mrs. Lisette D. Dammas. (Already mentioned.)

No. 10: Charles J. Duda. Residence: Dobbs Ferry, New York. A bookkeeper for Davis and Lawrence Company.

No. 11: James Mitchell. An accountant with Harris, Kerr, Forster & Company. When previously employed by the U.S. Post Office, he was passed by "the Loyalty Probe."

No. 12: James F. Tessitore. Residence: Mount Vernon. An estimator for the Alco Gravure Division of Publications Corporation. During World War II, "printed millions of topics for the Government."

As for the alternate jurors, these were:
Alternate No. 1: Mr. John F. Moore. Residence: Bronx; a business representative for the Consolidated Edison Company.[6]

Alternate No. 2: Mr. Emerson C. Nein. Residence: Bronx; an officer and auditor for the Empire State Bank.

Alternate No. 3: Richard Lombardi. Residence: White Plains Road; a government employee (Post Office).

Alternate No. 4: Mrs. Edna Allen, whose husband worked for the Consolidated Edison Company, and whose son served in the Army's Chemical Corps. Residence: Bronx.

III

> "The most dangerous enemy to truth and freedom amongst us is the compact majority."
>
> —*Henrik Ibsen*

Such then was the jury chosen to consider the fate of the Rosenbergs and Sobell. Fulfilling the instructions of the Court, all of them swore that their minds were completely open; that they had not formed any opinion favorable to the Government or unfavorable to the defendants; that they felt neither friendly nor unfriendly to Communism.

And such also was this jury of their peers: Almost every one apparently a safe, dependable, corporation-employed, authority-oriented person. So many of them accountants, auditors, or executives, but not one employed in the arts and professions. No school-teachers, no journalists, no architects, no scientists, no nurses, no engineers, no musicians. No one in the crafts, such as a jewelry designer or an X-ray technician. And certainly, no manual worker such as a carpenter, a furrier, a longshoreman, or a welder.

In sum, all twelve jurors were politically pure and inviolate. And with all of them so certain that their minds were as unsullied as "a white sheet of paper with nothing on it," perhaps Judge Kaufman was intuitively correct in his choice of words—that their task was merely a matter of adding a column of figures.

NOTES AND REFERENCES

1. No one connected with the defense was aware of this fact at the time of trial. This writer chanced upon it in *Who's Who* in October of 1952, a year and a half after the trial.
2. Record, pp. 44 and 57. *Note:* For examination of the jurors, see pp. 43–158.
3. Among the alternate jurors, another woman, Mrs. Edna Allen, was also chosen.
4. In view of the prolonged period persons usually serve on Grand Juries, Mrs. Dammas would appear to be almost a professional juror.
5. It is worth considering how this single black man must have felt among his eleven white co-jurors with himself on trial, so to speak. As an employee of the Consolidated Edison, it is certain that he must have been aware of the dangers of "voting the wrong ticket." This would be especially true in 1951.
6. Together with Mr. Dean and Mrs. Allen, this makes almost a 19 per cent representation for the Consolidated Edison Company.

ADDENDA

In the 1974 PBS television documentary previously mentioned, some of the surviving Rosenberg trial jurors were interviewed. The thrust of these quite recent remarks reveals the political attitudes they held in 1951 which, admittedly governed their verdict. For example, Vincent Lebonitte, foreman of the jury, recalled: ". . . the idea of a Communist connoted something evil or dirty. It was a dirty word, actually."

Charles Duda, Juror No. 10, stated: ". . . the Korean War was going on, and—uh—communism was—uh—communism. Uh—it was a bad thing. . . . Taking over all these European nations and making slave states out of 'em; so—uh—I think the feeling against communism was more prevalent then than it is today."

In the book describing these reactions, there is also the disclosure that "the prosecution, but not the defense, had access to FBI reports on each" of the "300 prospective jurors" from which the Rosenberg jury had been selected. Thus the screening had already been done. (See Goldstein, *op. cit.*)

In an in-depth New York *Times* article dealing with the selection of juries in recent political trials such as the "Camden 28" and the "Gainesville 8," it is noted that none of the dissident defendants were convicted. The defense, with the aid of social scientists, had made special efforts to eliminate jurors showing the "classical authoritarian personality" and the "very over-rigid, irrationally law-and-order people" such as constituted most of the Rosenberg trial jury. (See article "Jury by Trial," by Edward Tivnan, New York *Times* Sunday Magazine, November 16, 1975.)

13 " 'TREASON!' CRIED THE SPEAKER"

I

> "Treason against the United States, shall consist *only* in levying War against them, or in adhering to their Enemies, giving them Aid and Comfort. No Person shall be convicted of Treason unless on the Testimony of two Witnesses to the same overt Act, or on Confession in open Court." [*Emphasis added.*]
> —*United States Constitution, Art. III, Sec. 3*

From the very outset of trial, prosecutor Saypol and Judge Kaufman were determined to transform it into a trial of treason *and yet deprive the defendants of the safeguards of the Constitution.*

What was the precise charge against the defendants?

It was based on a violation of the Espionage Act of 1917, enacted during World War I:

Whoever, with intent or reason to believe that it is to be used to the injury of the United States or to the advantage of a foreign nation communicates, delivers or transmits . . . to any foreign government. . . . [R. 55]

Now let us compare this with the exact wording of Indictments No. 1, 2, and 3, all of which remained the same in this respect:

On or about June 6, 1944 . . . Julius Rosenberg [et al.] . . . did conspire . . . with intent and reason to believe that it would be used to the advantage of a foreign nation, to wit, the Union of Soviet Socialist Republics . . . (R. 52–53.)

At once we notice that the crucial clause—*to the injury of the United States*—has been omitted. In other words, there was no accusation that the Rosenbergs and Sobell had ever intended to do anything to injure the United States. Why did the Government omit this clause? For the simple reason that the Soviet Union was not an enemy nation, but a wartime ally in 1944–1945, the principal period of the alleged conspiracy.

The central concept of treason is betrayal of allegiance. That is why it is considered "a mortal accusation," and carries so terrible a stigma. And because the mere accusation of treason carries such a "peculiar intimidation," it was specifically named by the Founding Fathers as the *only* offense in the Constitution:

Such deep concern with this one crime came about partially . . . because experience had shown that an extremely broad power to punish for treason might become an instrument of oppression.[1]

Why were the framers of our Constitution so deeply concerned that some future governing body might use it as an instrument of oppression? Because every one of them had a price on his head as a traitor for "imagining the death" of George III of England:

It is true that in England of olden times men were

tried for treason for mental indiscretions such as imagining the death of the King. But our Constitution was intended to end such prosecutions.[2]

•

No matter what hostility may have been engendered against the Soviet Union by 1951, history records the following:

"The Russians were magnificent allies. They fought as they promised and they made no separate peace."
—Secretary of War Henry Stimson

"The hopes of civilization rest on the worthy banners of the courageous Russian Army."
—General Douglas MacArthur

Even with such dimly remembered facts, it would have been impossible to charge the Rosenbergs and Sobell with the crime of treason, *i.e.*, with adhering and giving aid to an enemy nation. Yet, in effect, they were tried for something more than treason, because *throughout the trial* their alleged membership in the Communist Party was made synonymous with "imagining the death of the King." Here are portions of Saypol's opening statement:

. . . The loyalty and allegiance of the Rosenbergs and Sobell were not to our country. . . . Rosenberg, you will hear . . . devoted himself to . . . betraying his own country. . . . These traitorous Americans. . . . the *treasonable acts . . . the most serious crime which can be committed against the people of this country.* [R. 177–184; emphasis added.]

During Saypol's pyrotechnics, the defense demanded that Kaufman instruct the jury on the correct charge:

The Court: The charge here is [conspiracy to commit] espionage. It is not that the defendants are members of the Communist Party or that they had any interest in Communism. However, if the Government intends to establish that they did have an interest in Communism, for the purpose of establishing a motive for what they were doing, I will, in due course, when that question arises, rule on that point.

And yet, despite these instructions, Kaufman gave to the implication of treason his judicial seal of approval:

Irrational sympathies must not shield *proven traitors.* . . . Indeed by your *betrayal* you undoubtedly altered the course of history. . . . Who knows but that millions more of innocent people may pay the price of your *treason.* [Emphasis added.]

To repeat—nowhere in the indictment or testimony is there charged or established any intent to injure the United States! [3]

II

Why did U.S. Attorney Saypol avoid the charge of actual espionage and choose rather the lesser "catch-all" charge, that of conspiracy to commit espionage? According to the trial record, Saypol had not a shred of evidence to prove the *actual* commission of the crime. Therefore he turned to the conspiracy charge, *i.e.*, an agreement to commit espionage, or as Clarence Darrow explains it,

If a boy should steal a dime a small fine would cover the offense; he could not be sent to the penitentiary. But if two boys by agreement steal a dime, then both of them could be sent to the penitentiary as conspirators.[4]

By means of this device Saypol was not required to produce any evidence beyond the word of Elitcher and/or the Greenglasses, because in Federal courts, as previously mentioned, corroboration of accomplice witnesses is unnecessary. Not only can specious evidence be introduced, but when there is an atmosphere of hostility, a conviction can be obtained on the mere allegation that the accused party agreed to do something illegal.

There was still another advantage to the prosecution in the use of the "conspiracy strategy." For with this charge comes into play a unique rule of evidence not otherwise permitted in an American court of law, *i.e.*, hearsay testimony. Here again is Clarence Darrow's comment:

If A is indicted and a conspiracy is charged . . . the state's attorney is allowed to prove what A said to B and what B said to C while the defendant was not present.

And now, with words that would be prophetic were it not that Darrow had to fight the Saypols and Kaufmans of his own time, we have this cogent presentation of the evil as it becomes compounded.

To make this hearsay or gossip competent, the state's attorney informs the court that later he will connect it up. . . . Thereupon the complaisant judge holds . . . if it is not connected up it will be stricken out. A week or a month may pass by, and then a motion is made to strike it out. By that time it is of no consequence whether it is stricken out or not; it has entered the juror's consciousness . . . it has made an impression on his mind.

As we saw, it was in this way that Saypol and Kaufman heaped upon the defendants all the innuendo of guilt elicited from Max Elitcher when they led him into their version of the "Hitler-Stalin pact." In this way, too, all of the hearsay testimony of Harry Gold and Elizabeth Bentley, *strangers* to Sobell and the Rosenbergs, was massed against them. So great are the dangers inherent in conspiracy charges that we have this judgment of the late Justice Robert Jackson of the U.S. Supreme Court:

The naive assumption that prejudicial effects can be overcome by instructions to the jury . . . all practising lawyers know to be unmitigated fiction.[5] [Emphasis added.]

We have seen how, in effect, Saypol and Kaufman turned the trial into one of treason. By calling it conspiracy, however, they obtained convictions on the basis of uncorroborated accomplice testimony of the Greenglasses, Elitcher, and Gold—the worst possible type of evidence. The following is in further support of our anatomy of frame-up:

They [the accomplices] are in a position to tell a story that is in the main true . . . but at the same time to insert into that story some limited but serious falsity—as, for example, an assertion that some particular ac-

256

cused person was present, when he really was not present, or to insert a damning word or two into an account of a harmless conversation which had in fact taken place, and thus to give a criminal atmosphere to a perfectly innocent conversation.

It is plain that Elitcher was still in danger of prosecution, and—as he says—was anxious to help himself out if he could; and . . . it is noticeable that the few words here and there that relate to espionage might well have been quite easily and neatly inserted in an otherwise true and innocuous story.[6]

•

To sum up, a trial of treason was achieved in the Rosenberg case by simply giving the same offense another name: to wit, conspiracy to commit espionage. And by so doing, the Government removed the protection of the "two-witness rule" in that section of the treason clause which demands for conviction either a confession in open court, or two witnesses to the same overt act.

Here again we see what great caution was exercised by the authors of the Constitution, who knew all too well the danger of forced confessions and therefore insisted upon full corroboration of the accusation of treason. The two witnesses could not merely testify to two or more different acts. No, both persons had to witness the same treasonable act. But, as we will see now in the case of Max Elitcher, his word *alone* sufficed.

NOTES AND REFERENCES

1. U.S. Department of Defense letter submitted to a Congressional hearing on February 3, 1954. (*I. F. Stone's Weekly,* April 5, 1954.)
2. From Federal Judge Youngdahl's ruling on the Owen Lattimore case. (New York *Times,* May 3, 1953.)

3. In his first appeal to the Supreme Court, Mr. Bloch pointed out:

> Congress in passing the Atomic Energy Act of 1946 did not see fit to prescribe the death penalty for atomic espionage except where there exists an intent to injure the United States.

(See Petition on Writ of Certiorari, No. 111, October 13, 1952, p. 14.)

4. Clarence Darrow, *The Story of My Life,* Scribner's, New York, 1932, p. 64.
5. Krulewitch v. U.S. 440, 453.
6. From an analysis of the Sobell case by Denis Nowell Pritt, senior member of the English Bar, a King's Counsel since 1927, a Member of Parliament, and chairman of the Hoard League for Penal Reform. (See *National Guardian,* March 22 and 29, 1954.)

ADDENDA

As a recent example of the enduring stigma of treason with which the Rosenbergs were burdened, even the featured critical article about J. Edgar Hoover in *Time* magazine, December 22, 1975, contains the misleading description: "Julius and Ethel Rosenberg, executed for treason."

(*Note:* For Roy Cohn's present view on the "horror of conspiracy trials," after he had been indicted for conspiracy *himself,* see *Addenda* to Chapter 20.)

14 "THE FRIEND OF HIS FRIEND"

> "Every Spaniard was called upon by the Edict to become an informer . . . to become accusers and betrayers—the friend of his friend, the brother of his brother, the son of his father." [1]

On Thursday morning, March 8, the prosecution's first witness, Max Elitcher, was called to the stand. On that same morning Saypol's opening statement of the day before was headlined in the New York *Times* as though it were sworn evidence:

THEFT OF ATOM BOMB SECRETS IN WAR STRESSED AT SPY TRIAL

Concerning Korea, the headlines presaged a possible extension of the war. Unless permitted to destroy the "sanctuary" of China's industries in Manchuria, MacArthur warned, the war might end in a stalemate.

In the *Times* article on the trial, there was also reference made to the long list of 102 witnesses to be called in behalf of the Government.[2] This list was, of course, impressive because it included such distinguished men as Dr. J. Robert Oppenheimer, Dr. Harold C. Urey, and General Leslie Groves, the three Americans most responsible for the Los Alamos project. When the trial ended, however, none of these important witnesses had been produced. Out of the 102 announced only 23 ever appeared.

Not only was Dr. Urey never called, but he informed this writer in the corridor outside Courtroom 110 on June 8, 1953 (the day of the hearing on the "New Evidence"), that he never even knew he had been announced as one of Saypol's witnesses! It is perhaps ironical justice that it was Dr. Urey who later became prominently involved in the fight to save the lives of the Rosenbergs, after he had studied the record and had found much of the Government's case incredible.

Summing up the damage done the defendants by this deceptive list: First, it succeeded in undermining whatever presumption of innocence may have still existed. Second, the maneuver tied the hands of the defense; for with the announced appearance of Dr. Urey and Dr. Oppenheimer, what hope could the defense have to induce other scientists to appear as rebuttal witnesses? And finally, the huge list had the effect of throwing the defense off balance and sending it up many blind alleys of wasteful preparation.[3]

II

As suggested in the Author's Note, the summary of testimony as it appeared in the *Columbia Law Review* was chosen for the following reasons: (1) It is concise, (2) it is unbiased and reasonably accurate, (3) it is from a highly respected legal periodical, and (4) it is assurance that every important point in the Government's case is fully presented.

COLUMBIA SUMMARY RE ELITCHER

[Max Elitcher] reported that in June, 1944, and September, 1945, Julius Rosenberg had solicited his services for espionage activities. Later in 1945, Rosenberg asked Elitcher to continue his employment in the Navy Department because of its fertility as a field for espionage. Elitcher also testified that in July of 1945 [this should be 1948] he had communicated his suspicion to Morton Sobell that he, Elitcher, was being followed. That night, according to Elitcher, Sobell went on what he said was a visit to Julius Rosenberg in order to deliver a 35-millimeter film can purportedly containing secret information (the inference being that Sobell feared apprehension and confiscation of the can because of Elitcher's suspicion of being followed). Elitcher, although he accompanied Sobell, did not see Rosenberg. . . .

Direct evidence against Morton Sobell, the other defendant in the case, *derived solely from the testimony of Max Elitcher,* who related that Sobell had asked him to enter the Young Communist League in 1939 and later had joined with Rosenberg in trying to get Elitcher to engage in espionage. In June, 1944, Rosenberg, seeking to convince Elitcher of the need and propriety of espionage activities, told him that Sobell was engaged in such activities. And, as previously mentioned, Sobell had transmitted important information to Rosenberg after Elitcher had reported his suspicions of being followed.[4] [Emphasis added.]

For convenience in analyzing Elitcher's testimony, the foregoing summary may be divided under these headings:

1. Julius' Spy Proposal of June, 1944.
2. The Espionage Request of September, 1945.
3. The Espionage Request of 1948.
4. The Catherine Slip Episode of July, 1948.

(*Note:* The last heading includes Elitcher's alleged auto ride with Sobell to Catherine Slip [a street] to deliver to Julius the 35-millimeter film can.)

•

1. JULIUS' SPY PROPOSAL OF JUNE, 1944

It will be borne in mind that this proposal appeared for the *first time* in the final indictment, returned January 31, 1951; in other words six months after Elitcher claimed to have told "the whole complete story" on July 20, 1950. Here is Elitcher's testimony:

[Elitcher]: Well, one evening, it was early, before supper, I received a phone call from a person who said he was Julius Rosenberg.

The Court: When was this?

The Witness: In June, 1944. He said that he was a former classmate. I remembered that name. . . . He came over after supper . . . and we had a casual conversation. After that he asked if my wife would leave the room, that he wanted to speak to me in private. She did and he then said to me—he talked to me first about the job that the Soviet Union was doing in the war effort and how at present a good deal of military information was being denied them by some interests in the United States, and because of that, their effort was being impeded. He said that there were many people who were implementing aid to the Soviet Union by providing classified information about military equipments, and so forth, and asked whether in my capacity at the Bureau of Ordnance would I have access to and would I be able to get such information and would I turn it over to him.

In describing this information, Elitcher continued:

Well, he asked about any plans or blueprints or anything that might be of value, and that all these things are needed. . . . He said that this information . . . should be taken to New York, to him, and he would have it processed photographically and the material would be returned. He said that this would be done in a very safe manner. . . . it would be processed immediately and could be returned almost within a short time . . .

It is here that we first see Sobell's name mentioned:

[Elitcher]: Well, in the process of convincing me of the perhaps need or the safety of these deeds, he told me that Sobell, who had been my former roommate, was also—

Mr. Phillips [Sobell's attorney]: Just a minute. I object to any conversation about Sobell in the absence of Sobell.

The Court: Let us understand this right now; in a conspiracy after it has been established that the conspiracy exists, conversations by one conspirator are binding on the other conspirator even though not in his presence. . . . Your objection is overruled. It is taken subject to proof that a conspiracy exists.

Q. [Saypol]: Was it at that time that he [Rosenberg] then mentioned that Sobell was helping in this way?
A. Yes.[5]

Here is the hearsay testimony so strongly condemned

by Clarence Darrow and Justice Jackson. Although no conspiracy has yet been proved, Elitcher may testify what Julius is supposed to have said about Sobell while the latter remains totally ignorant of the conversation. The mischief, as Jackson warns, is that there is no possible way for the accused to refute such hearsay since he was not present.

When we turn to Elitcher's cross-examination regarding Julius' June, 1944, visit, we see that Mr. Bloch elicited the admission that not only had he and Rosenberg been casual acquaintances at college but that in the *six years* following their graduation they had never seen each other, never corresponded and never telephoned one another. (*Note:* Except for one brief accidental meeting at the Wardman Hotel swimming pool in July, 1940, or four years earlier.) [6]

During cross-examination Mr. Bloch divided Julius' visit into two parts: (1) while Helene Elitcher was present, and (2) while she was waiting in the bedroom. Concerning the first part, Elitcher testified that there was only small talk for fifteen to thirty minutes, after which Helene was asked to "step out." And now Mr. Bloch questions Elitcher about the second part:

Q. And then you say Rosenberg, not having seen you for six years, hardly knowing you, launched into an overture to you to engage in getting information?

A. Yes.

Q. Didn't you testify before that you were shocked at this overture?

A. Well, yes. It was new. Something which—well, I think it would shock anyone, from the approach . . .

Q. How long would you estimate the conversation that you had with Rosenberg at your house that night lasted, while you two were alone?

A. *I would say no more than a half hour, probably less. It was relatively short.*

Q. Now, after your wife left did Rosenberg come right to the point and talk to you about possible espionage work . . . ?

A. Well, he started out with this discussion of the Russian war effort. . . . He sort of built up to it talking about that . . .

Q. How long would you say that part of the conversation lasted?

A. *A few minutes; say three or four; less than five minutes.* [Emphasis added.]

First, we are asked to believe that Julius, a mere acquaintance, had spent no more than three to five minutes in warming up Elitcher, and then concluded the conquest within the next twenty-five minutes!

Second, that Rosenberg was so indifferent to Elitcher's shocked reaction that he divulged the exact procedure which the spy ring used to transmit its secrets. Third, that Elitcher, despite his admitted knowledge of a possible death sentence, agreed to Rosenberg's proposal!

Finally, we are asked to ignore entirely the possible suspicions of Elitcher's wife as well as Rosenberg's unconcern to such suspicions. The so-called spymaster is not at all troubled while Helene, whom he has just met, waits in the adjoining bedroom. That she might be curious and eavesdrop never enters his mind, nor for that matter Elitcher's. Neither is there and mention of her showing normal inquisitiveness following this mysterious visit!

In his acceptance of the spy proposal, it is Elitcher's testimony that he warned Julius, "I can't make any trips to New York on my own without my wife's knowledge." If so, then would not Julius ask at his next meeting with Elitcher the natural questions: "How about your wife—was she suspicious? Did she want to know what we talked about?" The record reveals no such inquiry.

Further, why did Julius not simply suggest on the phone to meet for lunch the next day, or at a bar that evening? Why would a seasoned spy risk making his proposal within earshot of an unknown, and therefore a potentially dangerous person?

According to Elitcher, until that fateful night Julius had been "merely a vague person" to him. In the face of this, is it credible (1) that Rosenberg, the "super-spy," would behave so irrationally and so recklessly, (2) that Helene Elitcher would have remained so indifferent to what was going on, and (3) that a man as

264

timid and cautious as Elitcher would have plunged so unhesitantly into an association so perilous?

●

Early in the summer of 1944, Julius was assigned by the Signal Corps to go to Washington and do some work at the Bureau of Standards. The following is from his direct examination as to what actually took place:

Q. [Bloch]: About how long did you remain in Washington to complete your assignment?
A. [Julius]: Well, I don't remember the exact number of days, but I know it was about three to five days. . . . I was lonesome and I looked up in the telephone book for Mr. Elitcher's number, and I called him one evening.[7]

Here is more on this point as Julius is cross-examined later:

Q. [Saypol]: But you didn't know him very well, did you?
A. Well, he went to the same school I went to. . . . I thought of a couple of people's names who might be in Washington; I remembered the incident at the swimming pool at that time, that Elitcher was in Washington, and perhaps he had a telephone.

Q. How many days had you been in Washington when you decided you were lonesome and you wanted to look up somebody?
A. I believe it was about the second or third day of my stay there.
Q. Well, had you met any people in the Bureau of Standards with whom you were working?
A. No. [R. 1166–1172]

First, we observe that Julius did not undertake a special trip to Washington to make a spy proposal to Elitcher, but went there on an official assignment which could be verified easily by Government travel records. Yet Elitcher carefully omits this point even though it would have been the most normal thing to have asked, "What are you doing in Washington?" On the contrary, he makes it appear that Julius had come to Washington expressly to recruit him.

More important is the reasonableness of Julius' loneliness after being in Washington two or three days. Despite Saypol's labored sarcasm ("When you *decided* you were lonesome"), we see a normal impulse far removed from the air of intrigue given it by Elitcher in his opening statement that he "received a phone call from a person who said he was Julius Rosenberg."

Returning to Julius' direct examination:

Q. [Bloch]: Did you during the course of that evening ever say to Mr. Elitcher, in specific words or by implication, that you wanted him to engage in espionage work . . . ?

A. [Julius]: I never said anything of the sort.

Q. Did you discuss the war?

A. Yes, I did.

Q. Tell us what you said to Elitcher and what he said to you?

A. Well, we discussed the progress of the war, the fact that the German Army was taking a beating at that time, and that a terrific amount of power [was] being built up by the Allies to put the finishing touches to the war; and we discussed the fact that the Russians had been carrying a very heavy burden in the war.

And here again is Julius' cross-examination:

Q. [Saypol]: Now tell us, what did you talk about? . . .

A. He said to me, "What are you doing in Washington?" I told him, "I am here on an assignment," and I told him I was at the Bureau of Standards in ref—in regard to some work.

[*Note:* This is the point Elitcher so suspiciously omits.]

Q. Was there a time when either at your request

or at his request Mrs. Elitcher left your presence and left you alone?

A. There was no time that I requested it or he requested his wife to leave the room, but there was a time when she went in to do the dishes, from the living room to the kitchen.

Q. Now then, what did you talk about?

A. Talked about my job, where I was working at, the fact that he was working for the Government, what his rating was, what my rating was. We talked about Washington, D. C.; we talked about my family, and I asked him about his health and then we talked about the topics of the day.

Q. Well, what were the topics of the day?

A. The war.

Q. And what did you talk about in connection with the war?

A. What the latest news was about the war.

And so, to compare Julius' account of a prosaic visit, with that of Elitcher, we find both versions are *almost* the same. In Julius' account, he dropped up simply to seek the company of the only person he happened to know in Washington. The only time Helene Elitcher left them was when she went into the kitchen to do the dishes. In Elitcher's version this housewifely act is transformed almost into a command that she mark time in the bedroom.

It will be noted that Julius admits straightforwardly his pro-Soviet sympathy. Certainly if Julius, on trial for his life, had any consciousness of guilt, he could have been more discreet before that hostile jury, so bitterly prejudiced against Russia as it was during the height of the Korean War. He could just as well have omitted his voluntary statement that the Russians had made heavy sacrifices in World War II.

For in 1951, with our foreign policy reversed, and our former ally, the Soviet Union, become the enemy, what did it matter that the Russians had suffered 25,000,000 dead? Indeed, for most of that jury, it had been the "wrong war." We should have let Hitler destroy the Soviet Union; we should have dropped "the Bomb" on them when we had the chance. Now, they and Red China were backing the North Korean aggression.

Small wonder, then, that the jury preferred to believe Elitcher's version of this visit; this uncorroborated testimony of a timid little man (an admitted perjurer), who, at the request of a mere acquaintance, plunged headlong into a conspiracy, entailing a possible death penalty, in the fantastic time of twenty-five minutes!

•

Following the visit of June, 1944, Elitcher told of seeing Julius socially in New York that same summer, and also the following summer when he and his wife had stayed overnight at the Rosenberg apartment. But curiously enough there were no requests from Julius during any of these meetings to obtain military secrets.[8]

Thus, we have the paradox of a conspiracy during which nothing was conspiratorial! If we think of human actions in terms of cause and effect, the Elitcher story of his recruitment as a Soviet spy remains completely isolated from reality.

2. THE ESPIONAGE REQUEST OF SEPTEMBER, 1945 [9]

According to Elitcher's testimony, the second time Rosenberg showed any interest in him as a spy was *one year and three months* after the initial request. He claimed that Julius had again visited him in Washington, one Saturday morning in September, 1945, remained some "fifteen or twenty minutes," and said:

[Elitcher]: . . . that even though the war was over there was a continuing need for new military information for Russia and again was trying to get my views about it, whether I would want to contribute in the future.

. . . I said I would see and if I had anything and I wanted to give it to him, I would let him know.

268

. . . He was asking whether—what I was doing. This was quite some time later after the past visit [of June, 1944]. . . .

Q. [Saypol]: What did you tell him what you were working on at the time? . . .

A. Well, I told him that I was working on some sonar or anti-submarine fire control devices.

This is Elitcher's *total* direct testimony on the subject. Again, it is designed to create the impression that Julius made a *special* trip to Washington for the visit. However, according to Julius' direct testimony,[10] he had gone to Washington to see his Congressman for help on his appeal to the Signal Corps for reinstatement. The month before, he had been discharged by G2 on FBI charges of Communist Party membership. He had dropped in on Elitcher for a brief social call.

Arriving at the Elitcher's, Julius had found them about to drive over to the Federal Workers Union, where Helene was employed, and accompanied them to the union hall where, after a few minutes, they parted.

All of this innocuous detail is carefully omitted in Elitcher's direct testimony. But in his cross-examination, not only is most of this confirmed, but the improbability of any espionage discussion is clearly demonstrated by Elitcher's admissions of his wife's presence during all of the time they were together.

Conceding that Julius did ask Elitcher what he was working on, such a conversation between engineers would be quite commonplace. For Elitcher to have told Julius briefly and in a general way that he was working on anti-submarine devices is a far cry from a conspiracy to commit espionage.

To summarize this episode, we are asked to believe that Julius, the alleged spy-master, in a year and three months after recruiting Elitcher, never *once* asked him for the information originally requested, despite their two meetings in New York. And, in September, 1945, there is still no request to deliver the secret information. As to "the future," Elitcher casually says he will "let him know."

3. THE ESPIONAGE REQUEST OF 1948

Throughout Elitcher's testimony describing his clandestine conversations with Rosenberg and Sobell over a period of four years, there is a vague and amorphous quality. Here, for example, is how he describes conspiratorial conversations with Sobell in 1946 and in 1947:

[Elitcher]: Well, he said, I don't know in what words, or implied that it had to do with *this espionage business,* but I don't recall the exact nature of the words. [Emphasis added.]

[Elitcher]: Well, at about that time my wife and I were having some personal difficulties and I told it to him. . . . he became concerned and asked whether she knew anything about *this espionage business.* [Emphasis added.]

And here is the June, 1948, meeting with Julius:

[Elitcher]: I told him I had decided to leave Washington. He said . . . he needed somebody to work at the Navy Department for *this espionage purpose* and he wanted me to change my mind. . . . Sobell was along and I recall that he agreed with Rosenberg . . . . However, I convinced him that I was not going to change my plans. . . . Sobell left and Rosenberg and I had dinner together.

Q. [Saypol]: What was the conversation in the course of that dinner?

A. Well, among other things, we continued to talk about *this espionage.* . . . he asked whether I knew of places where important military work was done. I mentioned the Bell Telephone Laboratories to him . . . in Whippany, New Jersey. He was interested in my getting a position there and I said, "We'll see, maybe I can—I don't know." [R. 256–258; emphasis added.]

First, it is now four years since Elitcher's alleged recruitment, but thus far not one secret, not one illegal document has he delivered to anyone!

270

Second, the curious phrases: "this espionage business"—"this espionage purpose." Can we believe in a bona fide spy-master saying: "I need someone at the Navy Department for this espionage purpose"? Or that Sobell would say: "Does your wife know anything about this espionage business?"

Is this the way spies talk to each other? Imagine two bank embezzlers, with one asking, "Does your wife know anything about this embezzlement business?"

Again, we see that Elitcher's testimony consisted of little more than innuendoes. Elitcher may well have discussed with Julius the possibility of finding a better job at the Bell Telephone Company. Just at this time, Elitcher, in fact, was looking for work and eventually found it at Reeves. Hence, all he was doing on the witness stand was to start with these full truths and insert just a bit here and there concerning "this espionage business."

4. THE CATHERINE SLIP EPISODE OF JULY, 1948 [11]

In Chapter 8 we have already related a portion of this episode: how Elitcher drove up from Washington to visit the Sobells and his fear of having been followed by the FBI. In this section we will analyze his further testimony:

[Elitcher]: . . . I called Sobell aside and told him that I thought I had been followed by one or two cars from Washington to New York. At this point, he became very angry and said I should not have come to the house under those circumstances. I told him . . . I had planned to come to his house to stay; the fact that I was being followed couldn't change it; whoever was following me would probably know about it; in any case it was our only destination.

To begin with, why should a spy knowingly lead his pursuers to the home of his co-conspirator? Since Elitcher had stopped off at his mother's house, why didn't he remain there? Or, go to a hotel for the night

271

and proceed to the Sobells' the next day? He states he couldn't change his destination. Why not? Suppose he had found his mother seriously ill? Are we to believe that he would have apologized to the FBI trailing him? "Look, boys, you'll have to forgive me—my mother is sick, come back tomorrow."

[Elitcher cont'd.]: He [Sobell] was still angry and concerned. However, he didn't seem to believe that I had been followed. He told me I should leave the house, I should go to a place in the mountains perhaps, or some other place and stay.

On the one hand Sobell is agitated, but at the same time skeptical. Then, despite the skepticism, he asks Elitcher to go hide in the mountains, (meaning, no doubt, some summer resort). But this is *after* the damage has been done.

It is important to ask: Why does Elitcher introduce this congestion of contradictions? Quite obviously because he has been instructed to provide an atmosphere of guilt—to paint a picture of alarm now that the FBI is breathing down their necks. Yet, at the same time he retains Sobell's skepticism in order to prepare for the cloak-and-dagger material which he now presents:

[Elitcher cont'd.]: He [Sobell] finally agreed that I would stay. However, a short time later he . . . said he had some valuable information in the house, something that he should have given to Julius Rosenberg some time ago . . . it was too valuable to be destroyed and yet too dangerous to keep around. He said he wanted to deliver it to Rosenberg that night. I told him it was foolish under the circumstances; that it was *dangerous*, it was a silly thing to do. [Emphasis added.]

Now we see why Elitcher stressed Sobell's skepticism. For if Sobell is presented as too concerned about the FBI, then he would be foolhardy to risk delivery of the dangerous information (the 35-millimeter film can) that very night. No, Sobell's alarm must be shown as only momentary; there is no danger save in Elitcher's imaginary fears. And so, rather than destroy the valuable film, Sobell is determined to deliver it to Rosenberg immediately. But here the contradictions begin to pile up:

If Sobell is afraid the film is too dangerous to keep another moment, it can only be because he fears that the FBI may burst in to catch him red-handed. But if this be true, why is he hurrying to meet Rosenberg with the *same detectives hot on his heels?*

Observe also the coincidence of Sobell having this film can in his house precisely at the time of Elitcher's visit. Is it customary for spies to hold on to a "hot" can of film for "some time"? And, as we will now see, it was only a short drive to Rosenberg's home:

[Elitcher]: However, he insisted and . . . asked me to go along, He said he was tired, and that he might not be able to make the trip back. I agreed to go after argument, and we left the house. Upon leaving I saw him take what I identified then as a 35 millimeter film can.[12]

From Sobell's house in Flushing to the street known as Catherine Slip in lower Manhattan is "ten miles" by car and it was only 9 or 10 P.M., a fairly early hour. Why should Sobell anticipate that he "might" be too tired to drive back? Why does he demand that Elitcher accompany him after the latter has just driven in from Washington—an all-day journey of some 300 miles in mid-July?

Truly, as Sobell's attorney pointed out later, the situation added up to nothing less preposterous than Sobell's desire to have Elitcher along as a future witness against him!

[Elitcher cont'd.]: No reference was made to it [the film can]. . . . When he got into the car he put it in the glove compartment.

Here, apparently, Sobell reckoned that the FBI, should they be caught and frisked, will not think to check the glove compartment! Here is an explanatory note about their further precautions as Sobell started to drive, from Elitcher's cross-examination:

We did check as we went outside, as we drove, that no one was following, and apparently no one was, as we could see no one following as we proceeded from the house to [Catherine Slip]. . . .

In passing, one wonders why Elitcher failed to take similar precautions during his trip up from Washington. To return to his direct testimony:

[Elitcher]: He told me to park the car. . . . He took this can out of the glove compartment and left and I drove up the street and down and parked facing the East River Drive . . . He came back approximately a half hour later . . . and as we drove off I turned to him and said, "Well, what does Julie think about this, my being followed?"

Why didn't Elitcher go along with Sobell to see Julius? Was it to make both the episode and the locale sound especially mysterious—a B-picture scene on the waterfront with Sobell slinking off to meet the spymaster? But, whatever the facade, we now come to the *raison d'être* of this entire tale—Elitcher's instructions to bring Elizabeth Bentley into the picture, not as a party to the "conspiracy" but by the mere mention of her name by Rosenberg as *relayed* to him by Sobell.

With such a foundation, Saypol could call her as a witness to testify that she had once heard of a "Julius" giving illegal information to her lover, Jacob Golos.

(*Note:* Nothing of this Catherine Slip story, according to Elitcher's testimony, had been told to the FBI on July 21 when they had their "full discussion about Sobell.")

For clarity, let us return to Elitcher's question as they "drove off":

[Elitcher]: "Well, what does Julie think about this, my being followed?" He said, "It is all right; don't be concerned about it; it is O.K." He then said Rosenberg had told him that he once talked to Elizabeth Bentley on the phone but he was pretty sure she didn't know who he was and therefore everything was all right. We proceeded back to the house.

Q. [Saypol]: Just a moment. At that time was the name Elizabeth Bentley under discussion?

A. Well, it had been in the newspapers just prior to that time . . . and I knew from the mention of the name. . . . I knew from the papers that she had admitted to some—to being a part of an espionage ring, that is all. We drove back—*he drove back* and we discussed the point no further. [Emphasis added.]

First, why would Rosenberg, the spy-master, be so "sure" Bentley was ignorant of his identity? In her subsequent testimony, a certain "Julius" would telephone her whenever he wished to reach Golos; and Golos had told her that this "Julius" was an engineer residing in Knickerbocker Village. Why, then, if Julius had just read in the newspapers that the former "Red Spy Queen" was exposing the entire espionage network, would he feel so certain that she had not identified him?

In the next chapter we shall see Greenglass' conflicting statement that Julius had confided to him in May, 1950, that he was planning to flee the country because "probably Bentley knew him"! Thus from one witness (Elitcher) we have Julius' total lack of concern about Bentley, whereas from another witness (Greenglass) his virtual panic, and with no explanation reconciling these different versions.[13]

Second, concerning the return trip, we find Sobell miraculously refreshed. Instead of *Elitcher,* it is *Sobell* who is doing the driving. Let us turn to the cross-examination on this subject:

Q. [Kuntz]: . . . When you came up from Washington . . . you were scared to death at that time, were you not?

A. [Elitcher]: Yes.

Q. Did you suggest to him or did he suggest that

because you were followed it might be wiser that you stay home while he take this 10 mile trip?

A. I think I suggested. I didn't want to go because I had been followed. . . . He said he wanted me to go; *he was tired and he wanted to make sure that he would make the trip back.* [Emphasis added.]

Q. [Kuntz]: Sobell drove?
A. Yes.
Q. That was after he told you he was too tired to drive?
A. Yes.
Q. You didn't touch that wheel in that [entire] trip, did you?
A. Well, yes, I did, I parked the car, but other than that, no. [R. 361–366]

And so the only basis on which Elitcher is able to account for Sobell's incredible spy behavior is contradicted by himself!

At the conclusion of Elitcher's direct examination, we can see the extent to which the prosecution went in its tactic of proving "guilt by innuendo":

Q. [Saypol]: Was there anything about some equipment that you noticed in Sobell's home, that you can tell us about?
A. [Elitcher]: Well, he had photographic equipment, enlarging; he had a 35—a Leica camera, and an enlarger and material for processing film.
Q. In your experience with Sobell . . . is it accurate to say that material that you worked on in the Navy Department, that he worked on in General Electric in Schenectady, and that both of you worked on in Reeves Instrument, was classified?
A. Yes.[14]

Here, then, is an ominous warning to every camera enthusiast who happens to be employed on classified work: the mere ownership of camera equipment may be introduced as circumstantial proof that one is photographing secret documents.

If Sobell were truly a spy engaged in filming secret documents, would he do it in his own house, keep around all that incriminating photographic equipment? An enlarger is a sizable apparatus, almost as big as a suitcase. If Sobell was so terrified that an FBI search that night might result in the discovery of a tiny one-inch film can, what about all that telltale processing equipment so difficult to conceal?

Clearly, this last piece of testimony was introduced to give credence to that 35-millimeter film can. But now, let us turn to the inevitable "documents" which the "bad guys" are always managing to filch somehow.

[Saypol cont'd]: In the time that you worked with Sobell at Reeves Instrument Company, or at any time, did you ever see Sobel take any papers or documents?

A. [Elitcher]: Well, in the course of his duties, I did, as far as I know, I saw him take—he had a brief case, and he did take things out of Reeves Instrument. I presume that they had to do with his work.

We had another installation at Roosevelt Field, Long Island, and he went there quite often, and I know that he did have a brief case and he took material out, but what it was, or what the material was, I do not know.

As stated in courtroom parlance, this type of testimony is called "piling it on." This particular instance merits special scrutiny because it illustrates so perfectly the technique of innuendo used in frame-ups.[15] Despite Elitcher's verbose response, *the only damaging fact* we learn is that Sobell had a briefcase! And as Elitcher ruefully admits, "But . . . what the material was, I do not know."

We have stated before that it is the comparatively simple case against Sobell which provides the window through which one can best discern the nature of the entire frame-up. On August 19, 1950, the following Associated Press dispatch was released in connection with Sobell's arrest at Laredo:

He [Sobell] was employed as a project and research engineer on top secret gunfire control equipment manufactured for the armed services [at the Reeves Instrument Company].

The Reeves plant is considered spyproof—with brick walls, daily building searches and closely guarded doors.

The plant's personnel manager, Thomas J. Reilly, said yesterday that *Sobell could not have removed any written data because of the strict supervision of employees.* [Emphasis added.]

III

> "The highly novel technique of the belated recognition. . . ." [16]

On July 21, 1950, according to Elitcher's direct testimony, he was supposed to have had "a full discussion about Sobell" with the FBI. In cross-examination, however, he admitted it was almost six months later that he "remembered" the role of Elizabeth Bentley in the Catherine Slip episode. Let us glance at this technique of the belated recognition or tardy memory:

Q. [Bloch]: . . . You were given a high degree of latitude in . . . unfolding your story?
A. [Elitcher]: Yes.

Q. Now did you at that time tell the FBI agents about this conversation . . . "Rosenberg said not to worry about Bentley," or . . . anything about this automobile trip . . . ?
A. I did not.

Now Bloch asks if "the name Bentley was projected into [his] mind by somebody either in the FBI or on the prosecuting staff," but Saypol objects, Kaufman sustains, and Bloch, omitting the protested phrase, rewords the question:

Q. Well, was that somebody who mentioned the name Bentley connected with the prosecutor's office?
A. Yes. [R. 330–338]

Who was that "somebody," Bloch presses on, and when exactly was the Catherine Slip episode first mentioned to the FBI? Elitcher is evasive, but when Mr. Kuntz takes up the cross-examination he is finally cornered:

Q. [Kuntz]: This occasion of your trip to Catherine Slip, that loomed rather important in your mind, did it not?

A. [Elitcher]: Yes.

Q. As a matter of fact, according to your testimony, the only contact you have ever had in all this time with secret or dangerous stuff was on that trip, that ten-mile trip; right?

A. Yes.

Q. But you didn't tell this to the FBI on the first visit?

A. No, I did not.

Q. By the way, when you finally reported this incident of the trip, the ten-mile trip . . . to the FBI, you even omitted the name Bentley, didn't you?

A. If I did, it was purely accidental. I hadn't intended to omit it.

Q. . . . You told about this conversation with Bentley *after* the FBI mentioned Bentley?

A. Yes, but much later. . . . [R. 368–372; emphasis added.]

•

Before we complete this section of Elitcher's testimony, there is the vital question whether or not he actually received or delivered anything illegal during all the years of his participation in the alleged conspiracy. Here are the pertaining portions of his cross-examination regarding Rosenberg:

Q. [Bloch]: Did you pass any information, secret, classified, confidential or otherwise, of the Government of the United States, to the defendant Julius Rosenberg, at any time?

A. [Elitcher]: I did not.

Q. None whatsoever?

A. That is correct. [R. 276–277]

And here Mr. Kuntz pins Elitcher down regarding Sobell:

Q. [Kuntz]: . . . Did Sobell ever ask you for any document belonging to the United States Government?
A. No.
Q. . . . Did Sobell in any way offer you any documents belonging to the United States Government?
A. No.
Q. Did Sobell, by word, or action or intimation of any kind, suggest to you that you take United States Government material?
A. No.

Q. Did you get any documents from the United States Government?
A. No.
Q. Did you hand any document of the United States Government to Sobell?
A. No.
Q. Did you hand any United States documents to anybody in this world, belonging to the United States Government?
A. Not unauthorized.
Q. I am talking about illegally?
A. No. [R. 351, 356–357]

We have been asked to believe that the spy-master Rosenberg and his lieutenant Sobell continued to woo fatuously this evasive man for four years without a *single* result. This was no child's play. If they were spies, their lives hung in the balance. Is it conceivable, after years of such consistent failure on the part of Elitcher, that Rosenberg would furnish self-incriminating information about Bentley?

All during these four years Elitcher shows himself to be timid, reluctant and anxious about his wife's suspicions. And yet where does he choose to spend his two-week vacation with his family? At the home of his co-conspirator Sobell. In July of 1948 he was in abject terror that he had been followed to Sobell's house by the FBI. And yet where does he purchase his house a few months later? Around the corner, with back yards adjoining. And where does he choose to work? At Reeves—the very defense plant from which his co-conspirator steals classified material to photograph and pass on to the Russians!

Let us review Elitcher's two principal conspiratorial episodes: the spy proposal from Julius in 1944 and the 1948 visit with Sobell. In both cases we see the technique of inducing a cowed witness to extend innocent visits into criminal acts. Onto Julius' visit is hooked the spy proposal. Onto his own visit to the Sobells is hooked the trip to Catherine Slip and the name of Bentley. In the first episode he has Julius involve Sobell by hearsay. In the second episode he reverses it with Sobell involving Julius by hearsay.

In both cases, there is the time-worn trick of the belated memory.

The spy proposal, the very beginning of Elitcher's involvement, is not recalled until January, 1951, or six months after he is supposed to have told the whole truth about Rosenberg. The Catherine Slip episode, his last conspiratorial action, is not remembered until the end of 1950!

So then, what evidence of any actual espionage have we from Elitcher? None—save hearsay, inference, and innuendo. No supporting witnesses, no documentary proof, nothing but Elitcher's uncorroborated word. The word of a self-admitted perjurer intent upon saving himself from prosecution and gradually pressured into further elaborations.

Q. [Bloch]: . . . You were lying when you concealed your membership in the Communist Party?
A. [Elitcher]: Yes, I did.
Q. So you have lied under oath?
A. Yes.

Q. And you were also fearful about the oath you had taken?
A. Yes.
Q. Which was an absolute lie and perjurious; isn't that correct?

A. I knew the oath, yes.

Q. [Kuntz]: You want to save yourself, don't you?
A. Yes [R. 278, 279, 361]

IV

We have now examined every point of Elitcher's testimony contained in the *Columbia Law Review* summary.

How was it possible that the jury could not find *one reasonable doubt* in Elitcher's testimony? And how could Judge Kaufman, *solely* on the testimony of Elitcher, impose upon Sobell the maximum penalty short of death under the Espionage Act—a sentence of thirty years?

There can be only one answer. It was not a trial of evidence; the jury was too biased to even weigh the evidence. It was a political trial and the guilt of the defendants was the political guilt of dissenters from the moment they were accused and arrested.

If we examine the 65 pages of Elitcher's direct testimony, we find that 82 out of the total 177 questions asked by Saypol—*or almost half*—were related to "intent" or alleged membership in the Young Communist League or Communist Party.

It is for this reason that we have considered Elitcher's testimony of such vital importance in the analysis of the entire frame-up. Precisely because it stands alone and without corroboration it provides the clearest window through which one can see the extent of hostility and prejudice which permeated that chamber of doom. In other words, examining what was done to Morton Sobell one can better see the hollow pretense of the trial given the Rosenbergs.

●

> ". . . I had personality problems. . . . I found
> it difficult to meet with people, to have a
> good time. . . . Without the aid that I went
> to, it would be difficult for me to present my-
> self in front of this audience. . . ."
> —*Max Elitcher's testimony; Record, p. 380*

Before we take leave of Max Elitcher, one cannot
refrain from comment on the inhuman statement
quoted above wherein he describes the benefits of his
psychiatric treatment. One is painfully reminded of the
cynical psychoanalyst who admitted that his function
in the present neurotic *Zeitgeist* was to turn out "well-
adjusted bastards." We have already seen how Elitcher purchased the Sobells' furnishings at bargain
prices even while he was secretly conferring with Saypol's staff.

During cross-examination, Mr. Bloch endeavored
to show that promises had been made and that immunity from prosecution was to be Elitcher's reward.
Bloch did this by exposing two facts which occurred
just before trial: (1) Elitcher's employer at Reeves
had asked him to resign only two weeks before trial,
and (2) despite this loss of income Elitcher was so
certain of his deal and so confident of his future that
he had nevertheless purchased a brand-new car.
[R. 347]

During a discussion with Mr. Bloch, this writer inquired as to Elitcher's psychological motives in purchasing the new car just after his income had been
cut off. Certainly it was an indiscreet purchase when
Elitcher knew he must shortly testify that no promises
had been made to him. Mr. Bloch's reply was specu-
lative but worth noting: The new car may have had
a symbolic meaning for Elitcher, something in the
way of a guarantee of the status, security, and pros-
perity he could expect now that he had cast in his lot
with the Establishment.[17] In another sense, it was
perhaps a behavior pattern characteristic of those
tension-ridden persons who eat "reward" foods in
times of stress.

In any event, although Mr. Bloch did not have
concrete proof of the deal at the time of trial, the sub-

sequent exposure of Rogge's file memos disclosed the impatience of Elitcher to receive his reward. Only one week after his testimony, with the trial still at mid-point, Elitcher was already demanding payment for services rendered! However, it was not the usual thirty pieces of silver but, as indicated in Chapter 8, a permanent FBI seal of approval. Here are some excerpts of the memo written by Elitcher's attorneys. (See Appendix 6.)

MEMORANDUM

March 19, 1951

To: OJR [Rogge]
From: HJF [Fabricant]

. . . You suggested that it would be profitable to speak with McInerny [Assistant Attorney General]. . . . The importance of Elitcher's cooperation cannot possibly be underestimated. . . .

It is equally reasonable to assume that his cooperation in subsequent prosecutions by the government will be essential to the success of said prosecutions and it is also apparent that Elitcher will continue to cooperate.

Thus far, Mr. McInerny is not only reminded of the value of Elitcher's services but also of his stand-by readiness to help convict others. Hence in May, 1953, we see him as an accusing witness in the perjury trial of William Perl, another of his former classmates. One month after the death of the Rosenbergs, we learn of Elitcher's secret appearance before the Un-American Activities Committee, this time accusing "Communists" whose names "he could not supply" at the Rosenberg trial. Here are some excerpts from an editorial in the Pensacola *Journal* on July 13, 1953, shortly after the execution of the Rosenbergs:

Disclosure by [Max Elitcher] . . . of the existence of an underground network of Communists . . . is more than a little suspect. . . . The testimony was given in secret session . . . at the demand of the Justice Department which asserted national security was involved. This belated patriotism smacks too much of a second thinking. . . .

Returning to Rogge's file memo, here is the quid

pro quo put before McInerny, or, in colloquial terms, the "payoff":

> At the present time, Elitcher . . . needs a profitable employment. . . . If the Department of Justice or the FBI were to furnish Elitcher's prospective employers with a letter stating that they would be willing to appear or give testimony in his behalf at any future security investigation, it would be a most desirable achievement.

When Max Elitcher was about to descend from the witness stand, there was a question whether or not he might have to be recalled for further testimony. At this point Mr. Saypol declared with a grand gesture, "The witness will always be available."

No more fitting brand could ever have been stamped on him.

NOTES AND REFERENCES

1. A description of the Edict of Grace announced by the Spanish Inquisition; Heinrich Graetz, *History of the Jews,* Vol. 4, Chap. 10, The Jewish Pub. Society of America, Philadelphia, 1894.
2. For list of announced prosecution witnesses, see Record, pp. 51–52.
3. For example, anticipating the testimony of William Perl, former classmate of Julius Rosenberg.
4. "The Rosenberg Case," *op. cit.,* pp. 221 and 223. See also Elitcher's direct examination in Record, pp. 197–263.
5. For Elitcher's direct testimony concerning Julius' alleged spy proposal, see Record, pp. 206–210, 233–237.
6. For cross of Elitcher, see Record, pp. 264–394. For cross concerning Julius' alleged spy proposal, see Record, pp. 297–303.
7. For Julius' direct testimony concerning alleged spy proposal, see Record, pp. 1149–1152.
8. For Elitcher's direct re these two visits, see Record, pp. 238, 239–243. For Elitcher's cross re these visits, see Record, pp. 303–308.

9. For Elitcher's direct, see Record, pp. 243–244. For Elitcher's cross, see Record, pp. 309–315.
10. For Julius' direct testimony about the 1945 Washington visit, see Record, pp. 1152–1157.
11. For Elitcher's direct on the Catherine Slip episode, see Record, pp. 259–262.
12. *Note:* It will be observed that Elitcher, even by his own testimony, never *sees* the contents of the film can. Thus, in this most damaging portion of his testimony, he is not even a witness to an overt act of espionage. (See Record, p. 363, wherein Elitcher states he neither saw nor knew what "the material was.")
13. Compare Record, p. 261 (Elitcher re Bentley) with p. 529 (Greenglass re Bentley).
14. Record, pp. 262–263. (*Note:* See these pages also for subsequently quoted excerpts re Sobell's briefcase.)
15. In the Oppenheimer case, exposed by the Alsops as a "miscarriage of American justice," such evidence is described as "layer after layer of false appearances, chaff dressed up to look like corn." (See New York *Times,* January 2, 1955.)
16. Quoted from the New York *Herald Tribune* columnist Joseph Alsop with regard to the type of testimony sworn to by Louis Budenz against Owen Lattimore. (*The Nation,* April 10, 1954.)
17. "Why does an apostate turn against his former comrades? Psychiatric studies are wanting. . . . Conceivably, he is moved by hate, fear, revenge, or perhaps a pathetic desire to regain status and respectability." (Richard C. Donnelly, in *Yale Law Journal,* November, 1951, p. 1126.)

ADDENDA

With regard to Elitcher, here is an example of the favorable comment on this book quoted from the *New York University Law Review* of April, 1956—comment which the Pollack report carefully omits:

Mr. Wexley scores his most telling points in his analysis of the testimony of the witness Elitcher, whom the jury had to believe in order to convict Sobell.

The reviewer, Leonard Sachs, after discussing these points and finding Elitcher's testimony "inherently incredible," concludes:

Thus, even if Elitcher's testimony is believed, it would not seem to establish Sobell's guilt conclusively. That he was convicted on the basis of it strongly suggests he was prejudiced by his joinder [tried together] with the Rosenbergs.

Despite his frequent use of the *Review*, Pollack not only avoids these "telling points" regarding Elitcher, but resorts to an absurd quibble. He takes issue with my statement that Elitcher "virtually admitted" the existence of a "deal" allowing him to escape prosecution for perjury. He replies that while Elitcher "did admit" his fear of such prosecution, "at no time" did he actually testify that a deal had been made.

Such quibbling, found throughout the report, only demonstrates the frailty of Pollack's rebuttal: He seems to be *virtually admitting* the fact of the deal even though Elitcher hasn't used the dirty word on the witness stand. Moreover, the Rogge memo, *conceded* by Pollack as "authentic," explicitly spells out the quid pro quo of the deal. (See Appendix 6.)

15 "THE BROTHER OF HIS BROTHER"

I

"My conscience hath a thousand several
    tongues,
And every tongue brings in a several tale,
And every tale condemns me for a villain."
                                    —*King Richard III*

It was 2:30 in the afternoon of March 9 when the clerk called the prosecution's second witness, David Greenglass. Among the spectators there was a ripple of excitement and a craning of necks to see better the plump, wavy-haired prisoner take the stand. Then, as he raised his hand to swear the oath, all movement ceased and:

The great court chamber was so silent that the clock tick seemed audible in the brief pauses.[1]

In the midst of this dramatic silence, a young man stepped forward. His name was Roy M. Cohn, and he was just twenty-four years of age. It was no secret to the press how he had secured his important post of Assistant U.S. Attorney, so fresh out of law school. His father was Albert Cohn, "a judge in the Appellate Division of the New York State Supreme Court, a one-time protégé of the late Boss Ed Flynn and a power in the Democratic Party." [2]

Despite his deceptive appearance—"sleepy eyelids and carefully slicked hair"—there is a dynamic quality about Cohn's character which has been described as "a studied toughness of manner":

He bounces about the room like a movie gangster who suspects that the draperies conceal a rival hood.[3]

David Greenglass' testimony lasted all that Friday afternoon, all the following Monday and part of Tuesday morning. It was followed by that of his wife, Ruth Greenglass. Here is the summary of their direct testimony in the *Columbia Law Review*.[4]

1. THE SPY PROPOSAL TO RUTH

Greenglass, an army private, was stationed in 1944 at the Los Alamos, New Mexico, atomic project. In November of that year, Julius and Ethel Rosenberg learned of Ruth's plans to visit her husband, told Ruth that David was working on an atom bomb, and persuaded her to ask him to supply certain general information concerning the Los Alamos project for transmission to the Soviet Union.

2. DAVID'S CONSENT TO BECOME A SPY

After some reluctance Greenglass complied, relating the names of important scientists working on the project and giving information concerning security measures and the nature of his work.

3. THE EVENTS OF JANUARY, 1945

Two months later [*correction*: this should read only one month] in January, 1945, Greenglass, on leave in New York, supplemented this information with a sketch of a high explosive lens mold used in atomic experiments and a list of potential spy recruits.

4. THE TYPING BY ETHEL

This information was typed by Ethel Rosenberg.

5. THE JELLO-BOX RECOGNITION DEVICE

A few days later, Julius Rosenberg introduced Greenglass to Ann Sidorovich, who was expected to visit New Mexico to receive further atomic information. Because it was not certain that Mrs. Sidorovich would be the messenger, a Jello box-top was irregularly severed and half given to Greenglass, the arrangement being that the eventual emissary would possess the matching half when contacting him.

6. THE MEETING WITH THE "RUSSIAN"

During this same January visit, Rosenberg arranged a meeting between Greenglass and an unidentified Russian who questioned Greenglass about the lens mold.

7. THE VISIT OF HARRY GOLD

In June, 1945, Harry Gold, who had previously been in contact with Dr. Klaus Fuchs, British atomic scientist and spy, called on the Greenglasses in New Mexico and announced his purpose to transmit the secret data. On Gold's presentation of the matching half of the box-top, Greenglass gave him a detailed sketch of the lens mold and a further list of spy prospects.

8. THE DELIVERY OF THE NAGASAKI BOMB PLANS

In December, 1945 [*correction*: this should read September, 1945], Greenglass, again in New York on a furlough, prepared a cross-section sketch and twelve-page explanation of the [Nagasaki] atom bomb based on overheard conversations and surreptitious investigations at Los Alamos. Ruth Greenglass and the Rosenbergs aided in the preparation of the report.

9. THE THEFT OF THE PROXIMITY FUSE, ETC.

Julius Rosenberg at this time mentioned former espionage activities involving a stolen proximity fuse, adding later that he had transmitted other information to Russia, subsidized the college education of promising contacts, and engaged generally in espionage activities. After the war Rosenberg and Greenglass, with two other partners, engaged in an unsuccessful business venture.

10. THE PLANS TO ESCAPE

When the courier Gold was apprehended in May of 1950, Rosenberg advised the Greenglasses to flee, providing them with money and information concerning the smallpox injections necessary for entry into Mexico. Rosenberg indicated his own intention to flee, mentioning his fear that he could be identified by Jacob Golos, an exposed spy, and Elizabeth Bentley, an espionage courier who had spoken to him by telephone. [*Correction:* Nowhere in the record does Julius mention any fear about Golos, nor does Greenglass mention it in his testimony. In May of 1950, Golos had been dead seven years, having died in 1943.]

11. ETHEL'S TALK WITH RUTH

After the arrest of Greenglass on June 15, 1950, Ethel sought assurance from Ruth Greenglass that her husband would remain silent.

12. THE MONEY PAID THE GREENGLASSES

Compensation to Greenglasses for the entire venture totaled $5,850. [*Correction:* This should read $6,650.]

13. THE REWARDS GIVEN THE ROSENBERGS

Payment to the Rosenbergs consisted of two watches, a console table suited for espionage purposes, and a citation entitling them to special privileges in Russia.

14. THE ROSENBERGS' POLITICAL IDEAS

Finally, the Greenglasses testified that the Rosenbergs were members of the Communist Party and had often expressed their admiration for the Russian socialist system.

●

As indicated above, although the *Columbia Law Review* presents its summary in chronological sequence, it reserves to the last what should have been its first point, *i.e.*, the prosecution's opening salvo against the political ideas of the Rosenbergs. Therefore, we will start with David's direct testimony containing:

14. THE ROSENBERGS' POLITICAL IDEAS
   [R. 414–421]

After the routine questioning regarding birth, schooling, work, etc., Greenglass was asked to recall his sister's marriage to Julius in 1939, when David was seventeen:

Q. [Cohn]: Now did you have any discussion with Ethel and Julius concerning the relative merits of our form of government and that of the Soviet Union?

Upon prompt objection of the defense, Cohn cited "a treason conviction" of a Nazi spy named Haupt who showed sympathy "with Hitler and hostility to the United States":

The Court: What you are trying to bring out from the witness is the fact that the defendants expressed some form of favoritism to Russia in their discussions?
Mr. Cohn: Exactly, your Honor.
The Court: I believe it is relevant.

Here, in this citation involving aid to an enemy in a *treason* conviction is another instance of how the defendants were tried without the safeguards specified in the Constitution.

Q. [Cohn cont'd.]: Talking about Socialism over capitalism, did they specifically talk about Socialism as it existed in the Soviet Union and capitalism as it existed here?
A. [David]: They did.
Q. Which did they like better? Did they tell you?

Here Mr. Bloch objects to the question as leading and suggestive. Whereupon Kaufman *suggests* the answer:

The Court: I will sustain the objection on that ground, which they like better. *But you tell us whether or not on any occasion they told you that they preferred one over another.*
The Witness: They preferred Socialism to capitalism.
The Court: Which type of Socialism?
The Witness: Russian Socialism. [Emphasis added.]

What is significant here is Judge Kaufman's stress on issues which he knew were deliberately inflammatory. Let us concede that the Rosenbergs preferred socialism to capitalism; how can Kaufman equate this with the treason conviction of Haupt? When Eugene Debs and Robert La Follette ran for President on Socialist platforms, millions of Americans voted for them. Millions of Americans today believe in socialism, even Chinese communism, as superior systems to that of capitalism. Their right to their beliefs is guaranteed by the First Amendment. How can any court equate such beliefs with "intent" to commit treason?

> "David Greenglass' story . . . gripped the courtroom. . . . His sister, Mrs. Rosenberg, grew pale; once she covered her eyes with her hands."
> —New York *Times,* March 11, 1951

1. THE SPY PROPOSAL TO RUTH [R. 421–424]

Continuing with the *Columbia* summary, let us return to our first heading as Cohn questions Greenglass concerning his first knowledge of the alleged conspiracy. Allegedly, it was during Ruth's five-day visit to Albuquerque, New Mexico, for their second wedding anniversary lasting from November 29 to December 3, 1944, at the Hotel Franciscan. Then on the day before Ruth's departure, the fourth day of their reunion, she finally decided to relay the Rosenberg's proposal to David:

A. [David]: . . . We went for a walk . . . and my wife started the conversation. My wife said that . . . Julius Rosenberg invited her to dinner at their house . . . and later on there was a conversation between the three present, my wife, my sister and my brother-in-law. . . . Ethel started the conversation by stating to Ruth that she must have noticed that she, Ethel, was no longer involved in Communist Party activities. . . .

Here we see an example of hearsay testimony, with David reporting what Ruth had told him outside the presence of the Rosenbergs, with no way for them to disprove it. Before comment, let us include Ruth's testimony regarding this initial step, as Assistant U.S. Attorney James B. Kilsheimer conducts her direct examination:

A. [Ruth]: Yes. *Julius said that I might have noticed* that for some time he and Ethel had not been actively pursuing any Communist Party activities, that they didn't buy the *Daily Worker* at the usual newsstand; that for two years he had been trying to get in touch with people who would assist him to be able to help the Russian people more directly other than just his membership in the Communist Party. . . . [Emphasis added.]

We will overlook the two different versions, whether it was Ethel who made the first advance or Julius. But, in either case, it will become evident that this portion of the testimony was intended to fit in with Bentley's subsequent testimony, namely, that Communists are ordered to drop "open" Party work when they take up "underground" work as spies.

[Ruth cont'd.]: And he [Julius] said—I wanted to know how he knew what David was doing. He said that his friends had told him that David was working on the atomic bomb, and he went on to tell me that the atomic bomb was the most destructive weapon used so far, *that it had dangerous radiation effects*, that the United States and Britain were work-

293

ing on this project jointly and that he felt that the information should be shared with Russia, who was our ally at the time, because if all nations had the information then one nation couldn't use the bomb as a threat against another.

[*Note:* In David's testimony, we will see that she gives him a different reason why Russia should receive the information.]

He said that he wanted me to tell my husband David that he should give information to Julius to be passed on to the Russians.

And at first I objected to this. I didn't think it was right. I said that the people who are in charge of the work on the bomb were in a better position to know whether the information should be shared or not.

Ethel Rosenberg said that I should at least tell it to David, that she felt that this was right for David, that he would want it, that I should give him the message and let him decide for himself, and by the —Julius and Ethel persuaded me to give my husband the message and they told me the information—

I decided to give my husband the message, and Julius Rosenberg told me the things that he wanted me to ask my husband, the information that he wanted me to bring back.

Q. And what information did he ask you to obtain from your husband if he should be willing to do it?

A. He wanted a physical description of the project at Los Alamos, the approximate number of people employed, the names of some of the scientists who were working there—something about whether the place was camouflaged, what the security measures were and the relative distance of the project to Albuquerque and Santa Fe. [R. 679–680; emphasis added.]

Here is a remarkably swift compliance suspiciously similar to that of Elitcher. She objects, doesn't think it right, but promptly plunges into the conspiracy as a full-blown courier. As for the Government's charge that it was the Rosenbergs who "sent" Ruth on this spy mission, in her direct examination, she admits having "planned" to visit David for their wedding anniversary.

2. DAVID'S CONSENT TO BECOME A SPY

Concerning David's own plunge into the conspiratorial pool, here are his reactions:

> . . . At first—she asked me what I thought about that—at first I was frightened and worried about it and I told her . . . I told my wife I wouldn't do it. And she had also told me that . . . Julius and Ethel had told her that Russia was an ally and as such deserved this information and that she wasn't getting the information that was coming to her. [R. 425–427]

We recall that the motivation of the Rosenbergs, as given by Ruth, was to break the atomic monopoly of the United States, to give Russia a counterthreat, in short to create the present condition of atomic stalemate.

However, this was a *1951* concept, and therefore an anachronism in 1944, five years before the Soviet Union had set off an atomic explosion. In other words, what Ruth was induced to say on the witness stand in 1951 was attributed to Julius in 1944—at least six months before the first atomic explosion at Alamogordo!

On the other hand, David's statement concerning the Rosenbergs' motivation is not only at variance with that of Ruth, but is in harmony with the thinking of 1944, namely, that Russia, *as an ally*, "deserved this information."

Thus, on this most vital point—motivation—we see these two opposed versions betraying the fact that too many coaching officials were involved in the frame-up.

In 1944, undoubtedly the Rosenbergs did voice disapproval of anti-Soviet spokesmen in the Pentagon for delaying the opening of a Second Front. It will be recalled that the slogan in such circles was to let "Russia bleed itself to death." In most liberal publications during the war years there was bitter criticism of those hoping to turn the war against Russia. Hence the feeling that Russia deserved to be treated as an ally was hardly a treasonable concept in 1944. In 1950–1951, however, such political comments by the Rosenbergs, as recalled by the Greenglasses in their conferences with the FBI and the prosecution, were obviously utilized to provide the important element of "motive."

Continuing with David's reaction:

[David]: So later on that night after the conversation, I thought about it and the following morning I told my wife that I would give the information.

Q. [Cohn]: Does that complete the conversation to the best of your memory that took place between you and your wife?

A. That's right. *Then when I told her what the conversation was*—I mean, I told her I would do it, she asked for specific things that Julius had asked her to find out from me. [Emphasis added.]

Examining this last response, it would appear that Greenglass fumbled, almost giving away the fact that it was *he* who had told *her* "what the conversation [with the Rosenbergs] was"!

But to reconstruct Greenglass' overnight decision: Here were two young people faced with a terrifying prospect. For days, Ruth was reluctant even to tell her husband about the proposal. And when she did, David expressed fear, worry, and outright refusal. Then he thought about it.

Thought about what? What caused him to change his mind overnight? According to Saypol the motivation of the Rosenbergs lay in their indoctrination as Communists and their blind obedience to orders from Moscow. But on what basis shall we accept the swift submission of the Greenglasses?

Ruth makes no claim that she had ever had any desire to aid the Soviet Union. From the start she didn't think it was right—in fact, had "refused." There were no appeals to Ruth to give one's all for the "Cause." Nothing but her in-laws saying that they were sure David would want to help and therefore the least she could do was to tell him about it.

The least she could do for whom? David? Was it her bounden duty as a wife to give her husband this golden opportunity to join a dangerous spy ring?

It is strange that so much is attested about the Communist affiliations, ideas, and beliefs of the Rosenbergs and Sobell, while nothing in the way of such "motive" is offered to explain that of David Greenglass.[5] The only testimony regarding his reasons for becoming a spy begins to emerge in cross-examination:

Q. [Bloch]: From the time that you told your wife that you were not interested and that you wouldn't do this work, to the following morning when you told her you would, did you consult with anybody?

A. I consulted with memories and voices in my mind. [R. 539]

It is difficult to assess Greenglass' reply other than unsurpassed impudence. In his summation, Mr. Bloch reminded the jury of the incident: "He was arrogant. He felt he had the Government of the United States behind him." [R. 1468]

Q. [Bloch]: . . . Did it occur to you at the time that you finally said to your wife "I will do this" and then transmitted to her certain information, that there was a possible penalty of death for espionage?

A. Yes.

Q. Are you aware that you are smiling?

A. Not very.

All through Greenglass' testimony there was intermittent smiling or grinning. In his summation, Emanuel Bloch made reference to this conduct as nothing less than animal-like, as he pointed to the horror of a man "who comes around to bury his own sister and smiles." Here is the New York *Times* of March 13 and 14 on this point:

The first public disclosure of . . . the super-secret Nagasaki-type atomic bomb came yesterday from the *smiling* lips of a witness. . . . Flashing his customary *smile,* the moon-faced witness said. . . . [Emphasis added.]

When we search the record for an explanation of Greenglass' overnight reversal other than his nocturnal "memories and voices," finally we find this admission:

Q. [Bloch]: And did you continue to think that what you were doing after November 29, 1944 . . . that you were doing the right thing?
A. I was having my doubts.
Q. When did you begin to have doubts?
A. Almost as soon as I started to do it. . . . I started to have doubts almost as soon as I said that I was going to give the information.

Thus, even while Greenglass is trying to provide believable motivation, he seeks to present himself as the reluctant pawn. And at this point Kaufman decides he needs help:

The Court: Now you saw Mr. Rosenberg in January [1945] within a short period of time after you had these doubts that you speak of; did you relate to him on that occasion that you had doubts about the propriety of it?
[Greenglass]: No, I did not say anything to him because . . . when I first started to do it, it was one of the motivating factors for doing it.
I had a kind of hero-worship there and I did not want my hero to fail, and I was doing the wrong thing by him. That is exactly why I did not stop the thing after I had the doubts.
Q. [Bloch]: You say you had a hero-worship?
A. That is right.
Q. Who was your hero?
A. Julius Rosenberg.

Let us now turn to the direct testimony of Ethel

as Judge Kaufman tries to use her to bolster David's hero-worship:

> The Court: Did he [David] sort of look up to you?
> A. [Ethel]: Yes.
> Q. And your husband?
> A. He liked us both. He liked my husband.
> Q. Sort of hero-worship?
> A. Oh, by no stretch of the imagination could you say that was hero-worship.
> Q. You heard him so testify, did you not?
> A. Yes, I did. [R. 1322]

Observe how Kaufman moves artlessly from "sort of look up to you" to "sort of hero-worship." Ethel makes no attempt to deny that her brother looked up to her and liked Julius, but when she fails to concede that this constitutes hero-worship, Kaufman gets in the last blow: "You heard him so testify, did you not?"

Is there anything in the record which corroborates this hero-worship of Julius? Nothing. On the contrary, it is replete with instances of David's deep-seated resentment and hostility, all of which came to the surface almost as soon as he entered the business venture with Julius:

> A. [Greenglass]: There were quarrels of every type and every kind. I mean there was arguments over personality, there was arguments over money, there was arguments over the way the shop was run, there was arguments over the way the outside was run. [R. 664]

Even if we concede the likelihood of hero-worship during David's teen-age period, is it conceivable that Greenglass, now two years married—seeing the war drawing to a close and eager to settle down and raise a family—would be so swept away by an adolescent hero-worship that he would knowingly take all the risks previously described?

And what about Ruth's influence as a wife? Can we

believe that the hard-headed Ruth would be convinced by such childish arguments as: "I did not want my hero to fail, and . . . doing the wrong thing by him"?

Finally, there is the Joint Committee Report's special section labeled "Motives." And although it speculates on what Greenglass' motivations may have been, the latter's claim of hero-worship—the *only* motive stated in the record—receives no consideration whatsoever! [6]

•

As we continue with this first claim of the Greenglasses regarding actual espionage, we will see that it was based on normal conversations such as would occur between a soldier and his wife who had not seen each other in some eight months.

Q. [Cohn]: Would you tell us . . . what your wife asked you?

A. She asked me to tell her about the general layout of the Los Alamos Atomic Project, the buildings, number of people and stuff like that; also scientists that worked there, and, that was the first information I gave her. [R. 425—426]

And here, in contrast, is Ruth's direct testimony:

Q. [Kilsheimer]: Now will you tell us . . . what information your husband gave you on that following day?

A. [Ruth]: Yes. He said that Los Alamos had formerly been a riding academy, that it was forty miles from Santa Fe and about 110 miles from Albuquerque,[7] that the project itself was on the top of a hill and it was secluded; you could hardly see it until you were almost on top of it; that there was a guard at the entrance at all times, and everyone was checked going in and out.

He told me the names of the scientists, Dr. Urey, Dr. Oppenheimer, Kistiakowski, Neils Bohr.

[*Note:* Here Ruth includes Dr. Urey, even though David first learned about his presence at Los Alamos in December, *after* her departure; see R. 411.]

David told me that he worked in an experimental shop, that he made models from blueprints that scientists brought in to him.

Q. And did he tell you the approximate number of people who were working at Los Alamos?

A. Yes, he did.

Q. Do you remember now what figure he gave you on that?

A. No, I don't recall.

Compare the two versions: Whereas Ruth gives a detailed description, David, who supposedly furnished the information, gives no details at all! Actually, all that happened was that a soldier told his wife in the most general terms where he was working and what he was doing. For example, take Ruth's memory of the exact mileages. The distances which David had to drive each weekend between Los Alamos and their Albuquerque flat were real to her, and therefore remained fixed in her mind.

[Ruth cont'd.]: I told him that Julius was interested in the physical description of the project at Los Alamos, the approximate number of people employed there, whether the place was camouflaged, what the security measures were, and the type of work that David himself did, and then my husband gave me the information.[8]

What could the Russians possibly gain from the knowledge that the project had once been a riding academy? And why should they want to know whether it was camouflaged? Did they contemplate sending a spy satellite to photograph it back in 1944? Let us note also that David's version never answers the alleged question regarding camouflage. And of what possible value was the information that there was a guard at the entrance and that all personnel were checked? Is this unusual for a military installation? Such wartime measures are common at every defense plant.

Finally, what did Julius allegedly learn about David's work? Only that he "worked in an experimental

301

shop [and] that he made models from blueprints that scientists brought in to him." What kind of shop? What type of blueprints? What sort of experimental models? Thus, here again, valueless information which any soldier might have told his wife quite casually before or after Ruth moved to Albuquerque.

In essence, the testimony discloses two striking improbabilities: First, if Julius, as a spy-master, were after the secret of the atomic bomb, then his questions would have been primarily directed to that end. Second, if the Russians had such a super-spy as Dr. Fuchs reporting to them since early 1944, then they must have known already that the nuclear physicists Drs. Oppenheimer, Bohr, and Urey were connected with the Los Alamos project.

Another contradiction: Until the moment of Ruth's message from Julius, David professes to have known nothing about the work going on at Los Alamos. And yet, on the "following morning," suddenly he has the *secret* names of Drs. Bohr, Oppenheimer, and Urey right on tap!

Returning to Ruth's testimony, it will be recalled that Julius informed her that the atomic work David was engaged in had "dangerous radiation effects." Hence, it is reasonable to ask: Would not a wife be anxious to hear about her husband's safety and health at the project? Do we find such normal anxiety in Ruth's testimony? Not a word. Nor, for that matter, is there any hint in David's testimony concerning the radiation effects to which he might be exposed.

Under cross-examination, Greenglass admits that he had full access to the technical area. Thus, not only was the danger of alpha, beta, gamma, and neutron rays well known at the project, but every possible precaution was taken. Therefore, to accept the Greenglass' testimony, we must also accept that David and Ruth were totally indifferent both to the danger and to the precautions.

In line with this point, we are asked to believe that Ruth did not mention the knowledge she possessed, "that David was working on the atomic bomb," until the *fourth* day of their reunion. And while it is reasonable to believe that a young wife might put aside all other matters to celebrate her wedding anniversary, it is just inconceivable that she would not even *mention* the possibility of the "dangerous radiation effects" for three days!

In their entire testimony, there is no explanation for this extraordinary delay other than the passing comment made by David concerning Ruth's reluctance to tell him about Julius' spy proposal:

She told me she didn't think it was a good idea. And that she didn't want to tell me about it.

Let us ponder this a moment. Here is a momentous decision involving risk of the death penalty. Not once, in relaying the spy proposal, does Ruth give utterance to any expression of anxiety. Only that it might not be "a good idea." Would she not have said: "Look, Dave, maybe you better think it over; we're not playing with marbles. If you still want to do it, you can always tell them so when you come home on furlough; it's only a few weeks off."

Now Greenglass' annual furlough was due only twenty-nine days later, on January 1, 1945. It is a cardinal principle among spies to avoid unnecessary risks and to involve as few persons as possible. Why should the Rosenbergs have involved Ruth in the conspiracy, when they could have spoken to David confidentially in so short a time?

It may be argued that the Russians were in desperate haste to secure information on the atomic bomb as quickly as possible. But we have seen that Julius' queries had nothing to do with the bomb. Furthermore, we have it from J. Edgar Hoover that Julius' superior, Yakovlev, was informed by Gold that Dr. Fuchs was expected "home for a Christmas visit." (*Note*: This would be Christmas, 1944. Hoover writes further in the *Reader's Digest* that Fuchs and Gold "reestablished contact in Cambridge . . . shortly after Christmas.") As for the date when Ruth transmitted David's "information" to Julius in New York, we find it to be on or about December 10, 1944. [R. 3]

Strange that the KGB, entrusted with the most important mission in history, should take this unnecessary risk with the Greenglasses for such valueless information, when all they had to do was wait some two weeks for Dr. Fuchs' expected arrival on or before December 25. Here is the Joint Report describing the value of Dr. Fuchs to the Russians:

In August 1944, Fuchs moved to Los Alamos . . . and worked there until June, 1946. He took part in the making of the earliest atomic bombs; he was privy to ideas and plans for improved atomic weapons, and he possessed insight into the thinking of the period as regards the hydrogen bomb. . . . No information . . . was withheld from him. . . .[9] [Emphasis added.]

In David's testimony describing his January furlough in New York, we note a most lackadaisical attitude on the part of Julius. Instead of seeing his new recruit promptly, we find this:

Q. [Cohn]: After your arrival in New York, did there come a time when you saw the defendant Julius Rosenberg?
A. Yes, he came to me one morning and asked me to give him information, specifically anything of value on the atomic bomb, whatever I knew about it.
Q. About how long after you had arrived in New York did this conversation take place?
A. *A few days* after I arrived. [Emphasis added.]

Thus, not only was there no haste concerning David, but according to Ruth's testimony, Julius' disinterest was such that he did not come to see her until "two or three days" after her return from Albuquerque in December.
Finally: Why did the Rosenbergs take this unnecessary risk with Ruth? Suppose David flatly refused? Hero-worship when he was a youth of seventeen? But that had been five years before. And why recruit him by proxy via Ruth? For, if she refused, they would have exposed themselves in vain. Moreover, how could they take a chance on what Ruth might feel toward them after a possible quarrelsome divorce?
To sum up: The Greenglass testimony is unworthy

of belief at every stage. Not only do the Greenglasses present conflicting testimony about the Rosenbergs' motivation but, on the face of it, Ruth's version is a fabrication in tune with the Government thinking of 1951. Improbabilities exist at every turn, from their lack of concern about the radiation effects to the unbelievable three-day delay. As for the information allegedly transmitted to Julius, we have seen that it was not only valueless but that it was basically the product of normal conversations between husband and wife.

In short, it was the easiest kind of testimony for the Greenglasses to supply the prosecution, because all they had to do was add to a harmless anniversary reunion a falsity here and a distortion there.

3. THE EVENTS OF JANUARY, 1945 [10]

We have seen that Julius allegedly waited a few days after David's arrival in New York, then received this additional information:

    1. "A list of scientists who worked on the project."

    2. "Some possible recruits . . . for Soviet espionage."

    3. "A sketch of the [High Explosive] lens mold," plus a written description "on a separate sheet of paper."

Concerning the scientists, these turned out to be the same names allegedly given to Ruth in Albuquerque. It would be understandable if Julius had asked for additional names, but the repetition would indicate that Greenglass was instructed to "build up" the quantity of information given Julius on this occasion.

Concerning the spy recruits, it is significant that Roy Cohn does not ask Greenglass for any specific names, nor are any furnished. In Elitcher's testimony, too, there is this recurrent theme of having Sobell ask for possible spy recruits, and there, too, no names are given. Thus another "build-up"—this one establishing the formula that sympathy-to-Communism equals willing-spy-recruits.

As for the sketch of the lens mold, right at the

outset we find exaggeration. Instead of "a number of sketches," as first claimed, soon they are reduced to but a single sketch:

> Q. [Cohn]: Now, Mr. Greenglass, have you at our request prepared *a copy of the sketch* of the lens mold which you furnished to Rosenberg on that day in January? [Emphasis added.]

At this point we come to some legal hocus-pocus. This "copy" was not, of course, made of the original sketch at the time of the alleged crime, but "prepared" on the eleventh floor of the Tombs just before trial, *i.e.*, six years later. And, as the case proceeded, this "copy" was admitted into evidence as Government Exhibit 2. In an attempt to demonstrate that a "copy" was not corroboration but merely a self-serving device, the defense asked Greenglass:

> Mr. E. H. Bloch: When did you prepare this?
> A. During this trial, yesterday. [R. 439–440]

Although Kaufman conceded that it did not constitute proper corroboration, nevertheless he admitted it as "chart evidence" which would be enlightening to the jury. However, Bloch pointed to the rule that chart evidence must be explanatory only, and must not be submitted as a *true copy* for the obvious reason that the jury might accept it as such. But despite defense objections, Kaufman sided with the prosecution, and the sketch which Greenglass had prepared only "yesterday" became *evidence*. It did not matter two weeks later that Julius denied receiving any such sketch. The denial was only verbal, whereas the exhibit shown to the jury appeared real and tangible!

(*Note:* Later, other "copies" of other alleged sketches given to Gold and Rosenberg were also admitted into evidence as Government Exhibits 6, 7, and 8.)

Soon we will take up the question of Greenglass' capacity to obtain and transmit the complex data he claimed to have delivered in 1945 and to have duplicated exactly in 1951 without assistance, but at this point it may suffice to give a brief illustration of his limitations:

Q. [Bloch]: You did not even know the formula for the curvature [of the lens mold], did you? . . . You had to be a scientist to know the formula, isn't that right?
A. That is right. [R. 628]

4. THE TYPING BY ETHEL [R. 443, 450–451]

In this stage of the *Columbia* summary, we will deal with the Government's primary accusation against Ethel Rosenberg—namely, her typing of David's written descriptions of the two sketches he gave to Julius: (1) that of the lens mold given in January, 1945, and (2) that of the cross-section of the Nagasaki atomic bomb given in September, 1945. For the present, we will deal only with the January incident after Julius came to see David and the latter had agreed to prepare the sketch and description of the lens mold:

[David]: . . . And my wife, in passing, remarked that the handwriting would be bad and would need interpretation, and Julius said there was nothing to worry about as Ethel would type it up, retype the information.

Following this, Greenglass tells how he and Ruth, in response to a dinner invitation, went to the Rosenberg apartment "two or three days" later:

A. And Ethel remarked that she was tired between the child and staying up late at night, keeping— typing over notes that Julius had brought her—this was on espionage.
Mr. E. H. Bloch: I move to strike that out [espionage].
The Court: Did she say that [espionage]?
The Witness: She said "in this work." She also stated that she didn't mind it so long as Julius was doing what he wanted to do.

Here is Ruth's direct testimony concerning this incident:

> [Ruth]: Well, Ethel said that she was tired, and I asked her what she had been doing. She said she had been typing; and I asked her if she had found David's notes hard to distinguish. She said no, she was used to his handwriting. [R. 691]

It will be recalled that David's description of the sketch was on *one sheet* of paper (actually only a few sentences). In addition, we see that Ethel had no difficulty with "his handwriting." And since the Rosenbergs had received the information two or three days before, we may presume that Ethel had typed it promptly in a matter of a few minutes. Hence, why should Ethel have found it necessary to stay up so "late at night" and why should she still feel tired two or three days later?

With regard to Greenglass' insertion of the word "espionage," it is significant how he quickly changes it to the phrase "in this work." Like Elitcher, he had been over-rehearsed and so intent on serving the prosecution that he, too, inserts the word "espionage" whenever possible.

No doubt it was true that Ethel was tired from both housework and child-caring, and she may have even been up late the night before typing Julius' grievance appeals for his union. This subject would have been normal for Ethel to mention or even to complain about to a brother and sister-in-law. And it was apparently this sort of small talk which was later elaborated into an act of espionage. Thus the full horror of Ethel's tragic fate becomes so striking in Greenglass' final remark:

> . . . She also stated that she didn't mind it [the typing] as long as Julius was doing what he wanted to do.

This statement, even if we take it at face value as true, has only one possible interpretation: that Julius was the *prime mover* of the conspiracy and that Ethel

308

went along or put up with it only because she desired to please her husband, and *not* because she was the driving force behind Julius. And yet, despite this clear statement made by the *only* witness accusing Ethel, Judge Kaufman characterized her as a "full-fledged partner in this crime" and found her equally deserving of death.

(*Note:* Since the testimony of David and Ruth was that of man and wife, it may be viewed as that of a single witness.)

5. THE JELLO-BOX RECOGNITION DEVICE [11]

Certainly the most vivid portion of the Greenglass testimony was the Jello-box episode. It was the feature most played up by the press, but needless to say, no news account included the fact that Greenglass' partner in the episode, Harry Gold, was his bunkmate for almost nine months before trial.

In the anatomy of frame-up we drew special attention to the point that although the mass of perjured testimony consists largely of half-truths, half-lies, distortions of truth, extensions of truth sprinkled with nuances, innuendoes, and insinuations, there is nevertheless an unavoidable core of outright collusion during which the testimony is deliberately manufactured. Perhaps nowhere in the Government's case is this manufactured product more concretely illustrated than in the episode of the Jello-box.

The first part of the episode, according to the Greenglasses, took place during the early evening of January 5, 1945, at the Rosenberg flat, where David and Ruth had been invited for dinner. Thus we have an innocent foundation of a normal family visit upon which was subsequently built this cloak-and-dagger meeting of plotting conspirators.

Arriving at the Monroe Street flat, David and Ruth were introduced to an old friend of the Rosenbergs, a Mrs. Ann Sidorovich, who had dropped in for an afternoon chat with Ethel. According to the Greenglass testimony, after about a half hour of social conversation, Mrs. Sidorovich departed and Ethel prepared to serve dinner.

So far, we observe that everything is quite prosaic. The husband of Mrs. Sidorovich, Michael, also an engineer, had been a high-school chum of Julius. The Sidorovich couple had once resided at the same address. In the record, we see the undisputed evidence of their frequent visits with nothing of any incriminating nature.

However, as soon as the Rosenbergs were left alone with the Greenglasses (according to their testimony), the conspiratorial part of the evening began. In other words, with Mrs. Sidorovich no longer a possible witness to disprove the Greenglasses' testimony—only then are we told that Julius divulged her role as a fellow-conspirator. Here is the gist of the Greenglasses' further testimony:

That in a few months Ruth was to take up residence with her husband in Albuquerque. That Mrs. Sidorovich would probably be the courier sent out to receive such further information as David might have ready. That arrangements would be made for the two women to meet in a movie theater in Denver where they would exchange purses, with Ruth's purse containing the secret information.

That another plan to meet in Albuquerque was discussed, and here David had suggested that the best possible rendezvous would be in front of a certain Safeway store.

That when Julius mentioned the possibility that someone other than Mrs. Sidorovich might be the courier, Ruth had asked how would they be able to identify the substitute.

That Julius then proposed the Jello-box recognition device, which, according to the Greenglasses, was arranged as follows:

That Julius had removed the instruction side of a Jello box and had cut it into two irregular halves. That Ruth was given one half to retain until the day the substitute courier would arrive with the other matching half. And that the decision of the exact time of the rendezvous was to be held in abeyance until Ruth's departure for New Mexico.

For the purpose of our analysis, the following chronology is necessary to explain the events that ensued, according to the Greenglasses' testimony:

1. About January 20 David's furlough time expired and he returned to Los Alamos.
2. In the first week of February, according to Ruth, Julius visited her flat to give her specific instructions about the meeting in front of the Safeway store. It was to take place late in April or early in May.
3. On February 28 Ruth left New York to find work in Albuquerque.
4. On April 18 Ruth suffered a miscarriage and apprised Ethel of that fact by letter.
5. Whereupon Ethel, we are told by Ruth, replied that "a member of the family" would visit her on the third or fourth Saturday in May.
6. Obeying these instructions, Ruth went to the Safeway store on both these dates (once with David), but no courier showed up.
7. On June 3, we are told, a stranger (Harry Gold) appeared at the Greenglass apartment bearing the matching Jello-box half, and David gave Gold additional material on the High Explosive Lens.

Right at the outset, there is a sharp contradiction. In describing the conversation before Mrs. Sidorovich left, Ruth tells that it consisted of: ". . . Just the usual pleasantries and playing with the child [Michael Rosenberg, then two years old] and talk about ordinary things." Then, after Mrs. Sidorovich's departure:

[Ruth]: Julius Rosenberg said that he had Ann Sidorovich come to his apartment just so that we would be able to recognize her and she know us when she came out to us to get information. . . .

Now let us turn to a page in the record just previous to the above:

Q. [Kilsheimer]: Had you met Ann Sidorovich prior to that evening?

A. [Ruth]: Yes. [R. 687]

Why, if the two women had *previously* met, was it necessary for Julius to arrange this mutual inspection meeting? On the other hand, if Julius was uncertain that Ann Sidorovich would be the courier, why would he do what is absolutely forbidden in espionage? Why would he expose her to the Greenglasses and vice versa? Or, to pursue the point to its final absurdity, if he could think up the Jello-box recognition device for Mrs. Sidorovich's substitute, why didn't he simply arrange the same device for her?

Finally, why the avoidance of all conspiratorial conversation until *after* Mrs. Sidorovich had gone? Since everything had been exposed anyway, why couldn't the details of the two women exchanging purses in the Denver movie be thoroughly ironed out by them directly? In short, why did all the spy talk take place in Ann Sidorovich's *absence?*

For a very simple reason: If the Greenglasses had included Mrs. Sidorovich in the actual arrangements, then the defense could have called her as a witness to deny it! But since she was not present, her testimony would have no bearing. Which explains why she was not called as a defense witness. Even so, the prosecution thwarted any such possible step by announcing both Mr. and Mrs. Sidorovich on its list of Government witnesses. Thus the defense was deceived into believing that even these good friends of the Rosenbergs had been pressured into testifying against them. And, of course, Mrs. Sidorovich was never called to corroborate the Greenglass testimony.[12]

Whichever way one examines the Greenglass testimony, it falls apart. Why was the cloak-and-dagger meeting in the Denver movie so promptly discarded? Why all these spy-thriller precautions with Ruth traveling all the way to Denver, when only a moment later the Safeway rendezvous in Albuquerque becomes perfectly safe? And why, when the alleged rendezvous between Gold and Greenglass does take place, is it in the latter's own apartment with Gold having been given Greenglass' real name and address?

Which brings us to the ultimate in this plethora of

nonsense: *Why was the Jello-box recognition device necessary at all?* Why not a password? If Gold and Bentley were Soviet spies, then why was their use of passwords not also used by Julius? Finally, the reasonable mind must ask itself, why would Julius bother to send Mrs. Sidorovich or any courier when Ruth was available? Why couldn't she simply bring further information directly to Julius in New York or to Ethel in Denver rather than arranging an exchange of purses with Mrs. Sidorovich? Because such a safe and sane method would have eliminated both the Jello-box and Harry Gold from the Greenglass story, and thereby removed from the Government's case its "necessary link."

●

In the courtroom the fanciful tale of the Jello-box episode was given the same illusion of reality as Greenglass' "eleventh floor" copies of the sketches. A *sample* Jello box, despite defense objections, was admitted into evidence as Government Exhibit 4. Whereupon Greenglass was handed a pair of scissors by Roy Cohn and told to cut the sample Jello-box side into two halves as Julius had allegedly done. The half he claimed to have received from Julius was designated Exhibit 4A; and the half supposedly last seen in Julius' possession became 4B.

Meanwhile, the jury, as it gaped wide-eyed at the Jello-box ceremony, had long since forgotten about Ann Sidorovich as a possible courier. "Sidorovich" was a fine Russian-sounding name to include in the conspiracy. It had served Saypol's purpose. What had happened to the plan for the exchange of purses in the Denver movie? Nothing! It had served to heighten the melodrama and, as J. Edgar Hoover has written, people tend to believe the bizarre rather than prosaic truth.[13] What had happened to the Safeway store rendezvous? Nothing! But it left yet another bit of intriguing detail to linger in the minds of the jury.

> "I am in blood
> Stepp'd in so far that, should I wade no
> more,
> Returning were as tedious as go o'er."
> —*Macbeth*

In Chapter 6 on David Greenglass, explaining the process of his self-entrapment, we quoted passages from his confidential statement to Rogge. As indicated, this statement came to light with other Rogge memos almost two years after the trial. In it, Greenglass apparently informed Rogge what he had "confessed" to the FBI during his twelve-hour interrogation at the time of his arrest.

At the trial he insisted that he had withheld nothing substantial during this interrogation. However, his own report to Rogge reveals this to be false. For it not only fails to mention the most important secret he claims to have delivered to Julius—the cross-section of the Nagasaki atomic bomb—but there is not a single reference to the Jello-box episode as it later involved the Rosenbergs! [See Appendix 2.]

In other words, if we are to believe the Greenglass testimony about Julius initiating the Jello-box incident, we are faced with the paradox that the FBI would have remained content with a full story of the conspiracy, but one which omitted the two most important events of that conspiracy!

6. THE MEETING WITH "THE RUSSIAN" [14]

The grand strategy of the prosecution at the Rosenberg trial was to prove a chain of guilt. It was for this reason that the Jello-box episode was found necessary. The links of this chain were to be: (1) Rosenberg connected with the Russian official, Yakovlev; (2) Yakovlev with Gold; (3) Gold with Greenglass; and finally, (4) Greenglass with Rosenberg.

However, although the prosecution had indicted Yakovlev in absentia, and although Gold was ready to testify about *his* meetings with that official, the only way it could show any link between Julius and Yakovlev was through the *inference* that the Jello-box card subsequently given Gold was originally delivered to Yakovlev by Rosenberg.

Evidently the prosecution felt the need for a more convincing link to fill this gap of inference. In short, a "Russian" had to be invented to serve either as Yakovlev or as the missing link.

This was accomplished by simply having Greenglass create a "Russian" out of a "man." How do we know that this embroidery took place? By comparing Greenglass' confidential report to Rogge with his trial testimony nine months later. Here are excerpts from this report concerning an alleged rendezvous taking place during Greenglass' furlough in New York in January of 1945:

I then mentioned a meeting with *a man* who I didn't know, arranged by Julius. . . . The place was a car, an Olds owned by my father-in-law, at somewhere above 42nd St. on 1st Ave. in Manhattan. I talked to *the man* but I could recall very little about which we spoke. [Emphasis added.]

Here, we detect not the slightest hint of any Russian. Now to Greenglass' testimony at the trial:

Q. [Cohn]: Did he [Julius] tell you who this person he wanted you to meet was?
A. [Greenglass]: He said it was *a Russian* he wanted me to meet. [Emphasis added.]

As we see, the "Russian" linked to Julius at the trial was *only* a "man" at the time of Greenglass' arrest. To expose the extent of Greenglass' perjured testimony, there is another officially acknowledged memo which reveals that Greenglass was asked if "the man" was a Russian. It is a memo written the very next morning after Greenglass' interrogation. Rogge's associate, Herbert Fabricant, had come to interview Greenglass in the FBI suite. Here is the last sentence of this memo:

He [Greenglass] *did not know* if the man was a Russian and told the FBI that *he didn't know*. [Emphasis added.]

•

In our examination of the Jello-box testimony we have postponed analysis of the final incident—the matching of the two halves by Gold and Greenglass. Since we have arrived at that section of the *Columbia* summary referring to Gold's alleged visit to New Mexico in June, 1945, let us now analyze his testimony regarding that "Land of Enchantment."

NOTES AND REFERENCES

1. New York *Times*, March 10, 1951.
2. "The Self-Inflated Target," *Time*, March 22, 1954.
3. See "The Adventures of Cohn and Schine," in *The Reporter*, July 21, 1953.
4. *Columbia Law Review*, pp. 220–221. For David Greenglass' direct, see Record, pp. 394–466, 489–537; for Ruth Greenglass' direct, see Record, pp. 677–714.
5. See Rogge's insistence that the Greenglasses had always resisted "attempted indoctrination" by the Rosenbergs:
   David and Ruth Greenglass, yes, wanted to see a better world, but they did not want to see a Communist one. (Record, pp. 1625–1626.)
   See also Records, pp. 540, 551–553.
6. Joint Report, p. 11.
7. In later testimony, Ruth admits that she learned these distances during her stay in Albuquerque, presumably from innocent conversations. (Record, p. 754.)
8. Under cross-examination, the defense exposed what was obviously a "studied rehearsal" by asking Ruth to repeat these instructions, which she did almost *verbatim*. Compare Record, pp. 682 and 683 with pp. 727 and 728.
9. *Op. cit.*, pp. 1, 6.
10. For David's direct, see Record, pp. 427–429, 438–454.

11. For David's direct, see pp. 443–450; Ruth's, pp. 686–690.

12. Ann Sidorovich testified before the Grand Jury in 1950 that the Greenglass story of their meeting was completely false and, despite continuing pressure by the FBI, steadfastly denied ever having any connection with any espionage.

13. J. Edgar Hoover, *Persons in Hiding*, Little, Brown & Co., Boston, 1938. In writing about Gaston B. Means, "a former important FBI official," whom Mr. Hoover describes as "the greatest fakir of all times," we are given this insight into the success of Mr. Means' "grotesque" and "concocted" stories: "He played upon the love for melodrama which exists in almost everyone. . . . Means was sufficiently canny to realize that a plausible story might easily be checked; his task therefore was to make his adventures so unbelievably melodramatic that their very outrageousness made them seem overwhelmingly sane."

14. For David's direct, Record, pp. 452–454; cross-examination, pp. 651–653.

ADDENDA

With regard to the Greenglass testimony, the most crucial of all, here is another favorable comment on our analysis in the *New York University Law Review* of April, 1956, which the Pollack report avoids mentioning:

Wexley is also on relatively strong ground in his analysis of the Greenglass testimony.

Whereas the reviewer disagrees (without stating anything specific) with "some of [my] arguments" he stresses that "there is a remainder which presents disturbing questions." For example, the absence of a credible motive:

It is odd that Greenglass, a non-Communist, could be so easily led into a life of high crime.

And to this, the reviewer adds the footnote: "As his

317

motive, Greenglass lamely mentioned 'hero-worship' of Julius." As for David's claim to have "secured the secrets of the atom bomb from overhearing scientists' conversations," there is the reviewer's total agreement with almost every point we have presented.

•

In an FBI memo of July 22, 1950, referred to in the Pollack report, we find a most significant disclosure regarding letters received by David Greenglass from his wife and from the Rosenbergs while he was working at the Los Alamos Atomic Project. Here is Pollack's excerpt from one of Ruth's letters to David in May, 1943:

Dearest, remember what Julius told you, as a Communist it is up to you to set an example to other soldiers.

As for the letter written by Julius and Ethel, in November, 1943, we are told that they were writing David about having attended "a Communist rally where Paul Robeson, the notorious Communist, opened the meeting by singing."

The pejorative description of the late Paul Robeson as "notorious" must, of course, be Pollack's, but regardless of this bias toward an American folk-hero, these disclosures further expose the essential weakness of the Government's case, *i.e.,* that Julius was a super-spy at the head of a nationwide spy ring.

If this were so, surely Julius would have been more cautious, knowing that army mail could be censored. But, since in these letters, the Rosenbergs made no effort to conceal their Communist sympathies or activities, and indeed, spoke and wrote of them openly, it follows that they had no feeling of guilt or fear of apprehension as Soviet spies.

Second, there is the detailed Greenglass testimony that the Rosenbergs (in recruiting Ruth) had explained how they had cautiously dropped *all* Communist activities before becoming spies so as not to invite suspicion regarding their espionage work. If true, then their *continued* Communist activities completely contradicts whatever logic there may have been to such testimony.

Finally, we see that David *kept* these "incriminating" letters, not only during the years of his alleged espionage (1944–1946), but even to the moment of his arrest in 1950. In this event, it is inconceivable that the Greenglasses, as spies, conscious of guilt, would retain such potentially damaging evidence.

Thus, ironically, these letters referred to so triumphantly by Pollack, instead of providing further motivational proof of guilt by intent, achieve an opposite result. The fact that the Rosenbergs were so open and candid about their leftist leanings, negates the charge that they acted secretly and furtively as Kremlin-directed spies. It also explains why these letters obtained by the FBI in July, 1950, were *never* produced by the prosecution at the trial in March, 1951.

16 ALL IS NOT GOLD . . .

I

> "Wilder and wilder the story became . . .
> on and on went the melodrama. . . ." [1]

On the morning of March 15—indeed the Ides of March—Harry Gold took the witness stand. In discussing his appearance with observers at the trial, the author found that the most outstanding reaction was that he looked like a dead man. His manner of delivery was devoid of emotion, with the sound of a mechanical recital as though it were coming from a phonograph record. But it was the expression in his eyes that was the most striking; they were like the eyes of a dead fish.

Some idea of the interest his testimony aroused can be measured by the "star" billing in the New York *Times* headline of March 16, 1951:

ADMITTED SPY, GOLD IS STAR U. S. WITNESS

His direct examination was conducted by Saypol's senior assistant, Myles J. Lane, and for the most part can be described as a series of conversations between Gold and Yakovlev. [2] Although many of these conversations concerned Gold's meetings with Dr. Fuchs

319

and in no way implicated the Rosenbergs, neverthe-less Judge Kaufman permitted them to be recited in detail on the grounds that the absent Yakovlev had been named in the indictment. Thus, under the "con-spiracy ruling," although Fuchs, Gold, and Yakovlev were perfect strangers to the Rosenbergs, their alleged conversations were admitted as evidence.

7. THE VISIT OF HARRY GOLD [R. 820–829]

According to Gold's testimony, he visited the Green-glasses in Albuquerque after having previously met with Fuchs in Santa Fe.

Let us now examine the testimony of this trip step by step, beginning with Gold's briefing by Yakovlev on May 27, 1945.

Previous to this briefing, Gold tells us that he had notified Yakovlev about a prearranged rendezvous with Fuchs for June 2 in Santa Fe. And that it was at this May 27 briefing that Yakovlev instructed him to take on the additional mission to Greenglass:

[Gold]: I told Yakovlev that I did not wish to take on this additional task. Yakovlev told me that the matter was very vital and that I had to do it. He said that a woman was supposed to go in place of me but that she was unable to make the trip. He said therefore, he said that I had to go.

I told Yakovlev that it was highly inadvisable to endanger the very important trip to see Dr. Fuchs with this additional task. Yakovlev told me that I didn't understand that this was an extremely im-portant business, that I just had to go to Albu-querque, in addition to going to Santa Fe, and he said, "That is an order"; and that was all. I agreed to go.

Since no testimony exists that there was vital in-formation ready at this particular time, why should Yakovlev be so insistent about obtaining some doubt-ful information from Greenglass, and thereby endanger the certainty of obtaining critical information from Dr. Fuchs? Moreover, in earlier testimony Gold tells us: "I was having difficulty at this time getting off from work."³

Suppose Gold just could not manage the extra time required to see Greenglass? Were there only two couriers available in the entire spy ring—Ann Sidorovich and Harry Gold? Or are we to believe that the Russians were determined to save an extra railroad fare at the risk of endangering the most valuable secret in world history?

As for Gold's attempt to paint Yakovlev as a stern commissar giving brusque orders, this convenient procedure—the explaining away of improbabilities by the "built-in justification"—is reminiscent of Elizabeth Bentley's tactics at the Brothman trial. It will be recalled how she tried to explain away the illogic of the Brothman-Gold rendezvous by the flat assertion that it was a "decision of the Communist Party and that [Brothman] must abide by it."⁴

Another improbability: that the "woman" (by inference: Ann Sidorovich) "was unable to make the trip." Did not the Greenglasses tell us that Julius was doubtful about her on January 5, almost five months earlier? Wasn't this the reason for arranging the Jello-box device?

When we search for an explanation to this improbable testimony, we find it, of course, on the "eleventh floor." It was Gold's task to bolster Greenglass' testimony about Ann Sidorovich by insinuation.

It is interesting to follow the mechanism of this character assassination. First comes the testimony of the Greenglasses, who relate what Julius had supposedly told them about Mrs. Sidorovich being a courier. Then comes Gold, who glibly invents a series of conversations with a Russian official. Which Russian official? Any one (what difference?)—but preferably one who has left the country some years ago.⁵ And now, during one of these imaginary conversations, Gold needs only to mention that Yakovlev told him about a certain woman courier and lo—another link in the chain has been forged!

II

Here is Gold's further testimony following his agreement to obey Yakovlev's "order" to undertake the double mission:

[Gold]: Yakovlev then gave me a sheet of paper; it was onionskin paper, and on it was typed the following: First, the name "Greenglass," just "Greenglass." Then a number "High Street"; all that I can recall about the number is that the last figure—it was a low number and the last figure, the second figure was "0" and the last figure was either 5, 7 or 9; and then underneath that was "Albuquerque, New Mexico."

The last thing that was on the paper was "Recognition signal. I come from Julius."

In addition to this, Yakovlev gave me a piece of cardboard, which appeared to have been cut from a packaged food of some sort. It was cut in an odd shape and Yakovlev told me that the man Greenglass, whom I would meet in Albuquerque, would have the matching piece of cardboard. Yakovlev told me that just in case the man Greenglass should not be present when I called in Albuquerque, that his wife would have the information and that she would turn it over to me. Yakovlev gave me an envelope which he said contained $500, and he told me to give it to Greenglass. Yakovlev told me that I should follow a very devious route on my way to Santa Fe and to Albuquerque. He said that I should first go to Phoenix, Arizona; then to El Paso, and from there to Santa Fe. Yakovlev said that I should do this to minimize any danger of being followed.

The last thing that took place on this last Saturday in May was that Yakovlev and I arranged for two meetings upon my return from the Southwest.

Q. [Kaufman]: Was there any route to be followed from Santa Fe to Albuquerque?

A. [Gold]: He didn't specify, your Honor. There

is only one way that I know of to get from there. They are 60 miles apart and there is a bus runs between them.

Let us first examine Gold's artful pretense that he cannot recall the exact address of 209 North High Street. It is almost amusing to see how disingenuously he labors to remember it, as though anyone would expect such a feat after six years from a single, brief visit to a stranger's address. Observe the play acting as he recalls that the second figure was precisely an "0," and then the floundering with the last figure being a 5, 7, or 9.

But Gold had spent nine months with Greenglass on the eleventh floor of the Tombs! Are we to believe that Greenglass never mentioned his Albuquerque address to Gold? Or that Gold never discussed his visit there with the FBI? Here is Greenglass' memo to Rogge written back in June, 1950:

I stated [to the FBI] that I met Gold in N.M. at 209 N. High St., my place.

Concerning the alleged "recognition signal"—at once we see that these *actual words* were written down together with the password "I come from Julius," and Greenglass' address! What if Yakovlev or Gold were caught with this information? An Albuquerque address of a soldier employed at the Los Alamos Atomic Project would be bad enough, but we are also asked to believe that a Soviet Vice-Consul would be so idiotic as to write down the incriminating words "Recognition signal"!

Furthermore, if Yakovlev had to write down the address, why couldn't he limit it simply to "209 North High St"? Why did he have to make it so specific by adding "Albuquerque, New Mexico"? If Gold could commit these elementary instructions to memory (as he was allegedly advised), why couldn't Yakovlev do the same and thereby avoid carrying such damning evidence on his person?

Concerning the password itself—"I come from Julius"—why is it that no other spy-master or courier uses his real name? Yakovlev is "John"; Semenov is

"Sam"; Bentley is "Helen"; Golos is "Timmy"; and Gold himself is "Raymond" or "Martin" or "Dave from Pittsburgh." Why is it that *only* Julius Rosenberg uses his real name? The answer is obvious. It was Gold's task to link a "Julius" with Yakovlev in order to complete the chain of guilt. If some fictitious name had been used, for example, "Joe," how could the prosecution prove that "Joe" was indeed Julius Rosenberg?

In analyzing the "Recognition signal" we will see that the record itself exposes the palpable fraud of the Jello-box routine. Let us return to the Rosenberg apartment, where Ruth was supposed to have asked Julius how to recognize the courier substitute for Mrs. Sidorovich. Here is David's version of Julius' reply:

> [David]: So Julius said to my wife, "Well, I give you something so that you will be able to identify the person that does come." [R. 446]

In contrast, here is Ruth's version telling how Julius gave her the half of the Jello-box side which she placed in her wallet:

> [Ruth]: . . . And he said, "This half will be brought to you by another party and he will bear the greetings from me and you will know that I have sent him." [R. 689]

It will be seen that David's version contains no recognition signal such as "I come from Julius." It states *only* that the courier will carry an identifiable article, namely, the half of the Jello-box side. On the other hand, Ruth's version implies the use of a password. But why is this password not *explicit* in Julius' instructions if it was designed to be relayed to Gold in the precise words: "I come from Julius"?

"Greetings"; this is the key word in Ruth's version —and yet when the recognition signal is given to Gold, there is no hint of this word.

As we skip ahead to the subsequent testimony of the Greenglasses and Gold describing the latter's arrival at their Albuquerque apartment, we see that on this vital point there are three different versions:

[Gold]: I said, "I came from Julius." [R. 825]

[David]: He said, "Julius sent me." [R. 457]

[Ruth]: He said he bore greetings from Julius. [R. 699]

Now a password is a password and, when it has been written down as a "Recognition signal," certainly the bearer should remember it accurately, especially one with so phenomenal a memory as Gold. As for David, who claims to recall every detail of the cross-section of the Nagasaki atom bomb after six years, we see that he cannot recall anything resembling Gold's password, except the name of Julius.

And finally there is Ruth—sticking to her version, rehearsed with Kilsheimer, while Cohn rehearsed with Greenglass, and Lane rehearsed with Gold. One can readily visualize one of these worthies cautioning his witness, "Now don't worry about getting too exact on every detail or else it might sound like you all got together. The recognition signal? Well, don't worry about what the others will say. Just don't forget the name 'Julius': that's the important thing."

Is this too unpleasant to accept? Then let us remember the many conferences which Greenglass admits. And let us also bear in mind Greenglass' handwritten report of what he originally stated to the FBI: "Also, I didn't know who sent Gold to me."

•

Concerning Gold's description of the "piece of cardboard," notice how he resorts to the dissimulation that it "appeared to be a packaged food of some sort." Why does he do this? Because, in his effort to be oh-so-precise, he would have us believe that his half of the card did not include the word "Jello." However, according to Ruth Greenglass, the side which Julius cut up was the "Directions" side, and if the reader will glance at any package of Jello he will see that these directions contain the word "Jello" no less than *eight times and on all parts of the card!*

Concerning Gold's testimony about the $500 given him by Yakovlev, we are later told that it consisted of twenty-five $20 bills placed in a sealed envelope. Now let us suppose that Gold had been followed and arrested. (*Note:* Yakovlev's alleged instructions were that Gold take "a devious route . . . to minimize any danger of being followed.") Would not the sealed envelope containing those twenty-five $20 bills be somewhat difficult to explain? Would not a highly trained spy rather keep the bills in his wallet so that it would appear to be his own traveling funds instead of a payment to be delivered to someone?

Concerning the "devious route" Gold was warned to take, obviously this item was designed only to beguile the jury, since Gold ignored these instructions entirely! In his testimony there is no further mention of the matter. However, in Mr. Hoover's *Reader's Digest* article, there is this explanation: "On the appointed June day Gold arrived in Santa Fe. He had rejected John's [Yakovlev's] suggestion that he use a circuitous route because he was low, as usual, on funds. . . ."

Gold's final statement—that taking the bus directly to Albuquerque was the only way he knew to reach that city from Santa Fe—is contradicted by this writer's on-the-spot inquiry. While Santa Fe has no railroad station for passengers, it is connected by bus service to Lamy, eighteen miles away. (The train then goes on to Albuquerque.) Since, according to Hoover's *Digest* article, it is implied that Gold traveled by train, it follows that he would have had to take that connecting bus. Hence, Gold would *know* that it was possible to reach Albuquerque by train via Lamy.

Therefore, when he stated that he knew of no other transportation between the two towns than the bus route, it was a statement of ignorance which we may take as further proof that Gold never took a train to meet Fuchs in Santa Fe or a bus to meet Greenglass in Albuquerque!

One might add that just as the exchange of purses in the Denver movie was swiftly discarded, so was the "devious route." And naturally so, because the sole purpose of all this cloak-and-dagger material was to serve just enough highly spiced hors d'oeuvres so that the jury would not become too critical of the rest of the menu.

III

"These lies are like the father that begets them: gross as a mountain, open, palpable."
—*Henry IV (Part I)*

In order to give substance to the testimony of the Greenglasses that Gold had visited them in Albuquerque, it was crucial to the prosecution that some concrete evidence of his presence there be presented. Not only would it tend to prove "the necessary link" between Yakovlev and Greenglass, but it would support Gold's claim that he had met Dr. Fuchs in nearby Santa Fe during this same trip.

We have seen Mr. Hoover's effort to prove Gold's presence in Santa Fe by means of the fictitious museum map. Now we will see the prosecution's efforts to prove Gold's presence in Albuquerque by means of a fictitious hotel registration card.

Continuing with Gold's testimony concerning his double mission, he first described his rendezvous with Dr. Fuchs in Santa Fe on June 2, 1945. Now he relates how he took the bus down to Albuquerque that same Saturday afternoon:

[Gold]: I arrived in Albuquerque early in the evening of the 2nd of June, and about 8:30 that night went . . . to the designated address on High Street. There I was met by a tall elderly white-haired and somewhat stooped man. I inquired about the Greenglasses and he told me that they were out for the evening but he thought they would be in early on Sunday morning.
Q. [Lane]: Then what did you do?
A. Then I returned to downtown Albuquerque. . . . I stayed that night [Saturday]—I finally man-

aged to obtain a room in a hallway of a rooming house and then *on Sunday morning* I registered at the Hotel Hilton.

Q. Now, did you register under your own name?

A. Yes, I did.

Q. What name did you use?

A. *Harry Gold*.

Q. Now what did you do on Sunday? That is June 3, 1945?

A. On Sunday about 8:30 [A.M.] I went again to the High Street address. [Emphasis added.]

Let us now analyze these two crucial points:

1. That Gold registered needlessly at the Hotel Hilton on Sunday morning, with no intention of remaining in town over Sunday night. (As he testified, he left for New York "immediately.")

2. That Gold registered not only needlessly, but dangerously under his *true name*.

With regard to the first point, there could be no rational reason for Gold to register except the one indicated, namely, that the prosecution needed a hotel registration card to prove his presence in Albuquerque.

To demonstrate this, let us review the reasons why Gold's conduct in registering is so incredible. First, we recall his testimony that he had arranged for a meeting with Yakovlev on his "return from the Southwest." Somewhat later he explains that this prearranged meeting called for his return to New York at the specific time of 10 P.M. on the evening of June 5, a Tuesday. Now, this meeting was a most important one because Gold tells that it was then that he turned over to Yakovlev the atomic secrets from both Fuchs and Greenglass. [R. 829]

But in order to effect this delivery on schedule, Gold would have to take the *"Chief,"* the only fast train out of Albuquerque, which left at 9 A.M. Therefore, not only did Gold have precious little time to spare that Sunday morning, but any delay such as remaining another night in Albuquerque would have made it *impossible* for him to keep his precisely timed rendezvous in New York! [6]

Second, Gold had no reason to anticipate that he would meet with any delay at the Greenglasses' to warrant his paying for a room at the Hotel Hilton before he had seen them. We recall his testimony that Yakovlev had told him "that just in case Greenglass should not be present . . . his wife would have the information" ready.

Therefore, if Gold expected to receive the information promptly, why didn't he simply go to the Greenglass apartment and pick it up? He had been told the night before that the Greenglasses were out only for the evening. Why, then, did he not do first things first? Not only was there no reason to remain another night, but he knew he had to meet Yakovlev, in New York at the prearranged time, and therefore could not delay his return.

Finally, to believe in Gold's authenticity as a spy, he must have been always aware of the serious risk he was taking by registering at such a conspicuous hotel. He, himself, has told us how he warned Yakovlev that "it was inadvisable to endanger the very important trip to see Fuchs with this additional task." And in his meeting with Fuchs, Gold tells that he had received "a bunch of papers" containing atomic information. Moreover, he was carrying the $500 for Greenglass as well as the suspiciously cut Jello-box card.

If, therefore, Gold was indeed a trained spy for more than ten years, and if he had all this precarious material on his person, would he not be anxious to get out of town as quickly as possible? And if so, why would he undertake the slightest additional risk, especially one so dangerous as registering in the Hotel Hilton that Sunday morning, *and in his own name?*

Let it be emphasized that Albuquerque was an Army town in wartime, situated near the most heavily guarded secret area in the United States. This was confirmed at the trial by Colonel John Lansdale, a prosecution witness:

A. My assignment was . . . to be responsible for all phases of the security of the atom bomb project. . . . We took extraordinary measures. *We placed undercover agents in all the surrounding towns.* [R. 881, 887; emphasis added.]

If Gold were a highly trained spy, he would have known that the town was literally crawling with FBI and CID (Counter-Intelligence) men disguised as Army personnel, taxi drivers, hotel clerks, porters, waiters, shop clerks, etc. As for Gold's customary precautions, here is his own testimony describing one of his rendezvous with Yakovlev:

. . . But before I went there I was to scout the place very carefully for about an hour, to make sure that there were no signs of surveillance. [R. 832]

And here is Gold's testimony on his practice of never revealing his true name or address:

In all cases when I introduced myself, I used a false name and in all cases I never indicated my true place of residence. [R. 815]

Now with this self-portrait of a most cautious spy, let us reconstruct the scene of Gold walking into the largest hotel in Albuquerque that Sunday morning with not a piece of baggage and offering his real name and true place of residence.[7]

First, it is before 8:30 in the morning, a time when a stranger in town would be especially noticed by the desk clerk, bell captain (either one of whom could be an undercover agent) or, for that matter, the hotel detective. And what would they see? According to descriptions of Gold: "a fat, little man . . . with a pouting face . . . withdrawn, mousey . . . with dark, almost swarthy skin, receding forehead and anxious eyes," and with "a peculiar slouch."

Let us visualize this conspicuous figure waddling across the empty lobby, wearing a suit considerably crumpled from his four-day train and bus trip. Let us see him ask for a room in Eastern accents and then register "Harry Gold" with a Philadelphia address. And let us see the exchange of looks between bell captain and desk clerk when the stranger proves to have no baggage. Finally, let us visualize the result of the chambermaid's report on the next morning that the stranger did not even sleep over.

In fact, there is not the slightest suggestion in the testimony that Gold even went up to the hotel room! Despite Lane's examination—showing precisely how many minutes his morning visit to the Greenglasses comprised, and precisely how many minutes he spent with them in the afternoon—somehow the garrulous Gold never even mentions returning to the hotel to check out. Indeed, since he had no baggage, what was there to check out?

To sum up, it would seem almost as though Gold had been intent on leaving not only a trail of suspicion behind but even an address where he could be reached and checked on. Which brings us to our second point:

Why did Gold add to all these unnecessary risks that of registering his true name and address? To repeat, for the obvious reason that the prosecution needed such a registration card to submit as evidence that Gold was indeed the person who had registered at the Hotel Hilton on that date.

And this is why the card had to bear Gold's true name and not a fictitious one. Because a card with any other name, for example "Raymond Smith" or "Joe Doakes," would have been immediately challenged. With so much depending upon it, the defense would be justified in demanding proof that the signature was truly that of Gold, and not just anyone's signature. In this event, the prosecution would have been forced to bring in handwriting experts to furnish such proof, and, in, turn, the defense might have seen fit to bring in its experts.

Hence, two serious risks would have faced the prosecution: First, as the result of disagreement among the experts, possible doubt might be left in the minds of the jury. Second, and worse, the defense experts might discover, through a careful examination of the ink and/or the paper stock, that the card could not have been signed in 1945, but was indeed a 1950 forgery, and thus have thrown the Government's entire case into a cocked hat!

At the conclusion of Gold's testimony the record

shows another significant fact about this supposedly authentic hotel card. When Saypol introduced it as Government Exhibit 16, he was very careful not to present the *original card*, but rather a *photostatic copy*. His excuse was that he had "the original on its way, together with a witness if required," and that time would be saved if the defense would accept it as a genuine copy. [R. 867–869]

In this manner he avoided the danger that the defense might summon document experts and examine the card for traces of forgery. With the photostatic copy it would be impossible for such experts to examine the age of the ink or paper as they could with an original.

Since the record shows that the defense accepted the photostat as a true copy, evidently the bluff was successful. Needless to point out, neither the original card nor the witness was ever seen by the defense, the defendants, or the jury! As for Saypol's excuse, it is, on the face of it, a specious one—because he had fully eight months to obtain the card before trial. Surely, if the card were a genuine one, he would have known long before trial that he would need it as the *only* bit of documentary evidence substantiating the Albuquerque meeting between Gold and Greenglass.

It is idle to speculate what ruse or legal stratagem Saypol might have resorted to had Mr. Bloch insisted on the original. But of one thing we can be certain: that Gold's alleged registration at the Hotel Hilton was the source of no little anxiety to Mr. Saypol. To cast light on this fact, let us turn to the book written by Saypol's clandestine publicity man, the New York *Post* reporter Oliver Pilat.[8] Here is that portion relating to Gold's alleged registration at the Hilton on June 3, 1945:

He had registered under his right name, without baggage, *the previous evening*, after a visit to the North High Street address around eight o'clock. . . .[9] [Emphasis added.]

The previous evening! But we have seen how Gold testified that he stayed Saturday night in a rooming house, and did not register at the Hilton until "Sunday morning"! And yet Pilat declares in his preface that he is reporting the case accurately, and that all "the details and the quotations [of testimony], save for a rare connecting phrase, come from the record." And here, also in his preface, is this revealing acknowledgment:

The experts consulted included Irving H. Saypol, the prosecutor at two atomic trials, and now a N. Y. Supreme Court Justice.

What is of significance here is not so much that Mr. Pilat has made this conscienceless attempt to bolster Saypol's case by presenting a better story for Gold, but that it serves to expose one of the most gaping "holes" in all this sordid deception.

One of the first questions that occurred to this writer with regard to the authenticity of Gold's registration card was just how long hotels normally retain the thousands of cards which accumulate over the years. Upon inquiry at the largest hotels in Albuquerque (Hotel Franciscan and Hotel Alvarado), it was learned that *only* the Hilton kept guest cards longer than the three-year period required by the New Mexico State hotel laws. Evidently, while most hotels are anxious to be rid of the enormous stacks of cards after the three-year requirement, it appears that the Hilton chain is exceptional in having its hotels retain the cards for as long as five and ten years.

In other words, if, as it would appear, Gold's hotel card was a forgery, it becomes clear why the Hotel Hilton was chosen. *For, had he claimed to have registered at any other Albuquerque hotel in 1945, there would have been no way to prove his presence in New Mexico in 1950, five years later!*

(*Note:* It is a relatively simple matter to obtain or duplicate these hotel registration cards, since they are printed in lots of hundreds of thousands by large firms, and considerable stocks are kept both at the printer and at the hotels. This writer had no difficulty at all in obtaining three or four such cards at the Hotel Hilton in Albuquerque in early 1953.)

IV

> "He lied with such a fervour of intention,
> There was no doubt he earned his laureate
> pension."
>
> —*Lord Byron*

In our examination of Gold's alleged visit to the Greenglasses, we will compare the testimony of all three participants.[10] We will begin with Greenglass' version of Gold's arrival on Sunday morning:

A. [Greenglass]: There was a knock on the door and I opened it. We had just completed eating breakfast, and there was a man standing in the hallway who asked if I were Mr. Greenglass, and I said yes. He stepped through the door and he said, "Julius sent me," and I said "oh," and walked to my wife's purse, took out the wallet and took out the matched part of the Jello box.

Q. [Cohn]: After you produced that, did Gold do anything?

A. He produced his piece and we checked them and they fitted, and the identification was made.

Q. In other words, he had—

A. He had the other part of the box.

Q. And you had last seen that in Rosenberg's apartment that night in January, 1945?

A. That is right.

Let us try to visualize this scene exactly as described. But if we are asked to believe it, then let us consider the state of mind of Greenglass:

Scene: It is 8:30 A.M. on Sunday. A corporal employed as a machinist at the Los Alamos Project has just breakfasted with his wife. Since April he has waited for Rosenberg to send a courier. Two Saturdays before, his wife had waited in vain in front of the Safeway store. The following Saturday, just a week

before, he had joined his wife in the vigil but still
no courier.

When he had entered the espionage conspiracy he
was "frightened," "worried," and beset by "doubts."
And with good reason: (1) He has heard and read
the warnings of the death penalty for espionage. (2)
He is aware of the intensive surveillance of all personnel whether at work or in surrounding towns. (3) He
must know that he is a marked man—potentially
suspect for the simple reason that his "A-20" card (his
personal background record) contains a "red dot"
placed there by G-2 because of his onetime membership in the YCL. He must know this either through
direct interrogation by Intelligence officers or via la-
trine rumors from "premature anti-Fascists" interrogated by G-2 on information received from the
Central Subversive File Checks of the FBI. If he does
not quite know this for a fact, he must certainly
reckon with its possibility, particularly in view of
what was regarded as the politically suspect background of his sister and brother-in-law. (4) Although
the record does not mention it specifically, by this
time he may have heard from Ethel that Julius had
been discharged from the Signal Corps by Army Intelligence on FBI charges of Communist Party membership.

Since no courier arrived to meet him at the Safeway store on the specified dates, for all he knows
Julius may have been caught or may be under such
serious surveillance that the mission was canceled.
Therefore his state of mind that morning, when the
unexpected stranger appeared at his door asking for
him *by name*, must have been one of paralyzing uncertainty. And yet we are asked to believe this testimony as re-enacted:

(Knock on door. Greenglass crosses to open it.)
Man (in hallway): Are you Mr. Greenglass?
Greenglass: Yes.
Man (as he steps in): Julius sent me.
Greenglass: Oh. (Crosses to wife's purse, takes
out half of cut card and shows it to "man," who
produces his half.)

If the reader can imagine seeing this scene even played on TV straight and serious, he could not but find it ridiculous. For observe how Greenglass hurries to display his half *before* the "man" has produced the necessary other half! Suppose the "man" were one of Colonel Lansdale's security officers seeking to trap him? This would be Greenglass' first thought, because for months he has expected the courier at one place only, the Safeway store. And yet without the slightest hesitation he exposes himself as a spy merely on the basis of the visitor saying "Julius sent me"! And if it were true that there was a definite password written down *precisely* for Gold to memorize—namely, "I come from Julius"—then why do we not hear it in its correct form from Greenglass?

By way of a concluding comment, observe the final prompting question to establish the inferential link between "Julius" and Yakovlev. To be sure, Cohn could not whisper his cues into Greenglass' ear (as he was to do with McCarthy three years later [11]), but considering his obvious impatience one must concede he showed considerable restraint.

Now let us examine Ruth's version of the same incident:

> [Ruth]: . . . We had just finished breakfast and someone knocked at the door. My husband opened it and he [the "man"] said he bore greetings from Julius.
> He came into the apartment and he produced half of the Jello box side. *Then* my husband went to my wallet and got the other half and they matched them and they fit. [Emphasis added.]

At once we detect how Ruth's testimony repairs her husband's error. Whereas in his version David produces his half first, Ruth restores the logic by reversing the order. It must be noted that, between David's testimony on this point and Ruth's, five full days had elapsed. And now to the version of Mr. Gold: .

> A. [Gold]: On Sunday about 8:30 I went again

to the High Street address. I was admitted, and I recall going up a *very steep flight of steps,* and I knocked on a door. It was opened by a young man of about 23 with dark hair. He was smiling. I said, "Mr. Greenglass?" He answered in the affirmative. I said, "I came from Julius," *and I showed him the piece of cardboard in my hand,* the piece of cardboard that had been given me by Yakovlev in Volk's Cafe. He asked me to enter. I did. Greenglass went to a woman's handbag and brought out from it a piece of a cardboard. We matched the two of them.

Q. [Lane]: Will you describe that cardboard which Greenglass showed you?

A. It appeared to be from the same part of the same packaged food *from which the piece of cardboard that I had had originally been cut.*

Q. [Kaufman]: When you say Greenglass matched the two, just what did he do?

A. He showed it to me and we put them together, as nearly as I can remember.

Q. How did you put them together? To see whether the ends met, is that what you did?

A. No. Just roughly. I mean you could see at a glance that they were the same thing.

Q. [Lane]: And the two pieces matched, you say?

A. The two pieces matched. [Emphasis added.]

For future reference, let the reader bear in mind Gold's description of the "very steep flight of steps." [12]

In Gold's description of the Jello-box ceremony, we detect how he, too, has evidently been instructed to repair the blunder in Greenglass' version. It is amusing to see how Gold still feigns ignorance that his half was part of the Jello box even though (according to his testimony) he has seen the two parts fitted together and containing the word "Jello" eight times.

Regarding the Jello-box scene as Gold describes it, the spectacle of a veteran spy standing in the hallway holding out his half of the Jello box card in the palm

337

of his hand *before* entering the room is even more unacceptable than in Greenglass' version.

It is appropriate to comment on Judge Kaufman asking Gold to repeat the matching of the Jello-box sides. Gold has just stated clearly that he and Greenglass matched the two halves. Thus, supported by this request, Lane has it repeated for the third time.

With such frequent support from Kaufman, is it any wonder that Saypol could remain confident that, whatever blunders and oversights he and his assistants might make, the verdict would be practically directed by the Court?

V

In the *Columbia* summary of the prosecution's case describing Gold's visit, the final item reads that Greenglass had given him "a further list of spy prospects." All through the record there are these lists of spy recruits allegedly requested by Rosenberg, or by Sobell, but *never* do we hear any names of these mysterious persons.

Apparently losing no time that Sunday morning, Gold asked Greenglass if he had the information ready. The latter replied he would "have to write it up," and proposed that Gold return at three or four o'clock that afternoon. It is at this point that Gold was allegedly offered a list of potential recruits:

> [Gold]: . . . He started to give me the names of these people. . . . I cut him very short indeed. I told him that such procedure was extremely hazardous, foolhardy, that under no circumstances should he ever try to proposition anyone on his own into trying to get information for the Soviet Union.

Despite this stern warning, what do we find when we skip to Gold's afternoon visit:

> [Greenglass]: . . . I also gave him a list of pos-

sible recruits for espionage. . . . I gave this list of names and also sketches and descriptive material.

In the morning Greenglass is reprimanded for even offering the list, but in the afternoon he gives Gold the list notwithstanding. But here is Gold's full report on what he received from Greenglass:

Q. [Lane]: En route to New York did you at any time inspect the material which you had received from Greenglass?

A. [Gold]: Yes, I did, on the train from Albuquerque to Chicago and somewhere in Kansas, I believe. I examined the material which Greenglass had given me. I just examined it very quickly.

Q. [Kaufman]: Well, now, can you describe a little better what was in the Greenglass package?

A. Yes. The material given me by Greenglass consisted of three or four handwritten pages plus a couple of sketches. The sketches had letters on them which were referred to in the text of the three or four handwritten pages. The sketches appeared to be for a device of some kind.

Nothing whatsoever about Greenglass' list of recruits. No doubt the conflict here was due to Gold's refusal to go along with Greenglass' embroidery. For, to his precise way of thinking, such lists were not proper material to be delivered to a courier; Greenglass should have testified that he gave such lists only to Rosenberg.

In concluding the testimony of Gold's morning visit, the latter adds this final point:

[Gold]: The last thing that took place that morning was just as I was preparing to go, Mrs. Greenglass told me that just before she had left New York City to come to Albuquerque she had spoken with Julius. This meeting that we had in the morning on the 3rd of June 1945, this Sunday morning, took about fifteen minutes.

There is no mention of any such conversation in the testimony of Ruth or David. Moreover, when one studies the sense of this testimony, one can find no reason for Ruth to have made this gratuitous remark. What is obvious is that following the Greenglasses' testimony the prosecution felt the name "Julius" should not be limited to Gold's password, but also be tied to a remark attributed to Ruth.

And in an effort to lend authenticity to the non sequitur, Gold methodically offers the time of the day, the day of the week and the date of the month and year, merely to make the trivial point that the visit had taken "fifteen minutes."

•

Here is the substance of David's testimony describing Gold's afternoon visit: that after Gold had left that morning, Greenglass prepared the sketches of the lens mold together with its descriptive material. That about 2:30 or 3 o'clock Gold returned to pick up the information which Greenglass had placed in an envelope. That in exchange for this envelope Gold gave Greenglass the sealed envelope containing the $500.

Q. [Cohn]: Was there any further discussion with Gold?

A. Well, he wanted to leave *immediately* and I said, "Wait, and we will go down with you," and he waited a little while. We went down, and we went around by *a back road* and we dropped him in front of the USO [United Service Organizations]. We went into the USO, and he went on his way. As soon as he had gone down the street my wife and myself *looked around* and we came out again and back to the apartment and counted the money.

Q. How much was it?

A. We found it to be $500.[13] [Emphasis added.]

Here, in David's testimony, and likewise in Ruth's, the $500 is paid in the afternoon. However, in Gold's testimony, the payment is made during the *morning* visit:

340

[Gold]: Greenglass then told me . . . he would have the material on the atom bomb ready for me that afternoon. . . . Then I gave Mr. Greenglass the envelope. . . . the one that contained $500.

Certainly this cannot be dismissed as a minor discrepancy. The Greenglass testimony is specific and detailed—the envelope was given to them in the afternoon. But Gold's testimony is equally specific and detailed; the envelope was given in the morning. It is not a question of which party is lying. In this charade, they are all lying. The Greenglasses sought to minimize the unsavory motive of profit that had been forced upon them by not having the $500 paid in advance. But Gold, the stickler for exactitude, played his part religiously. For the prosecution, as we shall see, was more anxious to preserve the credibility of Gold as "the necessary link" in this crucial phase of the so-called conspiracy than to support David's "hero-worship" of Julius as his sole motive for entering it.

•

We come now to another aspect of the prosecution's purpose in introducing Government Exhibit 16, the Hotel Hilton registration card dated June 3, 1945.

Why was this particular date so important for the prosecution? Because it had to synchronize with another date, namely an Albuquerque bank record of Ruth Greenglass which showed a deposit of $400 on the next day, June 4, 1945. Evidence of this deposit was then introduced as Government Exhibit 17. If, therefore, Government Exhibits 16 and 17 could be linked together—Gold's registration of June 3 and Ruth's deposit of June 4—then how could any juror doubt that the $400 deposit came from Gold's $500 payment made the day before? Let us therefore turn to this summary of Ruth's testimony to demonstrate the flaws in this "documentary link."

On the very next day after Gold's visit she deposited $400 in the Albuquerque Trust & Savings Bank. With the balance, she purchased a defense bond for $37.50, and used the remaining $62.50 for household expenses. [R. 701–702]

Here again we do not quarrel with full truths. Conceded that Ruth Greenglass opened a bank account with a deposit of $400 on June 4, 1945. However, as we have sought to show, the nature of modern frame-up is essentially a technique of taking full truths and giving them criminal meanings. And in this instance Gold's registration card was obviously forged to fit the date of Ruth's $400 deposit.

If one is inclined to speculate where the Greenglasses obtained their $400, a good part or all of it may simply have been their monthly salaries plus Ruth's army allowance. (*Note*: Ruth, at this time, was employed as a secretary-typist by the OPA office in Albuquerque.) On the other hand, it may have been derived from David's black-market sales of pilfered army equipment, which subject we will deal with in a later chapter.[14]

If it were not so, why would the Greenglasses hurry to *start* a bank account with this spy money the very next morning? In subsequent testimony the Greenglasses claim to have hidden $4,000 of Russian escape money in their apartment. Why, then, didn't they hide this $500? As for the defense bond, this little gesture, of course, was self-serving; as though to say: "See, our patriotic conscience still stirred us."

This "documentary link" with Ruth's bank deposit served the prosecution in still another sense. Since it became circumstantial evidence of the receipt of Russian money, an authentic aura was cast over *all* the other monies the Greenglasses claimed to have received "from the Russians" through Julius Rosenberg, and without the necessity of furnishing the slightest proof.

•

As we conclude with Gold's alleged afternoon visit, we see how each member of this trio adds a little tidbit here and there, very much as some stage actors do when they pad their roles by "ad libbing" an extra line or two. Here is Gold receiving the "material on the atom bomb":

342

[Gold]: . . . I took the envelope. Mr. Greenglass told me that he expected to get a furlough sometime around Christmas, and that he would return to New York at that time. He told me that if I wished to get in touch with him then I could do so by calling his brother-in-law Julius, and he gave me the telephone number of Julius in New York City.

Q. [Lane]: Do you recall now what that number was?

A. I cannot. . . . I told Greenglass that very likely I might be returning to Albuquerque in the early fall of 1945 and if I did so there was a possibility that I might stop in and see him.

Q. And did you receive some information at that time, some papers from Greenglass?

A. I have already related that he gave me an envelope which contained, *which he said* contained information on the atom bomb.

Q. And then what did you do?

A. The three of us, Mr. Greenglass, Mrs. Greenglass and myself, left the Greenglasses' apartment and we walked along a *slanting back street* in Albuquerque, and there in front of a small building [the USO] I left the Greenglasses.

Q. And did you return to New York?

A. Yes, I did.

Q. *Immediately?*

A. Yes, I did. [Emphasis added.]

Concerning David's expected furlough, the record shows that it took place in September of 1945 rather than at Christmas. It is highly unlikely that a soldier awaiting his annual furlough, only three months later, would have said it was to be "around Christmas." Therefore, how would it be possible for Gold to drop in on the Greenglasses "in the early fall" in Albuquerque when at that time David would be on furlough in New York?

Once again Gold drags in the name of "Julius," but now he adds "brother-in-law" in order to pinpoint the name directly to Julius Rosenberg. But even so, why would such a dangerous method of contact be suggested? Since Greenglass knows nothing about

Yakovlev, and since Gold has said, "Julius sent me," and is in possession of the half of the Jello box last seen in Julius' hand, David can properly assume that Gold and Julius know each other. *Why then would it be necessary for David to tell Gold how to reach Julius?*

Moreover, if we are to believe Gold's rigid practice of always working through a "superior," would he not have cut Greenglass "very short indeed" at such an offer? Here is an example of the "very set pattern" Gold glibly recounted to the beguiled jury:

> [Gold]: A system was set up whereby Yakovlev could get in touch with me if he wanted me quickly, but I couldn't get in touch with him because I didn't know where. Yakovlev told me that in this way the chain was cut in two places. The person from whom I got the information . . . did not know me by my true name, nor did he know where I lived, nor could he get in touch with me and I couldn't get in touch with Yakovlev. Yakovlev said this was a good thing. [R. 817]

Obviously then, it would not be a "good thing" for Gold to have taken Julius' telephone number and then phoned him at Christmas and said, "Hello, Julius? This is Dave from Pittsburgh. I want to get in touch with your brother-in-law, Greenglass." [15] Incidentally, since Julius' number was listed in the New York telephone directory, David would hardly have to give it to Gold to carry with him needlessly.

Observe how Gold hastily corrects his testimony to add *"which he said* contained information on the atom bomb." Can we believe that Greenglass, acutely conscious of surveillance (including eavesdropping informants or hidden microphones), would be so careless as to mention the atom bomb?

In this writer's visit to 209 North High Street, it was ascertained that no less than four other families shared this house with the Greenglasses. The walls are very thin, since it is only a remodeled one-family home. Moreover, the Greenglasses' adjoining neighbors shared a hall bathroom which has a common wall with the Greenglass apartment.

Under such circumstances, it is inconceivable that spies would use such wording as "This contains information on the atom bomb." Any alert juror, with his prejudices put aside, could have deduced that Gold had been instructed to include the damaging phrase "atom bomb."

A brief comment is in order concerning the "information on the atom bomb." It consisted allegedly of additional sketches of the High Explosive Lens and, as in the case of the sketch supposedly given Julius in January, "copies" were also submitted into evidence as Government Exhibits 6 and 7. And here, too, it was admitted by Greenglass that the "copies" were prepared before or during trial and that he had "relied solely upon memory."

However, according to Greenglass' testimony, we find that these sketches represented but *one part* of a series of "constant experiments going on" in the many machine shops at Los Alamos. In other words, despite the six years that had elapsed, his claim is that he remembered each and every detail of this *one part* exactly:

> The Court: Is this to your present knowledge *an exact replica* of the sketch which you turned over even to the extent of the comments on the side?
>
> [Greenglass]: It is. [Emphasis added.]

In the next chapter, dealing with Greenglass' alleged delivery of the Nagasaki atomic bomb plans, we will see by the affidavits of prominent physicists that they themselves would find it impossible to recall exactly and solely from memory an experiment six years after they had worked on it!

VI

As indicated previously, this writer undertook an investigative trip to the so-called scene of the crime, which involved retracing every step Gold claims to have taken in Albuquerque and Santa Fe. Not only did this investigation prove that Gold's testimony was a fabrication, but that it was shoddily prepared with the customary contempt for the public intelligence.

We have already noted our discovery that Gold's "very steep flight of steps" was a falsification. This writer can affirm that the only flight of stairs at 209 N. High Street is the very opposite of "steep" and consists of four wide and shallow steps, a large landing at the turn, and then eight more shallow steps ending at Greenglass' floor. It is clear that Gold never saw the inside of that house and tossed in the steep stairs to lend authenticity to his visit.

In addition, we made a thorough check of Gold's "slanting back street." Although this writer reconnoitered the surrounding neighborhood, he found no such slanting back street or back road. All of the streets are laid out in the usual rectangular fashion. Moreover, inquiry was made of a few old-time residents, and none of them had ever heard of any back street in that neighborhood.

Concerning the Greenglass testimony introducing an air of intrigue in taking "a back road" and how they "looked around" furtively "in front of the USO," we see the admission of the possibility of surveillance. Confirming this, here is a report of the extent of the surveillance existing at the time from Dr. J. Robert Oppenheimer, head of the Los Alamos Project, as quoted in the New York *Times*:

Telephone calls were monitored, mail was censored *and personnel who left the area . . . knew that their movements might be under surveillance.*[16] [Emphasis added.]

It was allegedly a Sunday afternoon, with the USO crowded with Army personnel, among whom there could be one or more of Colonel Lansdale's under-cover men. Can we believe that Greenglass would risk walking there in the company of another spy carrying on his person atomic secrets in Greenglass' own handwriting? In addition, Gold was also carrying Dr. Fuchs' atomic information. Do experienced spies behave this way in any of the authentic cases on record? Here is Gold's testimony contradicting his own conduct:

If I was going to actually get information, very usually a brief meeting was scheduled, the idea being to minimize the time of detection. . . . [R. 815]

In Mr. Hoover's article describing Gold's alleged meeting with Dr. Fuchs in Santa Fe on September 19, 1945, there is this description of proper spy conduct:

Just before the two men parted, Fuchs gave Gold a packet of vital information. It was *standard practice* for the incriminating parcel to be withheld until *the last minute*. [Emphasis added.]

But we have seen that Gold permitted Greenglass to give him the incriminating parcel in the apartment and instead of making this the *last minute* of their transaction, they take a promenade together to the USO!

•

While we are on the subject of Gold's alleged September 19 meeting with Dr. Fuchs, it is appropriate to reexamine Gold's Hotel Hilton registration card in the light of additional and hitherto unknown information which this writer has obtained.

Since the record does not show what address Gold put down on the card, this writer initiated an inquiry as to this point. The results uncovered the fact that the prosecution had prepared *two* photostats of *two* registration cards, one for June 3 and one for September 19, 1945. The photostat of the September 19 card was not introduced in evidence and is not mentioned or referred to in the record. However, it furnishes almost conclusive corroboration of our thesis explaining why the Hotel Hilton in Albuquerque was chosen. Because it turns out that Gold's alleged registration card of September 19 was *also* at that hotel, *despite the fact that he had no reason to be in Albuquerque on that date!*

Here is a breakdown of the two alleged registration cards, both containing Gold's true name:

On the June 3 card, the home address is given as: "6823 Kindred St., Phila. 24, Penna." The business connection is given as: "Terry & Siebert."

On the September 19 card, however, the home address is given as: "132 Bowden Street, Phila. 24," and the business connection is given as: "A B A Laboratories, N.Y."

Now, in Gold's testimony at the Rosenberg trial [R. 841], the home address on the June 3 card is confirmed as his true place of residence, and that he had lived there from June of 1944 until at least "December of 1946." As for the address on the September 19 card, the only similarity to it is in Gold's cross-examination at the Brothman trial when he was asked:

Q. Did you ever live at Boudinot Street?
A. [Gold]: I lived at 5032 Boudinot Street.[17]

So far, then, we have the curious situation of Gold registering twice at the *same* hotel within a period of three and a half months; on the first occasion allegedly giving the true and exact address where he could be further investigated, and on his second visit allegedly giving a spurious address which could not fail to arouse serious suspicion if the two cards were checked by the FBI.

But it is from his business connections that even further suspicion would have resulted. Despite the fact that Gold was employed by the Pennsylvania Sugar Company on both June 3 and September 19, we see that he put down "Terry & Siebert," a small chemical laboratory. Although this firm no longer exists in Philadelphia, this writer managed to locate one of its former owners and learned the following:

1. That Gold was never an employee there.
2. That on occasion he did some minor odd jobs for this firm.

3. That these jobs entailed routine laboratory work.

4. That Gold was never sent by the firm anywhere.

5. And that the firm had no connections of any kind in the Southwest and knew of no trips Gold had undertaken there.

In short, therefore, even a cursory investigation of Gold following his June 3, 1945, registration would have placed him in a serious predicament. But how much more so as the result of what he put down on his September 19 card, *i.e.*: "A B A Laboratories, N.Y." Because, according to his own testimony at the Rosenberg trial, such an act would have been equivalent to having written down "Spy Headquarters"!

Let us see why. Here is how Gold describes his final meeting with Yakovlev on Dec. 26, 1946:

That at about five o'clock in the afternoon, he received a telephone call from Yakovlev under the pseudonym of "John" at the laboratory of A. Brothman and Associates in New York, otherwise known as the A B A Laboratories.

That an appointment was made for later that night, and in a bar on Second Avenue, Yakovlev asked Gold to plan for an espionage mission to Paris in March of 1947. And that the discussion involved the problem of how Gold was to manage "to get off from work to make this trip to Paris."

[Gold]: I told Yakovlev that once the pressure of work at Abe Brothman and Associates had eased up a bit—and then Yakovlev almost went through the roof of the saloon. He said, "You fool." He said, "You spoiled eleven years of work." He told me that I didn't realize what I had done, and he told me that I should have remembered that some time *in the summer of '45* he had told me that Brothman was under suspicion by the United States Government authorities *of having engaged in espionage* and that I should have remembered it. . . . And he dashed out of the place. I walked along with him for a while and he kept mumbling that I had created terrible damage. . . . Yakovlev then told me that he would not see me in the United States again, and he left me.

Q. [Lane]: That was your last meeting with Yakovlev?

A. That is right. [R. 841–844; emphasis added.]

To clarify this alleged break, it occurred because Gold had taken a job with a spy (Brothman) who was "hot" and under possible surveillance *since the summer of 1945*. Without going into the contradictions in this portion of Gold's testimony, let us return to the registration card of September 19, 1945. If we are to believe his testimony, we must accept that, despite Yakovlev's dire warning that Brothman was under suspicion, Gold nevertheless put down this "hot" business connection on the September 19 Hotel Hilton card.

Furthermore, we discover in Gold's previous testimony concerning the September 19 rendezvous with Dr. Fuchs that he had no reason whatsoever to go to Albuquerque. Here is the record as he relates Yakovlev's instructions prior to that trip during their meeting of August 1945:

The conversation concerned the fact that I was to take, soon to take a trip in September to Santa Fe to meet Dr. Fuchs. I told Yakovlev that since I was going to see Dr. Fuchs I might as well go to Albuquerque and see the Greenglasses. *At this time Yakovlev told me that it would be inadvisable to endanger the trip to see Fuchs by complicating it with a visit to the Greenglasses in Albuquerque.* [R. 835; emphasis added.]

And so we see that Gold not only had no reason to stop off in Albuquerque, but that he was specifically warned that it would be dangerous to go there.

And yet, according to the photostat of the alleged September 19 card, we are asked to believe that Gold nevertheless went to Albuquerque and again registered in his own true name at the Hotel Hilton.

It must be understood that when one is traveling from Chicago to Santa Fe, Albuquerque is a considerable distance farther. In other words, had Gold stopped at a hotel in Santa Fe, he would have saved himself not only the unnecessary train travel to and from Albuquerque, but an additional bus trip from that city to Santa Fe and back, as well as the extra expense.

Why, then, one asks, was there this needless September 19 card prepared for the Hotel Hilton in Albuquerque? For this simple reason: It was the only hotel near Santa Fe that retained guest cards for more than three years. In other words, whoever prepared these *fraudulent* cards in 1950 was forced to choose a hotel which could be proved to have kept such registrations since 1945.

To summarize, if we are to believe in the authenticity of these two registration cards we must accept the following incredible conduct on the part of Gold:

1. That a trained spy such as Gold would recklessly have returned to the scene of the crime.

2. That despite the knowledge that his June registration may have aroused suspicion, he would have nevertheless returned to this same hotel in September, only three months later.

3. That he would have knowingly invited additional suspicion by using two different home addresses and two different business connections.

4. That he would have put down not the firm which truly employed him, but one whose owner was a spy whom he knew to be under Federal suspicion at that very time.

5. That despite the fact that staying at the Hotel Hilton on September 19 represented hundreds of miles of additional traveling and extra fares, he would have nevertheless spent this unnecessary time and money.

6. And finally, that he would have done all this despite the specific warnings and instructions of his superior, given him in the August meeting just before his departure.

•

Earlier in this chapter we discussed the improbability of Gold's registering on that Sunday morning of June 3, 1945, when he must have known that he had to catch a morning train in order not to miss his "prearranged" rendezvous with Yakovlev in New York. Here is his testimony concerning that rendezvous:

Q. [Lane]: When did you arrive back in New York?
A. [Gold]: I arrived in New York on the 5th of June, 1945, in the evening. . . .
Q. Where did you meet him?
A. I met Yakovlev along Metropolitan Avenue in Brooklyn. . . .
The Court: What time was it?
The Witness: It was about 10 o'clock at night. [R. 829]

Thus, we see how precise Gold is about the time and the date he met Yakovlev. And with regard to his leaving the Greenglasses at the USO, his testimony shows this to have been between 3:15 and 4:15 P.M., Sunday, June 3.

Since it was also Gold's testimony that he had left "immediately" for New York that Sunday afternoon, this writer decided to check the railroad schedules for that date to see what was the earliest train Gold could have taken to reach New York in time for his Tuesday night rendezvous on June 5. At the Albuquerque Santa Fe Railroad station, the timetable of June, 1945, was accurately recalled by the trainmaster.[18] This timetable given to this writer proves the following facts:

1. That it was *impossible* for a passenger traveling by train to New York to have left Albuquerque on a Sunday afternoon and to have reached New York on a Tuesday night.
2. That there was only one fast train leaving Albuquerque on Sunday which could arrive in Chicago on Monday, in time to allow Gold to make a connection that would bring him to New York City the next day, Tuesday. (*Note:* See Gold's previously quoted testimony that he traveled by train via Chicago; Record, p. 828.)

3. That this train was the *Chief*, but its departure from Albuquerque was 9:00 A.M. Mountain Standard War time.

4. That, since this one fast train had departed long before Gold left the Greenglass apartment, there was only one other train he could have taken that Sunday, the *California Limited*, a very slow night train which left Albuquerque at 8:10 P.M. and did not arrive in Chicago until thirty-six hours later, or 7:30 A.M. on Tuesday.

5. *That no train leaving Chicago on Tuesday at or after that hour could have gotten Gold into New York before June 6, or Wednesday morning!*

In short, then, Harry Gold's testimony about his June 5 rendezvous with Yakovlev, during which he swears he transmitted the secret information from Fuchs and Greenglass, *is a provable perjury!* Coupled with such other lies as the "very steep stairs," and the "slanting back street," as well as all the contradictions contained in his alleged conversation with the Greenglasses and all the improbabilities of his conduct as a spy, the only conclusion one can come to concerning his visit is that it was fashioned entirely out of whole cloth!

VII

By way of a postscript to Gold's testimony, there is the question of why Mr. Bloch decided not to cross-examine him, despite the prosecution's insistence that he was the "necessary link" in the so-called chain of guilt around the Rosenbergs. The question has been posed to this writer by not a few lawyers and therefore bears mentioning in more than a lengthy footnote.

In the series of interviews this writer had with Emanuel Bloch the problem was frequently discussed in all its ramifications. The attorney explained his decision as follows:

That in a legal sense Gold had never actually connected Julius Rosenberg with the alleged Yakovlev-

Gold-Greenglass conspiracy. That even if one believed Gold's testimony regarding his visit to the Greenglasses, his claim was that his half of the Jello box had been given to him by Yakovlev and not by Julius Rosenberg. That although Gold had included the name of a "Julius" in his alleged password it was not that of Julius Rosenberg and therefore could have been that of any other person or a fictitious name. That Gold never claimed to have met the Rosenbergs or even to have heard about them as members of the alleged conspiracy. And that, in view of these circumstances, it would have been contrary to all established criminal court strategy—indeed, sheer folly—to have challenged Gold in cross-examination and thereby invited that glib and agile witness to involve the Rosenbergs "spontaneously."

In discussing Mr. Bloch's decision and reasons with other attorneys this writer found several sided with Bloch's opinion, especially in view of the importance Gold enjoyed at the time of trial as the officially accepted accomplice of Dr. Fuchs. However, this writer took issue with Mr. Bloch as follows:

That each time Gold mentioned the name "Julius" the jury itself must have filled in the name of Rosenberg. That each time Gold mentioned his half of the Jello box the jury must have visualized Rosenberg delivering it to Yakovlev directly or by means of an intermediary. That, with the Greenglasses' testimony about the cutting up of the two halves by Julius, the inference of the Rosenberg-Yakovlev link must have dominated the jury's mind. That, regardless of the fact that Gold had not connected Julius Rosenberg (except by inference) with the conspiracy, the jurors, being laymen, must have viewed the failure to cross-examine him as a concession to Gold's veracity. And that while it might not have made any possible difference to the verdict of the jury, which was already preconditioned by the official acceptance of Gold, nevertheless an incisive cross-examination of his concoctions (disclosed at the Brothman trial) and his admitted talents as an "accomplished deceiver" might seriously have damaged the prosecution's case before the public.

In reply, while Mr. Bloch conceded that these arguments had real merit, he pointed out that they were the product of hindsight and our intensive investigation which was not possible at the time of trial. In this respect, it is worth quoting the following opinion:

Advocacy is a skill and art; easy to criticize, difficult to fairly appraise. Indeed, a post-mortem of criminal trials . . . would undoubtedly reveal flaws of varying magnitude in the trial techniques of respected members of the bar.[19]

In later discussions, particularly after this writer's trip to Albuquerque had revealed the extent of Gold's fabrications, Mr. Bloch voiced his feelings about the frame-up as follows:

For thirty years I have been an officer of the Court. True, I had seen nefarious practices in the criminal courts, but basically I believed in the administration of justice and in the integrity of most officials sworn to uphold it. Yes, I thought that Gold was possibly mixed up in some kind of espionage, but I knew that he was a liar about that Jello box business. And certainly that Greenglass was dragging in the Rosenbergs to save his own hide. But how could I dream that officials in the Department of Justice would lend themselves to the perpetration of a complete hoax concocted by this weird character, Gold? I suppose that was my biggest mistake—having those illusions, underestimating the cynicism and power for evil in high places.

Maybe that's why I believed to the last minute that they wouldn't dare go through with the executions. I couldn't believe in that much evil.

NOTES AND REFERENCES

1. J. Edgar Hoover, describing the fabrications of "the amazing Mr. Means," in *Persons in Hiding*, Little, Brown & Co., Boston, 1938.
2. For Gold's direct testimony, see Record, pp. 798–848.
3. "At this time," Gold was employed at the Pennsyl-

vania Sugar Company. How was a routine $50-per-week laboratory assistant able to take off time from his work for so many long trips, this particular one to Santa Fe and Albuquerque covering six full days? (See Section VI, this chapter.)

4. Similar tactics of exposed perjurers have been analyzed by Frank J. Donner in his article "The Informer," *The Nation*, April 10, 1954.

5. The record discloses that Yakovlev sailed back home (incidentally, on the United States Lines) together with wife and children in 1946, or over four years prior to the trial. (Record, pp. 946–947.)

6. This was proved by this writer's interview with the Albuquerque dispatcher of the Santa Fe Railroad, who recalled the Santa Fe Railroad timetable of June, 1945, and, fortunately, found an available copy in his files.

7. "He had registered under his right name, without baggage. . . ." (See Pilat, *op. cit.*, p. 4.) Since Mr. Pilat's preface reads that U.S. Attorney Saypol was his expert consultant, we will not contest the curious fact that Gold traveled six days without even a change of linen!

8. This relationship is revealed by the final paragraph in the Rogge file memo of August 23, 1950: "Also, I had lunch with Ruth, Pilat, and HJF. We looked at Pilat's articles. They look OK, but HJF as a precaution told *Lane* previously he would insist *Pilat* who already had 2 conferences with *Saypol*, showed the draft of the articles to *Saypol* or *Lane*." (Emphasis in the original. See Appendix 5.)

9. Pilat, *op. cit.*, p. 4.

10. For David's direct on this visit, see Record, pp. 456–465. For Ruth's, see pp. 699–701. For Gold's, see pp. 824–829.

11. ". . . The public, which for thirty-six days watched Mr. Cohn whispering into Mr. McCarthy's ear, would hardly dispute the fact that Mr. Cohn was very valuable to Mr. McCarthy." (Editorial, New York *Times*, July 16, 1954.)

12. According to this writer's observations on a visit to the former Greenglass apartment in Albuquerque, this description of the stairway is a complete falsification. (See Section VI of this chapter.)

13. In Section VI, dealing with this writer's trip to Albuquerque, this "back road" as well as the bland indif-

ference of Gold in accompanying the Greenglasses to the USO, is discussed in more detail.

14. See Daniel Yergin's article in *New Times* (May 16, 1975), concerning Greenglass having been "deeply involved in a theft ring at Los Alamos" and the discovery of other bank deposits in Albuquerque banks of "several thousand dollars during that year" of 1945, sums "unrelated to their official salaries."

15. In his testimony, Gold states that he introduced himself to the Greenglasses as "Dave from Pittsburgh." (Record, p. 826.)

16. Ironically, the "father of the A-bomb," Dr. Oppenheimer himself was under close surveillance. Even his chauffeur was an undercover man. (See Oppenheimer reply to AEC charges; New York *Times*, April 4, 1954.)

17. Brothman Record, p. 909. (*Note:* Compare with "132 Bowden St.")

18. See photostat of Santa Fe timetable of June, 1945, in Appendix 11.

19. United States v. Stoecker, 216 F. 2d 51 (C. A. 7th, 1954).

ADDENDA

The Pollack report denies flatly that Harry Gold was a pathological liar, adding that "Neither Wexley nor any of the files" provide support for such a contention. Thus Pollack ignores Gold's sworn admissions of uncontrolled lying as well as the official psychiatric report describing Gold's "neurotic personality." (See Chapter 3 and *Addenda.*)

And with Gold's "remarkable memory for details," Pollack continues, "it is hardly possible that he would have invented the story out of whole cloth without tripping himself somewhere on detail." Here, Pollack is equally indifferent to all the gaping holes which he himself has labored so hard to patch up, *e.g.*, the Hilton registration cards, the timetables, etc. However, two pages later in his report, Pollack shows second thoughts about Gold's infallibility:

It may be that Gold was not the best example of a perfect international spy as depicted in fiction and on the screen, but it should be remembered that the Soviet Union was willing to use untrained members [of the Communist Party] as emergency spies because it considered the rank and file to be expendable.

So—in all the vast "network" of the KGB operating in the U.S., there was not a *single* trained spy available to pick up "the most important scientific secrets ever known to mankind." Not even in Julius' "nationwide" spy ring could one be found. It was all an emergency. The KGB had to turn to the rank and file of the American Communist Party. But, as we know from the Brothman trial, Gold was *not* a member of the Communist Party. On the contrary, he was eloquently anti-Communist.

Also, we are told, such "emergency spies" were considered "expendable." In other words, it didn't matter to the KGB if Gold were caught, the atomic secrets lost and the entire spy ring exposed! Now Pollack continues:

Assuming arguendo that he [Gold] was an emotionally unstable person, there is no doubt that he was attracted to the spy idea because it suggested "a controlled dignified form of activity, like [a] laboratory itself." (Pilat, supra, pp. 24–38.)

Here, it would appear that Pollack, in seeking support from Pilat to provide this weird motive, in effect concedes how *unstable* Gold really was! Some pages later, Pollack makes another attempt to explain Gold's unbelievable conduct as a genuine spy:

Also, Gold was no ordinary professional spy. He was naive in spying and not too anxious to cover his traces.

Thus, on the one hand, we have from Gold's sworn testimony in three trials (the Brothman, Rosenberg and Smilg cases) and from Hoover's *Digest* article, that Gold was carefully trained by his Soviet superiors in the technique of espionage ever since 1935. But on the other hand, here is Pollack, working for a full year to "counteract" this book, and with all the FBI files at his disposal, telling us the very opposite. Both versions, of course, are false. But in Pollack's efforts to present Gold as a believable witness, he is forced to destroy him as a believable spy—

even to the point of reducing him to a simpleton inviting arrest.

Wherever possible—and space does not permit citing all the numerous instances—Pollack falls back on the question which he calls his "ace in the hole": Why did the defense "not dare to cross-examine Gold?" *"Defendant's counsel did not dare to cross-examine him."* "One wonders why Mr. Wexley overlooked this item in his review of the official Record of the case." [Emphasis by Pollack.]

It was *not* overlooked. The question of Gold's cross-examination is discussed in depth in this writer's interview with Emanuel Bloch and covers two full pages in the final section of this chapter. Despite the meticulous study of this book, not a word of Bloch's explanation is dealt with in the Pollack report. Thus, it is Pollack who "overlooked" this significant section. If one wonders why, perhaps it was that Mr. Bloch's painfully admitted illusions concerning the integrity of "officials in the Department of Justice" struck too close to home.

•

In the Government's official "White Paper" on the Rosenberg case, there appears a separate chapter (XXXIII) devoted to "The Hilton Hotel Registration Card." One would expect a powerful rebuttal to our analysis regarding this crucial card, but not so. Unable to rebut, refute, or deny the validity of the vital points made demonstrating that the card was an "FBI-inspired forgery," Pollack merely repeats them one by one with an air of disdainful dismissal:

Wexley charges that Gold never registered at the Hilton. . . . Wexley contends that the registration evidence was concocted. . . . Wexley claims. . . . He further charges that. . . . (etc., etc.)

Continuing in this tone, he concludes with this protest:

Thus we are told that the hotel registration was a complete forgery. . . . that the card could not have been signed in 1945 but was indeed a 1950 forgery. These are brazen but serious charges.

Very well, brazen or not, now at last they are serious.

And yet, as Pollack concludes his chapter, all he comes up with is a quibble about whether Gold carried baggage ("How does he [Wexley] know that?")—which item we have dealt with in this chapter, with its source given in Note 7, *i.e.*, Mr. Pilat, on whom Pollack leans so heavily throughout this report.

Pollack also asserts that Bloch was to blame for his own stupidity or failure to see through Saypol's strategem with the photostat. (This is Pollack's only offered proof that the Hilton card was not a forgery!)

Perhaps the clearest indication of Pollack's inability to cope with the thorny problem of the statement:

He (Wexley) cannot understand why Gold should have registered in his own name or why he registered at all since he was leaving for New York the same day.

As stated in this chapter, we "understand" all too well the reason why the forged card contained Gold's own name. It was, as amply demonstrated, so that the prosecution could "prove his (1945) presence in New Mexico in 1950" and thus provide some tangible basis for his testimony at the Rosenberg trial.

In short, despite Pollack's refutation by reiteration, what we see is a studied avoidance of the all-important question: Why did Gold, the self-proclaimed veteran spy, register "needlessly and dangerously" in his own name and with his own address? A question, as I have charged, which compels only one answer: that the Hilton card had to be an FBI-Gold forgery.

(See *Addenda* to the Epilogue concerning our discussion with Bloch in Washington on June 17, 1953, to present our findings about the Hilton card and the Santa Fe timetable to the press and in a motion for a new trial.)

•

As noted in "The Letter 'W'," the 1975-released FBI memo of July 2, 1950, provides further confirmation that Gold's "impossible" train trip from Albuquerque to New York (as well as Pollack's efforts to plug the hole with the plane detour via Washington) was entirely concocted. In this memo, Ruth's letter to David of November 4, 1944, described her wartime difficulties in getting a train seat from Chcago to Albuquerque:

I may not be able to get a reservation . . . that seems to be next to impossible. . '. . they have asked for tickets four weeks hence and were unable to receive them. . . . I got to Chicago Saturday . . . [9 A.M.]. I went directly to the Santa Fe depot and hung around but . . . every window I got the same answer "Sold out."
. . . . [At 4 P.M.] all the agents were [still] saying "sold out". . . . So I got back on the line and at five after 5 I got a seat—I was never so relieved in my life.

Thus Ruth was forced to wait all day in Chicago, from 9 A.M. to 5 P.M., to obtain a train seat. And yet, according to the Pollack report, despite the greater drawbacks to wartime plane travel, Gold obtained his reservation at the Chicago airport with a mere phone call. However, even if one accepts this miracle, Gold would have had to arrive in Chicago aboard the *California Limited* at the scheduled time of 7:30 A.M. Here are Ruth's letters of December 4 and 6, 1944, describing her return trip from Albuquerque to Chicago on that *same* train:

I went down to the [Albuquerque] depot but I didn't fare so well. . . . I'll be darned if I know what to do. . . . Since the California Limited is a fairly crummy train . . . all I could get is a coach seat. . . .

We were about three hours late getting into Newton, Kansas and there the cylinder in the engine burned out. . . . We were due in Kansas City at 6 [P.M.]. . . . We pulled in at 12 [Midnight] and. . . . didn't pull out until 2 o'clock [A.M.]. . . . [Now] I'm at NEW YORK CENTRAL [in Chicago]. . . . but still ain't got a reservation [to New York]. . . .

Exactly six months later, on June 3-5, 1945, this same "crummy train" is supposed to arrive in Chicago precisely on schedule for Gold to catch his alleged plane to Washington!

17 "LET HER AND FALSEHOOD GRAPPLE"

I

> "So Truth be in the field . . . Let her and Falsehood grapple. . . ."
>
> —*John Milton*

We now approach the very heart of the Government's case where truth and falsehood really come to grips. Since the death penalties for the Rosenbergs were based on a crime "not to the injury of the United States," and since these were to be the first carried out in peacetime, the prosecution found it necessary to enlarge the crime. In order to justify the punishment of death, the charges included the stealing of the secret construction of the plutonium bomb used to destroy Nagasaki. Here is the *Columbia* summary of this charge:

8. THE DELIVERY OF THE NAGASAKI BOMB PLANS [1]

In [September] 1945 Greenglass, again in New York on a furlough, prepared a cross-section sketch and twelve-page explanation of the [Nagasaki] atom bomb based on overheard conversations and surreptitious investigations at Los Alamos. Ruth Greenglass and the Rosenbergs aided in the preparation of the report.

In his testimony it was Greenglass' claim that, despite the passage of more than five years, he remembered this cross-section and detailed description to the extent that he could reproduce in 1951 an *exact* copy of what he had delivered to the Rosenbergs in September of 1945. This "copy" was admitted into evidence as Government Exhibit 8. Although we will deal here with other important matters, our primary concern will be an analysis of these two questions:

1. Is it credible that an ordinary mechanic with Greenglass' total lack of scientific education could have performed the feat he claimed, *i.e.*, merely by asking questions of gullible scientists or by listening to snatches of their conversations?

2. Is it credible that Greenglass could have reproduced Government Exhibit 8 in exact detail almost six years later, without assistance and solely from memory?

Let us turn to the direct testimony. Here it is in substance:

That during David's September furlough the Greenglasses stayed at the flat of his mother. That on the morning after their arrival Julius dropped up to ask what information David had brought and that it be written up.

That Julius gave David the sum of $200. That Ruth protested giving the information to Julius. That David said, "I have gone this far and I will do the rest of it, too."

That after Julius left, Greenglass drew a cross-section of the Nagasaki-type bomb and wrote twelve pages of descriptive material. That, in addition, he "gave some scientists' names, and also . . . some possible recruits for espionage."

That about 2 o'clock that afternoon David and Ruth drove to the Rosenberg apartment. That Julius took the report into another room and came out saying, "This is very good. We ought to have this typed up immediately."

That David heard Ruth reply: "We will probably have to correct the grammar involved."

That while Ethel did the typing, Ruth and Julius aided her by having it "typed down in correct grammatical fashion":

[Ruth]: Well, Ethel was typing the notes and David was helping her when she couldn't make out his handwriting and explained the technical terms and spelled them out for her, and Julius and I helped her with the phraseology when it got a little too lengthy, wordy.

That with this procedure completed, the handwritten notes were burned in a frying pan, then taken by Julius into the bathroom where he flushed the ashes down the toilet.

Such is the gist of the Greenglass testimony, which was wholly and completely denied by the Rosenbergs, except for their recollection that their in-laws did pay them a visit or two during this September furlough in 1945.

Let it be emphasized that there was no supporting evidence or any witness to this episode. Thus again we must consider that an innocuous visit of a soldier home on furlough paying a family call became the basis of a conspiratorial meeting.

Concerning Ruth's opposition to David's spying, we see transparent lying. If she is so opposed, why does she come along? Is it because she must be a witness to the typing ceremony so that she may later testify about it at the trial?

According to his testimony, Greenglass is still giving Julius (for the third time) the names of scientists and possible spy recruits. However, when cross-examined, he can repeat only the *same* scientists' names given to Ruth in November of 1944, and to Julius in January of 1945. As for the mysterious recruits, again no names are mentioned.

Concerning the alleged typing by Ethel, we come to what is perhaps the cruelest act in the history of frame-up: Greenglass' gratuitous incrimination of his sister. For even if Ethel's guilt had any basis in fact, neither the FBI nor anyone else could have had any knowledge of it without his "voluntary" disclosures. However, Greenglass' testimony betrays how mercilessly he "piled it on" in compliance with the prosecution's instructions.

First, why was it necessary for Greenglass' September report to be typed, whereas his June report to Harry Gold remained untyped? Why no mention about Greenglass' illegible handwriting when Gold and Yakovlev discussed the June report in such detail? [R. 831]

Second, one cannot help wondering why Ruth, an expert typist, made no effort to allow Ethel to do her housework or tend to her two-year-old son. (*Note:* According to Ruth's testimony, the little Michael was present.) After all, Ruth was thoroughly familiar with her husband's handwriting, and surely, Ethel had to pay some attention to her child while the typing went on from 2:30 to 5 o'clock. Under such circumstances, one would think that Ruth would have taken over the typing entirely.

But no, Ethel had to do all of the typing, for she had to be cast in the role of a "full-fledged partner" of Julius. (And Ruth's role had to remain a minimal one.)

Let it be understood that the Government's case against Ethel was, from the start, a very weak one. All they had was her alleged persuasion of David to enter the conspiracy. To insure conviction Saypol needed something more—a physical act connected to the delivery of the secrets. But since she was tied down by housework and a child, about the only thing they could "hang" on her was this act of typing. Accordingly, this had to be "blown up" by every means possible. Here is an illustration from Saypol's summation:

This description of the atom bomb . . . was typed up by the defendant Ethel Rosenberg that afternoon. . . . Just so had she on *countless* other occasions sat at that typewriter and struck the keys, blow by blow, against her own country, in the interests of the Soviets. [R. 1523; emphasis added.]

In the record these "countless" occasions actually number two, both without corroboration. In fact, only *one* occasion is claimed to have been witnessed by the Greenglasses.

Let it be emphasized that the primary basis for putting Ethel Rosenberg to death was this alleged typing. And yet, in David's confidential report to Rogge of what he told the FBI, there is not the slightest mention of Ethel or these conspiratorial visits. As pointed out previously, this report contains:

1. No mention of Ethel's complicity whatsoever.
2. No mention of Ethel's typing of the January report on the lens mold, nor anything about the episode of the Jello-box arrangement by the Rosenbergs.
3. No mention of Ethel's typing of the September report on the Nagasaki bomb, nor anything about that episode.

In other words, we see that everything concerning Ethel's typing, *contrary to Greenglass' testimony,* was the result of his many months of conferences with Roy Cohn and the FBI.[2]

•

In this matter of Ethel's typing, there is a suspicious pattern one can trace to other trials supervised or conducted by United States Attorney Saypol. In the Hiss trial there was the alleged typing by Priscilla Hiss of the so-called "pumpkin papers." This allegation was categorically denied by Mrs. Hiss, and here is Alger Hiss' final comment before sentencing:

I want only to add that in the future the full facts of how Whittaker Chambers was able to carry out forgery by typewriter will be disclosed.[3]

But, forgery or not, the "evidence" of Mrs. Hiss' typing was a trump card in the prosecution's case. Thus it is not unlikely that Saypol calculated, "If the trick worked before, why not try it again?" In the Brothman trial he had Bentley "confess" that she typed espionage notes dictated by Brothman and given to the Russians via Golos, who, of course, was conveniently dead at the time she testified.[4]

Somehow this repeated pattern of lady-spy-always-types-espionage-notes brings to mind the mystery story writer utilizing the same plot device in one book after another. So it is when one compares certain passages in the Brothman tryout with similar ones in the Rosenberg trial. For example, Greenglass' curious preoccupation with burning and flushing things down the toilet:

Q. [Cohn]: Do you know what happened to the original notes after the typing was completed?
A. [Greenglass]: The original notes were taken and burnt in the frying pan and then flushed down the drain.
Q. Who did that?
A. Julius did that. [R. 513]

Strange, how cautious Julius was about these ashes, and yet in the Greenglasses' later testimony we will see how indifferent he was about keeping in his apartment a microfilming apparatus to photograph Ethel's typed reports. But, to trace this particular pattern in the Brothman record, here is Miss Bentley being asked what happened to her notes:

Q. Did you hand them on to Mr. Golos in stenographic form or did you transcribe them?
A. [Bentley]: I transcribed them on the typewriter and then carefully burned the stenographic notes.[5]

And here is Greenglass again, questioned about the Russian escape money Julius allegedly gave him:

Q. [Cohn]: Now what did you do with the $4,000?
A. [Greenglass]: Well, at first I had intentions of flushing it down the . . . I started to flush it down the toilet bowl.

But he didn't, and later we are told that this $4,000 was paid by the Greenglasses to O. John Rogge as his retaining fee. Thus it was quite fortunate for Rogge that Greenglass had had this change of heart, standing there cast in thought as he pondered: To flush or not to flush . . .

II

"As to her husband, she stated that he had a 'tendency to hysteria.' . . ." [6]

Since our examination of the testimony now deals with the vital question of David's scientific claims, let use review briefly his educational background. His accomplishments, as previously mentioned, were: (1) he had failed all eight out of eight elementary technical courses in the first year of high school and (2) he had attended a trade school where he was taught the rudiments of auto mechanics. [R. 611]

To demonstrate the absurdity of Greenglass' claims, Mr. Bloch asked him: Did he ever get a degree in science? An engineering degree? Did he ever take courses in calculus? Differential calculus? Or thermodynamics? Or nuclear physics? Or atomic physics? Or quantum mechanics? Or advanced calculus? To all of these questions, Greenglass replied, "I did not."

Q. Were you classified in the Army as a machinist?
A. I was classified—I had two classifications.
Q. What were they?
A. One was automotive machinist and one was machinist and toolmaker. [R. 611–614]

How, then, was it possible for this scientifically ignorant person to have comprehended the complex data involved in the construction of the Nagasaki atom bomb when he claimed to have gathered the data merely by *listening?* And how was he able to reproduce it *exactly* almost six years later and entirely from memory? For, Government Exhibit 8 was purported to be an exact "copy" of the bomb's cross section, describing its component elements, their action and interaction as well as the principles of operation of the bomb itself!

Even to a layman these claims must sound incredible, but to qualified scientists they are simply fantastic. In their opinion, not only would it have been impossible for Greeenglass to have understood what he was stealing in 1945, but impossible for even a trained scientist to have reproduced such material after so many years entirely from memory!

Here is the opinion of one of the scientists responsible for the success of the Manhattan District Project, the Nobel Prize winner Dr. Harold C. Urey, who appeared at a Congressional hearing on March 3, 1946:

Detailed data on the atomic bomb would require 80 or 90 volumes of close print which only a scientist or engineer would be able to read.

And here is an excerpt from Dr. Urey's urgent telegram sent to President Eisenhower on June 12, 1953, one week before the execution of the Rosenbergs:

THE CASE AGAINST THE ROSENBERGS OUTRAGES LOGIC AND JUSTICE. . . . A MAN OF GREENGLASS' CAPACITY IS WHOLLY INCAPABLE OF TRANSMITTING THE PHYSICS, CHEMISTRY AND MATHEMATICS OF THE ATOM BOMB TO ANYONE.

To get back to Greenglass' claims, how was he able to "snoop out" the complicated secrets of the Nagasaki bomb? Here is his explanation:

[Greenglass]: In the course of my work at Los Alamos I came in contact with various people who worked in different parts of the project and also I worked directly on certain apparatus that went into the bomb, and I met people who talked of the bombs and how they operated. . . .

I would usually have access to other points in the project and also I was friendly with a number of people in various parts of the project *and whenever a conversation would take place on something I didn't know about I would listen very avidly and question the speakers as to clarify what they had said. I would do this surreptitiously so that they wouldn't know.* [R. 493, 494; emphasis added.]

Here we are asked to believe that there was never anyone present who might regard Greenglass' behavior as suspicious. We recall from Colonel Lansdale's testimony the extraordinary degree of surveillance at Los Alamos, and that every scientist and technician *knew* of the existence of such surveillance.

Here is a description of the security measures taken at Los Alamos: The "tech area" was separated "by heavily reinforced wire fences" and inside of this region "only certain persons" had access. "Every tenth inhabitant belongs to the security division. . . ." And if anyone was ever seen to be talkative someone was certain "to step in and admonish him with a gesture . . . of turning a key: 'Shut up!' " [7]

Concerning Greenglass' claim that he could obtain atomic secrets by merely being "friendly with . . . various people . . . who talked of the bombs," it is noteworthy that the prosecution did not produce a single one of these people to confirm this claim.

By way of a final comment, we must not forget that it was virtually impossible for Greenglass even to *understand* the specialized language which these physicists spoke. It is as unintelligible as Sanskrit. Thus even if Greenglass could have induced these scientists to explain the secrets they were working on, it is doubtful that they could have found the means of communicating them to him. For the only thing Greenglass had learned as a machinist at Los Alamos was his particular work in machining a portion of the brass lens mold used for casting soft iron of a certain porosity. In direct testimony he admits his basic ignorance as to the nature or principle of what he was working on during his drive with "the Russian":

> [Greenglass]: He wanted to know the formula of the curve on the lens . . . but the things he wanted to know I had no direct knowledge of and I couldn't give a positive answer. [R. 453]

While we are examining Greenglass' scientific capacity, it is relevant to point out how Judge Kaufman prevented any test of it. This occurred when Saypol called to the stand a former liaison officer attached to the Los Alamos Project, one John A. Derry. He was asked his opinion on the value of the secret material represented by Government Exhibit 8. Mr. Derry's testimony was that the information contained in Greenglass' prepared "copy" would have been considered valuable and a classified top secret back in 1945. *This was to be expected, since the prosecution would not have dared to have Greenglass prepare a copy of something that was not a secret!* [8]

When, however, the defense attempted to ask Mr. Derry the all-important question relating to Greenglass' capacity to prepare such a "copy" unaided, this is what happened:

> Q. [Bloch]: Would you say as a scientist, a graduate engineer who . . . had the experience that you have detailed to us here, that a machinist without any degree in engineering or any science would be able to describe accurately the functions of the atom bomb and its component parts—
> The Court: Objection sustained.
> [*Note:* This is Kaufman's objection.]
> Mr. E. H. Bloch: May I finish it?
> The Court: Yes.
> Q. [Bloch]:—Both in relation to their independent functions and to their inter-related functions?
> The Court: Objection sustained. [R. 916]

It was a courageous question for the defense to ask, for it went to the core of the Government's case. It also bore great risk. Derry was Saypol's witness and if he had replied in Greenglass' favor it would have been a disastrous blow to the Rosenbergs. Evidently Kaufman feared the reply more than the defense did, seeing how quickly he moved to seal off this one effort in the entire trial to shed light on this key question. This action was based on the technicality that it was a matter belonging in summation. In short, on the basis of a legalistic quibble the presiding judge withheld from the defense its one opportunity to probe into this crucial question.

While on the subject of scientific opinion, it is significant to note that two government officials had been invited to sit at the prosecution's table. They were introduced to the Court as Mr. Charles Dennison, Chief of Litigation for the Atomic Energy Commission, and Dr. Beckerly, also attached to the AEC [R. 437]

Three years after the trial this writer came upon a startling news item in the New York *Times* of March 17, 1954. It concerned a speech given by one "Dr. James Beckerly, Director of the Atomic Energy Commission Classification Office." After explaining that Dr. Beckerly was the man "responsible for classifying nuclear data," the *Times* went on to report:

Dr. James Beckerly said it was time to stop "kidding" ourselves about atomic "secrets," and time to stop believing that Soviet scientists are incompetent.

The atom bomb and the hydrogen bomb were not stolen from us by spies, Dr. Beckerly emphasized.

Since Dr. James Beckerly was the AEC official who attended the Rosenberg trial, we can only ask in dismay why he did not volunteer to say the same thing in the courtroom? How could he sit there with this knowledge and maintain a stony silence? Why did he wait until nine months after the death of the Rosenbergs to make an admission that should have been his moral duty to announce *before* their execution?

•

Even if we wish to believe in the miracle of Greenglass' espionage feat of 1945, the second question remains: Could he have reproduced, in 1951, the cross section and the oral description of the Nagasaki atomic bomb wholly from memory, as he claimed at the trial?

Since there was no time given the defense during trial to elicit expert opinion on this question, efforts were made during appeal to secure independent judgment from accredited scientists. Fortunately, there were several distinguished British and French scientists (safely beyond the punitive arm of investigating committees) willing to study the record and report their findings. Here are some excerpts from their affidavits, sworn to and signed before United States Consular authorities in London and Paris.[9] This one was sworn

372

to by Dr. Thomas Reeve Kaiser, a nuclear physicist formerly at the Clarendon Laboratory at Oxford:

I have read the transcript of the testimony of David Greenglass, of Walter Koski and John A. Derry upon the trial of Julius Rosenberg and Ethel Rosenberg.

Question: Could a person of Greenglass' background and experience have produced in 1945 the sketch of a cross section of the Nagasaki type of atom bomb, together with twelve pages of matter explaining the functions and workings of such a bomb and its component parts, drawing solely from memory and without the aid or assistance of any person or written matter or technical or scientific source of coaching?

Answer: . . . It is inconceivable that a man in the position of the said David Greenglass, without specialist training and experience, could have accomplished this feat in 1945.

Question: Could a person of Greenglass' background and experience have produced in 1951 a replica of a cross section of the Nagasaki type of atom bomb . . . drawing solely from memory [etc.]?

Answer: . . . It is likewise inconceivable that the said David Greenglass could have reproduced the matter in question in 1951 without the aid or assistance of any person or written matter or help from any technical or scientific sources.

On this key issue of credibility, each scientist was also asked about his *own* ability to perform the feat of memory claimed by Greenglass.

Question: Could you, as a trained scientist, produce a sketch of a cross section of this type of atom bomb together with the approximate explanatory matter, drawing solely from memory alone five or six years subsequent to having terminated work or any connection with a technical problem of such complexity?

Answer: . . . While I could without difficulty produce sketches outlining the principles, involved in developments in which I participated some five or six years ago, I could not do more than this *without reference to notes made at the time*.

For example, without reference to such notes I could not make detailed drawings of specific equipments. I certainly could not, *without reference to notes,* make a replica of the sections of any specific apparatus. [Emphasis added.]

Another such affidavit was signed by Dr. James Gerald Crowther, a mathematician, a physicist, and the celebrated author of many scientific works. He was also Director of the Scientific Department of the British Council (a government agency) throughout the war. His opinion was the same as that of Dr. Kaiser.

Still another affidavit came from Dr. Jacques S. Hadamard of the University of Paris and former honorary chairman of the International Congress of Mathematicians of Boston and the Royal Society of London. It is substantially identical to those of his British colleagues.

Another affidavit to the same effect was signed by Dr. John Desmond Bernal, a professor of physics at Birkbeck College, University of London, and a former Scientific Advisor to the Ministry of Home Security and Combined Operations from 1939 to 1945.

Since, as demonstrated, it was impossible for Greenglass to have reproduced in 1951 Government Exhibits 2, 6, 7, and 8 without the assistance of coaches, books, drawings, etc., it is reasonable to assume that such assistance was provided during his sojourn with Gold on the eleventh floor of the Tombs. And since Greenglass swore that he had prepared these exhibits without assistance, this would not only constitute perjury but also raises the question whether or not subornation of perjury was involved.[10]

In other words, the essence of the case against the Rosenbergs (Government Exhibits 2, 6, 7, and 8) appears to have been literally manufactured for the trial by Greenglass with the assistance of certain government officials. But, whether due to Greenglass' limitations or to the precautions taken by the various participants, the frame-up was inherently a botched piece of work. Here is the opinion of the science editor of *Life*, March 26, 1951: "Greenglass' implosion bomb appears illogical, if not downright unworkable."

And here is the reaction in *Scientific American*, May, 1951: "What the newspapers failed to note was that without quantitative data and other necessary information, the Greenglass bomb was not much of a secret."

It may be contended that the Rosenbergs were just as guilty even if Greenglass' snooping was limited to only a portion of the atom bomb. But this was *not* the prosecution's case. Greenglass claimed that he was successful in stealing the secret of the *entire* Nagasaki bomb and that he had prepared the "copy" of it unaided. We believe we have proved his claims utterly incredible. Indeed, the fact that his handwritten memo does not contain mention of this most important act of the conspiracy is in itself proof of subsequent fabrication. In addition, this memo exposes a further perjury when Greenglass testified that he had told the FBI about the September visit to the Rosenbergs on the night of his arrest. [R. 594]

In view of this last claim, it is highly significant that the alleged September episode—the core of the Government's case as well as the most important act of the conspiracy—is not included in the list of Overt Acts charged in Indictment No. 3, dated January 31, 1951, which was only six weeks before trial. What is one to conclude from this singular fact but that the prosecution, desperate to win a conviction at all costs, decided to add the Nagasaki-bomb episode to Greenglass' testimony in the very last weeks before trial! [11]

Is it any wonder that the fabrication turned out to be so shoddy, when one considers all the apparently hasty decisions of the prosecution to keep Greenglass "piling it on"? How readily he complied in his eagerness to win the lightest possible sentence for himself will now be seen in the series of additional crimes which were conjured up for the Rosenbergs.

NOTES AND REFERENCES

1. For David's direct, see Record, pp. 489–500, 510–513. For Ruth's, see Record, pp. 702–705.
2. (Greenglass): When I came down to talk to the FBI I talked about a number of things; whatever their

interrogation led to . . . I signed statements, plenty of statements. (Record, pp. 601–602.)

3. See Earl Jowitt, *The Strange Case of Alger Hiss*, Doubleday, New York, 1953, p. 344. See also Alistair Cooke, *A Generation on Trial*, Knopf, New York, 1952, p. 338. See also article "What The FBI Knew and Hid" by John Lowenthal, *The Nation*, June 26, 1976.

4. Brothman Record, p. 364.

5. *Ibid.*, p. 483.

6. From memo of Robert H. Goldman, Rogge's associate, based on a confidential interview with Ruth Greenglass two days after her husband's arrest. (See Appendix 3.)

7. Jungk, *op. cit.*, see chapter "The Place Marked 'Secret,' " pp. 98, 102. See also *Now It Can Be Told*, by Lt. Gen. Leslie R. Groves, Harper & Bros., New York, 1962: "My rule was simple . . . each man should know everything he needed to know to do his job and nothing else."

8. In other words, the defense did not contest that Greenglass could be coached to *copy* a cross section and *memorize* it from material smuggled in to the eleventh floor of the Tombs.

On this assumption, Mr. Bloch was ready to stipulate that Government Exhibit 8 was secret material and offered that it be impounded.

Bloch's viewpoint was that although the Atomic Energy Commission had declassified the material, nevertheless the Rosenbergs would not insist on forcing public disclosure of the exhibit. His theory was that whatever Greenglass might have been instructed to prepare and testify to had no connection with the Rosenbergs.

As for his offer to impound, it took the prosecution by surprise, as evidenced by this initial reaction:

Mr. Saypol: That is a rather strange request coming from the defendants. (Record, p. 499.)

Seeing Saypol's confusion, Judge Kaufman took control, saying, "Let me handle it." Whereupon he requested the spectators to leave the courtroom during the interval Greenglass' testimony on Exhibit 8 was presented.

The actual value of the so-called secret material

can be estimated from the fact that Kaufman (and the AEC) permitted the reporters to be present and requested them to exercise "good taste . . . on the matter of publishing portions of this testimony." (See references to *Life* and *Scientific American* in this chapter.)

After the trial this defense strategy met with strong criticism in a pamphlet in which "the scandalous manner . . . the judge took advantage of [Bloch's] errors" was the principal thesis. (See Irwin Edelman, *Freedom's Electrocution*, P.O. Box 2505, Los Angeles, Calif.)

Among lawyers impressed with this point, was Mr. Fyke Farmer who later raised the question of the applicability of the Atomic Energy Act of 1946 and precipitated the stay of execution granted by Justice Douglas. (See New York *Times*, June 17–19, 1953.)

9. For full affidavits of Dr. Thomas Reeve Kaiser, Dr. Jacques S. Hadamard, Dr. James Gerald Crowther, and Dr. John Desmond Bernal, see Transcript of Record, Supreme Court, October term 1952, No. 687, pp. 113 to 127.

10. See charge in defense appeal that "this testimony was perjurious and must have been known to the authorities to be false." (Transcript of Record 687, p. 83.)

11. See discussion in "The Letter 'W' " dealing with the request of Saypol's assistant, Myles Lane, made to the Joint Congressional Committee, to add sufficiently important testimony to warrant the death sentence. This meeting was held on Feb. 8, 1951, four weeks before the trial.

ADDENDA

In the PBS television interview of 1974, referred to earlier, the eminent physicist Philip Morrison, who worked at the Los Alamos Atomic Project during World War II, gave this opinion regarding Greenglass' alleged bomb sketch:

This is a crude caricature of the structure of one particular model, without enough detail to make it possible to reproduce or even to understand it as it was drawn, since it contains some errors. But what more could you expect from a man who [had] . . . no direct contact at that time whatever with any but the simple mechanical parts that he might've seen if he'd worked in the shop or made the lens molds.

●

A statement to the difficulty in obtaining qualified scientists to testify in behalf of the defense was given to me by Gloria Agrin, the young lawyer who assisted Mr. Bloch: "There was just no way to get to any nuclear expert at the time. No one would talk to us then." One prospective witness who did qualify stated that he wanted to consider it, but on the next day, said anxiously, "I can't talk to you."

●

As the result of a 1966 motion in behalf of Sobell, Exhibit 8, the alleged copy of the Nagasaki bomb sketch and explanation were made public. These were shown recently to Dr. George Kistiakovsky, former Director of the 600-man X (Explosives) Division at Los Alamos. His opinion was that it was "uselessly crude." As with the previously released copies of the lens mold sketches, he stated that their value to the Soviet Union would have been "almost nil." Dr. Kistiakovsky, once science advisor to President Eisenhower, explained further that the Los Alamos development of the atom bomb was based largely on a theoretical paper which was "identical" to one that had been "independently published in the Soviet Union. . . . in 1942 or early 1943"—i.e., two to three years before Greenglass' alleged espionage.

It should be noted that Dr. Kistiakovsky was announced as one of the important scientists on the prosecution's list of witnesses. He was not called to testify.

Another prestigious scientist, Dr. Victor Weisskopf, Institute Professor of Physics at M.I.T. and deputy leader of the Theoretical Division at Los Alamos, described the alleged sketch as "ridiculous, a baby drawing, it doesn't tell you anything." (See article by Daniel Yergin, *New Times,* May 16, 1975.)

18 "CONSIDER YOUR VERDICT . . ."

I

> " 'Not yet, not yet!' the Rabbit hastily interrupted. 'There's a great deal more to come before that!' "
>
> —*Alice in Wonderland*

In its efforts to insure the maximum penalty of death for the Rosenbergs, as demonstrated, the Government turned the trial into one of treason. And yet the Government could not include in its charge intent to cause "injury to the United States." For, if the major crimes were committed during wartime, then that would be exactly the period when the United States was on the most friendly terms with Russia, its ally.

There was hence the danger that the death penalty for giving aid to an ally might seem excessive. The viewpoint might become widespread that had the Rosenbergs been convicted in 1944–1945, the period of cordial relations with the Soviet Union, their punishment would have been not more than a few years' imprisonment.

In short, it would appear too obvious that the Rosenbergs were being punished *ex post facto*. Furthermore, the danger of this viewpoint was a real one because the Atomic Energy Act of 1946 prescribed the death penalty *only* where there existed intent to injure the United States. (*Note:* It was because of this that Justice Douglas felt bound to give his famous stay of execution.)

It was for this reason that the prosecution made certain that there would be testimony extending the Rosenbergs' crimes into the period of the Cold War.

It did not matter that this testimony was tenuous and without practical results. What mattered only was that the defendants had to be accused of conspiracy during the postwar period when the Soviet Union was being excoriated as an enemy nation.

In our presentation of the *Columbia* summary, we designated the heading with regard to the postwar espionage as:

9. THE THEFT OF THE PROXIMITY FUSE, ETC.
[R. 510–519]

To give the reader a general conception of the above "etc.," here is a breakdown of Greenglass' testimony:

1. That Julius requested Greenglass to remain at the Los Alamos Project as a civilian worker, but that Greenglass refused.
2. That Julius offered to send him to a university with Russian money to report on the progress of nuclear physics, but that Greenglass refused.
3. That Julius told him that one of his "boys" had obtained information concerning the "sky platform project"—a project to establish an orbiting satellite "between the moon and the earth."
4. That Julius told him that "one of his contacts" had obtained the mathematical solution to the problem of atomic-powered airplanes.

It should be noted that all of these charges were confined to conversations between Julius and David, with *no witness* to corroborate. To examine these charges, let us begin with the September, 1945, visit:

[Greenglass]: . . . At this time Julius told me that he had *stolen* the proximity fuse when he was working at Emerson Radio. . . . He told me that he took it out in his briefcase. That is the same briefcase he brought his lunch in with, and he gave it to Russia. [Emphasis added.]

Here too we see the pattern for Saypol's questioning of Elitcher, when the latter was asked if he had seen Sobell take secret material from Reeves in his briefcase. That Elitcher disclaimed knowledge of what papers Sobell carried in the briefcase did not matter.

It was the "briefcase" that mattered. Now, on the foundation of Saypol's insinuation, Roy Cohn constructs another use of the briefcase. Instead of smuggling out unseen documents, this one conceals an unseen explosive device.

Let us recall from Chapter 14 the flat statement made by the personnel manager of Reeves, namely, that the plant was considered "spyproof," and that "Sobell could not have removed any written data because of the strict supervision of employees."

And as for the Emerson plant, according to an inquiry made to its executives after the trial, so thorough were the precautions that every part of every proximity fuse manufactured was checked and double-checked, with a 100 per cent inventory control of all parts as well as the completed product.

Concerning Julius' request—that Greenglass remain as a civilian spy at Los Alamos—what can one say to disprove testimony couched in such vague terms as, "He told me to do such-and-such and I refused"?

Doubtless there were innocent talks between Rosenberg and Greenglass concerning the latter's future, because we know that both went into business after the war. In view of the high wages paid at Los Alamos to civilian machinists, Julius may well have advised him to remain there. Six years later, it would be a simple matter to insert a sinister twist into such normal discussions.

Concerning Julius' alleged offer to educate Greenglass as a nuclear scientist, here is the substance of the latter's testimony: that the particular college Julius suggested was the University of Chicago; alternate colleges were the Massachusetts Institute of Technology and New York University, which "had a nuclear engineering course he wanted me to take."

To take any of this seriously, one must ask: How could Julius propose a course in nuclear engineering for Greenglass, who had not even passed elementary high-school science?

Also, the period of these conversations coincided with their business animosities, *i.e.*, 1946 to 1949. Such rash confidences by Julius to a hostile brother-in-law is highly improbable, especially since Greenglass, according to his testimony, had performed his last act of espionage back in September, 1945.

II

In our study of the anatomy of frame-up, we have tried to demonstrate how it is built up, not of pure fiction, but of half-truths and even full truths. In the charge that Julius had told Greenglass that one of his "boys" had stolen information for "the sky platform project," we have a perfect illustration of this technique. Let us therefore follow Cohn as he leads Greenglass into an accusation even more breathtaking that the theft of the Nagasaki atomic bomb:

Q. [Cohn]: Did Rosenberg mention to you any Government projects concerning which he had obtained information from any of his contacts?

A. [Greenglass]: Well, once in the presence of my brother [Bernard], he mentioned a sky platform project.

Q. Did you have any conversation with Rosenberg about the sky platform project?

A. Yes, I had a conversation with him *later*. I asked him *in privacy* . . . I would say this was '47, late '47. He told me he had gotten this information about the sky platform from one of the boys, as he put it.

Q. Did he tell you just what information had been given to him by one of the boys concerning the sky platform project? Did he describe it to you at all?

A. Yes, he did. *He described it in front of my brother, too.*

Q. How did he describe it?

A. He said that it was some large vessel which would be suspended at a point of no gravity between the moon and the earth and as a satellite it would spin around the earth. [Emphasis added.]

It will be seen that the technique here is the same as with Mrs. Sidorovich when she left *prior* to the arrangement of the alleged Jello box. Whereas Bernard is present, we observe that the espionage talk comes "later" and "in privacy." In other words, it is testimony that seeks to support itself with the *apparent* presence of a third party. However, let us see out of what full truths this charge was created. First, a similar conversation actually took place during a lull at the shop:

> [Julius]: . . . I don't remember the specific incident but at that time . . . in the newspapers there was some talk about the Germans [having] done some work on some kind of suspended lens in the sky to concentrate the rays of the sun at the earth, and that is what I believe was the discussion we might have had at that time. Greenglass used to read the *Popular Mechanics* and the *Popular Science* and he always talked about things like that at the shop.
>
> Q. [Bloch]: Did you ever say at that time that you got the information from one of your boys?
>
> A. I did not. [R. 1108]

Thus, from some idle shop talk about space science, there is created another postwar act of espionage. Today, some three decades later, with our critical need for solar energy, the principle in the above German plan is almost exactly that contemplated at present by space physicists, *i.e.*, a *suspended satellite* would collect and relay to earth solar energy in the form of microwaves. Indeed, "at that time," many of the popular science magazines contained articles dealing with future space laboratories such as our present Skylab and the Soviet Salyut. In short, such discussions were commonplace, and it needed only the insertion of one of Julius' mysterious "boys" with the *innuendo* that secret plans had been "obtained" to transform that harmless discussion into an act of espionage.

(*Note:* In "The Letter 'W'," we have covered this aspect of Julius' alleged postwar crimes.)

In examining Greenglass' final charge—the *implied*

383

theft of the Pentagon's plans for an atom-powered airplane—we can observe the same technique of utilizing the presence of a third party prior to the so-called espionage conversation:

> [Greenglass]: He [Julius] once stated to me in the presence of a worker of ours that *they* had solved the problem of atomic energy for airplanes, and *later on* I asked him if this was true, and he said that he had gotten the mathematics on it, the mathematics was solved on this.
>
> Q. [Cohn]: Did he say from where he had gotten this?
>
> A. He said he got it from one of his contacts. [Emphasis added.]

Here again, the conspiratorial portion takes place "later on" and in the absence of the unnamed worker. Also significant is the innuendo technique, *i.e.*, no actual charge of espionage or even that the information is a classified government project. Only the mysterious word "contacts" is sufficient to make of Julius the spy-master of a widespread ring. And here too, we should note, there is just enough of a lie applied to a full truth to provide the illusion of espionage. For in 1951, it was a well-publicized fact that the Pentagon was planning a nuclear-powered aircraft.

As for the realization of these plans, a decade later, in 1961, after spending over one billion dollars, it was announced officially that the project was canceled and that the "possibility of achieving" such a "militarily useful aircraft in the foreseeable future is still very remote." [1] And today, some thirty years after Julius' "contacts" were supposed to have obtained the *solution* to the development of such a nuclear-powered plane, there are still no signs that the U.S. or the U.S.S.R. are at all concerned about the "problem."

III

Perhaps due to the complexity of the court record, the *Columbia* summary does not present the Government's case in chronological sequence. Hence, we have chosen to stay with Greenglass' testimony as he goes on to describe:

13. THE REWARDS GIVEN THE ROSENBERGS [2]

According to Greenglass' testimony these were the strange rewards Julius received from the Russians:

1. One wristwatch for Julius.
2. One citation carrying certain privileges should Julius ever visit Russia.
3. One wristwatch for Ethel.[3]
4. One console table.

Regarding Julius' watch, Greenglass described it as as "a round dial watch with a sweep second hand, and . . . a leather strap." Now he is asked in cross-examination:

Q. [Bloch]: Did you ever see the watch that you say Ethel got from the Russians?

A. [Greenglass]: I might have seen it but I didn't —I didn't—

Q. Didn't what?

A. Well, I wasn't told that that was the watch.

Q. Can you describe the watch that you saw on Ethel's hand or any time when she had a watch on her hand in her possession?

A. I can't describe that watch, no.

Now Bloch asks Greenglass to be more specific about the citation:

Q. . . . Did you ever ask him to show you that citation?

A. I never asked him to show it to me, no.

Q. Did you ever see it?

A. I did not see it, but he said there was—there were certain privileges that went along with that. [R. 629–632]

It is surely appropriate here to quote from Dr. Urey's famous letter to Judge Kaufman concerning the grave doubts he was struck with upon studying the record: "Is it customary for spies to be paid in console tables and wrist watches?" [4]

In the blanket denials by the Rosenbergs concerning these rewards, one learns that Ethel's watch was bought by Julius as a birthday gift for $30. It should be noted also that the prosecution did not dispute this purchase.[5]

Concerning Greenglass' evasiveness and inability to describe Ethel's watch, there was also his statement that it was Ruth who had brought it to his attention as a gift from the Russians. Why, then, didn't he notice it on Ethel in all the years from 1945 to 1950? And if it be true that Ethel told about or showed the watch to Ruth, then why is there no corroboration of this in the latter's testimony?

Concerning the "citation," we come upon another pattern pointing to the eleventh-floor collusion that took place between Gold and Greenglass. First, one must ask why didn't Julius, so boastful as he displayed his watch, also display his citation, especially since he received it "along with that watch"? And why was there no curiosity on the part of David to see such an unusual document? All of which causes one to wonder why wasn't Greenglass awarded a citation? After all, he had given the Russians the most valuable secret in world history. And if it be argued that citations were reserved only for the "dedicated," then why is it that Harry Gold, the *anti*-Communist, was "awarded" the Order of the Red Star? Here is the very climax of Hoover's *Digest* article describing this award:

Gold had been awarded the Order of the Red Star for his outstanding work on behalf of the U.S.S.R. . . . one of the privileges of the award was free trolley rides in the city of Moscow!

Free trolley rides! Are we to assume that one of the privileges Julius would have received would have also been free rides—perhaps on the Moscow subway?

IV

In analyzing this phase of the testimony against the Rosenbergs, we find much of it centered about the so-called Russian console table. How important an issue it became can be seen from the fact that the total testimony concerning it constituted some seventy-five pages of the record! Not only was this table described by the Greenglasses as a Russian reward, but also as a secret piece of microfilming apparatus. In direct conflict is the testimony of the Rosenbergs, who maintained that it was an ordinary cheap table which they had purchased at R. H. Macy's for $21.

It should be stated that the table was never produced by the prosecution, nor was it ever explained why it was not available. Instead, the "evidence" consisted of a group of photographs of various tables purporting to *resemble* the Rosenberg table. These photographs became Government Exhibit 28. Other than this "sample" evidence there was *only* the unsupported word of the Greenglasses that it was a Russian gift. Here is Greenglass' cross-examination as Mr. Bloch asks:

Q. And was that console table used for eating purposes?
A. That console table was used for photography.
Q. For photography?
A. That's right. Julius told me that he did pictures on that table. [R. 630–631]

We see that he describes the table as simply *a table*! His only reference to photography is that pictures were made "on that table." There is nothing "special" about it. Now let us turn to Ruth's direct examination:

Q. [Kilsheimer]: Did you have a conversation with the Rosenbergs concerning that table?
A. [Ruth]: Yes, I did.

Q. *And was your husband also present?*

A. I think he was, yes. . . . I admired the table and I asked Ethel when she bought a *new piece* of furniture; she said she hadn't bought it, she had gotten it as a gift and I said it was a very nice gift to get from a friend, and Julius said it was from his friend and it was a special kind of table, *and he turned the table on its side to show us why it was so special.*

Q. And what did he show you when he turned the table on its side?

A. There was a portion of the table that was hollowed out for a lamp to fit underneath it so that the table could be used for photography purposes, and he said when he used the table he darkened the room so there would be no other light and he wouldn't be obvious to anyone looking in.

Q. And did Julius Rosenberg tell you what he photographed using the table?

A. Yes. He took pictures on microfilm of the typewritten notes. [R. 706–707; emphasis added.]

At once we see that David was present. And yet, in his description, there is no indication that the table's underside was hollowed out! In David's version, the Greenglasses were told that the table was "from the Russians," whereas in Ruth's version, it becomes a gift from a "friend." Later, we will see that this change was designed to accommodate the anticipated testimony of a prosecution witness, Mrs. Evelyn Cox, an elderly black woman who had helped Ethel with her housework in the year 1944–1945 when the latter was ill.

Concerning Ruth's description of the "hollowed-out" portion, one cannot tell whether or not there was a hole cut through the top for a light to shine upwards. If there was such a hole, then it would certainly have aroused the curiosity of Mrs. Cox while cleaning the apartment. Her testimony, however, is devoid of any hollowed-out portion. And if there was no hole cut through, how was the lamp "underneath" supposed to function for "photographic purposes"?

This explains why the prosecution did not dare to

bring in a table "doctored" to fit Ruth's testimony. Its impracticability could have been demonstrated by any photographer. Most microfilming apparatuses are self-contained units requiring no "hollowed-out" table for light concealment. Instead of taking the risk of "faking" a table, the prosecution relied on the jurors' imagination while they studied the photographs of "similar" tables which Saypol passed among them. And obviously, Ruth's last point was aimed at Ethel to stress that it was *her* typewritten notes which had been microfilmed.

So much then for the Greenglass version. Now let us turn to Julius telling of his purchase of the console table in 1944 or 1945 from R. H. Macy:

Q. [Bloch]: How much did you say you paid for it?
A. [Julius]: Somewhere in the neighborhood of $21.

Q. Now, was the table that you purchased at Macy's the same console table that was in your home at the time the FBI finally came around to arrest you?
A. Yes, it was. [R. 1054, 1136–1137]

Observe that the table was purchased as early as 1944 or 1945. This period is later confirmed by Mrs. Cox. [R. 1408]. But it will be recalled that Ruth testified about having admired the table as a "new piece of furniture" *in 1946*.

During the cross-examination of Julius, Saypol asked:

Q. [Saypol]: Let us have a little talk about this console table. . . . Do you remember what day of the week it was that you bought it [in 1944 or 1945]?
A. Well, I can't recall. It is too many years ago. . . .

Q. Now, do you remember who the salesman or the saleslady . . . ?

A. Mr. Saypol, I can't remember a thing like that.

What day of the week did the reader buy a chair or a table six or seven years ago? Who was the salesman? What average person can recall such items after many years?

In the ensuing questions posed by Saypol there was the effort made to give the impression that the table was something "special." It was then that Saypol offered into evidence Government Exhibit 28, consisting of pictures of rather expensive tables for the jury to examine.

Q. [Saypol]: Don't you know, Mr. Rosenberg, that you couldn't buy a console table in Macy's if they had it, in 1944 or 1945, for less than $85?
A. I am sorry, sir. I bought that table for that amount [$21]. That was a display piece, Mr. Saypol, and I believe it was marked down. [R. 1205–1206, 1211]

It should be noted that Saypol's question about the impossibility of the table costing less than $85 was soon answered in an affidavit by R. H. Macy.

In Ethel's direct testimony she made the firmest denials. It was not a special table. There was no hollowed-out portion. Julius never used the console table or any table for photographic purposes. No microfilming was ever made of any typewritten notes at any time. [R. 1331–1332]

During cross-examination, Saypol showed her the pictured "samples":

Q. [Saypol]: . . . Which of these tables *resemble* the console table that your husband, you say, bought at Macy's?
A. [Ethel]: . . . These look a lot more fancy than what I had, but I would say that this, or this (indicating) had some similarity.
Q. You told everybody that you bought it in Macy's for $21?
A. I wouldn't say that I told everybody. I don't

390

know whom I might have spoken to and whom I may not have, but I know I bought it at Macy's. [R. 1357–1360; emphasis added.]

Two years after this testimony, the truthfulness of the Rosenbergs concerning the console table was proven beyond all possible doubt in a public courtroom eleven days before their executions. And it should be noted that Judge Kaufman remained so rigid that he even refused to *look* at the newly discovered console table despite the R. H. Macy affidavit showing that its markings proved it authentic.[6]

With the sensational discovery of the actual console table, the following facts become incontrovertibly clear:

1. That the Greenglass table testimony was false and perjurious.
2. That the prosecution "knowingly sponsored this false testimony" and that it was utilized to forge "a false link . . . between the Rosenbergs and the 'Russians.' "[7]
3. That the actual console table was available to the prosecution for at least four months following Greenglass' arrest.
4. That the table could easily have been produced in evidence to support the Greenglasses if their testimony had contained any element of truth.
5. And finally, that every item about the table sworn to by the Rosenbergs was the truth.

Let us start with David's arrest on June 15, 1950. There was no mention of the console table to the FBI, according to his confidential statement to Rogge. If, as Greenglass claims [R. 577–578, 604–605], he made six or seven additional statements early in the summer of 1950, withholding nothing, it follows that the prosecution must have been fully aware of the incriminating console table during this period.

According to her testimony, Ruth Greenglass made a written statement of her full story in mid-July of 1950 [R. 740—747]. If Ruth told everything, then it follows that the FBI knew about the hollowed-out table possibly a day or two before Julius' arrest on July 17, but as much as four weeks before Ethel's arrest on August 11!

During both these arrests, the FBI made a thorough search of the Rosenberg apartment. Several crates of books, phonograph records, personal papers, watches, snapshots, and clothing were carted away, *but not the table*! [R. 1134, 1177, 1293]

Until the end of October, 1950, when it was finally decided to give up the apartment and sell the furnishings, it is an uncontested matter of record that the table remained there available to the prosecution at any time.[8]

If the prosecution had been told about the table by the Greenglasses prior to the end of October, most certainly the damning evidence of it would have been brought into the courtroom.

In short, this is what undoubtedly happened: (1) The testimony about the console table being a Russian gift used for microfilming was never thought up during the first *four months* following Greenglass' arrest. (2) Only at some time subsequent to October of 1950 did the prosecution decide to add it as additional embroidery to the Greenglass list of postwar accusations. (3) Since the prosecution believed that all the Rosenbergs' furniture had been sold five months before trial, it remained confident that the defense could never recover it and use it to contest the Greenglass testimony.

On April 13, 1953, some two months before the Rosenbergs were executed, the *National Guardian* published the startling story of how one of its staff, Mr. Leon Summit, happened to find and authenticate the Rosenberg table. As mentioned earlier, in October, 1950, it had been decided that the flat be given up and that the furnishings be sold for whatever a second-hand man would pay. One of Julius' sisters was assigned the unwelcome duty.

However, this sister, hoping that Julius and Ethel would be acquitted, had decided to hold on to certain items, and stored them in the basement of her home. Among these items were a vacuum cleaner, a bicycle, two chests of drawers—*and the console table*.[9]

Since this sister, Mrs. Goldberg, did not attend the trial (nor did any of Julius' relatives) for the simple reason, as she told this writer, that she was not up to the strain, she remained totally ignorant of the testimony concerning the console table. As for those newspaper accounts which mentioned the table, it was Mrs. Goldberg's reply that she had not associated the "Russian" version with the one in her basement.

Three months after the trial, however, Julius' mother set up an apartment for herself and her two grandsons, Michael and Robby, who were taken out of the shelter home to live with her. This was in June, 1951. And, to help furnish the new home, the chests of drawers, the vacuum cleaner, and the table were moved to this apartment in uptown Manhattan.

Since Sophie Rosenberg, Julius' mother, was equally ignorant of the table testimony, she too had no knowledge of the table's significance when her daughter helped with moving the stored articles. Which brings us to the affidavit of Leon Summit.[10]

It was in the early part of March, 1953, exactly two years after the table testimony, that Mr. Summit chanced to mention it to Mrs. Goldberg. To his astonishment, he was told that not only had the table never been sold, but that it was safely in the apartment of her mother. Instantly, Mr. Summit hailed a cab and hurried uptown.

"Oh, the little table?" Sophie Rosenberg replied. "It's right over there with the telephone standing on it."

Whereupon, Mr. Summit turned the table over to search for possible markings which might disclose its source of purchase. (Of course, there was no hollowed-out portion.) Finding more than he had hoped for, Mr. Summit called the *Guardian* office to send up its cameraman, who duly photographed the table and its markings.[11]

The chalked markings on the underside of the table were found to be the code symbols used by R. H. Macy & Co. On March 16, 1953, an affidavit was obtained from Mr. Joseph Fontana, a furniture buyer at Macy's, who was employed in that capacity during the years 1944 and 1945. The substance of Mr. Fontana's affidavit is as follows:

1. That examination had been made of the table's markings which were found to be: "NN 4046—760—F4 [or E4]—1997."
2. That "NN" meant "Macy's occasional furniture department."
3. That "4046" was "the pattern number assigned" by the manufacturer "to this style in the year 1940."
4. That "760" meant the "Brandt Manufacturing Company Cabinet Works of Hagerstown, Md."
5. That "F4 or E4" was "a symbol of a Macy season." If "F4," that would denote "the fall season of 1936." If "E4," this was "last used as a symbol in the early part of 1944." However, "the use of 'E4' would be consistent with the manufacturer's pattern number."
6. And that "1997" stood for "Macy's retail selling price of $19.97."

And here is the concluding paragraph of the affidavit:

This console table was one of the lower priced tables sold in Macy's furniture department sometime during or subsequent to the year 1944, if the symbol "E4" is correct.[12]

And so we see the proof of Julius' statement when he had testified that the price had been "somewhere in the neighborhood of $21." When one adds the 2 per cent city sales tax to the $19.97, the sum comes to exactly $20.37. Furthermore, Mr. Fontana's deposition flatly refutes Saypol's challenge that no one could buy a console table in Macy's "for less than $85."

And finally, as it was possible to see from the photographs themselves, in no sense whatsoever was the table "hollowed out" or a "special kind of table," thus proving beyond all question that the Greenglasses committed the most palpable perjury.

By way of a postscript, it should be mentioned that the table was taken to the home of Mrs. Cox, Ethel's former housekeeper, by Mr. Summit and Reverend H. S. Williamson, an ordained minister of the Constitution Church of Manhattan. Mrs. Cox not only recognized the table as being identical to the one she had known in the Rosenberg apartment, but she also hinted nervously at the pressure the FBI had exerted upon her ever since she had been called by the prosecution as a witness.[13]

•

It is difficult enough in an ordinary case for an innocent defendant to obtain absolute proof that he did not steal a certain sum of money, or that he was not in the vicinity of the victim's home. If he is fortunate, he may be able to furnish proof by means of independent witnesses attesting that he was somewhere else at the time. But in a case where the charges consist wholly of conspiratorial conversations, *how does one prove such conversations did not take place?* It is impossible unless, as in the above instance, the frame-up was carelessly improvised or the puppets were pushed too far or were too eager to fetch another "soiled bone of information." For let us not forget that the Greenglasses were acutely aware that much was at stake in this conflict of family pitted against family in which they had permitted themselves to become entrapped.

Week after week, month after month, while awaiting trial, one can be certain that this awesome question plagued them: What if the jury acquitted the Rosenbergs? What then? What would happen to them, having already confessed their full guilt? Not only would they be looked upon as self-confessed "traitors" but as perjurers so perfidious that they had attempted to shift the blame to an innocent sister and her innocent husband! Someone would have to be the scapegoat for the prosecution's failure and the public's revulsion. How quickly would Judge Kaufman turn his self-righteous wrath upon them, not only to "throw the book" at David but press for the immediate indictment and arrest of Ruth!

Little wonder then that the Greenglasses were disposed to stop at nothing at this final stage of their testimony. And, as we will see, even more reckless concoctions were to come.

NOTES AND REFERENCES

1. New York *Times,* March 29, 1961.
2. In the next chapter we will return to the *Columbia Law Review* summary concerning the remaining headings, *i.e.,* Nos. 10, 11, and 12. *Note:* For David's direct examination, see Record, pp. 520–523.
3. In Ruth's testimony there is no mention of the wristwatches or the citation.
4. For Dr. Urey's full letter, see *National Guardian,* January 8, 1953. See also letter to Editor of New York *Times,* same date.
5. For Julius' direct examination about the "rewards," see Record, pp. 1133–1136. For Ethel's, see Record, pp. 1341–1343.
6. Motion for New Trial, filed June 5, 1953. See Transcript of Record, Supreme Court, October Term, 1953, No. 497, p. 11.
7. *Ibid.,* pp. 35–36.
8. See affidavits of the Rosenbergs, and of Julius' mother, brother, and sister, all annexed to Motion for New Trial, Transcript of Record, No. 497.
9. See affidavit by Mrs. Ethel Goldberg (Julius' sister), in Transcript of Record, No. 497, pp. 61–63.
10. See affidavit of Leon E. Summit, Transcript of Record, pp. 46–49, together with Exhibits I and II, concerning Mrs. Cox's recognition of the table.
11. See photographs of table (Exhibits A to F), Transcript of Record, pp. 51–56.
12. See affidavit of Mr. Fontana, Transcript of Record, pp. 45–46.
13. See affidavit by Reverend H. S. Williamson, Transcript of Record, p. 57.

ADDENDA

Concerning the proximity fuse, when one turns to the Pollack report to examine what other evidence was culled from the FBI "departmental files," one finds only that Julius, as a Signal Corps inspector at Emerson, had "wide access to all the jobs" and that he was "in charge of inspection of proximity fuses" at the time. And that is all. No evidence whatsoever is produced to corroborate Greenglass' unsupported testimony that Julius had stolen the fuse or any part of it, whether in his briefcase or any other way.

It will be recalled that Julius was discharged from the Signal Corps in March, 1945 on the basis of FBI surveillance resulting in the charge of Communist Party membership. Assuming this to be true, is it likely, as the "inspector in charge" and as the alleged head of the spy-ring involved in stealing atomic secrets at the time, that he would have risked being caught red-handed with a proximity fuse, or any parts, found in his briefcase by the guards and undercover intelligence agents in the plant?

As an indication of Greenglass' readiness to "pile it on" his brother-in-law, there is his statement to congressional investigators, made long after the trial, of what Julius had told him in addition to the theft of the proximity fuse, the sky platform project and the Russian gift of the console table. In 1948, according to this statement, Julius had had "an agent working on the Aswan Dam" in Egypt, *i.e.*, years *before* the Aswan project had begun! (See Yergin article, *New Times,* May 16, 1975.)

•

Also noteworthy is the prosecution's elaboration of the proximity fuse "evidence" presented to the Joint Congressional Committee on February 8, 1951, one month before trial. To impress the Committee with the extent of the alleged spy ring ("the limit to which these people have gone"), Myles Lane not only cites a "tie-in" between Julius Rosenberg, the Sidoroviches, and a scientist from Cleveland, but also suggests an accomplice (an "in") at

Emerson Radio who helped Julius steal the proximity fuse:

> Also, Rosenberg worked for an outfit in New York that were making those proximity fuses. . . . Rosenberg had an "in" on that. He didn't get that by walking in and taking it. He had a proximity fuse, and he *showed* it to this man Greenglass. [Emphasis added.]

With this elaboration, Lane outdoes Greenglass. First, despite years of efforts by the FBI, no evidence was ever found to link the Sidoroviches or William Perl (the scientist from Cleveland) with any espionage. Second, according to Greenglass' testimony, there is no mention of any accomplice at Emerson. Third, the statement that Julius "showed" the proximity fuse to Greenglass is manifestly false. Even Roy Cohn, aware of the intensive security arrangements at Emerson, did not encourage Greenglass to go beyond the charge that Julius had "told" him about using his briefcase to steal the fuse.

19 "THE TONGUES OF THE WEAK-HEARTED"

> ". . . Terror loosed the tongues of the weak-hearted. . . . It was a summons to the most hateful vices of mankind to become allies of the court: . . . to gain salvation by betrayal." [1]

It has often occurred to this writer that the chief reason one finds the Greenglass testimony so apt to fall apart at the seams is that it was worked out *backwards*. In other words, the last episodes were worked out first and the earlier events were tailored to fit the necessities of the moment. For example, the Greenglasses paid Rogge the fee of $4,000. The actual sources had to be concealed, since it was derived partly from the Greenglasses' black-market loot and partly from their "various relatives" who met in Rogge's office "to discuss" his retaining fee.[2]

. . . Well, how to account for so large a sum without mentioning these sources? It came from the Russians. How? Through Julius. With what explanation? To finance the Greenglasses' "flight." And where to flee? To Mexico, of course. Why Mexico? Because Sobell happened to have gone there and that fact had already been made into the headline:

A-SPY NABBED FLEEING U.S.

. . . So far, so good, but now to explain why the Greenglasses did *not* flee. Should it be the reason Saypol was to offer in his opening statement—that "a vigilant FBI broke through the darkness," that their "attempts to escape were nipped in the bud"? Well, this could do for the Rosenbergs, but the Greenglasses had to show remorse. (You see, they never intended to flee—not really.) Well, then, why did they take the $4,000? Oh, David didn't really want the tainted Russian money but Julius forced it on him. In fact, David was so revolted by it all he started to flush it down the toilet. And why didn't he? Because David (and here we are back to where we started) needed the money to give to Rogge as a retaining fee. . . .

•

The testimony of the flight instructions was presented by Cohn and Greenglass in a number of suspense-laden installments. It will be recalled that the *Columbia* summary includes the payments of monies to finance the "flight." Since the greatest portion of these payments are integrally bound up with the instructions for flight we will examine both headings simultaneously, *i.e.*:

10. THE PLANS TO ESCAPE, AND
12. THE MONEY PAID THE GREENGLASSES

Installment One

In February, 1950, according to David's direct examination, Julius Rosenberg came to his apartment and suggested they go for a walk:

[Greenglass]: It was a few days after Fuchs was taken in England. . . .

He [Julius] said, "You remember the man who came to see you in Albuquerque? Well, Fuchs was also one of his contacts"; and this man [Gold] who came to see me in Albuquerque would undoubtedly be arrested soon, and if so would lead to me.

And Rosenberg said to me that I would have to leave the country; think it over and we will make plans to go.

Well, I told him that I would need money to pay my debts back so I would be able to leave with a clear head, and Rosenberg said . . . he would get the money for me from the Russians.

. . . Oh, I also said to him, "Why doesn't this other guy—fellow leave, the one who came to see me in Albuquerque?" And he said, "Well, that's something else again," and I went home after that. [R. 523–524]

How would Julius *know* that Dr. Fuchs was Gold's contact, when he had never met Gold or Fuchs. The record does not show that Julius and Yakovlev knew each other. But even if they did, why would the Soviet official unnecessarily divulge so vital a secret? [3]

Concerning the statement that the arrest of Fuchs would "undoubtedly" lead to the arrest of Gold, there is the false premise that Fuchs would identify Gold sufficiently to cause his arrest and that Gold, when arrested, would implicate Greenglass. But with Fuchs' arrest, Julius would have read that Fuchs' contacts were primarily with "Russians" and that other talks had been "with persons of unknown nationality." [4]

In short, what Greenglass did on the witness stand was to put in Julius' mouth the familiar sequence of events as given to the press by the FBI: that the arrest of Fuchs had led to the arrest of Gold, and that the latter's confession had led to the arrest of Greenglass.

Concerning the last bit of dialogue—when Greenglass asks why Gold doesn't also make ready to flee—here is an obvious attempt to plug the hole he himself has created. The implication of the query is that if Gold would flee, then there would be no cause for alarm. But since with all this illogic, there cannot be a logical answer, he simply has Julius reply enigmatically, "Well, that's something else again."

Installment Two

Here is Greenglass' direct testimony continued, after fully two months have passed since Julius' alleged February warning:

[Greenglass]: . . . It was about the middle of April [1950]. . . . Julius came to see me and he said I would have to leave the country and—well, that was about the gist of the conversation.

Q. [Cohn]: Had he given you any money up to this point?

A. No, no money was given to me up to this point. [R. 524]

By implication, the testimony is self-serving. Without the promised money to pay his debts, says the honorable Greenglass, he'll just sit tight even if it means disaster for all of them. But what is taking Julius so long to secure the money? Back in February he was so certain that Fuchs was *sure* to identify Gold. Gold was *sure* to be arrested and this would *undoubtedly* lead to David. Extraordinary how indifferent the spy-master is to danger all during these two months!

But what is more extraordinary is that Julius' indifference continues despite the knowledge of an FBI visit to Greenglass in February regarding the latter's theft of the uranium.[5] Is it conceivable, if Julius feared the imminent arrest of Gold, Greenglass, and himself, that the two brothers-in-law would completely refrain from discussing the alarming implications of this FBI visit, not only at the time of Installments One and Two, but during any of the installments Greenglass describes in the testimony that follows?

Installment Three

According to Greenglass, his next flight instruction was given him at the end of April, 1950, when Julius had come to see him concerning the stock transfer they had been quarreling about for many months:

> [Greenglass]: . . . He came up to my apartment in order to get . . . some shares that I had for a business enterprise I was in with him, and he at this time told me that I would have to leave the country as soon as possible, he would get the information for me to leave.
>
> . . . He said I would have to go via Mexico but he didn't give me the complete information as to that until a little later.

Again a conspiratorial conversation is hooked onto the full truth of the long-drawn-out business dealings the two had been having since their dissolved partnership. It was at this time, too, that Ruth prepared a number of promissory notes for the $1,000 which Julius had agreed to pay for David's stock transfer. In Ruth's testimony it appears that Julius' debt of the $1,000 preyed on her mind. And in the next installment, when the Greenglasses receive their first payment for the "flight," it turns out to be $1,000, the exact amount Julius was unable to pay them for their share of the business! In short, the $1,000 Julius owed them at this *precise* time was transformed into the incriminating $1,000 of Russian money.[6]

But what is it that causes Julius to instruct David "to leave as soon as possible" just at this time? It cannot be Gold's arrest, since that event was not made public until May 24, almost a month later. But whatever the reason for Julius' concern at this time, why didn't he bring the money promised almost three months earlier?

Thus, again, we see a "spy-master" who won't come out of the cold. Instead of making ready to flee the country at this late date, his chief anxiety seems to lie in obtaining a share of stock having the dubious value of $1,000 in the petty remnants of a business mortgaged to the hilt!

The next discussion took place at the Greenglass apartment on May 24, 1950, the morning after Gold's arrest. On this occasion, it was alleged, Julius entered with a copy of the New York *Herald Tribune* in which there was printed a picture of Gold:

Q. [Cohn]: What did he say?

A. [Greenglass]: He said, "This is the man who saw you in Albuquerque."

I looked at it and said I couldn't tell from that picture, and he said, "Don't worry. I am telling you this is the man and you will have to go out— you will have to leave the country," and he gave me a thousand dollars then and said he would give me $6,000 more.

We then went for a walk. . . . He said that I would have to get a tourist card—to go to Mexico. . . . In other words, not to get the tourist card at some Mexican Consulate in this city but to wait till we got to the border.

He told me that in order to get the tourist card you have to have a letter or you have to be inoculated again at the border—a letter from the doctor saying you were inoculated.

Q. For what, did he tell you?

A. For smallpox.

Q. Did he tell you how he found that out?

A. He said he went to see a doctor and a doctor told him about it and I said I would attend to that. [R. 525–527]

Concerning Julius' warning to Greenglass not to apply for a tourist card at the Mexican Consulate in New York but rather at the border, this question arises: If Julius feared such an application might be reported to the FBI (in response to an alert), why would he assume the same thing would not take place at the border?

But more important, Greenglass' testimony regarding the inoculation certificate is completely discredited by fact. Here are the Mexican tourist requirements stating the "Customs and Immigration Regulations" as they existed up to and including the year 1952:

VACCINATION: Automobile tourists are not subject to any vaccination requirements on entering Mexico. However, on returning to the United States tourists must present evidence satisfactory to the Quarantine Officer of a successful vaccination within the past three years prior to arrival.[7]

In other words, it was *not* a Mexican regulation that required a vaccination certificate to enter that country, but rather a United States requirement for *re-entering* this country! Only as late as 1953 did the Mexican public health authorities make mandatory a certificate of vaccination; in other words, three years *after* the alleged flight instructions of 1950.

The reader will recall from Chapter 7 that, when Sobell went to Mexico in June, 1950, he found no necessity for arranging for any smallpox vaccinations until he and his family prepared to return to the United States. Why, then, if Julius had arranged Sobell's "flight" as charged by Saypol, would he give Green-glass *unnecessary* and *false* instructions? [8]

Concerning Greenglass' further instructions allegedly received on May 24, we now come to that portion which, for brevity, will be referred to as "Operation Finger":

[Greenglass]: He then told me I would have to have passport pictures made up. . . . Of myself, my wife and my family,[9] and also he gave me a certain form letter to memorize and sign "I. Jackson" [10] at the end of the letter. This letter was to be used when I get to Mexico City. I was to write to the Secretary to the Ambassador of the Soviet Union and state in that letter . . . about the position of the Soviet Union in the U.N. . . . I was to sign the letter "I. Jackson."

Then I was to wait three days at . . . some place away from the center of town. . . . Then I was to go with a guide to the city in my hand . . . with my middle finger in the—between the pages of the guide—go to a place called Plaz de la Colon and

404

look at the statue of Columbus there—and this
would be about 5 o'clock in the afternoon, three
days after I had sent the letter.

. . . I was then to wait until some man was to
come up close to me. And then I would say "That
is a magnificent statue," and that I was from Oklahoma and I hadn't seen a statue like it before, and
this man was to say "Oh, there are much more
beautiful statues in Paris." That was to be our
identification.

Then he was to give me my passports and addi-
tional money so that I could go on with my trip.
I was then supposed to continue on probably via
Vera Cruz. . . .

Q. [Cohn]: A seaport in Mexico?
A. That is right. [R. 527–528]

Why is Greenglass instructed to remain away from
the center of town? If Julius feared that Greenglass
might be recognized by the Mexican secret police or
the FBI in Mexico, then this would presuppose the
international alert mentioned earlier and destroy the
logic of the attempt to secure entry at the border.
And with such an alert, would not Greenglass be
watched closely no matter what part of town he chose
to live in?

Concerning the password instructions: If it was
necessary to arrange a recognition device such as
the matching of the Jello-box halves for Gold and
Greenglass, why not a similar matching device for
Greenglass and the Soviet Embassy contact? Or to
state it reversely, if a password and counterpassword
were sufficient in old Mexico, why would they have
been insufficient in New Mexico?

As for Cohn's pinpointing of Vera Cruz as the
seaport from which Greenglass was to depart, here
again we have the tailoring of testimony to fit earlier
events. Since Sobell had sought steamship passage in
Vera Cruz, the same port was worked into Greenglass' testimony as part of his escape route. In his
summation to the jury, Mr. Bloch exposes this maneuver:

[Bloch]: But "Mexico" was inserted in your mind to poison you, you see, because Sobell was down in Mexico.

. . . If Greenglass was telling the truth about the signals with a book, and a finger in the book down before a statue in Mexico City . . . how is it that Sobell, who is supposed to, be conferring with Rosenberg, how is it when he went to Mexico, if he were trying to get out of Mexico because of this crime, how is it he did not know about the [finger] and the statue? Does that make sense to you? [R. 1491]

In Saypol's summation, there is this reply:

[Saypol]: Sobell went to the airport of Vera Cruz, *just as Greenglass had been instructed to do* . . . exhibiting the conduct that fits the pattern of only one thing . . . flight from an American jury when the day of reckoning had come. [R. 1529; emphasis added.]

But if Sobell had been instructed "just as" Greenglass, how is it that Julius failed to arrange forged passports for the Sobell family as he is supposed to have done for the Greenglasses? Indeed, if there is any truth to Saypol's argument, then Sobell, having received passports and passage from the Soviet Embassy in Mexico City, would have had no difficulty at all in leaving the country. And yet, from Chapter 7, we recall how Sobell was at a total loss during his seven-week stay in Mexico and how he made so many panic-stricken moves in his attempt to find political asylum.

In his opening statement Saypol had promised the jury he would furnish evidence to prove that there was

. . . *An elaborate prearranged scheme to flee the country* . . . [and that] these efforts . . . *followed a carefully planned pattern.* [R. 183; emphasis added.]

And yet the very opposite was proved—because whereas Greenglass, according to his testimony, is admirably taken care of in every respect (forsooth, even to the detail of his middle finger) Sobell, according to the Government's case, receives no aid in his flight whatsoever!

•

For the next stage of Operation Finger, let us now journey with Greenglass to Sweden and his next statue. Having arrived in Stockholm, he was to send "the same type of letter" to the Soviet Embassy there, again using "I. Jackson" as his pseudonym:

[Greenglass]: I would then go three days later to the statue of Lineus [11] [etc., etc.] and I would repeat that it was a beautiful statue, a magnificent statue— something to that effect, and the man would say, "There are much more beautiful ones in Paris," and that was to be our contact. Then he was to give me my means of transportation to Czechoslovakia, and that is where I was to go.

Q. [Cohn]: Did Rosenberg tell you what you were to do when you arrived in Czechoslovakia?

A. He told me to write to the Ambassador of the Soviet Union and say that I was here. . . . My full name was to be signed, "I. Jackson." . . . Well, that was the end of the conversation on that day except that—he [Julius] said that he probably— that he had to leave the country himself and he was making plans for it, and I said, "Why you?" He said that he was a friend—that he knew Jacob Golos, this man Golos, and probably Bentley knew him.

In this extension of Operation Finger, it appears that Greenglass has given up his role as an Oklahoman, perhaps as a result of becoming a world traveler. And why the long 1500-mile detour by ship from Vera Cruz to Stockholm? Why not the shorter and direct route via Paris and thence to Prague? In this case, however, Greenglass' password concerning "more beautiful" statues in Paris would not be appropriate, and he would have to rehearse another one, with the danger of tripping himself up. But again, there is little sense in questioning nonsense.

It is in the concluding portion of this episode that one is particularly struck by the lack of probability. Finally, after more than three months of bland indifference to danger, Julius is *himself* considering the possibility of flight.

We are asked to believe that in all this time there was no concern about his own family's safety, despite his certainty that Gold would be arrested and the fact that the FBI had shown its suspicions about Greenglass' uranium theft back in February.

But it is now May 24 and Greenglass has just seen the news of Gold's arrest and "confession." If it is true that Gold came to his apartment with the name of "Julius," then Greenglass knows full well that his brother-in-law has been or will be exposed. After all, it was *he* who had identified "Julius" to Gold as his "brother-in-law." Furthermore, he should recall that he gave Julius' telephone number to Gold. And yet, mark his professed surprise as he claims to have asked, "Why you?"

And note the reply attributed to Julius. Instead of the "spy-master" expressing the *real* reason—his fear that the FBI would connect him with Gold's password "I came from Julius"—we find him apprehensive about the remote possibility of Bentley's recollection of him through her association with Golos who had died seven years before!

In 1948, according to Elitcher's report of the Catherine Slip episode, we recall that Julius "was pretty sure" Bentley did *not* know who he was and therefore "everything was all right." [12] If so, there should have been no fear of exposure from that quarter. But again, as with Elitcher's testimony, it is transparent that Bentley's name was dragged in here for only one reason—so that the prosecution might lay a foundation for her subsequent appearance as a government "expert" on the Communist Party "underground apparatus."

Installment Five

It will be recalled that at the start of Julius' alleged instructions on May 24, Greenglass had been told "to have passport pictures made up" of himself and his family. In further testimony Greenglass elaborates these instructions, stating that he was to take five sets of such photos, with each set containing five copies.

And so, in accordance with these alleged instructions, on Sunday, May 28, he and his "whole family" went to a photo shop in the neighborhood, had "six sets of pictures taken" and picked them up "later that evening." [R. 529–531]

Six sets instead of the requested five! Let us bear this in mind while we examine Greenglass' alleged next meeting with Julius, when the latter came to call for the "pictures."

Installment Six

This next meeting, according to Greenglass' testimony, took place on May 30, two days later.

Q. [Cohn]: Now I think you told us that he had asked you to have five sets of pictures taken . . . ?
A. [Greenglass]: That is right.
Q. How many, in fact, did you have taken . . . ?
A. I had six sets of pictures taken.
Q. How many did you give to Julius?
A. Five sets.
Q. What did you do with the sixth set?
A. I kept it in the drawer.
Q. Was that set after your arrest given to the FBI?
A. I gave it to the FBI.

Mr. Cohn: May I exhibit them to the jury . . . ?
The Court: Yes. [R. 530–532]

At once we see how important this "sixth set" was to the prosecution and how convenient that Greenglass had kept it until his arrest on June 15. If we proceed on the thesis that Julius never instructed

409

Greenglass to take any passport photos, there arises the question: How did the latter happen to have them to give to the FBI?

We know that from the moment the FBI interrogated Greenglass in February, 1950, about the stolen uranium, there was an increasing state of desperation on the part of the Greenglasses. From the Rogge file memo of June 19, 1950, we know also that the FBI intimidated the Greenglasses by the means of obvious surveillance "for several weeks" before David's arrest [Appendix 3].

Considering the hue and cry for "Communist spies" which followed Fuchs' arrest, it is not surprising that Greenglass had a frantic impulse to flee the country. Thus again, the method of working backwards was employed. The FBI had come upon Greenglass' passport photos on June 15. Months later these were used to show that an escape route had been planned. "Five sets" were invented for Julius' flight instructions and Greenglass was allowed to present the sixth as a "life preserver." [13]

The validity of this can be seen when we recall David's claim that it was *he* who gave the sixth set to the FBI after his arrest. But here is what Ruth claims on direct examination:

A. We gave five to Julius and I gave the sixth set to the FBI. [Compare R. 531 with R. 712]

Both these claims are false. David could not have given the FBI the photos *after* his arrest because immediately following his arraignment he was transferred to the West Street jail. As for Ruth, she was in the hospital when David was picked up. In her testimony describing her next day's interview with the FBI at the hospital, there is not a word about any photos. After this visit she did not see the FBI until mid-July, and still no word about the passport photos. [14]

It is clear that the Greenglasses sought to demonstrate by their alleged deception of Julius that they had been remorseful even before David's arrest. However, when we turn to David's memo to Rogge, concerning what he told the FBI on June 15, there is not the slightest mention of any photos, flight plans, escape money, forged passports, statues of Columbus, guidebooks, middle fingers—in short, *nothing* concerning any aspect of any of these installments!

In sum, we can safely conclude that the Greenglass passport photos did not become the "sixth set" until it was decided months later to fabricate Operation Finger.

Installment Seven

On Sunday morning, June 4, according to Greenglass, Julius arrived at his flat with "$4,000 in a paper, brown paper wrapping." After putting the package "on the mantelpiece in the bedroom," Julius asked Greenglass to "go for a walk" so that the latter might "repeat the instructions" concerning the escape route. [R. 532–533]

(*Note*: Since this installment is elaborated in the one to follow, we will examine both together.)

Installment Eight

On June 7, one week before David's arrest, Julius visited the Greenglasses for the last time:

[Ruth]: He came to our house. . . . He came and spoke in whispers. He said he thought he was being followed and that he was going to bring $2,000 more but he didn't because he was being extra careful. [R. 714]

For the first time we see a new element introduced —Julius' fear of surveillance. Here is David's elaboration:

[Greenglass]: Later, he came back. I was under surveillance at the time and . . .

Q. [Cohn]: Did you think you were being followed at that time?

A. I did think I was being followed. . . . I noticed some people following me on a Sunday evening; and he came back—Julius came back during that week . . . and as he came into the apartment he said, "Are you being followed?" I said, "Yes, I am." He said, "I just came back from up-State New York to see some people, and I was going to Cleveland, Ohio, but I am going—I am not going to go there any more"; and he said to me, "What are you going to do now?" I said, "I am not going to do anything. I am going to sit—I am going to stay right here," and he left.

Q. [Cohn]: Did you see him again after that?
A. Only in court here. [R. 533–534]

(*Note*: According to the Rogge memo of June 19, 1950, Ruth divulges that they "had been under surveillance by the FBI for several weeks." Therefore, why this "sudden" realization on June 7, only *one* week before David's arrest?)

According to Greenglass' testimony, *four months* have gone by since Julius' first warning to leave the country. Only now, on June 7, does the spy-master reckon with the possibility that FBI agents may have been on their trail. To demonstrate how incredible this is, let us review Julius' alleged spy conduct through the last few installments:

On May 24, the day of Gold's arrest, despite the fact that Gold may have implicated them, Julius remains oblivious to the possibility of FBI surveillance. So much so that he sends the Greenglass family to have their passport photos taken without the slightest concern that the FBI might follow them and thereby learn of their flight plans.

On this same day, too, he has come from the Russians with $1,000 in cash, apparently with no anxiety that Greenglass and himself may be under close surveillance as the direct result of Gold's arrest. Moreover, despite his specific warning to the Greenglasses to flee, he makes no escape plans for himself.

On May 30, still unconcerned, he not only comes to Greenglass' flat to obtain the passport photos, but still in defiance of surveillance he delivers them to the Russians and picks up the $4,000.

(*Note:* To accept Julius as the big wheel of the spy-ring, this instance alone challenges the reasonable mind. For surveillance *did* take place, and had there actually been such a meeting, the FBI could have caught both Julius and the Russians red-handed with the photos and the $4,000!)

On June 4, still oblivious to the risk of the FBI on his trail, Julius brings to Greenglass the package of $4,000. Here, too, the FBI could have pounced on them as the money was delivered.

And just previous to June 7, despite Julius' knowledge of Gold's arrest *two weeks before*, he nevertheless risks an apparent espionage trip to upstate New York without the slightest regard as to surveillance and to the exposure of his "people" there.

Thus, only as late as June 7—to repeat, four months after the FBI had interrogated Greenglass—Julius finally comes to the realization that they have been under surveillance! But still he appears unable to grasp:

1. That surely Gold has told the FBI about his espionage with Greenglass in Albuquerque and the matching of the Jello-box sides.

2. That surely Gold has told the FBI about the password containing the name "Julius" and the conversation about Greenglass' "brother-in-law."

3. That surely the FBI must have followed the Greenglass family to the passport photographer's shop on May 28, and was therefore fully primed to arrest them in the event of flight.

Hence, if one ascribes any truth at all to the Greenglass testimony, Julius must have known that "the jig was up" on June 7. But what change takes place in his thinking? None—according to Ruth's testimony —save that he was going to be "extra careful" about delivering the additional $2,000!

And so, with the end of Operation Finger, we have, on the face of it, the most shoddy array of incredible conduct, conflicting testimony, illogical situations, and sheer improbabilities ever presented in a court of law.

II

Thus far, we have covered all but one of the payments allegedly received by the Greenglasses. According to Ruth's testimony, there was also a sum of $800 paid to David by Julius back in 1948 [R. 725—726].

Strangely enough, although this payment was made to David *outside* of Ruth's presence, there is *no mention* of it in David's testimony! Furthermore, Ruth does not even know the reason for the payment. Nor is there any explanation why this important payment is lacking in David's testimony. It was, after all, a sum four times the $200 they were paid for the Nagasaki bomb, and although Ruth claims that this mysterious sum of $800 had been deposited in their bank account in New York, no substantiation was produced.[15]

As indicated earlier, the prosecution's device of connecting Gold's hotel registration card and Ruth's $400 bank deposit had well insured the credibility of all subsequent payments. In other words, the prosecution was now supremely confident that it no longer mattered how improbable the accusations—they would all be accepted by the jury without question.

11. ETHEL'S TALK WITH RUTH [16]

We come now to the final point covered in the *Columbia* summary of the Greenglass testimony. It also happens to be the final item in Ruth's direct examination, the gist of which is as follows:

That in the middle of July, 1950, about one month after David's arrest, Ethel had come bearing "gifts" of a pie for Ruth and other sundry gifts for Ruth's three-year-old son.

That Ethel had said she had been advised by her lawyer "to get assurances . . . that David would not talk." That Ethel had said "it would only be a matter of a couple of years" for David, and proposed that if he would join Julius in a stand of innocence, everybody "would be better off."

Here, again, is an innocent conversation twisted into an incriminating overture, with an implied admission of guilt on the part of the Rosenbergs. For in Ethel's testimony regarding this talk, there is this totally different version:

1. That Ethel did not visit Ruth at her house with any such proposal, but had happened to find her at the flat of Tessie Greenglass, Ethel's mother, who had just returned with Ruth from seeing David in jail.

2. That Ethel had come to inquire about her brother's health and to ask when she might visit him.

3. That contrary to being advised by Mr. Bloch to get assurances that David would not talk (confess), that Ethel had given her own assurances that no matter what the newspapers were saying about David's guilt, she would "stand and help in any way" she possibly could.

4. And that when Ruth had "flared up" insisting that David was innocent and would fight the charges, Ethel was relieved to hear this from Ruth's "own lips."

5. And that, as they parted, Ethel had offered to borrow money to contribute to David's defense, but that Ruth had responded "coldly" and left abruptly.

Here, then, are the two versions of this tragedy-laden scene between the two sisters-in-law. But even if we disbelieve Ethel's denials, the fact is that Ruth's accusations came eight months after this conversation, *i.e.*, after eight months of cooperation with the prosecution in exchange for immunity and the promise of a light sentence for her husband.

Her effort to add something, *anything*, to Ethel's guilt beyond the typing is not only transparent, but the added accusation that Mr. Bloch advised this overture (to obstruct justice) as the last thrust of her testimony, clearly demonstrates the determination of the prosecution to throw in everything, including the kitchen sink.[17]

III

Such, then, was the full testimony of the Greenglasses. Here is the opinion of the Court of Appeals as to its weight:

Doubtless, if that testimony were disregarded, the conviction could not stand. [R. 1648]

It is a fundamental concept of American justice that if one finds any basis for reasonable doubt regarding any material matter in a witness' testimony, one has the right to conclude that *all* the testimony is open to suspicion and, therefore, may be entirely disregarded.

On this point, the law required Judge Kaufman to charge the jury that "*all* of the circumstances established by the evidence in this case, *taken together*, must satisfy" the jury beyond any reasonable doubt. [R. 1549–1550; emphasis added.]

Having examined every point in the *Columbia* summary of the Greenglass testimony, we now must face this all-important question: *Are we completely satisfied that the Greenglasses told the truth, the whole truth, and nothing but the truth beyond any reasonable doubt?*

According to the law, unless we can answer an unequivocal "Yes," there is no choice but to doubt and discard the prosecution's entire case.

NOTES AND REFERENCES

1. Heinrich Graetz describing the Edict of Grace passed by the Spanish Inquisition; *op. cit.*, Chapter 10.
2. See Rogge memo, Appendix 3; also Addenda to Chapter 21.

3. See Record, p. 838, wherein the defense requests the Court to instruct the jury "that Dr. Klaus Fuchs is not a defendant or a conspirator in this proceeding."

4. New York *Times,* February 12, 1950.

5. Record, pp. 1227–1228.

6. Compare Record, pp. 768, 781, and 786, with pp. 782–783. (See also comparison of sums in conclusion of Section I of Chapter 21.)

7. *MEXICO,* published by Automobile Club of Southern California, 2601 S. Figueroa St., Los Angeles, Calif. Copyright 1952, p. 73.

8. In Chapter 21, Section II, we will deal with this subject more extensively with the testimony of Dr. Bernhardt.

9. It should be noted that Greenglass' "escape" was to include Ruth and their two children, the youngest only a few days old.

10. Perhaps some light can be cast on the choice of the name "Jackson." At first, this writer was puzzled why Greenglass should have been instructed to use any pseudonym at all, since it plays no part in the subsequent identification. One day, the pseudonym of Trotsky's assassin came to mind, namely, "Frank Jackson." It is quite possible that Greenglass associated the name of "Jackson" with the concept of a Soviet spy in Mexico.

11. Linnaeus (Carl von Linné), the Swedish botanist. (For this stage of the "flight," see Record, pp. 528–529.)

12. Compare Record, p. 261, with p. 529.

13. The expression "life preserver" was used by Whittaker Chambers to describe his "pumpkin papers."

14. Record, pp. 729–730, 740–743. See also Rogge file memo in Appendix 3, in which Ruth describes the FBI visit to the hospital, but makes no mention of any photos.

15. It should be noted that neither this payment nor any other Rosenberg payment described in the testimony was contained in Greenglass' "confession" to the FBI, according to his confidential memo to Rogge.

16. For Ruth's direct, see Record, p. 714. For Ethel's direct, see Record, pp. 1337–1341.

17. See Record, pp. 1343–1344, wherein Mr. Bloch puts this question squarely before the jury.

ADDENDA

In the Government's rebuttal to this book, there are at least three instances where Pollack asserts that Sobell's Mexican trip closely follows Greenglass' "Operation Finger" *e.g.*:

1. "Sobell and his family flew to Mexico in a manner which parallels somewhat Rosenberg's instructions to Greenglass."
2. "In going to Mexico, he (Sobell) followed to some degree such a pattern."
3. Sobell's actions "during his stay in Mexico are indicative of a carefully planned attempt to flee the western hemisphere."

What is at issue here is the crucial question of credibility in Greenglass' cloak-and-dagger description of Julius' alleged flight instructions. For, as we have seen, Greenglass' testimony is at complete variance with the *reality* of Sobell's haphazard conduct in Mexico. Hence the dilemma: On the one hand, Pollack must somehow give support to Saypol's flat statement that Sobell was following an "elaborate prearranged scheme to flee the country." On the other hand, there is the trial record which proves the very contrary.

Pollack's solution is a familiar one. In "The Letter 'W'," it was observed that he resorted to outright distortion of our text concerning Saypol. Here, to defend Saypol again, he uses the same device: "Wexley states as a fact that Sobell was given a carefully planned pattern of escape from the United States such as Greenglass testified Julius Rosenberg gave him." (For the actual text, see section VI in Chapter 7.) Having thus set up a straw man by presenting this *opposite* meaning, Pollack proceeds to knock it down: "There is no testimony on record to prove that anyone gave Sobell any particular pattern of flight. . . ." Exactly the point we have emphasized.

The significance of all this is quite clear. Pollack cannot resolve the dilemma. For if Greenglass' "Operation Finger" with its step-by-step instructions attributed to Julius becomes incredible when applied to Sobell's panic-stricken conduct in Mexico, then all the other Greenglass charges must be viewed with the utmost suspicion.

20 "CONFESS—OR ELSE!"

I

> ". . . In spite of the self-interest of our ac-
> cusers to maintain intact the structure of the
> case against us, cracks appear through
> which the truth is slowly seeping." [1]

In the course of this work it has become this writer's
firm conviction that it was Roy Cohn who was one
of those most responsible for that mockery of justice
called the trial of the People of the United States
versus Julius Rosenberg, *et al.*

Not for nothing did the ambitious Cohn achieve his
notorious reputation. According to United States Army
charges, he was capable of employing the most unscrupulous methods to apply pressure and coercion,
even against the person of the Secretary of the Army.
And according to the affidavit of Harvey Matusow, a
government witness in Communist trials, it was Cohn
who "worked" with him in preparing a good part of
his false testimony:

. . . in several sessions with Cohn, *we developed the
answer which I gave in my testimony,* tying Trachtenberg
to that passage. *We both knew that Trachtenberg had
never made the statements which I attributed to him in
my testimony.* [2] [Emphasis added.]

Regarding another charge of Cohn's subornation of
perjury, the New York *Times* of February 1 and 4,
1955, reports that:

"Matusow said he testified falsely concerning a
lecture at the Jefferson School, which he had
attended. *This testimony, he said, was formulated
by Mr. Cohn* and Matusow memorized it for the
trial." (Emphasis added.)

Both at the Army-McCarthy hearings and in a series of signed articles written for the Hearst press, we find Cohn's boast that it was he who was largely responsible for the death of the Rosenbergs. Included among his other accomplishments, as he lists them proudly, was "The William Perl Perjury Case." [3]

When last we mentioned Perl, he was being harried by Saypol, Lane, and Cohn just before the start of the Rosenberg trial. We know, from Perl's testimony at his own trial, that the FBI had threatened him repeatedly: "They strongly recommended to me that Rosenberg and Sobell were going to 'fry,' as they put it. . . ."

In describing his state of mind resulting from this coercion, Perl referred to "the domination of [his] life by the FBI" and testified further that "The FBI's strong emphasis that Rosenberg and Sobell faced the death penalty horrified and shocked me."

With the Rosenberg trial only a few days away, the pressure on Perl steadily increased. Here is his testimony recalling a meeting in the United States Attorney's office where he was surrounded by Lane, Foley, Kilsheimer, Cohn and "various FBI agents":

Q. Do you remember what was said?
A. [Perl]: Yes . . . mainly Mr. Roy Cohn informed me that—well, that if I did not confess I would be indicted.
Q. And what did you say?
A. . . . That I had nothing to confess, but whatever he or anybody had against me, I would very much like to hear in open court.[4]

And yet, despite this steadfast denial of complicity and his refusal to swear falsely, Perl was nevertheless included in the prosecution's misleading list as a government witness against the Rosenbergs. Although this maneuver failed to produce compliance, the full significance of what had happened behind locked doors did not become known until the facts became part of the official transcript of the Rosenberg appeal to the Supreme Court long after their trial.[5]

It was a crucial moment for Saypol as the testimony of David Greenglass drew to a close and Ruth prepared to follow him. There had been the hope that Sobell would break, but this had not happened. Hence, there remained only William Perl. And since it was now apparent that he would not cooperate as a government -witness, the prosecution decided to present his "testimony" by newspaper!

Thus on Tuesday, March 13, in the midst of David Greenglass' testimony, Saypol "requested" the Grand Jury to indict Perl on four charges of perjury. And although the indictment was properly sealed on orders of Judge Goddard, nevertheless it was taken by Saypol to Judge Kaufman's chambers the very next day.

And so we find that it was Judge Kaufman himself who opened the indictment and signed the bench warrant for the immediate arrest of Perl. Not only was such an action not within his purview but he was sponsoring what the sealing of the indictment was designed to prevent—the *timed* arrest of Perl and its inevitable damage to the defendants on trial for their lives in the case before him.

That same night four FBI agents came to the home of the young Columbia physicist and hauled him off to jail. In full cooperation with Kaufman and Saypol, the official announcement of the arrest was made from Washington by J. Edgar Hoover personally. Included were the following highlights, according to the New York *Times* of March 15, 1951:

1. That Perl was "one of the two top aerodynamics experts in the country."
2. That Perl's "father was a native of Russia."
3. That his name had been "changed from Mutterperl."

The next morning there were not only sensational headlines in the newspapers but the broadest radio and television coverage. Thus we find this irony: Judge Kaufman, who had instructed the Rosenberg jury to avoid reading newspapers at home "about this case," was at the same time the judge who contributed directly to "testimony by newspaper" in a case being tried in his court.

Some newspapers carried such banner headlines as:

COLLEGE SCIENTIST ARRESTED AS LIAR IN ATOM SPY CASE

Even the New York *Times* was apparently deceived into connecting the Perl story with the Rosenberg trial in side-by-side columns under the front-page headline of March 15:

COLUMBIA TEACHER ARRESTED, LINKED TO 2 ON TRIAL AS SPIES

PHYSICIST CALLED PERJURER IN DENYING THAT HE KNEW ROSENBERG OR SOBELL

. . . Mr. Saypol said also that Perl had been listed by the Government as a potential witness in the current atomic espionage trial.

"His intended role on the stand," Mr. Saypol added, "*was to corroborate certain statements made by David Greenglass and the latter's wife,* who are key Government witnesses in the trial." [Emphasis added.]

GREENGLASS' WIFE BACKS HIS TESTIMONY ON THEFT OF ATOM BOMB SECRETS

Through their combined testimony Ruth and David Greenglass gave the jury . . . an illuminating picture of how Soviet spies operate.

It is doubtful that anyone takes seriously the myth that jurors, returning home each evening, avert their eyes and stop their ears whenever they see a headline or hear a broadcast concerning the case they happen to be deliberating.[6] Regarding trial by newspaper, there are several court opinions in Federal cases condemning such unscrupulous methods.[7]

When trial resumed the morning after Perl's arrest,

the defense endeavored to raise an immediate protest to Saypol's maneuver and suggested that a conference be held in Judge Kaufman's chambers, because "this is a very serious matter to the defendants." [R.756–757]

With hindsight, we know that the defense should have moved for a mistrial, but it was in the dark. For all it knew, Perl could have become panic-stricken and already have concluded a "deal" with Saypol. If so, he could be put on the stand the next day, ready to swear to anything to "corroborate" the Greenglasses' accusations. Aware of this weakness, Saypol felt on safe ground when he replied to the defense's protests with a bluff to have it out "in open court."

Unfortunately, too, the defense relied unwisely on the honor of the Court. Because when Saypol gave assurances that Perl's indictment had been returned "in the regular course of the administration of justice," Kaufman made an appeal to the defense "to accept his word" that this was the truth.

Needless to say, this representation constituted a "deliberate falsehood," as the defense subsequently charged, and only the passage of time uncovered the strategy of the "deceit." For, although an early date had been set that morning for Perl's trial, no trial took place in the two years that followed—not until a month or so before the Rosenbergs' execution.

•

In the Rosenbergs' second appeal we can see how serious was the "calculated fraud" in the unsealing of Perl's indictment and the "timed" order of arrest by Saypol, Kaufman, and Hoover. This was the opinion of the Circuit Court of Appeals on December 31, 1952, regarding the prejudice created against the defendants:

. . . The publication of the indictment was *deliberately* "timed.". . . Such a statement to the press in the course of a trial, *we regard as wholly reprehensible*. . . . Such assumed tactics cannot be too severely condemned.[8] [Emphasis added.]

And yet, despite recognizing these wrongs, the Court of Appeals lacked the courage to right them by granting a new and fair trial. Fearing to upset the applecart, the Circuit Court even denied a stay of execution to allow the appeal to go to the Supreme Court. It is important to study the rationale of this denial:

When publicity believed to be prejudicial occurs during a trial, the defendant may move for a mistrial or may request the trial judge to caution the jury to disregard it. In this case the defendants did neither. We may assume that, in this case, *a cautionary instruction would not suffice, and that if defendants had moved for a new trial, it should have been granted. But they did not so move.* [Emphasis added.]

Then, after quoting Saypol's statement to the press and condemning it as "wholly reprehensible," the opinion concludes:

Nevertheless we are not prepared to hold that it vitiates the jury's verdict when there is no allegation or evidence that any juror read the newspaper story, and the defendants deliberately elected not to ask for a mistrial [after conferring with the judge outside the presence of the jury].

On the one hand the Circuit Court declares that so serious was the potential prejudice that "a cautionary instruction" to the jury by Kaufman would *not* have sufficed. But on the other hand it contradicts itself by resorting to the excuse that no juror came forth to *admit* having been prejudiced!

In short, we see here little more than a legal quibble: that because the defense counsel had been stupid, gulled, and too timid to challenge Saypol's bluff, and too trusting of Kaufman—and that because the defense had neglected to move for a new trial (*which would have been granted by a higher court had Kaufman denied the motion*)—two human beings were to be consigned to their deaths! [9]

However, as the execution date drew near, Judge Learned Hand, the senior member of the Second Circuit Court of Appeals, resumed his place on the bench. After reviewing the issues involved in the appeal together with Judges Augustus Hand and Jerome Frank, their unanimous decision was that "possible prejudice" had been present during the trial and that a stay of execution was mandatory. According to the New York *Times* of February 18, 1953, Judge Frank stated at the hearing of the reconsidered appeal:

There is substance to this argument [of the defense] and for my part, I believe the Supreme Court should hear it.

Needless to say, the prosecution was quite startled at this turn of events. Only the day before Judge Kaufman had set the new date for the execution. Now, to its astonishment, here was the famed Judge Learned Hand sending the appeal on to the Supreme Court with this indignant comment:

People don't dispose of lives, just because an attorney didn't make a point. . . . You can't undo a death sentence. There are some Justices on the Supreme Court on whom the conduct of the Prosecuting Attorney might make an impression.

And as the prosecution began to bluster that the case had been continuing long enough and that it was time to execute the Rosenbergs without further delay, Judge Hand reprimanded him sternly:

Your duty, Mr. Prosecutor, is to seek justice, not to act as a time-keeper.

It was a triumphant moment for the defense, but a brief one. For when the appeal reached the Supreme Court on March 28, as we know now from the subsequent disclosure made by Justice Hugo Black, its members voted to deny it without even reviewing the trial record and therefore without affirming "the fairness of the trial." [10]

For those Americans who have been repeatedly deceived by official declarations that the Rosenbergs received their full measure of justice in the course of their appeals, here is Justice Black's full statement appearing in the New York *Times* on June 20, 1953, the morning after the death of the Rosenbergs:

It is not amiss to point out that this Court has never reviewed this record and has never affirmed the fairness of the trial below. Without an affirmance of the fairness of the trial by the highest court in the land there may always be questions as to whether these executions were legally and rightfully carried out.

And so we see that, although the Rosenbergs (and Sobell) were permitted to knock on the doors of the highest court, these doors were never actually opened to them. And when Justice William Douglas attempted to pry them open with his last-minute stay of execution, the most extraordinary pressure was exerted upon the Supreme Court by the Department of Justice to keep them tightly closed.[11]

NOTES AND REFERENCES

1. Petition of Ethel Rosenberg for Executive Clemency joined by Julius Rosenberg, January 9, 1953, p. 20.
2. Harvey Matusow, *False Witness*, Cameron & Kahn, New York, 1955, p. 246.
3. New York *Journal-American*, July 25, 1954.
4. Perl Record, available at U.S. Courthouse, Foley Square, New York City.
5. Transcript of Record No. 687, pp. 177–184.
6. *Note:* It is not generally known that the members of the Rosenberg jury were permitted to go home each night, and in *no real way were restricted* from reading about the case or listening to radio and TV news broadcasts. (See Record p. 153.)
7. "It is idle to say that there is no direct evidence to show that the jury read these articles. . . . The jury separated at the close of each session of the court, and it is incredible that . . . they did not see and read these newspaper publications." (Meyer v. Cadwalader, 49 Fed. 32, 36.)
8. Transcript of Record, No. 687, p. 334.
9. Following President Eisenhower's denial of clemency on February 11, 1953, a new execution date was set by Kaufman for the week of March 9, 1953.
10. On this second appeal, Justice Douglas joined with Justice Black in dissent.

11. For a penetrating analysis and condemnation of the unprecedented emergency session of the Supreme Court called to vacate Justice Douglas' stay, see the *Columbia Law Review, op. cit.,* Section vi: "The Supreme Court in Special Session," pp. 241–260.

ADDENDA

With the passage of years, there have been some curious ironies reported by the press regarding Roy Cohn and his various tangles with the law. Whereas, once, as Chief Counsel for Joe McCarthy's subversive activities subcommittee, he readily championed charges of conspiracy—today, after having been himself indicted three times during the 1960's on "charges of bribery, conspiracy, extortion and blackmail," he states that "he has an absolute horror of conspiracy trials."

Whereas, once, together with Kaufman and Saypol (and later, McCarthy), he "sneered" at "Fifth Amendment Communists," when he himself was called to testify before the Grand Jury, he "repeatedly resorted to the Fifth's privilege against self-incrimination"—today, he favors abolition of the Grand Jury process, saying that "it is a rubber stamp for the prosecutor."

His first trial ended with a mistrial. Finally, in 1969, after massive legal maneuvers and the aid of influential friends (such as J. Edgar Hoover), he managed to obtain an acquittal. (See articles, "The Roy Cohn Case—Ironies Galore" and "The Metamorphosis of Roy Cohn," in the New York *Times,* September 14, 1969, and May 13, 1974, respectively.)

The most recent incident of Cohn's embroilment with the law involved a Probate Court decision in Florida concerning a contested codicil drawn by Cohn to a multimillionaire's will shortly before the latter's death. Here, it appears that Cohn, once the "scourge of Godless Communism, and a defender of the American way of life," could not extricate himself. Charges against him by the petitioners involved "trickery and fraud" in obtaining the aged millionaire's signature to the codicil. The judge of the Probate Court, using "strong judicial language," condemned Cohn for having "misrepresented to the decedent . . . [etc.]." According to legal experts, the news account adds, the ruling was "tantamount to saying that he [Cohn] had committed a civil fraud." (See New York *Times,* June 25, 1976.)

On June 30, 1977, Judge Saypol died at the age of 71.

21 "ALLIES OF THE COURT"

I

> "Surely it is striking to note that had the Rosenbergs been tried across the street, in a New York State court where corroboration is required, a conviction would have been unlikely on this record."
> —*Columbia Law Review, op. cit., p. 234*

With the above observation, the *Columbia Law Review* emphasizes the fact that the testimony of Elitcher, Gold, Bentley, and the Greenglasses was never corroborated by any independent witness. Accordingly, in its entire presentation of "The Facts" of the case, there are only four brief sentences describing the combined testimony of all the other eighteen witnesses called by the prosecution.

Moreover, as the *Columbia Law Review* points out, the Government's case consisted solely of "accomplice testimony"—in other words, of such inherently unreliable character that no conviction would have been likely in a New York State court, nor in twenty other states where accomplice testimony requires nonaccomplice corroboration. For our thorough satisfaction, however, here is a brief review of the testimony of these eighteen minor witnesses:

1. Walter Koski: The scientist whose testimony dealt with the improbability that Greenglass could have "snooped out" the atomic information as easily as he claimed. The record shows that he corroborated nothing save that Greenglass' "copy" of the alleged

lens sketch was "reasonably accurate." Since no one claims that Greenglass was not capable of *copying* such a sketch, this testimony is valueless as corroboration. In no way does it suggest that Greenglass ever gave such sketches to the Rosenbergs or to Gold. [R. 466–488]

2. John A. Derry: The liaison officer whom Bloch requested to give his opinion of Greenglass' scientific capacity. It will be recalled that Kaufman prevented the reply. Since his testimony merely confirmed that Government Exhibit 8 would have been considered a valuable secret in 1945, as such, it had nothing to do with the alleged guilt of the Rosenbergs, and had no corroborative value. [R. 905—916]

3. Col. John Lansdale, Jr.: The security officer, whose testimony about the strict security measures at Los Alamos made David's claims that he could roam around the project at will, quite incredible. As for corroboration of the Rosenbergs' guilt, there was none. [R. 879–902]

4. Lan Adomian: A Russian-born American citizen employed by the Amtorg Trading Corporation as a translator. Having met Yakovlev in 1944, he identified the latter's photograph. No further testimony. [R. 947–949]

5. Mrs. Dorothy Abel: The younger sister of Ruth Greenglass, whose direct examination contained the following points: that, at age seventeen, she was present when Julius had come to Ruth's apartment in 1945, just before the latter rejoined David in Albuquerque. That Julius asked her to read a book in privacy. That she went "into the bathroom and closed the door." That "from time to time" she talked with Julius and Ethel "concerning Russia." That the Rosenbergs had said the Soviet Union was "the ideal form of government." [R. 787–792]

Obviously, none of this had any corroborative value. Concerning the item of remaining in the bathroom, here again is an innocent visit made to appear conspiratorial. According to Ruth's testimony, Julius came to inform her of the date a courier would meet her at the Safeway store in Albuquerque. What actually happened, according to Julius' testimony, was that

Ruth had telephoned him, saying she wanted to see him about something. Some evenings later, when Julius came up, she whispered: "I would like to talk to you alone. Tell the kid [Ruth's sister] to go into the bathroom." Whereupon Julius did so and was left alone with Ruth. Here is Julius describing what Ruth wanted to confide:

> A. Ruthie told me something to this effect: "Julius, I am terribly worried. David has an idea to make some money and take some things from the Army"; and I told her, "Warn David not to do anything foolish. He will only get himself in trouble. I have read some accounts in the newspapers about some G.I.'s doing foolish things and taking parts and gasoline from the Army, and their getting themselves in trouble," and I told her, "Don't tell—make sure tell him that he doesn't do anything of that sort." [R. 1087–1089]

Here is Julius' testimony on cross-examination:

> Q. [Saypol]: And did it occur to you that he would probably try to steal gasoline—is that what you said?
> A. Parts, that's what occurred to me.
> Q. What kind of parts?
> A. Tools.

While on this subject of Greenglass' thefts from the Army, which Julius had mentioned to Ethel that same evening in 1945, let us see how Judge Kaufman intervened to aid the prosecutor:

> The Court: Wait . . . You mean between that incident and the discharge of David Greenglass from the Army [in 1946] you never had occasion to discuss this desire on the part of David Greenglass to take things from the Army?
> The Witness: No, because it didn't enter my mind; it was just like a passing incident.

Now, Saypol, picking up the cue, demands why

Julius did not inform on David at the time the FBI first questioned him:

Q. [Saypol]: Did you tell the agents about that [David's "idea" of stealing] when they interviewed you on June 16th?

A. [Julius]: They didn't ask me about that.

Q. Did you think you should have volunteered it to them?

A. Well, when a member of the family is in trouble, Mr. Saypol, you are not interested in sinking him.

The Court: Were you trying to protect him at that time?

A. Well, I didn't know what he was accused of, your Honor. I had a suspicion he was accused of stealing some uranium at that time. [R. 1219–1226]

What is the essence of this loaded question by Kaufman? Was it not to say in effect: "Very well, Rosenberg, you claim you are innocent of espionage, and yet you were 'trying to protect' your brother-in-law. You claim you are not guilty, but when you could have 'volunteered' information to the FBI about David's taking things from the Army, you did not do so."

Perhaps the naked hostility continually leveled at the Rosenbergs by Kaufman can be summed up in this way: At no time during the testimony of the Greenglasses, Elitcher, or Gold did Judge Kaufman ever display the slightest doubt concerning their truthfulness. On the other hand the Rosenbergs, despite the presumption of innocence, were treated as though their guilt were a matter of judicial notice. Furthermore, Kaufman *knew* that Elitcher was a self-confessed perjurer paying for his freedom with his testimony. And, as we recall from the Brothman trial, Kaufman was only too aware of Gold's powers of concoction.

Concerning the lengths to which Kaufman went in his role as Judge-Prosecutor, all through Julius' and

Ethel's cross-examination they were caught between a crossfire so intense that it was often difficult to tell who was conducting the interrogation, Saypol or Kaufman.

●

6. Louis Abel: The husband of Dorothy and the brother-in-law of the Greenglasses, to whom they had allegedly given a sum of $4,000 to hide in a hassock in his home a few days before David's arrest. His testimony was that, at 2 o'clock in the morning of June 16, 1950, Greenglass had telephoned him to engage Rogge as his attorney. That later, he had delivered the $4,000 to Rogge's partner and Rogge's secretary, Mrs. Pagano. And that the $4,000 was wrapped in "a piece of brown paper." [R. 792–798]

First, if this $4,000 had any reality as "Russian money," can we believe that after Greenglass' telephone call to Louis Abel the FBI would not have trailed him and seized it as material evidence?

It should be clear that Abel's testimony is as much a cock-and-bull story as that part dealing with hiding the money in his "hassock." For the truth is, as we know from Rogge's file memos, that whatever monies were paid the lawyer were largely derived from the Greenglass' relatives. [Appendix 3]

(*Note*: At the trial, both Mr. and Mrs. Abel were represented by Rogge. Thus, together with the Elitchers and the Greenglasses, Rogge represented six announced prosecution witnesses. See also *Addenda* to this chapter, showing that Louis Abel's testimony as well as Mrs. Pagano's, according to a Justice Department memo recently released, appears to be contradicted by Rogge.)

To sum up Louis Abel's testimony, in no way did it link the Rosenbergs to the $4,000. Hence it was not corroborative testimony.

●

In line with our thesis that half-truths and full truths become the basis for half-lies and full lies, we have mentioned that the $1,000 debt, which obsessed the

432

Greenglasses to the point where they threatened suit, was undoubtedly the basis for the first $1,000 payment of "flight" money. Under cross-examination of Greenglass concerning his business losses, we can trace the second payment of $4,000 to its inspiration:

A. [Greenglass]: My brother Bernie . . . had gotten $5,000 from my relatives to invest. . . . [Later] the $5,000 was invested in G. & R. [Greenglass and Rosenberg] . . . and we bought machinery with that $5,000. . . . In other words, we owed a third of that $5,000 which later on turned out to be $4,000.

Q. [Bloch]: And did your brother Bernie borrow that money in part from your mother?
A. The money was borrowed while I was still in the Army. I had no knowledge that the money was going to be borrowed, but when I got out and went into the business I obligated myself for this money. [R. 662–663]

Perhaps it is appropriate here to quote Judge Kaufman's instructions to the jury, "You add a column of figures and you get a result":

Debt owed Greenglass by Julius $1,000
Debt assumed by Greenglass for his
    family's loss of investment 4,000
            Total $5,000

First alleged payment of flight money . . . $1,000
Second alleged payment of flight money . . 4,000
            Total $5,000

•

7. Mrs. Helen Pagano: The secretary of O. John Rogge, who testified that Louis Abel delivered the package of money containing $3,900. (*Note*: According to their testimony, the Greenglasses used $100 for personal use.) Since there is no mention of the Rosenbergs, the fact that the money was delivered to Rogge has no corroborative value. [R. 1420–1424]

8. Dr. George Bernhardt: This doctor, a neighbor of the Rosenbergs, had treated Julius for some months for hay fever. Here is the reference to Dr. Bernhardt in the *Columbia Law Review* from page 222:

> George Bernhardt, Rosenberg's physician, testified that Rosenberg had sought information in 1950 concerning injections necessary for admission into Mexico. . . . Rosenberg testified that he had sought this information for the benefit of David Greenglass—that Ruth had informed him that her husband was in trouble for stealing while in the Army. [See also R. 848–857]

Unfortunately, Mr. Bloch was unaware of the fact that a smallpox vaccination had *not* been required for entry into Mexico, but this writer would have shared that ignorance had it not been for his trip to Mexico in 1951, mentioned in Chapter 7.

We have emphasized this before, but it bears reemphasis: How is it that a seasoned spy-master, who is supposed to have prepared the "carefully planned pattern" for the flights of Sobell, the Greenglasses, and others, was completely unaware that a vaccination certificate was *totally unnecessary* for entry into Mexico? [1] Here is Julius' direct examination:

A. [Julius]: Then I asked Dr. Bernhardt about vacations in Mexico, what are the requirements? And he told me that you need to have a smallpox injection. Well, I asked him would he make out a certificate for smallpox injection for somebody he didn't vaccinate. He said, No, he would not.

Q. [Bloch]: . . . Did you ask the doctor about Mexico because of the conversation that you had had with David earlier?
A. Yes, I did.
Q. But you didn't tell it to the doctor . . . that it was a friend of yours . . . or a relative, who was contemplating going to Mexico?
A. I didn't tell him "a relative." I just told him "a person." [R. 1121–1123]

To reconstruct Julius' thinking and behavior at the time: Here was his wife's brother David, scared to death not only because he had been involved in some black-market ring but especially because of the uranium sample he had stolen and that ominous visit from the FBI to David in February. With the headlines full of Red spy hunts, it was natural that Julius should share David's fear that these thefts would become magnified.

While it is true that Julius, in attempting to secure a falsified vaccination certificate, may have been violating the law, such an act is deeply ingrained in the American tradition, *i.e.*, helping the persecuted during a wave of political hysteria. Furthermore, Dr. Bernhardt's testimony tends to support Julius' innocent conduct. Because whereas Julius recalls that he made his request in person at the physician's office, the latter insists it was "a telephone conversation" and that it took place "in the latter part of May."

Now we recall from Greenglass' testimony that the FBI surveillance which he and Julius were so concerned about occurred also in the latter part of May, 1950. Surely such a telephone conversation would be the last thing a spy-master would have risked, considering the very real possibility of FBI wiretapping.

In short, it is impossible to believe that Julius was the wary spy-master he is made out to be, when we see him leaving this very damaging trail behind him. For, as we have pointed out, he could have obtained accurate information concerning inoculation requirements by simply picking up a Mexican travel folder in any travel agency. In this regard, it is also unfortunate that Dr. Bernhardt was as ignorant as Julius of the requirements for entering Mexico. For had he told Julius that one needed a vaccination certificate *only* in order to *return* to the United States, this knowledge could have been made available to the defense. In any event, there is nothing in Dr. Bernhardt's testimony to corroborate any of the charges of espionage.

II

9. Mrs. Evelyn Cox: The housekeeper, the elderly black woman who had worked for Ethel in 1944 and

1945. A rebuttal witness, her intended role on the stand was to have her provide confirmation of the Greenglass testimony that the console table had been a gift from the Russians. However, when we examine her testimony, we find a most extraordinary situation. Not only is there no such confirmation, but the *critical point* about the console table—the alleged hollowed-out portion—was never seen by Mrs. Cox. In his summation Mr. Bloch stresses this point:

[Bloch]: . . . Don't you think that if this console table was as described by Ruth Greenglass, Mrs. Cox, who probably cleaned that house God knows how many times . . . don't you think it would have caught her eye that there was a hollow there for a purpose? Did you hear Mrs. Cox testify to anything of the kind? She did not. [R. 1483–1484]

As for the table being a gift "from the Russians," here is Mrs. Cox's direct testimony:

Q. [Saypol]: When you saw this new table, did you have some talk with Mrs. Rosenberg about it?
A. [Mrs. Cox]: Yes, I admired the table. I asked her where it had come from. . . . and she said that a friend of her husband gave it to him as a gift. . . . It was a sort of wedding present. . . .
Q. Did she ever say to you that she bought it in Macy's?
A. No.
Q. Did she ever say to you that her husband bought it and paid $21 for it in Macy's?
A. No, she said it was a gift to her husband from a friend.

Even if we assume that Ethel had said the table was "a gift . . . from a friend," it is hardly synonymous with a "gift" from the "Russians." In any event, on cross-examination, there arose the danger that Mrs. Cox's responses might favor the defense. Notice the deft hand of Kaufman in this excerpt:

Q. [Bloch]: May I ask you, Mrs. Cox, in the two

years in which you worked for Mrs. Rosenberg did you find Mrs. Rosenberg to be an honest woman?

A. Very.

Mr. Saypol: I object.

The Court: Are you making a character witness out of her?

E. H. Bloch: Yes.

The Court: Then you have got to ask her about her [Ethel's] reputation in the community.

Mr. E. H. Bloch: I will.

The Court: And she won't know her reputation in the community because she doesn't live in the community.

Q. [Bloch]: Mrs. Cox, did you discuss Mrs. Rosenberg with any of the people around Knickerbocker Village?

A. I didn't know anyone around.

Mr. Bloch: All right, that is all. [R. 1406–1420]

One would expect that an unbiased judge seeking the truth, and that an unprejudiced prosecutor seeking to protect the innocent, would have welcomed this isolated instance of testimony concerning Ethel's character. But how promptly they prevent Bloch from eliciting a kind word about Ethel.

From the disclosures made in the previously mentioned affidavits of Mr. Summit and Reverend Williamson concerning the apparent coercion undergone by Mrs. Cox, one cannot help concluding that she was induced to "remember" that the table was a "gift" from a friend. (*Note*: Mrs. Cox was testifying in 1951 about a random conversation six or seven years earlier.)

If the table had really been a Russian gift containing a hollowed-out area for microfilming, is it likely that Ethel would have stated it was a *gift*? Would she not rather have lied with a casual shrug, "Oh, it's just something Julie picked up at a knockdown sale." Indeed, anticipating that someone might ask curiously about a new table, would not the Rosenbergs (as spies) have prepared themselves with some such explanation?

But, regardless of suspicious signs of instructed testimony, there is the all-important fact that Mrs. Cox *never* noticed anything unusual about the table.

Why didn't Saypol put this key query to Mrs. Cox: "Did you ever notice a hollowed-out portion in the table into which someone could fit a lamp for photographic purposes?" It is possible that he attempted to do so in a pre-trial conference and that he received only a sharp glance which told him, "Look here, Mister—so far and no further."

III

Such, then, was the testimony of nine of the eighteen government witnesses.[2] Reviewing them briefly, Koski, Derry, and Lansdale never mentioned the Rosenbergs. Adomian only identified a photograph of Yakovlev; Dorothy Abel did not corroborate Julius' alleged conspiratorial conversation with Ruth because she was in the bathroom and didn't hear it. Louis Abel claimed to have received from the Greenglasses a sum of money and allegedly delivered it to Rogge, but it was not connected with the Rosenbergs or espionage. Mrs. Pagano merely testified that Rogge's fee had been delivered. Dr. Bernhardt knew only that Julius had inquired about a vaccination certificate for a "person" contemplating a trip to Mexico. And finally Mrs. Cox, whose testimony failed to confirm that the console table was a gift from the Russians or that it had a hollowed-out top such as the Greenglasses had described.

In short, the charge of the Rosenbergs' conspiracy to commit espionage was in no way corroborated by any of these nine government witnesses.

●

In preceding chapters we have presented portions of the testimony of Elizabeth Bentley. She was neither a major witness nor was she, as a self-styled Red Spy Queen, correctly an independent witness. Indeed, her reputation had become widely accepted as that of a professional witness.

According to the fact that her testimony had the special, unique purpose to prove the crimes of the Rosenbergs and Sobell by means of the technique of "guilt by association," it has been felt that she deserves a chapter all to herself.

NOTES AND REFERENCES

1. See Saypol's accusations that Julius had also planned the flights of William Perl and other friends, named Joel Barr and Alfred Sarant. These accusations, never proved, were denied by Julius and exposed by the defense as inflammatory. (Record, pp. 1193–1200, 1490–1491.)
2. The testimony of eight of the remaining witnesses is related almost exclusively to Sobell and will be taken up separately. The last one, the passport photographer Schneider, was a surprise rebuttal witness, whose testimony completed the trial. Therefore, we will analyze his testimony at the end of the chapter dealing with the Rosenbergs' defense.

ADDENDA

According to a Justice Department memo dated June 28, 1950, the testimony of the Greenglasses connecting their attorney's fee with the $4,000 of Russian money allegedly given them by Julius can now be seriously questioned. This cash sum was allegedly delivered to the Greenglass attorney, Rogge, the morning after David's arrest on June 15th, according to the testimony of Louis Abel (the Greenglass brother-in-law) and Helen Pagano, Rogge's secretary. As now disclosed, their testimony is also open to question.

The memo describes a meeting on June 26, 1950, ten days *after* the alleged payment of $3,900 ($100 withheld for personal use) was delivered to Rogge's office "wrapped in brown paper." This memo written by Assistant Attorney General McInerny reads in part:

Mr. Rogge advised he was retained to represent Defendant Greenglass and that he was to get a fee of $7,500. However, as yet, he [Rogge] has not received any part of it.*

As seen, there is no mention of the $3,900 allegedly delivered to Rogge on June 16th, ten days before. In short, whereas the Greenglasses and/or their relatives eventually did make payments to Rogge, the first one of only $1,000 was not made until June 28th according to a receipt of that date. And there is no known receipt for the $3,900.

In passing, the familiar pattern may be noted: The same type of damaging connection was made regarding the $500 of Russian money allegedly paid by Gold to Greenglass and Ruth's deposit of $400 the next day in the Albuquerque bank. In both instances there was the same sum of $100 deducted for personal use, inserted to dress up the episode with a touch of prosaic reality.

22 "THE RED SPY QUEEN"

I

> "This is her business; her business is testifying."
> —*Emanuel Bloch; Record, p. 1480*

On Wednesday morning, March 21, Miss Elizabeth Bentley took the stand. On the front page of the New York *Times* that morning there was no mention of her testimony, even though it comprised some sixty pages in the record. [R. 964–1024]

* The McInerny memo was released in 1973 to Dr. Emily Alman, Douglass College, N.J.

Perhaps the unusual press indifference to Bentley's appearance can best be explained by the fact that she had simply worn out her news value. With the great number of times she had been trotted out before investigating committees, Grand Juries and, more recently, the Remington trial, she had come to be looked upon as just another "career informer." [1]

At the time of trial, Bentley was forty-four years old. Following her graduation from Vassar in the early thirties, she went to Italy. There, while at the University of Florence, she was so impressed by Mussolini's "efficiency" that she became a member of the University Fascist Group.[2] It is her claim that she joined the American Communist Party in 1935. In 1938, Bentley met the man she describes as her lover, one Jacob Golos. According to her testimony at the Rosenberg trial, although Golrs operated a travel agency, he was one of a three-man control commission of the Communist Party which "kept the membership in line." Until his death in 1943, Bentley claims, she collected information from members of the Communist Party to be passed on to him.

In May, 1945, she testifies further, she met an American captain "doing undercover work for the United States Government" and during the next three months was taken out socially by him, despite her claim that she was "working for the Russian secret police" at this time.[3]

And so it was, we are told, that in the latter part of August, 1945, evidently as a result of the persuasiveness of the "captain," Miss Bentley decided to go to the FBI and "work with them" instead of with the Russian secret police.

After 1945, it appears, Bentley became a double agent, reporting regularly to the FBI. In the spring of 1947 her Grand Jury testimony led to the questioning of Gold and Brothman, which, as we know from Mr. Hoover's article, resulted in "no bill." But in 1950, as we have seen, Gold thought up his *new* story involving the "small white card" found in his cellar closet, and this time Brothman was convicted.

And here some important questions arise: How is it, if Bentley told the truth to the FBI in 1945 and then repeated it to the Grand Jury in 1947, and if the FBI made its search of Gold's house in 1947, that they did not find the small white card in Gold's folder, marked "A.B.'s stuff," *at that time?* And how is it, if the FBI searched Gold's house in 1947, that they did not find the "museum map" of Santa Fe lying behind the bookcase ever since June, 1945?

Bearing in mind the first question, let us turn to Roy Cohn's testimony at the Army-McCarthy hearings:

As a result of working with Miss Bentley and Mr. Gold, there resulted the prosecution . . . of Abraham Brothman. . . .

And here in Mr. Cohn's signed *Journal-American* article is his version of the discovery of the small white card:

I was certain that one part of Elizabeth Bentley's story was fantastic. . . . She told me she had turned Brothman over to a new Communist courier whose name she did not know. All she knew was that . . . the man would say, "I bring regards from Helen."

. . . Shortly after Fuchs talked and Gold was arrested, *in the attic* of Gold's house in Philadelphia, a little frayed card was found with these very words scribbled on it a decade before in Gold's writing, fully corroborating every detail of Bentley's story. It was an amazing confirmation of a fact. [Emphasis added.]

Amazing indeed! Cohn cites this incident as though Bentley had never revealed the full details of her "espionage work" to the FBI almost five years before Gold's arrest! [4]

If this "little frayed card" was in Gold's conspicuous red folder for a full decade, then how is it that the FBI failed to find it back in 1947? And how did the card suddenly ascend from Gold's basement up to Cohn's "attic"? (*Note:* We recall Gold's sworn version of its cellar location at the Brothman trial in Chapters 3 and 9.) But wherever the card was "found," we see that it was Cohn's "working with Miss Bentley and Mr. Gold" that resulted in its belated discovery in 1950.

Are we being unduly suspicious of Roy Cohn who *worked* with the three principal witnesses testifying against the Rosenbergs—Gold, Bentley, and Greenglass? Let us take note of the next case he boasts about at the Army-McCarthy hearings:

After that, sir, I went into the prosecution of William W. Remington. . . . He had been one of Miss Bentley's espionage contacts. . . .

As we know, Remington was convicted *solely* on the basis of Bentley's accusations. But, as we also know, the foreman of the Grand Jury which *indicted* Remington was later revealed to have been Bentley's "financial and literary collaborator"! And so we ask of Cohn and Saypol: How did John Brunini, who was known to be helping Bentley to write her book for "a percentage of the sale," come to be selected for this particular Grand Jury, which not only indicted Remington but also Ethel and Julius Rosenberg? [5] And how did Mr. Brunini come to be appointed foreman, or the pivotal man, of this fateful Grand Jury?

To sum up this preliminary section dealing with Bentley's background, the reader will recall from the anatomy of frame-up that it is the political atmosphere which generates, and at the same time cloaks the frame-up. For only in such an atmosphere could a Roy Cohn be promoted to Special Assistant to the Attorney General of the United States in order to prosecute Owen Lattimore on political charges so violative of the Constitution that Federal Judge Youngdahl threw out every major count in the indictment.[6]

II

". . . On appeal, the Rosenbergs [charged] that the trial court permitted the Government to erect 'a monstrous superstructure of inflammatory and prejudicial evidence,' and Sobell [charged] that he was tried as a political dissenter rather than as a spy."
—*Columbia Law Review*, p. 223

With these introductory remarks, the *Columbia Law Review* proceeds to examine what was without doubt the entire purpose of the prosecution, to wit: the equation of Communism with treason. And, as stated earlier, although this purpose pervaded and dominated the trial, nowhere is it as clear as in the testimony of Bentley. Here it is as condensed by the *Columbia Law Review:*

. . . In order to connect Party membership and activities with motive for espionage, the Government put Elizabeth Bentley on the stand. She testified that the American Communist Party was part of the Communist International, serving only the interests of Moscow, whether through "propaganda or espionage or sabotage," and carrying out the directives of Moscow; that the members were instructed to do everything possible to aid Russia; and that those who disobeyed instructions were expelled from the Party.

That such testimony was extremely damaging to the defendants is conceded by the *Columbia Law Review*, even though "guilt by association" is contrary to our basic tenet that guilt can be only personal and individual.[7]

How, then, did Judge Kaufman permit Bentley's prejudicial testimony to obliterate all presumption of innocence? Simply by means of this legal casuistry:

The Court: . . . This is as good a time as any to tell the Jury . . . as to the purpose for which this testimony was taken, that it is not to establish the guilt here of the crime charged because any of them might have been members of the Communist Party, but it is to show a link, as the Government contends, exists between aiding Russia . . . and being members of the Communist Party. . . .

And so, on this basis, for more than two-thirds of her testimony Bentley was permitted to fashion the "link" between *any* American Communist Party member and Moscow, even though not a word involved the individual guilt (or party membership) of the Rosenbergs or Sobell.

It was only as she began the final third of her direct testimony that Bentley actually mentioned the name of "Julius." Not Julius Rosenberg, but merely a "Julius." And not even a person she knew as "Julius," but only a *voice* on the telephone calling himself by that name. And this from a recollection as far back as 1942–1943, *or almost nine years previous* to her testimony! [8] Here is the substance of this testimony.

That while Golos was still alive in 1942, one of his contacts would phone her as a "go-between" and say: "This is Julius," and give her a message to transmit to her "superior." Here was the alleged procedure:

[Bentley]: . . . When I was called at 2 in the morning I often had to go out and go many blocks in the cold to get a pay telephone to call Mr. Golos. . . . *It was considered unsafe for me to call out of my own telephone.* [Emphasis added.]

As indicated, Bentley did not *know* who this "Julius" was. Evidently perturbed by this, Judge Kaufman asked:

The Court: Did you ever meet a person, did you ever meet anybody in person, whose voice you heard, and you can now say is the voice of the man who identified himself as Julius on the telephone?

A. No, I have *never* met anyone whose voice I heard, whom I could identify as Julius. [Emphasis added.]

Just how many thousands of men in and around New York City happen to be named "Julius" this writer cannot even estimate. However, even if we are to believe her testimony, any one of these thousands could have telephoned Bentley.

Concerning the unique use of Julius Rosenberg of his own given name in these alleged telephone calls, again we must ask: Why would he constantly use his true name when everyone else was using an undercover name? Golos used "Timmy" and "John," Bentley used "Helen," "Joan," and "Mary," and even admits:

"I had a sort of collection of names." And, as we recall, Gold was "Raymond," "Martin," and "Dave from Pittsburgh," whereas Semenov was "Sam," and Yakovlev was never anything but "John." Only Julius Rosenberg, we must believe, the alleged spy-master—only Rosenberg was so reckless as to use his own name of "Julius"!

Returning to Bentley's claim that she had to go out into the cold at 2 o'clock in the morning to relay Julius' message to Golos, here is how she embroiders this point:

> [Bentley]: [These calls] always came after midnight, in the wee, small hours. I remember it because I got waked out of bed.

Did Julius telephone from his apartment or did he also have to go out at 2 A.M. to find a pay phone in order to be safe? (*Note:* If so, why did Greenglass tell Gold to reach him in New York by telephoning his brother-in-law?) And, if it was considered "unsafe" for Bentley to call Golos from her phone, why was it safe for Golos to receive the message on his phone, or, for that matter, for Bentley to receive Julius' call at home?

Finally, why should Julius have made these calls "always after midnight"? Why couldn't he call her in the morning before going to work, or at lunchtime, or in the early evening? Or would such a reasonable time have sounded too prosaic to the jury? After all, if the mysterious "Julius" had to be invented, would it not sound ever so much more intriguing to say that the calls always came in the "wee, small hours"?

III

In further providing the prosecution with the need of the moment, namely, to connect "Julius" with the defendant on trial, Bentley testified to the following incident.

That Golos had once told her that "he had to stop

by to pick up some material from a contact, an engineer," who was this same "Julius." That one night in 1942 she "accompanied him to the vicinity of Knickerbocker Village." That Golos parked his car, left her in it, and went across the street to wait on the corner. That the contact finally arrived and the two men went down the street to a candy store. That later Golos returned "with an envelope of material."

If Judge Kaufman was perturbed about the vagueness of the telephone incident, the record at this point discloses his outright anxiety. For despite objections by the defense that the Golos-Bentley drive took place long before the indictment, Saypol was allowed a free hand in presenting the details. Only when the defense continued to object did Kaufman instruct Saypol that this testimony was not admissible. But the latter wouldn't stop. Worried that Saypol's clumsiness might cause an upset of the entire trial, Kaufman now warned him that Bentley had been unable to describe Golos' contact at Knickerbocker Village. Saypol, however, presses on:

> Mr. Saypol: She can describe him.
> The Court: Does she describe him in any way so that it is actually Rosenberg?
> Mr. Saypol: She describes him in such a way but she cannot say that that was the man.
> The Court: I know that.
> Mr. Saypol: She describes him by height.

At this point Cohn came to Saypol's assistance with a precedent from another case which brought about a legalistic flurry with the defense. Finally there was this outburst of irritation from Kaufman aimed at the prosecution's indifference to the danger of judicial error:

> [Kaufman]: Let's cut this short. . . . I think you will avoid any problem if you just get to the conversation part, if there was any telephone talk with a Julius . . . without this specific meeting here.

It is a pity that the court transcript, unlike a printed

play, fails to include a description of the manner in which the characters read the lines, else one might better appreciate the black humor of this scene: The bull-headed Saypol, so intent on bolstering Bentley's telephone incident with the drive to Knickerbocker Village that he cannot discern Kaufman's fear. Roy Cohn piping up with an ill-suited precedent torn out of context. And the flushed Kaufman, trying to keep from showing his anxiety at the introduction of evidence not only certain to invite reversal, but the most worthless evidence possible!

For here was Saypol attempting to establish an identification by a man's *height* and nothing else—and *at night*—and by a woman sitting in a car *a considerable distance away*—and all of it happening in 1942, *nine years* previous to her testimony!

IV

Such, then, was the sum total of Bentley's testimony: (1) The Golos-Bentley drive which Kaufman was constrained to rule out, (2) the telephone conversations with the mysterious "Julius" whose voice Bentley was unable to identify, and (3) her political testimony which had nothing to do with the individual guilt of the defendants but achieved the result the prosecution desired—the acceptance by the jury of the theory of guilt by association.

Before concluding with Bentley it is important to take heed of some subsequent disclosures which tend to reveal her as a complete fraud, not only in the Rosenberg case, but in all others.[9]

On April 19, 1955, the sensational announcement appeared in the New York *Post* that the "whole of Bentley's story concerning wartime espionage was being contested legally by William Henry Taylor, former official of the International Monetary Fund. Through his attorney, Byron Scott, demand was made by Taylor "for a public hearing before the Senate Internal Security subcommittee . . . to confront Bentley and deny her charges under oath." Charging that he had found no less than thirty-seven "discrepancies" in Bentley's testimony before Congressional hearings, Mr. Scott declared: "We are challenging the inconsistencies, the inaccuracies and the impossibilities of her story."

We have seen Bentley's claim that after becoming Golos' mistress in 1938, she had acted as his top courier. That among the thirty-odd espionage contacts which she made between 1938 and 1943 were Remington and Brothman. That she traveled from New York to Washington every two weeks with documents photographed on 35-millimeter film, with an average of forty rolls of film on each trip. And that Golos, to whom she delivered the film, was operating the World Tourist travel agency only as a front behind which he was arranging false passports for American Communists.

Now let us turn to some official records: In March, 1940, Jacob Golos was indicted by a Federal Grand Jury for failing to register as a foreign agent. In addition, he was flatly accused by the Attorney General of *engaging in espionage for the Soviet Union.* But whereas Golos denied the latter charge and no proof could be brought to substantiate it, he did plead guilty to the violation of the foreign agent registration law. Technically, he was guilty of the violation, even though World Tourist was frankly a travel agency arranging advertised tourist trips to the Soviet Union. He was fined $500, sentenced to four months' imprisonment, but was immediately placed on probation.

Thus, we are asked to believe that for approximately three years *after* Golos had been accused of espionage, Bentley, his principal courier, was carrying on all these extensive spy operations without the slightest knowledge or interest of the FBI! [10]

How is it, if Bentley's claims have any element of truth, that the FBI had no suspicions about her espionage dealings with Golos. Brothman, Semenov, and Gold from September of 1941—when the "small white card" rendezvous was arranged—until August of 1945 when, Mr. Hoover declares, her story came to him as a complete surprise? For that matter, if we believe her testimony (and Gold's), why did the FBI do nothing about this extensive spy ring until 1947?

But most important is this question: If, as early as August of 1945, the FBI *knew*, from Bentley's detailed recital, everything about those phone calls from "Julius," and if they knew also that "Julius" was an engineer living in Knickerbocker Village, then why didn't they undertake close surveillance of Julius Rosenberg, the only engineer with that name at that address?

Why didn't they follow this "spy" to his numerous rendezvous with his Russian superiors? Why didn't they see him receiving visits from Greenglass, home on furlough from the Los Alamos Atomic Project in September, 1945—the period when the latter was supposed to have turned over the Nagasaki bomb? Why didn't they catch Julius stealing the proximity fuse? Or while he was traveling to Schenectady and Cleveland to meet with his spy contacts? Or while he was entertaining student recruits? Or later, in the years 1947–1949, while Julius was stealing the plans for the "sky platform"? Or in the year 1950, while he was bringing the flight money to Greenglass, and bringing back the passport photos, and *telephoning* Dr. Bernhardt for an illegal vaccination certificate?

In short, if we are to believe Bentley, and J. Edgar Hoover's endorsement of her claims, we must ask why the FBI did *nothing* about the engineer named "Julius" for almost *five* years, from August, 1945, to June, 1950? Could it not ascertain that in that *same* year of Bentley's exposures, its own agents had delivered a report (in February, 1945) to Army Intelligence stating that Julius Rosenberg, an engineer employed at the Signal Corps and living at 10 Monroe Street, was a security risk as a Communist Party member?

One can go on and on with these queries, but it would be laboring the point. For it is inescapable that Elizabeth Bentley, presented as the "Red Spy Queen," was as much an FBI puppet as was Harry Gold, presented as the chief American courier for the "Rosenberg spy network."

Looking back at the political climate of the early

1950's, we would do well to contemplate the following excerpts from an article titled "A 17th Century Moral," which deals with the "Popish Plot" that was concocted in the then anti-Catholic England by the notorious Titus Oates:

Fear could be worked up practically over-night when Charles II ruled England, for the majority of the people thought the Roman Catholics believed arson and murder were justified. . . .

Titus Oates drew up an elaborate account of a plot . . . supposedly devised by the Pope . . . the murder of Charles, the blowing up of Parliament House [etc.]. . . .

This fantastic story was brought to the attention of the government by forged letters and other trickery and Oates was . . . put under oath, and bidden to Tell All.

Judges talked truculently to defendants and witnesses and admitted as evidence hearsay, unsupported rumor, and imputations of guilt by association.

The lot of Catholics in the days of Titus' glory was not a happy one. . . . The prisons were filled with teachers, attorneys and civil employees who refused to take the oath of allegiance. . . .

Oates' supporters demanded that Lord Stafford . . . be tried. . . . His execution was the last of the 37 deaths for which Oates was directly responsible. The number of persons he had made lose their reputation and livelihood is beyond all reckoning.

. . . Found guilty [of perjury, Oates] was sentenced to life imprisonment, varied by annual appearances in the pillory.[11]

NOTES AND REFERENCES

1. See Record, p. 1020, wherein Bentley was asked how many times she had testified previously. This was her reply: "Oh, good heavens, I don't know."
2. At the Remington trial, Bentley admitted her membership in the GUF, "Gruppo Universitario Fascista." (See Remington Record, U.S. Courthouse, New York City.)

3. Bentley never explained how she came to meet the unidentified captain, nor how it was that the Russian secret police knew nothing of her extracurricular activities with this captain.

4. At the Rosenberg trial Bentley stated that these conferences with the FBI numbered "more than ten" in 1945. In a series of articles written for the St. Louis *Post-Dispatch*, she wrote: "I knew I must tell my whole story to the FBI."

5. See New York *Times*, January 3, 1951.

6. New York *Times*, May 3, 1953.

7. Bridges v. Wixon, 326 U.S. 135, 157, 163. See also Kotteakos v. U.S., 328 U.S. 750, 773 (1946).

8. In its objections the defense argued vainly that the date of these telephone calls was at least eight months *before* the time charged in the indictment, namely, June 6, 1944.

9. See New York *Times* report of February 23, 1955, concerning disclosures made by Harvey Matusow to the Senate Internal Security Subcommittee in which Bentley is quoted as having confided to Matusow: " '. . . I have to continue doing this kind of work. I have to keep finding information to testify about.' "

10. In the request for a public hearing concerning Bentley's authenticity, Mr. Scott raises this same question. (New York *Post*, April 19, 1955.)

11. See article by Louise Fargo Brown, Professor Emeritus of History at Vassar College, in *The Nation*, April 3, 1954. See also *Encyclopaedia Britannica*, 1943 edition, Vol. 16, pp. 662–663.

ADDENDA

In his government memorandum, regarding Elizabeth Bentley, Pollack merely restates the vague claims about "a person who telephoned her and called himself Julius" and "someone" whom Golos had met in downtown New York, and whom she hadn't seen. Aware of the weakness of this testimony, none of which shows any connection with Julius Rosenberg, except by inference, Pollack tries to bolster it with Bentley's alleged activities as a spy courier in the "Communist chain of command." Then, Pollack continues:

Wexley flays the Government for using Elizabeth Bentley as a witness. He contends that Bentley's testimony was completely manufactured.

Here is Pollack's reply that her story, "bizarre as it may seem at times, was completely and thoroughly checked by the FBI. . . ." In other words, the legitimacy of the "Red Spy Queen" is verified only by those who crowned her.

As for the demand by Taylor's attorney for a Senate Committee hearing "to confront Bentley" ("challenging the inconsistencies, the inaccuracies and the impossibilities of her story"), Pollack finds it prudent to remain as silent as had Bentley. (See headline in New York *Post* of April 20, 1955: "Elizabeth Bentley Silent as Ex-U.S. Aide Blasts Her Charges as Fiction.")

23 "THE GOVERNMENT RESTS"

I

Perhaps by this time the reader will recall only dimly the testimony of Max Elitcher, whose examination had concluded on March 9. Now, on March 16, Morton Sobell's name was again heard by the jury. For an entire court week there was Sobell seated alongside the accused Rosenbergs, burdened with the full weight of guilt heaped upon them by the Greenglasses and Gold. Now, at long last, the name was called of one William Danziger (Government Witness 11).[1]

In substance, Danziger's testimony was as follows: that he had been a college classmate and friend of Sobell and that on June 20, he telephoned Sobell:

[Danziger]: Well, I called him at his home, to indicate that I needed an electric drill to do a repair job around my home, and he mentioned that he was getting ready to leave for a vacation in Mexico, and that he was leaving rather shortly . . . and if I wanted the drill, for me to come out and get it.

On that same day Danziger went out to the Sobells' house to borrow the drill and noticed them packing.

Q. [Cohn]: Did he tell you what means of transportation he was going to use?
A. Yes. He said he was flying. . . . He said he was going to Mexico—Mexico City.

The remainder of Danziger's direct testimony deals with the two letters he received with the names "Morty Sowell" and "Morty Levitov" written on the envelopes.[2] Concerning the Government's theory of flight, let us recall the original press release of J. Edgar Hoover at the time of Sobell's arrest:

Sobell fled the United States in June to avoid arrest *the day after the arrest of David Greenglass*. . . . The FBI said that Sobell was so alarmed by the arrest of Greenglass that he took a plane for Mexico City. [Emphasis added.]

The distortion of the time element here should not be overlooked. Sobell did not leave on the day after Greenglass' arrest, but almost a *week* later. In any event, this theory of Sobell's flight had become the nucleus of the prosecution's case against him. Here is Saypol elaborating upon this FBI release in his summation in order to make it fit Greenglass' "flight instructions" from Rosenberg:

[Saypol]: . . . You have heard the details, the instructions of Greenglass to get to Mexico . . . the statues, the three-day waits, the signals and so on. Just after Greenglass' arrest in June of 1950, Sobell fled. . . . The FBI caught up with him and brought him back, and you have him here. [R. 1534]

On the contrary, as we have seen, Sobell did *nothing* that corresponded to Greenglass' "Operation Finger."

Also, there is the officially accepted documentary evidence: (1) that he secured his tourist cards in his own name; (2) that he purchased his American Airlines tickets in his own name; (3) that he checked his camera equipment at the U. S. Customs in Dallas in his own name; and (4) that he had resided in Mexico for almost two months in his own name.

On the one hand, we are told that Sobell is fleeing in desperate alarm because of Greenglass' arrest, but on the other hand this fearful spy, knowing full well that his wire might be tapped, tells Danziger *on the telephone* not only where and how he is escaping but also that he is leaving shortly!

•

The next witness was put on the stand obviously to prejudice the jury against Sobell's lack of war service. This was Government Witness 12: Colonel Chandler Cobb, a Director of Selective Service, who had brought his records relating to Sobell's draft status during World War II. As we know, Sobell had been kept from active duty by the War Manpower Commission as a specialist essential to the war effort. After an authentic copy of Sobell's signature had been confirmed, the witness was excused. [R. 873–879]

There now followed one American and three Mexican witnesses whose testimony dealt with Sobell's trip. [R. 927–938]:

13. Minerva Bravo Espinosa, an employee of an optical store in Vera Cruz, who testified that Sobell had ordered a pair of glasses and had signed the order as "M. Sand."

14. Jose Broccado Vendrell, employed by the Hotel Diligencias in Vera Cruz, who testified that Sobell had registered as "Morris Sand."

15. Dora Bautista, a clerk employed by the Tampico Hotel, who testified that Sobell had registered as "Marvin Salt."

16. Glenn Dennis, employed by Mexican Airlines, who testified to Sobell's purchase of one ticket from Vera Cruz to Tampico under the name of "N. Sand," and another to Mexico City under the name of "Morton Salt."

In Chapter 7 we have already analyzed Sobell's motives for these pseudonyms during that week of panic when he was seeking political asylum. Although none of the testimony of these four witnesses had anything to do with the alleged conspiracy to commit espionage, the use of one alias after another virtually sealed Sobell's fate. His motives, of course, for using the pseudonyms, were never heard by the jury.

•

Regarding the testimony of Government Witness 17, Manuel de los Rios, the "friendly" neighbor who advised the naïve Sobell about seeking passage in Vera Cruz, we have already presented this narratively in Chapter 7. At best, as we have shown, it was highly suspicious. At worst, it was the work of an agent provocateur. [R. 919–927]

Regarding the final Government Witness (18), James Huggins, the Immigration Inspector at Laredo, we have covered his testimony also in Chapter 7: how the "manifest" card was typed in advance; and how he added on its reverse side the false notation: "Deported from Mexico." [R. 1024–1037]

Despite Huggins' admission that he had no information from *anyone* to warrant the notation of these incriminating words, Kaufman permitted this prejudicial "manifest" to be admitted as Government Exhibit 25-A.[3]

II

The following excerpts are from the *Columbia Law Review* and, in view of disclosures which follow, should be noted carefully:

After the trial was concluded, Sobell . . . claimed that his return from Mexico to the United States had not been voluntary—on the contrary, that he had been attacked, beaten unconscious and carried into the United States by several unknown assailants.

. . . Judgment against him was therefore void [Sobell

claimed] because having been "kidnapped" by Government agents, he was not validly within the jurisdiction of the district court.

. . . Since the Supreme Court has set aside a conviction resting upon evidence obtained while federal officers were violating federal enactments, Sobell may have prevailed with the argument that a judgment cannot stand when jurisdiction is obtained through a federal officer's violation of the anti-kidnapping law.[4]

Which brings us to the key question: Was Sobell kidnapped by hired agents of the FBI or did the Mexican Government deport him as claimed by the prosecution?

Here are the results of an investigation conducted by this writer, which were presented to the Court of Appeals in a motion for a new trial for Sobell.[5]

In Appendices 8 to 10, the reader will find translations of telegrams and correspondence from the official files of the Departments of State and Migration of the United States of Mexico, relating to the so-called "deportation . . . of the North American, Morton Sobell." These documents disclose the following:

1. That the Mexican authorities in Nuevo Laredo, the border town just opposite Laredo, Texas, knew *nothing* whatsoever about the illegal delivery of Sobell to the FBI. And that the FBI-employed "agents" who delivered Sobell did so by "evading the vigilance of the [Mexican] Migration Service." (*Note:* See telegram in Appendix 8.)

2. That the Department of Migration assured the Nuevo Laredo authorities that "in the future the requirements of migration will not again be omitted." (*Note:* See letter in Appendix 9.)

3. That the Mexican Government instituted an immediate investigation of the circumstances of Sobell's seizure. And, that so confused were the Mexican border authorities that the only way information could be obtained was from American officials in Laredo, Texas, and from a report in the Laredo Times—which, uniquely enough, announced the "deportation" of Sobell, *when no authorized official in Mexico* had anything to do with it!

457

In short, the most important officials in the Mexican Department of State were entirely dependent on what a foreign police deigned to tell their consul, and on what the latter could read in a foreign newspaper about a "deportation" supposed to have been carried out *officially* in Mexico City! (*Note:* See letter in Appendix 10.)

●

To sum up then, what was the prosecution's case against Morton Sobell? It consisted solely of the accusations of a self-confessed perjurer, Max Elitcher, in no way corroborated by any of the eight witnesses whose testimony we have just reviewed. To state it more bluntly, not only had the prosecution coerced Elitcher into framing Sobell, but it had criminally manufactured a "deportation" out of a brutal kidnapping, thereby creating in the minds of the jury the spectacle of a hunted fugitive captured with the help of the Mexican Government.

In concluding our analysis of the prosecution's case,[6] it is vital to point out that the *joint* trial of the Rosenbergs and Sobell took place over the continued protests of the latter's attorneys. According to their argument, if Sobell had to be tried at all he deserved a completely separate trial on the grounds that there allegedly existed two different conspiracies:

1. That of Rosenberg-Greenglass-Yakovlev-Gold.
2. That of Rosenberg-Elitcher-Sobell.

When, however, Judge Kaufman upheld the prosecution's argument that it was all one and the same conspiracy, not only was Sobell's cause gravely injured by the testimony dealing with the Rosenbergs, but, in turn, they were equally injured by Sobell's "flight," "capture," and "deportation." [7]

Impressed by the appearance of the five witnesses flown up at government expense from Mexico, as well as by the United States Immigration Inspector from Texas, the jury placed additional credence in Greenglass' testimony concerning "Operation Finger."

Following the introduction of Huggins' "deportation" card, the record reads:

> Mr. Saypol: The Government rests, if the Court please.

•

To be sure, the prosecution played a contemptuously careless game, but with full appreciation of point and counterpoint—a thrust here against the Rosenbergs, then a thrust there against Sobell. What would it matter if the Rosenbergs, now about to take the stand, endeavored to deny the mass of accusations piled up against them? In the eyes of the jury they were pariahs already contaminated as members of the "international Communist conspiracy" and adherents of a political philosophy already judged in the courts as "a clear and present danger."

. . . So let the defendants Rosenberg have their "day in court," for howsoever they might protest their innocence, on the basis of the officially promulgated and widely accepted premise—that Communists will always lie—the prosecution was confident that the verdict of guilt was inevitable. And as for Kaufman, as Saypol very well knew, the death sentences had been discussed with him and determined almost a month before trial!

NOTES AND REFERENCES

1. In this chapter we continue with those witnesses whose testimony relates specifically to Sobell. For Danziger's full testimony, see Record, pp. 857–867.
2. As indicated by the Charge of the Court, it does *not* constitute guilt that Sobell had taken safeguards as a political refugee. (In further support of this point, see *Columbia Law Review*, footnote 89, p. 237.)
3. It is quite clear from Huggins' cross-examination that he was instructed to insert the phrase "Deported from

Mexico" either by the FBI or by one of the prosecution's staff. (See Record, pp. 1027–1028, 1031, 1036.)

4. *Columbia Law Review*, p. 233, footnote 57. (The *Review* cites as a precedent: McNabb v. U.S., 318 U.S. 332, 1943.)

5. Motion for a new trial for Sobell was made by his attorney, Marshal Perlin, May 5, 1956. (28 USC § 2255).

6. Regarding the prosecution's rebuttal witness, the photographer Schneider, we will come to his testimony in the ensuing chapter.

7. Judge Kaufman's failure to instruct the jury on the possibility of the existence of two separate conspiracies was deemed by Judge Jerome Frank of the U.S. Court of Appeals a most serious and reversible error, calling for a new trial. (See Chapter 26, Section VIII.)

ADDENDA

Concerning Sobell's impulsive choice of pseudonyms, Pollack, after quoting our explanation from Section VI in Chapter 7, in which we associated "Morris Sand" with the seashore in Vera Cruz, makes this sarcastic challenge:

One wonders how Wexley would explain the use of "Marvin Salt" in Tampico and "Morton Salt" on a plane ticket from Tampico to Mexico City.

Here Pollack strives to give the impression that we had avoided mention of these other pseudonyms. Later, in a chapter called, "Omission of Material Matter in Wexley's Book," he goes even further and states falsely:

Wexley gives no explanation for Sobell's use of aliases, though he admits the stupidity of Sobell in doing what he did.

Regarding "Morris Sand," as shown above, not only did we explain it, but Pollack quotes our explanation verbatim. Likewise with "Marvin Salt," which, as explained in the *same* section, was "evidently another free association with the sea" in Tampico, another seaport. As for "Morton Salt," the reader will recall that I ascribed it to his "seriocomic" attitude at the time, associating it with the famous trademark, "MORTON SALT ('When it rains, it pours')."

What we see here is that Pollack is unable to rebut my conclusions that these pseudonyms (four of them containing Sobell's own initials and all of them suggestive of his own name or his wife's maiden name) were the obvious choices of a panic-stricken political refugee and *not* those of an experienced spy.

Indeed, Pollack's little slip, accepting Sobell's "stupidity" in choosing these names, gives additional support to our analysis.

As for Pollack's overall charge concerning the "omission of material matter" in this book, any objective comparison between it and the Government's report will confirm what we have demonstrated in so many instances— that it is rather Pollack who studiously omits important material matter wherever he finds it dangerous to the Government's case.

24 "THOUGH ALL THE WINDS OF DOCTRINE . . ."

I

> "Though all the winds of doctrine were let loose to play upon the earth, so Truth be in the field. . . ."
>
> —*John Milton*

It was March 21, a Wednesday afternoon. According to the New York *Times* of that date, Julius Rosenberg made a conspicuous figure at the defense table. He was described as "tall, thin and wearing glasses," with his prison pallor considerably set off by the dark line of his mustache.

Day after day he had lived through this incredible nightmare. First the evasive Elitcher virtually admitting the "deal" whereby he would be spared prosecution for perjury. Then David Greenglass, "piling it on" with his hopes for a minimum sentence. And that fantastic Harry Gold! It was really a nightmare, that phantasmagoria of the Jello box; and the mysterious "Julius" calling Bentley in the "wee, small hours," and Greenglass, posing as an Oklahoma tourist before the statue of Columbus in Mexico City . . .

And yet Julius knew that the odds had been stacked against them long before the trial. There was all the power of the media convicting them as "A-spies" from the moment of their arrests. There was the insuperable handicap of being accused by the Government of the United States, by its highest officials, the United States Attorney General, the Director of the FBI; in sum, by everything that could overawe an average juror in this war-scare atmosphere.

And what could they expect from this pompous and self-righteous judge who had hurried their counsel at every turn as though he feared that some juror might have time to detect some glaring contradiction. Hurry —hurry—hurry! This was the theme-note heard constantly from the bench, but most frequently whenever the defense appeared to be exposing one of these contradictions.[1] Only a moment before, when the prosecution had concluded its case and the defense prepared to make its motions, Kaufman had snapped:

> The Court: I want them [the motions] very brief.
> Mr. E. H. Bloch [repeating]: I don't know what the Court's idea is—whether you want them outside the presence of the jury.[2]
> The Court: Yes, and very brief.

Then there had followed the motions, each one met with the drone of Kaufman's denials:

. . . Motion for mistrial on the grounds that the prosecution had introduced the issue of membership in the Communist Party as a "link" to the crime charged; that even if the Court decided to strike all the testimony dealing with this matter, it had already served its inflammatory purpose.
Motion Denied! [3]

. . . Motion in behalf of Sobell: that since the only testimony implicating him had come from Elitcher, and since it had not included any evidence of atomic espionage, a separate conspiracy was involved and Sobell was entitled to a separate trial. And that, even if one were to believe Elitcher's testimony, no espionage had actually taken place.

Motion Denied!

. . . And when the venerable Harold Phillips representing Sobell, had tried to explain that this was why he had previously declared, "I don't know what we are here for," Kaufman had retorted aspishly:

The Court: So you found out, did you not?

. . . And finally, the motion that the indictment be dismissed:

[Alexander Bloch]: . . . on the ground that the Government [had] failed to prove the charge contained in the indictment beyond a reasonable doubt.

The Court: Denied. . . .

And so, at long last, after 248 days and nights of pacing his cell and waiting for his day in court, now his time had come. The Judge was again seated, the gavel tapped, the spectators quieted down—then a sudden stillness and Emanuel Bloch arose:

If the Court please, my first witness is the defendant, Julius Rosenberg.

II

There is the story of the rabbit, which, upon seeing the antelope racing past in terror, asked, "Why are you fleeing?"

"Hurry, save yourself!" said the antelope. "They are coming through the forest today to kill all the rabbits!"

"But what is that to you?" asked the rabbit. "You are an antelope."

"To be sure," replied the antelope, "but if they want to call antelopes rabbits, how are we to prove we are not?"

How does one go about proving a negative? Since no man can show conclusively that he did *not* request or transmit certain illegal information, there remains only the simple act of denial. How could Julius Rosenberg do more than deny that he had told Greenglass about his theft of the secret of the "sky platform"? How could he prove that he did *not* receive a citation? Or how could he *disprove* that Gold had had a rendezvous with Yakovlev?

And yet, this was the heavy burden placed on Mr. Bloch as he began to question Julius concerning each overt act charged in the indictment. Did Julius ever ask Ruth to enlist David in espionage? No, he did not. Did he see David on his January furlough? Yes, he did. Where? At his mother-in-law's house. Did members of the family invite the Greenglasses to their homes for supper? Yes, they did. Did he know that David was working on the Los Alamos Atomic Project? No, he did not know that.[4]

And so it went: question, denial; question, denial. Had Julius so desired, he could have denied flatly that the crucial September visit had ever taken place. Since no witnesses were present, it would have merely been the word of one couple against the other. But it was the defense's hope that the jury would understand how easy it was for the Greenglasses to dress up such innocent visits and extend them into conspiratorial acts. Yet Julius' forthrightness was to lead him into a dangerous exchange of political opinion with the Court, indeed into committing the sin of sins, the refusal of the heretic to recant.

It had begun as soon as Mr. Bloch was questioning Julius about Ann Sidorovich. Again assuming the role of prosecutor-in-chief, Kaufman interrupted, introducing issues which clearly violated the defendant's constitutional right of freedom of thought:

The Court: Did you ever discuss with Ann Sidorovich the respective preferences of economic systems between Russia and the United States?

A. [Julius]: Well, your Honor . . . I am not an expert on matters on different economic systems, but in my normal social intercourse with my friends, we discussed matters like that. And I believe there are merits in both systems. . . .

Q. I am not talking about your belief today, I am talking about your belief at that time, in January, 1945.

A. Well, that is what I am talking about. At that time, what I believed at that time I still believe today. In the first place, I heartily approve our system of justice as performed in this country, Anglo-Saxon jurisprudence. I am in favor, heartily in favor of our Constitution and Bill of Rights and I owe my allegiance to my country at all times.

Under the guise of establishing "intent," here is Kaufman conducting an inquisition into the most sacred right of all Americans—the right to believe whatever one chooses and to express that belief fearlessly and unashamedly.

In his book about Alger Hiss, Alistair Cooke presents a brilliant analysis of the phenomenon of American ex-heretics beating their breasts in penitence for the beliefs they once cherished proudly:

A man who could be shown to have been a doctrinaire Communist or a fellow traveler in the thirties would have a harder and harder time proving, in the fifties, that he had not been a member of the Communist underground. After the Hiss Trials . . . this was, in fact, exactly what happened. And in the Senate especially there was an alarmed minority ready to make political hay by blurring this distinction between an old sympathizer and an old spy.[5]

Perhaps it was foolhardly of Julius to have accepted Kaufman's challenge, for the ominous threat was unmistakable. Even the newspapermen appeared to be aware of this in their report: "When Rosenberg was being questioned about Communist activities, the jurors watched him closely."

On that same day, the actor Larry Parks was being questioned in Washington by the Un-American Activities Committee about membership in the Communist Party. Tormented, he "pleaded with the investigators not to force him to publicly 'crawl through the mud —to be an informer.' " [6] And if ever Julius Rosenberg had his chance to assuage Kaufman by crawling through the mud this was it. But instead of trying to protect himself by pointing out a difference between his belief of 1951 and that of 1945, he replied, unwisely but with profound honesty, that whatever he believed then, he still believed.

[Julius]: . . . And in discussing the merits of other forms of governments . . . with my friends . . . I felt that the Soviet government has improved [the] lot of the underdog there, has made a lot of progress in eliminating illiteracy, had done a lot of reconstruction work and built up a lot of resources, and at the same time I felt that they contributed a major share in destroying the Hitler beast who killed six million of my co-religionists, and I feel emotional about that thing.
Q. Did you feel that way in 1945?
A. Yes, I felt that way in 1945.
Q. Do you feel that way today?
A. I still feel that way.

Realizing that this firm stand could be misinterpreted by the jury, Mr. Bloch decided to clarify the issue:

Q. [Bloch]: Did you ever make any comparisons in the sense that the Court has asked you, about whether you preferred one system over another?
A. [Julius]: No, I did not. I would like to state that my personal opinions are that the people of every country should decide by themselves what kind of government they want. If the English want a King, it is their business. If the Russians want communism, it is their business. If the Americans want our form of government, it is our business. I feel that the majority of people should decide for themselves what kind of government they want.

Despite these avowals, Kaufman interrupted again:

The Court: Well, did you ever belong to any group that discussed the system of Russia?

The Witness: Well, your Honor, I feel at this time that I refuse to answer a question that might tend to incriminate me.

The Court: It seems to me I have been hearing a lot about that.

Here, as the case becomes Kaufman *versus* Rosenberg, Mr. Bloch strives to undo the malicious intent behind the last remark:

Q. [Bloch]: . . . When you answered the Court's question did you have in mind the Communist Party?

A. [Julius]: Yes, I did.

The Court: Well now, I won't direct you at this point to answer; I will wait for the cross-examination.

Q. [Bloch]: Do you want to say anything more about ideas on politics—if the Court wants it . . .

A. I can say this . . .

The Court: No, he has replied.

What exactly is on trial here? *A man's ideas or the crime charged?* Significant, too, is how Kaufman slams the door on the defense's willingness to explore more fully Julius' "ideas on politics." Now that he has cast the cloud of "Communist incrimination" over *all* of Julius' testimony, he curtly dismisses the offer with "No, he has replied." Thus, in effect, he is saying to the jury: "We have enough—we have him now. The accused *still believes* that the Soviet Union has improved the lot of the underdog; *still believes* that the Russians have eliminated illiteracy, and *still believes* that if the Russians want communism, it is their business! And, when I asked him about ever belonging to a group that discussed the economic system of Russia, you saw him immediately hide behind the Fifth Amendment like all the rest of his kind we have been

467

hearing a lot about. Indeed, we have enough—we need no more!"

III

It is during Julius' cross-examination that the hollowness of the prosecution's case becomes most apparent.[7] Here, in this section, is the *only* tangible "proof" which Saypol could offer that the Rosenbergs were tools of the Kremlin:

> Q. [Saypol]: Did you ever go out and collect any money for the Joint Anti-Fascist Refugee Committee?

> A. [Julius]: I don't recall collecting any money, but I recall contributing money.

Now that Julius has taken the bait, Saypol springs the trap. Striding melodramatically toward the jury, as we read in the New York *Times* of March 23, the prosecutor ". . . produced a collection can bearing the Committee's name and set it down on the jury-box rail with a loud thump." And moving well back for better effect, Saypol hurls this triumphant question:

> Q. . . . Did you ever see this before? . . . Do you remember when the agents arrested you and took that out of your house?
> A. [Julius]: That is correct.
> Mr. Saypol: I offer it in evidence.
> (Government Exhibit 27 . . . received in evidence.)

Here the record discloses that the prosecutor proceeded to read the wording on the label of the coin-can as though it were some secret spy directive:

> Mr. Saypol [reading]: . . . "Save Spanish Republican Child, Volveremos, We Will Return.— Joint Anti-Fascist Refugee Committee, 192 Lexington Avenue, Suite 1501."

And, turning to the witness. Saypol delivers the telling blow he had been building up to:

> Q. So that perhaps you did *a little more* than just contribute? [Emphasis added.]

It was an incredible performance and Julius stared astounded at this little tin can being submitted to the jury as "evidence" of guilt.

As the record discloses, the Rosenbergs had done "a little more"; they had contributed one dollar to aid the victims of Franco, but they had kept the collection can on their bookcase for visiting friends to drop in some coins!

IV

> "We have never known the ease of riches or even comfort. At times we have felt the pangs of want." [8]

On direct examination the usual preliminary questions had been asked concerning Julius' education, employment, and marriage. Since nearly all of this material has been covered in earlier chapters, perhaps only this should be added: that the undisputed record of the Rosenbergs as an average, hard-working, decent American family is without blemish.

In an embellishment of her accusations, Ruth Greenglass testified that Ethel had told her that Julius was running around "a good deal" and using up his energy "in this thing" . . .

> [Ruth]: . . . That he had to make a good impression; that sometimes it cost him as much as $50 to $75 an evening to entertain his friends. . . . [R. 691]

On cross-examination of Julius, Saypol tried to develop this theme of the spy-master entertaining his recruits by asking how many night clubs and "high class restaurants" Julius made "a habit of going to."

Yes, Julius replied, he had been to a night club, "the Federation of Architects had a dinner party at Cafe Society."

Q. Was that the only night club you were ever at?
A. That is the only night club I ever attended.

Q. . . . Did you ever go to restaurants where the prices were expensive?

A. Well, once when I was taking my wife out to a place near Emerson Radio called Pappas, and on another occasion I have eaten at a place called Nicholaus on Second Avenue.

For Julius, to whom a three-dollar meal in the late forties, was the height of extravagance, such dinners with his wife on these two occasions were indeed "expensive."

Julius' average weekly salary during his five years with the Signal Corps, 1940–1945, was $52.75. The Rosenbergs' monthly rent for their three-room apartment was $45.75. The value of the Rosenbergs' furniture can be estimated by their $25 secondhand piano, their $20 secondhand chest of drawers, and their $21 console table bought at Macy's.[9]

The cost of Ethel's clothes in the ten years of her marriage was "a maximum of $300" including an $80 "fur coat." The cost of Julius' five suits purchased in this ten-year period was $130. His only overcoat, purchased ten years before the trial, had cost $55. Their average gas bill was $2 per month. [R. 1083–1084, 1299]

Pitiful? Not at all. Ethel and Julius had an unusually happy home life even though it frequently "bordered on poverty." What was bitter was hearing the prosecution depict Julius as "the payoff man" of a widespread criminal combination fed by a seemingly endless supply of "Moscow gold." [10] Here is an example of how the Rosenbergs lived at 10 Monroe Street on the Lower East Side:

Q. [Bloch]: . . . You lived there approximately nine years?

A. [Ethel]: That is right.

Q. Did you do all the chores of a housewife?

A. Yes, I did.

Q. Cooking, washing, cleaning, darning, scrubbing?

A. Yes, I did.

Q. Now, outside of these three periods you last mentioned [one month following the birth of each child and four or five months of Ethel's illness], you did all of the housework yourself?

A. That is right.

Q. Your laundry and everything?

A. That is correct. [R. 1296]

"Ah, yes," mutters the skeptic, "but Julius could have kept Ethel scrimping and slaving and still have been the paymaster of all his recruits, contacts, and subsidized students. The Rosenbergs' modest standard of living could have been simply a front."

But if we accept this contention, what about all established "rules of conduct" regarding successful espionage agents? Would Julius, as a veteran spy, dare to toss around $50 and $75 a night so ostentatiously in direct conflict with his low income? Here is how this charge struck Dr. Harold C. Urey when he wrote to the New York *Times* on January 8, 1953:

The Rosenbergs appear to have been as poor as churchmice and the statement that Julius was spending $50 or $75 a night in night clubs seems to me to be a very doubtful one. Had he done this, he would have been obviously and unaccountably rich to all his associates.

V

> "There came a day, however, that a vigilant FBI broke through the darkness of this insidious business and collected the evidence. . . ."
>
> —*Opening statement by Saypol; Record, p. 183*

Even when one tries valiantly to accept the credibility of the prosecution's case, one is met with the implausible. For example, the FBI's *total* failure to discover any evidence pointing to the Rosenbergs' "guilt" other than the little coin-can and the nominating petition Ethel had signed ten years before the trial.

According to the facts disclosed by the record, not only was there no darkness, but there was the FBI spotlight focused on Julius as far back as 1944! FBI detectives had him under surveillance at least four months *before* his alleged spy proposal to Elitcher, and nine months *before* his alleged recruitment of Ruth and David. Here is Julius being asked about his dismissal from the Signal Corps in February of 1945:

Q. [Saypol]: And what was the reason?
A. [Julius]: It was alleged that I was a member of the Communist Party.

Here is Julius' sworn denial in his statement to Army Intelligence at the Signal Corps:

I am not now, and never have been a communist member. I know nothing about communist branches, divisions, clubs or transfers. I never heard either of the Division or the Club referred to. I had nothing to do with the so-called transfer. Either the charge is based on a case of mistaken identity or a complete falsehood. In any event, it certainly has not the slightest basis in fact.

For more than a year Julius challenged the report of the FBI, even making a special trip to Washington to see his Congressman to help him appeal his case.

It was at that time he was supposed to have recruited Elitcher. [R. 1152–1156]

It may be argued that Julius' denials and appeals were false; desperate measures to regain his job, but regardless of whether the FBI report was bona fide or not, one thing is clear: that such a report was made to G-2 and that Julius was fired promptly on the basis of an FBI surveillance which had commenced *during 1944*, if not earlier. Which brings us to this important question:

If Julius was under surveillance during the precise period of the alleged conspiracy, and if he was really a spy, then why didn't the FBI discover anything at all about his widespread espionage network in these six years?

And how is it, in these six years when there must have been surveillance of Julius, that the FBI could not produce *one single scrap* of incriminating evidence —whether check accounts, letters, notes, microfilms, names of recruits, Soviet citations, Soviet wrist-watches, cameras, microfilming apparatus, passport photos, the hollowed-out console table, or any evidence whatsoever?

In any event, this much is certain: that a good deal of Julius' comings and goings throughout the period of the alleged conspiracy must have been known to the FBI. Neither can there be any doubt that his phone was periodically tapped, that his mail was opened, that his bank accounts were photostated, and that every one of his friends and classmates whose names were later revealed at the Perl trial and at the McCarthy investigations at Fort Monmouth was thoroughly checked.

And yet, in all these years, the FBI failed to discover anything dealing in any way with espionage! For if they had found *something*, no matter how slight, Mr. Saypol would surely have used it to thump down on the jury rail as he did with the coin can labeled "Save a Spanish Republican Child."

VI

> "I have read the testimony given at the trial, and though I have no legal experience in matters of this kind, my competence is comparable to that of the jurors and the great public who are concerned about this matter.
>
> ". . . The government's case rests on the testimony of David and Ruth Greenglass, and this was flatly contradicted by Ethel and Julius Rosenberg. I found the testimony of the Rosenbergs more believable than that of the Greenglasses."
>
> —Letter of Dr. Harold C. Urey to Judge Kaufman, Dec. 16, 1952

In this fatal contest between the Greenglasses and the Rosenbergs, let us view the latter's testimony as a whole and see if it meets the acid test of credibility. Do we find any of the gaping holes, the flat contradictions, and sheer improbabilities we find in the testimony of Elitcher, Gold, Bentley, and the Greenglasses? Let us recall, for example, the crucial console table and ask which table is more believable.

Is it the prosecution's vanished table, never produced in court, even though it was available to the FBI for months? Is it Saypol's hypothetical, expensive mahogany table doing double duty as a Russian gift and as a microfilming apparatus? Or is it the discovered cheap gumwood table authenticated by the furniture buyer of R. H. Macy? Is it Ruth's hollowed-out table? Or is it the one Mrs. Cox wiped and dusted so often, with her testimony entirely devoid of any such unusual feature?

In our test for credibility, let us ask some reasonable questions about the Jello box. How is it that neither David nor Ruth ever mentions it to the Rosenbergs during their September visit in 1945? Only three months earlier, a "man" had suddenly appeared at their apartment, *contrary to instructions*. How is it that the Greenglasses fail to make the slightest reference to Gold's surprise visit, such as:

"Is he going to visit us again? How come he didn't meet us at the Safeway store as we arranged it? The Jello-box halves fitted just right, but why didn't you ever tell us about his recognition signal, 'I came from Julius'? And thanks for that $500, but I wonder if we did the right thing: I told this Dave from Pittsburgh that I might come to New York on a furlough this Christmas and that he could contact me via your telephone. I hope that was okay. Was it?"

During the alleged September delivery of the Nagasaki bomb data, which was only one month *after* the atomic destruction of Hiroshima and Nagasaki, isn't it strange that no normal remark was made about the fearsome Atomic Age we were then entering? All the world was discussing the staggering destructive possibilities of the very weapon David had described in his twelve-page report and which Ethel was typing at that very moment. And yet, we are asked to believe, here were these two couples peculiarly aware of this world-shaking secret, but not one reference was made to its extraordinary military and political potential. Certainly, if Julius and Ethel wanted Russia to have the bomb so desperately, they would normally have made *some* political comment regarding its tremendous significance.

In the *Columbia Law Review* examination of the Rosenberg case its editors stop short, with typical legal neutrality, at the vital question: Which tale was the truth and which the perjury? But perhaps its withheld opinion can be detected in its emphasis of the intolerable handicap the Rosenbergs were burdened with, namely:

. . . the federal rule which permits a defendant to be convicted upon the *uncorroborated* testimony of an accomplice. [Emphasis added.]

Explaining that this archaic rule, still bedeviling our Federal courts, stems from the ancient English common law, the *Review* carefully footnotes the following:

. . . There was a greater incentive in those times [for accomplices in turning King's evidence] not to attest to a falsehood, because involvement in judicial proceedings might eventuate in trial by battle, and the outcome of that conflict was generally thought by the intensely religious people of the era to depend on the veracity of the accused. If the battle were lost, the falsifier could then be hanged because of his own confessed crime.[11]

And so, seven or eight centuries after such barbarisms as "trial by battle," we see the spectacle of two young Americans executed by means of an ancient ruling which did not even afford them the protection offered in the common law!

VII

It was near the conclusion of Julius' cross-examination that the prosecution put into operation a plan, cunningly timed, to attack his credibility. It was to ask him whether or not he had, in 1950, taken passport photos. When he would reply in the negative, the prosecution would then present in rebuttal the passport photographer as a surprise witness, thereby delivering Julius a mortal blow.

Here is the gist of the trap questions Saypol asked of Julius: In May or June of 1950, did he have any passport photos taken at a shop at 99 Park Row? Did he tell the photographer that he wanted the passport in order to go to France to settle an estate? [R. 1277–1280]

At this point Julius sensed that Saypol had something up his sleeve. For with the mention of a location within walking distance of his home, it occurred to him he might have indeed been out with his family on a week-end stroll and that another innocent event was being distorted into one of guilt.

[Julius]: Well, when I [would] walk with the children, many times with my wife, we would step in; . . . [or] we would pass a man with one of those box cameras and we would take some pictures. We

476

would step into a place and take some pictures, and the pictures we liked, we would keep.

Q. [Saypol]: Passport pictures?
A. Not passport pictures.

On the very next day, when the photographer of 99 Park Row, one Ben Schneider, was put on the stand, the total effect of his testimony was that Julius had lied when he denied having taken passport photos there with his family.[12]

Of course, the plan was calculated to achieve a number of objectives: (1) To relate Schneider's testimony to the sensitive question of "flight." (2) To corroborate the Greenglass charge that the Rosenbergs had also planned to flee and thus lend credibility to all the rest of the Greenglasses testimony. (3) To lend credence to the prosecution's general charge concerning Sobell's "flight" to Mexico.

•

Unlike that of the rebuttal witness Evelyn Cox, the name of Ben Schneider had not been made known to the defense among the 102 persons announced originally by the prosecution. This was in clear violation of the statute which provides that all government witnesses must be named *before* the start of trial.[13] Saypol's excuse, supported by Kaufman, was that the Government did not know of the existence of Schneider until the day before he testified. Here is the substance of Schneider's direct examination on March 27:

That the very first time he had any knowledge that he was going to be a witness was at 11:30 A.M. on March 26, 1951, only the day before his appearance in court. That on that morning two FBI agents (Roetting and Gallaher) had come to his shop to show him photographs of the Rosenbergs. (*Note:* In a moment, we will discuss this fortuitous discovery of Schneider by the FBI, literally a stone's throw from their office, on the next-to-last day of trial!)

That while he, Schneider, had seen many photographs of the Rosenbergs in the newspapers, he had never recognized them. However, the reason he could identify them from the FBI photos was that the agents had shown him "a front view and a side view." That he had told the FBI he was positive it was the Rosenbergs who had come to his shop, together with their two children, on a Saturday in May or June of 1950, and that they had ordered three dozen passport photos at a cost of nine dollars. That Julius had given the following reason for their trip:

[Schneider]: . . . They were going to France; there was some property left; they were going to take care of it; the wife—that is, his wife was left some property.

Q. [Saypol]: Did you then deliver it [the photos] to Mr. Rosenberg?
A. Yes, sir.

Q. *And is that the last time you saw him before today?*
A. *That's right.*

Q. And is it *seeing him here with his wife* that recalls it to your memory that they were the persons who came in?
A. That's right; that's right. [R. 1424–1429, 1439; emphasis added.]

Not until after the trial, long after the Rosenbergs' first appeal to the Circuit Court had been denied, did Mr. Bloch learn that Schneider's testimony was "steeped in fraud, aided and abetted by the prosecuting officials." [14]

It is a stroke of irony that Oliver Pilat, confidential press agent of Saypol, should have been the one to expose the extent of Schneider's "perjury." This occurred when his book *The Atom Spies* was published in 1952 and the following passage came to the attention of Mr. Bloch:

While Julius was still on the stand, an FBI agent brought into the courtroom a photographer. . . . He wanted to look at Rosenberg to be sure, and when he took the look, he nodded. . . .[15]

The reaction of Mr. Bloch can be imagined: So, on March 26, Schneider had been *secretly* led into the courtroom to see Julius "on the stand," and only thus could he be *sure* of the identification! Then what about his repeated statements that it was seeing the Rosenbergs on *March 27*, which recalled them to his memory?

Now that the cat was out of the bag, there was the danger that Bloch's impending charge of Schneider's perjury in the second appeal might involve the agent responsible. Thus the FBI had this particular agent prepare an affidavit which would absolve the FBI, even if it did expose Mr. Saypol's hand. Here are the important passages of this affidavit by John A. Harrington, sworn to on December 1, 1952:

On March 26, 1951, during the course of the trial . . . I was informed [by Special Agents Roetting and Gallaher] that they had located a photographer who had identified a photograph of Julius Rosenberg as a person whose passport photograph he had taken. . . .[16] Mr. Irving H. Saypol . . . *directed* that the photographer he brought to the United States Court House to confirm the identity of Rosenberg. . . . Shortly thereafter . . . I brought Mr. Schneider into Courtroom 110, to the fore part of the courtroom. . . . I instructed Mr. Schneider to look round the courtroom and see if he saw anybody he recognized. . . . and, when he saw Julius Rosenberg, he stated to me that that was the man whose pictures he had taken.

At no time did I point out or in any other way indicate who was Julius Rosenberg or the place where he was located in the courtroom to Mr. Schneider. [signed] John A. Harrington.[17] [Emphasis added.]

The most significant disclosure here is the prosecution's need to have Schneider see Julius in person *before* taking the witness stand. And, obviously, this was Saypol's motive in concealing Schneider's clandestine visit. For if this fact had been made known to the jury, they would have had to wonder: "Wait, here is a witness so uncertain of the identity of the Rosenbergs that the prosecution dared not risk a crucial test of identification made in open court." [18]

To sum up the Government's machinations in this instance: First, the violation of the defendants' rights when Schneider was presented as a rebuttal witness without proper notice, thereby depriving the defense of a fair chance to investigate the possibility of his questionable background. Second, the violation concerning the exclusion of witnesses from the courtroom until ready to testify. Third, Schneider's "perjury." Fourth, the "knowing fraud" as charged by the defense. And finally, that Schneider was so doubtful about identifying the Rosenbergs, even after seeing their photos in the newspapers for weeks, and even after being shown front and side views of their photos, that their identification had to be prepared secretly the day *before* his trial testimony!

Returning to the affidavit, we see that Harrington attempts to exculpate himself by repeating that he did not give Schneider any indication of Julius' identity or the location where he might be sitting. But he *omits* the fact that Julius was sitting *on the witness stand!* Moreover, the record shows that Julius was being identified by name every few minutes with such direct references as:

Q. [Mr. Kuntz]: Mr. Rosenberg . . .

Q. [Mr. Saypol]: Now, Mr. Rosenberg . . .

Q. [Mr. Bloch]: Mr. Rosenberg . . . [R. 1281, 1282]

On cross-examination it was Schneider's admission that he kept no negatives, no receipts, no records, no sales slips; in short, that he relied entirely upon his memory, with *nothing* to substantiate that the Rosenbergs were the persons he had photographed nine to ten months before. [R. 1429–1440]

When Saypol inquired of Schneider: "What do you do mainly?" the reply was: "Passport photographs and identification photographs." And yet, when Bloch asked him to describe the signs outside his shop, this was the testimony:

Q. Do you have two signs in front of your store, in red, with white lettering, called "Photos"?
A. That's right.
Q. Do you have any large sign on the outside, saying "Passport photos"?
A. *Well, no. I haven't got that.* [Emphasis added.]

In order to satisfy himself on this point, this writer made a personal visit to Schneider's shop in August of 1954 and undertook the overt act of having one set of "passport photos" taken of himself.

The shop awakened suspicion at first glance. For example, the entire fore part was bare except for an empty counter with empty wall shelves behind it. Upon inquiry of the original owner of the store, it was learned that Schneider had once employed a shoemaker in the front, while he ran his photo studio in the rear. However, as Schneider informed this writer, he preferred to be alone the past six or eight years—having let the shoemaker go because "pals" dropping in would "kid" him with remarks such as "Hey, Benny—how's about a shine?"

In appearance, Schneider was a man of about fifty-five with a pink face and baldish head surrounded by a reddish fuzz. This writer recognized him instantly from a previous description and inquired, "Mr. Schneider?" He replied, "No, Walters."

"But the pawnbroker down the street told me you were Schneider."

"Oh, did Davis—the fat fellow send you?" Apparently reassured, he shrugged, "Okay, so I'm Schneider."

"Ben Schneider?"

"Sure—what's the difference?" He grinned.

On the walls were some stained photos of celebrities and prize fighters as they had appeared some twenty years before, also some fly-specked samples of Schneider's own photography.

In a small back room which was the studio, there

was a lighting arrangement of four or five blackened porcelain sockets fixed to a dust-laden overhead standard, which seemed to contain the first Edison electric lamps. The camera looked like something Brady would have regarded with skepticism back in the 1860's.

While this writer waited for the photos to be printed (three for one dollar), he asked if he might use the washroom. Whereupon Schneider suggested the tavern at the corner, since he was using the wash-basin for his chemicals. About twenty minutes later, when Schneider emerged from the washroom with the prints, they were still damp and badly scratched. During this wait, this writer wondered how Schneider could possibly have completed the Rosenbergs' alleged thirty-six prints in "20 minutes to a half an hour," when it took him fully twenty minutes to complete only these three prints!

In any event, it is just too incredible that the FBI men Roetting and Gallaher managed to find this *one* needle in the haystack of all the thousands of photographers in the city of New York and that he was found so conveniently on the last day of Julius Rosenberg's testimony! Besides, the qualified wording by Roetting in a separate affidavit [19] does not exclude the possibility that Schneider might have been "interviewed" in the past on *other* matters, including the possession and peddling of drugs.

Some final observations concerning Schneider's testimony: If Julius were really a Soviet spy-master, why would he choose precisely 99 Park Row—a photo shop so close to FBI headquarters—to place such a suspiciously large order of *three dozen* passport photos? Moreover, why would he do this in May or June of 1950, the period of Julius' greatest fear of "street" surveillance?

And why the unnecessary risk? If he was so proficient in microfilming, why could he not simply snap a few pictures of Ethel and the children and have Ethel snap his, then develop them in the privacy of his own home? In fact, since Sobell had a 35-millimeter camera and photographic equipment, why didn't Julius simply call on his services and thus eliminate all danger?

In his summation Saypol resorts to the most labored rationale to lend credence to Schneider's testimony regarding the three dozen photo prints. Asking the jury why was it necessary to order "more than one set of three pictures," Saypol offers the following explanation:

. . . That in order to make possible this skipping furtively from country to country, forged and false passports are necessary, and perhaps in perpetrating a forgery, a false passport, mistakes might be made, pictures might be mutilated, different passports might be required, depending on the route to be taken . . . and that is why I suggest you may *infer* more than the usual number is taken. [R. 1524; emphasis added.]

The illogic of this inference should be apparent. Why should Julius need a forged passport at all? According to the Greenglasses' testimony, the Rosenbergs were to meet them in Mexico. Since passports are *unnecessary* for Americans in entering that country, Julius could have simply traveled there with a tourist card. And in Mexico City there would have been no need of a forged passport, because the Soviet Embassy could have given him a *Russian* passport.

As for Saypol's speculation about the furtive use of different escape routes, why should Julius be uncertain about his own route, when it is charged that he had arranged Greenglass' escape route so precisely?

At the conclusion of Julius' redirect examination, Mr. Bloch announced that the defendant, Ethel Rosenberg, stood ready to take the stand. Her direct examination was interrupted, however, by the arrival of a "batch" of pictures taken from the Rosenberg home by the FBI, and, as Julius resumed the stand, these were offered in evidence to support his testimony. Since nearly all of the pictures were of the Rosenbergs and their children, and not the alleged passport photos, it is not surprising that Kaufman ruled against the defendants' exhibit.

Now that Ethel was about to be recalled, Saypol, in recross examination of Julius, used the opportunity to brand her beforehand by alerting the jury to his final question:

Q. Is or was your wife a member of the Communist Party?

A. [Julius]: I refuse to answer on the ground it might tend to incriminate me.

Mr. Saypol: Very well, I don't intend to press it.

The Court: Wait a minute. You are not going to press for an answer?

Mr. Saypol: No, I don't think so.

The Court [to Julius]: You may step down. (Witness excused.)

It was an obvious bit of play acting between Saypol and Kaufman: The prosecutor's grand gesture as he declines to press the question *which he may not press;* the feigned surprise of Kaufman as he encourages Saypol to press for the answer the witness *need not give.* And finally, Saypol's shrug of dismissal to imply that it is hardly necessary for the jury to hear Julius take the Fifth Amendment, since it would only be equivalent to a confession of guilt.

Here, then, in this final moment before Julius left the witness stand, is revealed the essential strategy of the prosecution: to present the Rosenbergs as Communists hiding behind the Fifth Amendment. It was this that was to remove all doubt of their guilt—their refusal to answer the hobgoblin question of the era:

"Are you or have you ever been a member of the Communist Party?"

NOTES AND REFERENCES

1. For some of the numerous instances wherein Judge Kaufman hurried the defense, see Record, pp. 431–433, 487, 584, 587, 635, 852, 917, 949–952, 1051, 1333.
2. For motion to dismiss indictment and motion for mistrial, see Record, pp. 1441–1447.
3. Here, Kaufman based his admission of Communist Party evidence on this astonishing comparison: ". . .

Just as I would admit testimony involving the Republican Party, the Masons, or the Elks. . . ." (Record, p. 1038.)

4. For Julius' direct, see Record, pp. 1051–1159; redirect, pp. 1282–1286, 1307–1308.
5. Alistair Cooke, *A Generation on Trial*, Knopf, New York, 1952, p. 40.
6. "Later [Parks] went behind closed doors to give them the names." (New York *Times*, March 22–23, 1951.)
7. For Julius' cross, see Record, pp. 1159–1282; recross: pp. 1308–1309.
8. From the Petition for Executive Clemency, January 9, 1953, p. 34.
9. See Record, pp. 1058, 1053–1054, 1054–1055, 1297–1298.
10. Petition for Executive Clemency, January 9, 1953.
11. *Columbia Law Review*, p. 233 and footnote 59.
12. With Ben Schneider, we now come to the last of the prosecution's twenty-three witnesses.
13. 18 U.S.C., Section 3432.
14. Transcript of Record, No. 687, p. 87.
15. Transcript of Record, No. 687, p. 86, with emphasis added by the defense.
16. There is no explanation how FBI agents Roetting and Gallaher made their curious last-minute discovery of Schneider. In the affidavit of Roetting he states that "this was the first occasion" he had ever laid eyes on Schneider, and that: ". . . so far as I know, no agent of the federal Government had interviewed him previously in connection with this or any related matter." (Transcript, No. 687, pp. 148–149. See *Addenda* below.)
17. *Ibid.*, pp. 149–150.
18. Such a pretended test was made from the witness stand with Schneider going through the mock ceremony of pointing out Julius and Ethel, as though this were the first time he had seen them since they had been to his shop the previous year. (Record, p. 1428.)
19. See Roetting's qualifying phrase "so far as I know" in his statement in above Note 16.

ADDENDA

Despite the FBI's distrust of the informer, Tartakow, and his "unsavory record" discussed in the *Addenda* of Chapter 10, an FBI memo credited him with providing the "key information" which helped them find Ben Schneider, the "passport" photographer.

According to a New York *Times* account of the memo, this "key information . . . was the tip" from Tartakow revealing Julius' admission of concern about having made passport photos prior to his arrest in July, 1950. Thus, we are told, this is how the FBI managed to track down the photographer, so that the prosecution could expose Julius' plan to flee the country. It was this "tip," according to the FBI memo, which had provided Schneider, and as Julius had later confided in Tartakow, it was Schneider's testimony which was "the most damaging evidence" against him.

Even assuming that Julius, the alleged spy-master, while on trial for his life, would be so reckless as to confide such self-incriminating information in a potential stool-pigeon, these question arise: Why would the FBI have waited so long for this information? Why would they need this "tip" to begin their last-minute search in March, 1951, for the photographer when they already had heard about Julius' flight plan nine months earlier? According to Greenglass' testimony, Julius had divulged his intention to flee at the time he had given flight instructions to David in May and early June, 1950. Hence, with the FBI allegedly aware of Julius' flight plan from David's disclosures, they had at least eight months to find Schneider and therefore had not the slightest need for the Tartakow "tip."

What is plainly evident is that this post-trial memo of April, 1951, concerning the "tip" was prepared to account for the highly suspicious presentation of Schneider as a "surprise witness" on the very last day of the trial, and to support the prosecution's excuse for not having included him in the required list of government witnesses. In other words, as with other FBI memos prepared after the trial, the "tip" story was designed as "insurance" for the prosecution in the event the defense might win an appeal or motion for a new trial.

486

Again, in line with my general thesis, Julius, at the close of the Government's case, may very well have stated his concern to one or another fellow-prisoner that Schneider's passport testimony had been most damaging, and with Tartakow picking up such a normal statement, it required only the insertion of the "tip" to turn it into an admission of guilt.

(See New York *Times*, December 14, 1975, and January 3, 1976.)

25 "THE EMPTY RITUAL"

I

"For the source of the Fifth Amendment in 16th Century England, and the history of its operation in the United States, are milestones on the progress of the individual from ecclesiastical and political tyranny to the attainment of equal footing and protection under the law." [1]

In the previous chapter reference was made to the brief portion of Ethel's examination which was sandwiched in at the conclusion of Julius' testimony.[2] Her direct examination was conducted by Alexander Bloch and dealt with her schooling, family, marriage, children, and household duties. But even at this early stage there were interruptions from Kaufman, slanted to exploit the inflammatory issue of Communism:

The Court: Did you know anything about the charges that had been leveled against your husband by the Government [the Signal Corps] in '45?

A. [Ethel]: Well, it was alleged that he was a member of the Communist Party.

The Court: Now, you typed the reply for him; is that right?

A. Yes.

The Court: And the reply which you typed denied that he was a Communist; is that correct?

A. That is correct.
The Court: And was that true?

It was not simply that Kaufman was seeking to trap a wife into testifying against her husband. The question was entirely irrelevant to the issue of guilt or innocence but, no matter how Ethel might reply, Kaufman knew the result would be injurious.

If she insisted that Julius' statement to the Signal Corps had been the truth—that he was *not* a Communist—then she would be taking on the FBI. Affidavits or testimony from professional informers could readily be produced stating that Julius had lied about his Party membership in 1945 and, therefore, was little deserving of credence now in 1951. On the other hand, if she sought protection in the Fifth Amendment, Kaufman could again indicate in a sarcastic aside to the jury, "It seems to me I have been hearing a lot about that."

Thus, when the defense objected and raised the question of the witness' privilege, Kaufman's purposes were suited admirably. Here is the record, as he adroitly pushes her into what amounted to a plea of guilt:

The Court: . . . Now we have the question of privilege.
Mr. Saypol: She hasn't asserted it, if the Court please.
The Court: I know she hasn't. Do you want to hear my question read back?
The Witness [Ethel]: Yes.

[Clerk reads: "And was that true?"]
A. [Ethel]: Was what true?
Q. [Kaufman]: The statements which you typed, that he is not a Communist?
A. . . . I refuse to answer on the ground of self-incrimination.
The Court: All right.

488

Actually, it was a choice between Scylla and Charybdis. With the Fifth Amendment condemned in that political climate as a veritable symbol of the sickle and hammer, it is not at all difficult to see why Kaufman commented with quiet satisfaction: "All right."

•

One may safely venture that Ethel's conviction, was achieved partially through the persistent violation by Saypol and Kaufman of the "no-inference rule" laid down by the Supreme Court on the use of the Fifth Amendment:

In the Federal courts . . . the law permits no inference of guilt from a claim of the privilege . . . and neither court nor counsel can make any adverse comment upon it. As a practical matter, to allow the inference of guilt would destroy the protection of the Fifth Amendment, because the witness would then be merely given a choice between a verbal confession and a silent one.[8]

And yet the greatest part of Ethel's cross-examination consisted of a review of her Fifth Amendment position before the Grand Jury, with each question calculated to produce the inference of guilt.[4] To the Grand Jury, we recall that Ethel had already confessed her "crime" of having signed in 1941 a nominating petition for the Communist Party candidate, City Councilman Peter Cacchione. Now, at the trial, although it could have no possible bearing on espionage, this petition was permitted into evidence as Government Exhibit 31. To borrow the phrase from Alistair Cooke, it was a perfect illustration of how a possible "old sympathizer" of the 1940's was turned into "an old spy" in the 1950's. For example:

Q. [Saypol]: Did you tell the grand jury in response to the question, "Did you ever sign a Communist Party nominating petition for elective office?

A. I did sign a Communist Party petition." Was that the truth?

A. I refuse to answer on the ground of self-incrimination.

Certainly, it was the truth that she had signed the petition. Saypol had just submitted it in evidence with her signature right on it! Moreover, Kaufman, only a moment before, had concluded a colloquy between Saypol and Bloch by addressing the witness directly on this point:

Q. [Kaufman]: Let me ask you this: Did you tell the grand jury the truth and the entire truth when you testified?
A. [Ethel]: Yes. [R. 1352]

What then was the purpose of all this repetition? Did the 1941 nominating petition signed by some 50,000 other voters show any connection between the alleged crimes and "intent" to commit such crimes? Of course not; it would be a mockery of the fundamental right of citizenship—the right to nominate a candidate of one's own choosing. The purpose, clearly, was to fasten the label of "Communist" on Ethel and to keep it ever present before the jury.

To sum up the totality of the prosecution's case against Ethel Rosenberg, it was: (1) the unsupported charges by the Greenglasses that she had helped enlist them and had later typed David's two reports.[5] (2) Proof of "intent" established by her admission that she had signed a nominating petition for a Communist candidate ten years earlier. (3) That having exercised her constitutional privilege, she was admittedly a "Fifth Amendment Communist" and, as such, was potentially inclined to commit treason or as the McCarthy-Cohn formula had it, was "part of the conspiracy to destroy this country."

•

At the very end of Ethel's recross-examination Saypol resorted to a well-worn trick used by prosecutors when their evidence is weak and insufficient: that of smearing the defense attorney as the Satanic influence responsible for the accused's refusal to confess guilt. Concerning the advice Mr. Bloch had given Ethel just prior to her Grand Jury appearance, Saypol asked:

Q. [Saypol]: Were there any other questions you were afraid of or apprehensive of when you talked to Mr. Bloch? Did you tell him about any other crime?

A. [Ethel]: No crime that I could have committed because I didn't commit any.

Whereupon, with this reply, Ethel was excused and Emanuel Bloch arose to announce:

Defendants Julius Rosenberg and Ethel Rosenberg rest.

A moment later Mr. Kuntz arose in behalf of Sobell and indicated that his client would not take the stand:

". . . If your Honor please, the defendant Sobell desires to rest on the record." [6]

II

> "I charge you further that no inference is to be drawn against any defendant who has exercised his or her constitutional privilege against any matters which may tend to incriminate him or her."
> —*Charge of the Court, Record, p. 1566*

In the three-week period of the trial the jurors had heard thousands of words concerning the defendants' alleged membership in the "Communist International Conspiracy."

(*Note:* No one can estimate how much of this subject the jurors heard on their radio and television sets, or read in their newspapers, not only during the trial, but through all the years of the Cold War.)

In page after page of the record there stand Kaufman's intimations, insinuations, and innuendoes concerning the Rosenbergs' political beliefs and affiliations. In page after page one can read Kaufman's disparaging comments and derogatory remarks about Ethel's taking of the Fifth Amendment.

What, then, shall one say to the unparalleled hypocrisy of the charge quoted above, or a previous one in which Kaufman cautioned the jury that they were "not to determine the guilt or innocence of a defendant on whether or not he is a Communist"?

In the political atmosphere of March, 1951, to repeatedly stigmatize the defendants, and then to expect them to obtain a fair and unprejudiced trial simply because the judge directs the jury to overlook the stigma which he himself has affixed, is beyond hypocrisy. Even the Court of Appeals, in its thinly veiled criticism of Kaufman's prejudicial conduct, found occasion to quote from Justice Jackson's famous statement:

. . . It may be that such warnings [to the jury] are no more than an empty ritual without any practical effect on the jurors.[7]

In actuality, the effect of Kaufman's lip service to a fair trial was almost as though he had winked at the jurors each time he repeated the ritual, or had whispered to them from the corner of his mouth, "Never mind these perfunctory charges. I've got to read them to you so that their lawyers don't upset the applecart by having the trial reversed in an upper court. Just legal hocus-pocus for the record; that's all."

It was in this cynical spirit and with this rapport between judge and jurors that the case of the United States against Julius Rosenberg, *et al.*, drew closer to its ominous and predictable end.

NOTES AND REFERENCES

1. Arthur Krock in the New York *Times,* editorial page, December 31, 1953.
2. For Ethel's direct, see Record, pp. 1293–1307, 1310–1343; redirect: pp. 1398–1399, 1401.
3. See article, "Does Silence Mean Guilt?" by Laurent B. Frantz, Law Librarian of Drake University, and

492

Norman Redlich, member of New York bar, *The Nation*, June 6, 1953.

4. For Ethel's cross, see Record, pp. 1344–1398; recross: pp. 1400–1402.

5. *Note:* These charges have been covered in Chapters 15 and 17. Every additional point in the *Columbia Law Review* summary regarding Ethel has been covered in Chapters 18 and 19.

6. *Note:* The decision of Sobell's attorneys not to have him take the witness stand was based on the prosecution's lack of evidence, since the only testimony against him came from the admitted perjurer Elitcher, who, according to the *Columbia Law Review*, was "hoping for non-prosecution." Since this was so, the *Review* concluded on this point that Elitcher's "testimony ought not to be given much weight." (*Op. cit.*, 237, footnote 89.)

In addition, Sobell's attorneys believed the jury would recognize that, since no atomic espionage was charged against Sobell, the joint trial had placed an unfair burden on him. That they exercised wrong judgment, considering the temper of the times and the natural prejudice of the jury, has been the opinion of many attorneys.

It has been felt that it would have been to Sobell's advantage if he had firmly denied Elitcher's accusations from the witness stand, even though he was not required by law to establish innocence. While it is highly doubtful that it would have made any difference to the jury, there is considerable opinion that it would greatly have benefited him with the public and the higher courts.

Concerning the circumstances which motivated his acceptance of his attorneys' decision, see Sobell's affidavit from Transcript of Record, pp. 7 and 8, Supreme Court of the United States, October Term, 1953. See also Morton Sobell's book, *On Doing Time*, Scribner's, New York, 1974.

7. Record, p. 1656. For Justice Jackson's full statement, see Krulewitch v. U.S., 336 U.S. 440 (1, 1650).

ADDENDA

As indicated in the *Addenda* of Chapter 11, a New York *Times* account of a recent FBI memo provides an apt example of Kaufman's gnawing fear that his true role in the Rosenberg-Sobell case will be finally exposed. The memo involves the prejudicial questioning of Ethel Rosenberg by Saypol and Kaufman concerning her Fifth Amendment stand before the Grand Jury.

In September 1957, a U.S. Supreme Court decision (the "Grunewald decision") held such questioning illegal. In December, 1962, a new member of the Court of Appeals, Justice Thurgood Marshall (subsequently appointed to the U.S. Supreme Court) sat in on an appeal hearing for Morton Sobell, then serving his twelfth year of the 30-year sentence Kaufman had imposed on him. At this hearing, Justice Marshall posed the following question:

. . . if Sobell had been tried last spring and we had him before us today [1962], wouldn't it be necessary for the court to reverse the decision, particularly in view of the Grunewald decision?

In reply to this question, the Assistant U.S. Attorney contesting the appeal answered, "Probably," thus conceding, at least morally, that Sobell's long incarceration had been unjust.

Whereupon, Kaufman promptly hit the roof, according to a report made December 21, 1962, by "a top FBI official" named C. D. DeLoach. The report tells of Kaufman's phone call to DeLoach saying that he had raised "hell" with Justice Marshall for having posed the question and that the reply of the Assistant U.S. Attorney had been a "stupid answer," one that "might very well be the straw that breaks the camel's back and as a result obtain Sobell's freedom."

First, we see Kaufman's contemptuous criticism of the government attorney for his cautious agreement with Justice Marshall. Second, his angered opposition to Marshall's enlightened and just attitude toward Ethel Rosenberg's constitutional rights. (The memo states that Kaufman "considered Marshall to be somewhat naive and certainly inexperienced on the bench.") Third, his implacable hostility toward Sobell even after twelve years of imprisonment. Fourth, and most significant, his dread fear that Marshall's question and the Government's reply might somehow cause the case to be reviewed by the Supreme Court and be re-tried. For if Sobell should win his appeal, not only could it lead to a serious examination of Kaufman's concurrence in the prosecution's harassment of Ethel, but also to the potential exposure of his prejudicial role in the entire Rosenberg case.

Indeed, his urgent call to this *top* FBI official was clearly an anxious, if not frantic, effort to alert the Attorney General through J. Edgar Hoover of the danger and for the latter to exert his enormous influence to keep the lid on the case tightly clamped. Since the call emphasizes Kaufman's great concern about "this unfortunate situation," it was surely not made merely to air his vexation at Justice Marshall.

As a fitting finale in the same *Times* account, we find in its last paragraph another revealing "document" from the FBI files dated May 4, 1975, stating that Kaufman had told the FBI that

. . . some counteraction should be taken to combat publicity by the National Committee to Reopen the Rosenberg Case.

(See New York *Times,* June 11, 1976.)

26 "O JUDGMENT!"

I

> "O judgment! thou art fled to brutish beasts,
> And men have lost their reason!"
> —*Julius Caesar*

On the day of the summations, the courtroom was jammed for the final act of the drama. During the trial, few of the spectators had appeared to regard the defendants with any open hostility, but on the final day, apparently sensing the note of doom, their antipathy became noticeable. One man, nodding familiarly to a guard, made a brushing movement with his hands, saying, "Well, today we finish 'em off!" And as the Rosenbergs were led into the courtroom and Ethel was seen to say something encouraging to Julius, a woman said, "Look at her smiling, the bitch! I wonder if she'll smile while she's hanging."

There were some, however, who seemed sympathetic to the defendants but did not dare to indicate this too openly. And many, deeply troubled by the trial and its implications, reacted as did the Rosenbergs' friends and relatives. They remained away from the trial, reluctant to face a harrowing emotional experience.

II

During his summation, Emanuel Bloch placed his main emphasis on the obvious motive for the Greenglasses' false testimony, their desperation to win salvation for themselves. And that the principal reason Julius Rosenberg became their luckless "clay pigeon" lay in the fact that

[Bloch]: . . . he was a guy who was very open and expressed his views about the United States and the Soviet Union, which may have been all right when the Soviet Union and the United States were allies, but today it is anathema. . . .

And, as we have seen, Julius' favorable views of the progress in the Soviet Union were anathema to "Pope Kaufman."

All through the trial, and also at the hearing on the motion to reduce sentence just before the executions (which this writer attended), Kaufman's prejudice was noticeable.[1] Whenever he had the opportunity he managed to denigrate the defense by tossing in some remark that would humiliate, ridicule, confuse, or throw them off balance. When it was not outright hostility, it was open sarcasm, restless rocking in his seat, tiresome yawning, and various other facial expressions signifying disbelief. At the trial itself, it should be emphasized that Kaufman's instruction to the jury not to form any adverse opinion because of any remarks he might have made or attitudes he might have displayed was but another aspect of the empty ritual.

As indicated, Mr. Bloch's summation had as its main effort the exposure of the fears, self-interest, and rationalizations of the Greenglasses. In the Charge of the Court, it is the duty of the trial judge to give the jury a summary of the two sides of the case. However, in this charge, Kaufman gave the prosecution's side *three times* as much space as that of the defense. [R. 1554–1562]

This discrimination against the defense was but a minor matter compared to the way he presented its contentions of the Greenglasses' motives in implicating the Rosenbergs:

[Kaufman]: . . . And that any testimony by the Greenglasses against them [the Rosenbergs] is due to the trouble they had with the Greenglasses while in business together, or for some other *unknown* reason. [Emphasis added.]

Unknown reason! But the major position of the defense had been presented in painstaking detail, not only in Bloch's summation, but in the latter's "Requests to Charge." [R. 1541–1542]

It was Kaufman's duty to instruct the jurors that they were to take into consideration the *self-interest* and *motive* of the witness in determining credibility, *i.e.*, the determination of Ruth Greenglass to win immunity from prosecution and that of David to win a light sentence. Hence, to misrepresent this basic point as an "unknown reason" was definitely a prejudicial act.[2]

III

"No one is ever innocent when his opponent is the judge."

—*Lucan: Pharsala*

What is most terrifying to contemplate about a man like Kaufman is the immense power he wields over the life or death, liberty or freedom of any person so unfortunate as to be brought before him. Let us not forget that his background was never that of a champion of the wronged, but rather that of a prosecutor and an ambitious politician. Where the trial is by jury, the Federal law does not permit a higher court to pass on the credibility of the witnesses; it may consider only judicial error. Hence, if the trial judge is wily enough to observe the letter of the law (while ignoring its spirit), the result is the achievement of almost tyrannical power. Only the President of the United States can set aside a sentence in a Federal court.

Small wonder, then, standing at the threshold of historical fame (or so he hoped), that Judge Kaufman was so determined to let nothing jeopardize this power, *even if it meant prejudicing the jury's deliberations!* Here is what happened after the case had been given to the jury:

At 4:53 o'clock, the jury commenced its deliberations. After dinner, shortly after 8 o'clock, the jury sent in a note requesting that the *testimony* of Ruth Greenglass be read to them, beginning at the point of the Rosenbergs' alleged spy proposal and ending with David's "first furlough in January 1945."

Since this request was received in the judge's chambers, the court stenographer was called in together with opposing counsel, and the proceedings were made part of the record [R. 1570—1573]. Here is what took place as Kaufman turned to the stenographer's transcript to refer to the requested testimony:

Mr. A. Bloch: I think that covers quite a bit. It goes to conversation before she [Ruth] went out West; conversation she had with her husband out West and also cross-examination on that point.

Mr. Lane: And the conversation she had when she came back from the West, and conversation as she testified to.

So far, we see Saypol's chief assistant Lane taking for granted that the jury's request *included* cross-examination as well as direct. But Saypol promptly interjects:

498

Mr. Saypol: I don't think they have asked for any cross.

And at once Kaufman picks up the cue to repeat:

The Court: They haven't asked for the cross.

Since none of the jurors was trained in the law, it was only natural for them to have asked for Ruth's "testimony" by referring to the subject matter, rather than specifying direct and cross-examination. If Kaufman were at all impartial he would have said as much to Saypol and there would have been no dispute.

However, he realized that if some of the jurors were now probing into Ruth's alleged swift compliance with the original spy proposal as well as David's unexplained overnight agreement, they must be troubled by doubts. Hence, this request might easily result in a split verdict and a hung jury!

And so we find Kaufman maneuvering to keep from the jury the information it really needed in order to evaluate this portion of the record. Here are his remarks after the elder Bloch pointed out the page where the cross-examination commenced:

The Court: I am not going to read the cross to them unless they request it.

Mr. A. Bloch: Well, I think when they ask for testimony, it means all the testimony on the subject.

This simple reply was much too reasonable for Kaufman to contest directly. Hence we find this compromise:

The Court: We will start reading at 972, the top, and then [finish] over here at 982.[3] Then I will ask the jury when we get finished [with the direct examination] whether that is what they want.

However, the defense was wary, sensing that Kaufman would give the jury only that part *favorable* to the prosecution and not the *telling* cross-examination:

Mr. A. Bloch: Will you ask them whether they want the cross?

The Court: I won't put it in their mouths, but I will ask them whether there is anything else they want.

Mr. A. Bloch: I think if you give them the direct, you ought to give them the cross. That is the whole testimony on that topic.

The Court: The jury is intelligent. If that is what they want, they will ask for it.

Mr. A. Bloch: They might not think [remember] there is any other testimony on that subject.

The Court: I am going to handle it in that way.

Mr. Phillips: Two testimonies go together. They didn't ask for the pages, they asked for the testimony.

And so we see Judge Kaufman's clearly stated promise that after reading the direct examination he would ask the jury "whether there is anything else they want." But here is what happened after Ruth's direct examination had been read to the jurors upon their return to the jury box:

The Court: Have we read what the jury wanted?
Jurors: Yes.
The Court: Very well, the jury may retire.

It would be difficult to believe this outrageous deceit actually took place were it not in cold print. It is only some fifteen minutes since Kaufman has given his promise, and yet, here he is retiring the jury, completely indifferent to what he has just *agreed* to put before them.[4] Now Emanuel Bloch rises to state formally:

Mr. Bloch: If the Court please, I make the request that the stenographer also read the cross-examination of Ruth Greenglass on this specific point—

Once more Kaufman has the opportunity to give the jury both sides of the testimony, but this is precisely what he is determined to prevent! Instead, he interrupts and strives to gag Mr. Bloch before the jury will realize what is going on:

> The Court: Your request is denied. That has not been requested by the jury. The jury will retire. We will give the jury exactly what they request.
> Mr. Bloch: I respectfully except.
> (Whereupon the jury retired from the courtroom at 8:30 P.M.)

Need one comment on this scene which speaks so plainly for itself, except to marvel at the hubris of this little Tartuffe who dared to say in his sentencing speech, "Justice does not seek vengeance. Justice seeks justice."

IV

> "Then went the jury out, whose names were Mr. Blind-man, Mr. No-good, Mr. Malice, Mr. Love-lust, Mr. Live-loose, Mr. Heady, Mr. High-mind, Mr. Enmity, Mr. Liar, Mr. Cruelty, Mr. Hate-light, and Mr. Implacable. . . ."
>
> —*John Bunyan, Pilgrim's Progress*

On that Wednesday March 28, 1951, after six and a half hours of deliberation, the jury failed to reach a verdict by 12:35 A.M., and so was "locked up" for the night in a midtown hotel. It is meaningful to note what front-page headlines they may have read before retiring. Here are a few from the New York *Times* of that day:

ACHESON EXHORTS AMERICAS TO MEET
SOVIET PERIL NOW

TENSION IS GRAVER THAN IN NOVEMBER,
MARSHALL'S BELIEF

And, on an inside page this bedtime story:

DANGER OF ATOM BOMB ATTACK IS GREATEST
IN PERIOD UP TO THIS FALL, EXPERT ASSERTS

On the next morning, Thursday, it is quite possible that with their breakfast the jurors read this headline in the *Times,* having first averted their eyes from the headline which referred to them as the "SPY JURY":

RED CHINA REJECTS M'ARTHUR'S OFFER
Radio Exhorts Troops to Také All of Korea

At 10 A.M. the jurors returned to the jury room. It may be appropriate here to dwell briefly on what the outlook of such a jury may have been at this particular moment in our frenetic history.

There they were, these eleven men and one woman, in general no different from millions of other Americans. Certainly, they were alert to the high stakes involved in this momentous case. The media had made that as abundantly clear as had the Court.[5] Should they decide in favor of the defense, in effect they would be condemning the United States Government, together with its Department of Justice, J. Edgar Hoover, and the FBI. On the other hand, a verdict in favor of the Government would be a patriotic blow against those eggheads who were still coddling Communists and a warning to other traitors. Obviously, there was little choice.

To be sure, their only responsibility was to weigh all the evidence. But they were faced with the testimony of FBI-endorsed witnesses such as Gold and Bentley. Could they dare to say they were unworthy of belief? If they found Bentley's testimony about her telephonic "Julius" incredible, then they were challenging *all* her charges against the thirty-odd "Communists" who had "infiltrated" the highest agencies in Washington, such as Alger Hiss. And how could they separate Gold's Jello-box visit to Greenglass from the now "official" story of how the Russians had stolen the A-bomb via the Fuchs-Gold-Yakovlev spy ring?

Besides, it was not their responsibility to decide the degree of guilt; that would be done by the judge in determining sentence. He had reminded them frequently that the jury was not to concern itself with the sentences, "no matter how distasteful" their verdict might be.

Wherever the jurors glanced in that courtroom they

saw their duty reflected. They saw it in the hardened expressions of the spectators, in the cold stare of the FBI men seated at the prosecution table, but, above all, they saw it mirrored in the eyes of Judge Kaufman. What was expected of them was all too clear. It was quite unnecessary to have it all spelled out in a specific command from the bench. As we have seen, Judge Kaufman helped the prosecution contaminate the verdict from the very start with the screening of the jury. Indeed, as it turned out, Kaufman was judge, prosecutor, and jury, all rolled into one.

•

> " 'I'll judge, I'll be jury;
> Said cunning old Fury:
> 'I'll try the whole cause and
> Condemn you to death.' "
> —*Alice in Wonderland*

At 11 o'clock the next morning, only one hour after the jury had resumed deliberations, it agreed upon a verdict. The jury entered the courtroom and the Clerk asked, "How say you?"

The Foreman: We the jury find Julius Rosenberg guilty as charged. We the jury find Ethel Rosenberg guilty as charged. We the jury find Morton Sobell guilty as charged.

Following the verdict, Kaufman gave this special accolade to the Director of the FBI:

Again I say a great tribute is due to the FBI and Mr. Hoover for the splendid job that they had done in this case.

At the Brothman "try-out," four months earlier, Kaufman had paid similar tribute to "Edgar":

I think that Mr. Hoover and the Bureau should be congratulated in their work on this case, and I ask you to please advise him of my sentiment.[6]

(*Note:* At the time the above was written, this writer sensed that there must have existed some strong

503

personal relationship between Kaufman and Hoover. With the passage of time, this hunch has been confirmed. There had been a "special friendship" between them for years before the Rosenberg trial. This explains not only the "Heil Hoover" saluting, but, more importantly, Kaufman's reflection of Hoover's fanatical views throughout the trial. In the *New Times* article mentioned in Chapter 11, according to one of Kaufman's old friends, we find that he had been "a great admirer, even an idolator of Hoover." And that "therefore the government's position" in the Rosenberg case fell on "receptive ears.")

On Thursday, April 5, 1951, Judge Kaufman ascended the bench to deliver his sentencing speeches. These were among the headlines in the New York *Times* that morning:

RAYBURN INTIMATES RUSSIANS MASS TROOPS IN MANCHURIA
A Third World War May Be Near, Speaker Implies in Statement to House

HOUSE UNIT SCORES REDS' "PEACE" DRIVE
Lists 550 Names, Including [Jose] Ferrer and Judy Holliday in Communist Fronts

Thus, if Kaufman felt he needed a highly charged atmosphere for what he intended to do, it was certainly present. In the calendar of the Cold War, it was a most expedient moment to provide the scapegoats for the Korean "police action" which had thus far cost more than 50,000 American casualties.

It was just a few minutes before 12 o'clock when Judge Kaufman cleared his throat and asked Julius and Ethel Rosenberg if there was anything they wanted to say before sentence was imposed:

Defendant Julius Rosenberg: No, sir.
The Court [to Ethel]: Do you care to say anything?
Defendant Ethel Rosenberg: No, sir.
The Court: Because of the seriousness of this case and the lack of precedence, I have refrained from asking the Government for a recommendation.

The responsibility is so great that I believe that the Court *alone* should assume this responsibility.

In view of the importance of the sentences I am about to impose, I believe it is my duty to give some explanation respecting them. [R. 1612–1616; emphasis added.]

In preceding chapters we have touched upon Kaufman's astonishing explanation which has appalled not only millions of lay persons but hundreds of jurists and statesmen in all countries. We have seen a judge determined to blame Communism for every ill bedeviling mankind. Viewing his attitude, it was as though there had never been any tension, any wars, or differences of ideology in the history of the world before the Rosenbergs were born. In his harassment of the Rosenbergs, we have seen his ill-concealed hatred of them as symbols of all the enemies of the System. But it is in his sentencing speech that this hatred becomes nakedly revealed:

It is so difficult to make people realize that this country is engaged in a life and death struggle with a completely different system.

Yet, they made a choice of devoting themselves to the Russian ideology of denial of God, denial of the sanctity of the individual and aggression against free men everywhere instead of serving the cause of liberty and freedom.

I also assume that the basic Marxist goal of world revolution and destruction of capitalism was well known to the defendants, if in fact not subscribed to by them. . . .

Here, then, was the real crime—Kaufman's *assumption* that the Rosenbergs had subscribed to world revolution and the destruction of capitalism. Evidently, when Julius had stated his belief that the people of each nation had the right to determine whatever type of government they desired, this belief served only to support Kaufman's obsession. Nowhere in the record is there evidence of the Rosenbergs' denial of God.

505

But even if they were atheists, every action in their lives attested to the fact that they prized the sanctity of the individual and the dignity of man. There was their continued concern for the refugee victims of Fascism. There was their dismay over the genocide of the 6,000,000 victims of Nazism. And, above all, there was their belief in the right of all Americans to think and speak as they pleased no matter how unpopular their beliefs might be. To a Kaufman, however, so fanatically devoted to the ideology of J. Edgar Hoover —the life-and-death struggle between the angels and the devils—the Rosenbergs' beliefs constituted evidence of evil.

•

It was exactly 12 noon. As the New York *Times* recorded the moment, Judge Kaufman read his reasons for the death sentences just as "the church bell of nearby St. Andrew's Roman Catholic Church tolled the noon hour, its longest toll of the day."

I consider your crime worse than murder. . . .
I believe your conduct in putting into the hands of the Russians the A-bomb . . . has already caused, in my opinion, the Communist aggression in Korea, with the resultant casualties exceeding 50,000 and who knows but that millions more of innocent people may pay the price of your treason. Indeed, by your betrayal you undoubtedly have altered the course of history. . . . We have evidence of your treachery all around us every day—for the civilian defense activities throughout the nation are aimed at preparing us for an atom bomb attack.

Even without the hindsight of subsequent events, the utter irresponsibility of these accusations must be plain. Did it never occur to Judge Kaufman that the wave of anticolonialism, nationalism, and social revolution that was sweeping Asia would have taken place without the existence of the A-bomb or the Rosenbergs?
To debate with Kaufman the reckless charge that the Rosenbergs *undoubtedly* altered the course of world history would be pointless. One cannot debate logically with out-and-out absurdities. In any event, the charge

has been adequately answered by Dr. James Beckerly, Director of the Atomic Energy Classification Office, to wit: That "it was time to stop kidding ourselves about atomic secrets," and that "the atom bomb and the hydrogen bomb were not stolen from us by spies." [7]

VI

> "Hangman, I charge you, pay particular attention to this lady. Scourge her soundly, man; scourge her till the blood runs down." [8]

In such sadistic language did the Lord Chief Justice of England impose the death penalty upon a woman for a minor crime of theft in the 1680's. It was a time, we are told, that had "a cruel, raw edge," and in that sense was not too far removed from our own Scoundrel Time.

In our examination of Ethel's alleged typing of the atomic reports, we recall from Greenglass' testimony that her role in the conspiracy was a minor one or, as Ethel was alleged to have said, "she didn't mind it [the typing] so long as Julius was doing what he wanted to do."

And yet, in his sentencing speech, in the face of this vital disclosure made by the *only* witnesses testifying against Ethel, Judge Kaufman found her equally deserving of the death penalty with Julius:

> The evidence indicated quite clearly that Julius Rosenberg was the prime mover in this conspiracy. However, let no mistake be made about the role which his wife, Ethel Rosenberg, played in this conspiracy. Instead of deterring him from pursuing his ignoble course, she encouraged and assisted the cause. She was a mature woman—almost three years older than her husband and almost seven years older than her younger brother. She was a full-fledged partner in this crime.

Equal guilt—equal punishment? Very well, but how does Kaufman equate Ethel's minor role with that of Julius, "the prime mover"? Where in the record is there anything to support the contention that Ethel *encouraged* Julius? According to the prosecution, it was Julius who "thought out" the entire spy ring [R. 182]. How, then, were Ethel's "crimes" equal to those of Julius?

Kaufman finds that she was a mature woman, almost three years older than her husband. If she had been three years younger, would Judge Kaufman have found *that* sufficient cause to sentence her to a lesser penalty?

Included in Mr. Bloch's plea for a fair and just sentence was this vital point: that had the alleged conspiracy been exposed during the period of its commission, *i.e.*, 1944–1945, a time when the Soviet Union was an ally of the United States, it would have been questionable whether the Rosenbergs would have found themselves in a criminal court at all. To this point Kaufman replied as follows:

> The Court: You overlooked one very salient feature, and that is that their activities didn't cease in 1945, but that there was evidence in the case of continued activity in espionage right on down, even during a period when it was then apparent to everybody that we were now dealing with a hostile nation. . . . There was evidence, for example, in 1948, with Elitcher. [R. 1606]

There is no way to describe this sophistry but to say it is shocking. When Kaufman cannot find justification for the death penalties for a crime taking place during the period of World War II, he seizes upon a minor facet of Elitcher's testimony, something which had *nothing to do with atomic espionage*, and advances this as the reason to put the Rosenbergs to death!

But even if we believe that Ethel took part in the conspiracy during the war years when the Soviet Union was our valued ally, the record is bare of any evidence whatsoever regarding her involvement *after* the war!

In other words, if one grants any logic to Kaufman's argument concerning the Rosenbergs' continued activity in espionage into the period when Russia became a "hostile nation," it can at best be applied *only* to Julius.

It cannot, according to the record or by any stretch of the imagination, be applied to Ethel!

VII

> "I have deliberated for hours, days and nights. I have carefully weighed the evidence. . . . I have searched the records—I have searched my conscience to find some reason for mercy. . . ."

With these words Judge Kaufman proceeded to impose "the punishment of death" upon Ethel and Julius Rosenberg together with the order that:

> . . . upon some day within the week beginning with Monday, May 21st [1951], you shall be executed according to law.[9]

In the New York *Times* of April 6 we read that the "burden of responsibility" appeared to weigh heavily upon Kaufman: "In the last week, he had a bit more than ten hours' sleep. Several times he went to his synagogue seeking spiritual guidance."

In almost every criminal case, the trial judge requests the Government for its recommendation of sentence. Why not in the Rosenberg case? According to Kaufman, there were both "the seriousness of the case and the lack of precedence." This, of course, was true. Never before in the history of the United States had a civil court, either in peace or in war, decreed a sentence of death for conspiracy to commit espionage. Not even for that gravest of crimes, treason, had there ever occurred a single execution.

Did Kaufman have an ethnic reason for assuming the full responsibility for the death penalties, in addition to his *agreement* to impose them almost a month before trial, as shown in "The Letter 'W' "?

Immediately after the sentences this opinion was voiced in many conservative Jewish newspapers. Here is the New York Jewish *Day* on April 16, 1951:

What led the judge to give the extreme penalty . . . ? Is it not perhaps the fact that the judge is a Jew and the defendants are Jews? . . . He himself . . . did not have the power to free himself from today's heated tensions . . . and was also afraid that perhaps, if he were not to give them the death penalty, he would be suspected of not having done so because he is a Jew. . . . he should under no circumstances have issued the death sentence. . . .

From the *Jewish Examiner* of March 14, 1952, here is the editorial opinion of Rabbi Louis D. Gross:

. . . Did [Judge Kaufman] think that the death sentence against the Rosenbergs was necessary to counteract the anti-Semitic charge of communism against Jews in general? Apparently the jurist has not learned that anti-Semitism has nothing to do with the truth.

These opinions were shared by non-Jewish people, such as James H. Wolfe, Chief Justice of the Supreme Court of the State of Utah:

Besides the general hysteria generated by fear and hate of communism which was interjected into that trial, it appears that there may have been the influence of anti-Semitism in a reverse sort of way . . . there may have been unconsciously an effort to lean over backward against the Jews who were accused. . . .[10]

A similar viewpoint was expressed by Stephen Love, a distinguished member of the Chicago bar and a Catholic layman. Here are the reasons he ascribes to Kaufman's unprecedented sentences:

(a) Did the trial judge fear that the United States Attorney would not recommend the death sentence, and thus make it practically impossible, or extremely difficult for the judge to impose it?

(b) Did he desire for himself the assumed glory of imposing a death sentence upon members of his own racial group and thereby demonstrating that he could be a firm and severe and unrelenting judge even as against them? Was this not a classic instance of a judge's leaning backward, a most unfortunate performance in a federal judge, in a capital case? [11]

VIII

> "He's just, your cousin, ay, abhorrently;
> He'd wash his hands in blood, to keep them
> clean."
>
> —*Elizabeth Barrett Browning*

After sentencing the Rosenbergs, Judge Kaufman called a short recess. There then followed a last plea by Mr. Phillips on behalf of Sobell, requesting "utmost consideration" in view of the fact that no testimony had been shown that his client had actually transmitted any illegal information to a foreign power. And that whereas the worst that had been charged by Elitcher was that he had merely *talked* espionage with Sobell, surely the Court would see fit "to impose almost no sentence or . . . such a small sentence" as would be fair and just. [R. 1619–1620]

To this plea, Kaufman made no reply but, turning coldly to Sobell, read his prepared speech:

> The Court: While I have not the slightest sympathy for you or any of your associates, as a judge, I must be objective. . . . I do not for a moment doubt that you were engaged in espionage activities; *however, the evidence in the case did not point to any activity on your part in connection with the atom bomb project.* I cannot be moved by hysteria or motivated by a desire to do the popular thing. I must do justice according to the evidence in this case. There isn't any doubt about your guilt, but I must recognize the lesser degree of your implication in this offense.
>
> I, therefore, sentence you to the maximum prison term provided by statute, to wit, thirty years. [Emphasis added.]

At first glance it is not clear whether Kaufman meant that the public was clamoring for Sobell's blood or for his freedom. In any event, Kaufman presents himself as aloof to everything but pure Justice, and he will administer it only according to the evidence. And yet he *knew* that there was no evidence other than that of a self-admitted perjurer when in charging the jury he had stated:

> If you do not believe the testimony of Max Elitcher as it pertains to Sobell, then you must acquit the defendant Sobell.

Furthermore, whereas Kaufman concedes the crucial point—that Sobell had no part in any atomic espionage —still he sentences Sobell to a penalty just short of death. And all the while it is as though he were incanting self-hypnotically: "I *must* be objective—I *must* do justice."

With his prosecutor's experience, Kaufman knew perfectly well that Saypol had obtained Sobell's conviction so easily because of the strategy of having him tried jointly with the Rosenbergs. In the dissenting opinion of Judge Frank reviewing the first appeal, Kaufman's failure to instruct the jury that they must also consider the question of two separate conspiracies constituted serious "prejudicial error":

> . . . for Sobell was jointly tried with major atomic energy spies whose acts and declarations were held binding upon him.

> . . . there was error, in this respect, which requires that Sobell be given a new trial.

> . . . *the judge, on his own motion should have submitted the question of one or several conspiracies to the jury.* [R. 1664—1666; emphasis added.]

In the *Columbia Law Review*, which is in full agreement with this opinion and holds that the other two judges of the Court of Appeals should have supported it, there is cited the Supreme Court attitude:

> . . . That when there is great danger that the jurors, consciously or otherwise, will transfer guilt from one conspiracy to another, prejudice to substantial rights may result.[12]

We have had occasion previously to point out that

the true nature of the Rosenberg trial can best be seen through the window of Sobell's treatment. It was just after Kaufman had declared that he would not be moved by hysteria that he suddenly dropped the mask to reveal the unreasoning hate which dictated his entire conduct of the trial. Here is the record as he concludes the sentencing of Sobell:

> [Kaufman]: While it may be gratuitous on my part, I at this point note my recommendation against parole. The Court will stand adjourned.

"Gratuitous" is a mild word to describe vindictiveness. Not content in condemning Sobell to a living death, Kaufman also wants to *insure* it by projecting himself as a "dead hand" controlling the determination of a parole board of a future decade—a board which might see fit to parole Sobell after ten, fifteen, or twenty years.[13]

Evidently it never occurred to Kaufman that some decades later Americans might tire of the tension diet of McCarthyism and Cold War, that the dogma of fear engulfing the country in the fifties might happily be dispelled by the sixties or seventies, and that millions of Americans might come to look upon him with the same horror they have regarded the infamous Judge Webster Thayer of the Sacco-Vanzetti case.

IX

At 2 o'clock on the afternoon of Friday, April 6, according to the New York *Times*, David Greenglass "stood on the same spot" where his sister had stood the day before. He stood with hands clasped behind his back, but showed no emotion. Some twenty feet away sat his wife Ruth, her hand gripping the rail in front of her.

In an effort to explain why Ruth Greenglass, a self-proclaimed spy and co-conspirator, had not even been indicted to stand trial, Saypol stated that it was by his decision she had been spared because she had convinced her husband to cease protesting his innocence.

It was, of course, a fancy bit of fiction. We know from the record and Rogge's file memos about the sordid bargaining that went on during the varying indictments to give Greenglass the same immunity as his wife. We know too about the promises that Greenglass would receive a year or two, at worst, and that there was even the possibility of a suspended sentence. Hence it was small wonder that O. John Rogge reacted so strongly when Saypol concluded his pre-sentencing speech with the recommendation "that the defendant be imprisoned for a term of 15 years."

Here is Rogge's protest against this "double-cross":

Mr. Rogge: May it please the Court . . . if the Government wants help . . . if it wants people in the position of David Greenglass to come forward and cooperate, it must give him a pat on the back.

Thereupon Rogge, according to the New York *Times* of April 7, expatiated on this theme for more than half an hour, not forgetting to include what he hoped would impress Kaufman:

. . . We are in a system that recognizes and respects the dignity of the individual. . . . I certainly say to your Honor . . . you would serve justice and you would temper it with mercy, if, let us say, you had a sentence in this case for David Greenglass of three years.

However, Kaufman remained unimpressed, no doubt resenting Rogge's implications that this had been the "deal" promised in return for Greenglass' "cooperation." During his sentencing speech, as he addresses Greenglass directly, it is not surprising to see again the sanctimonious phraseology of the Grand Inquisitor:

You have at least not added to your sins. . . . You repented and you brought to justice those who enlisted you in this cause. Justice does not seek vengeance. Justice seeks justice, but you deserve punishment. . . . I shall follow the recommendation of the Government and sentence you to 15 years in prison. [R. 1621—1638]

"As the last words fell," the New York *Times* reports, "Ruth Greenglass almost toppled from her front-row seat on the left of the courtroom." Evidently, when she had heard Saypol recommend the fifteen-year penalty, the harsh reality was unacceptable, but with the actual imposition of sentence the realization struck with full force.

Yet what could she or David do about it? She was going scot-free, but for the rest of her life there would dangle the Damoclean sword of the withheld indictment above her head, because in a capital crime there is no statute of limitations. And to whom should they complain? To their attorney, Rogge? He would only advise them to avoid anything that might jeopardize David's chances for parole. Moreover, in an exchange with Rogge, Kaufman had plainly indicated the *necessity* of a considerable sentence for Greenglass. For, as he pointed out, what was at stake was "a penalty that calls for possible death and also for maximum imprisonment of 30 years."

In other words, he was saying that the sentence could not be anything less than fifteen years for Greenglass in the face of the death sentences for the Rosenbergs and the maximum sentence for Sobell. Such unprecedented sentences imposed by a civil court in peacetime for crimes committed in favor of an ally had to have this "floor" of the Greenglass sentence to allay any suspicions about what had really happened behind closed doors.[14]

X

After the sentences had been pronounced on Ethel and Julius, they were taken down to the "tanks," the temporary detention cells in the basement of the courthouse. A fellow-prisoner, whom we shall call "Terry," had been brought there that morning together with Julius from the West Street jail. In recalling the moment when the deputy marshals led Julius past his cell, Terry described the following:

"I saw Julie when they brought him down. . . . He was trying to say something, but the words stuck. All he could do was to hold up two fingers."

At first Terry thought that the death sentences were only for Julius and Sobell, but an instant later Julius found sufficient voice and added to his gesture: "Ethel, too."

Waiting in the adjoining cells to be taken back to the West Street jail were the other prisoners who quickly realized what had just happened. After they heard the clangs of the cell doors closing on Julius and Ethel at opposite ends of the corridor, an oppressive stillness followed.

In the meantime Sobell had been brought down; and, since it was midday, the marshals had arranged for the three sentenced prisoners to have their lunch together with their respective counsel in one of the conference rooms farther down the corridor. Helen Sobell was permitted to be with her husband during this lunch hour.

While they were lunching there was a painful effort by one of Sobell's attorneys to relieve the gloom with small talk, and he muttered something about having lost twenty pounds during the trial. The small talk seemed to help; Julius commented wryly that he guessed he must have lost some weight too, because his suit felt a couple of sizes too large.

For the Sobells, somehow it was all too unreal; they just sat holding hands in silence and "sort of looked at each other," wondering if all of this were true and if the Rosenbergs realized the full and horrible significance of their sentences.[15]

Evidently, they did. A few moments later, when Emanuel Bloch began to blame himself for neglecting certain legal moves, Julius looked up from his coffee and shook his head. No, there was nothing that could possibly have altered the verdict in the existing climate. The FBI timing of their arrests had been obviously synchronized with the outbreak of the Korean War. The over-all plan called for the "breaking" of a sensational case against spies and traitors; and what could be more sensational than the charge that American Communists had stolen the secret of the A-bomb and had thereby imperiled the lives of every man, woman, and child in the United States? The sentences were inevitable. Now the groundwork was laid; anyone who was for peace *might be* a Communist, anyone who spoke or behaved *like* a Communist might be an enemy agent, and all such suspected persons had to be dealt with as potential traitors.

•

After lunch, the Rosenbergs were returned to their detention cells. In her cell, at the other end of the corridor, Ethel knew that Julius had experienced a terrible shock at hearing her death sentence. In her heart, she had expected it almost from the moment the trial began. She described it to Emanuel Bloch. Something about the judge had struck her—the way he would tilt back in his chair to look at the ceiling disinterestedly whenever the defense tried to make a point. All through the trial she had noticed this. It was as though Kaufman was just "going through the motions," as though the trial was an irksome preliminary to his sentencing speech. If there had been any hopes or illusions, she had surrendered the last of them at the time he had so determinedly prevented the jury from hearing Ruth's cross-examination.

One thing kept gnawing at her as she paced up and down the detention cell. It was the blow Kaufman had aimed at them as unworthy parents. He had said toward the conclusion of his sentencing speech:

Indeed, the defendants, Julius and Ethel Rosenberg . . . were conscious they were sacrificing their own children. . . . Love for their cause dominated their lives—it was even greater than their love for their children.

As she later told Mr. Bloch, it was a mean lie, a cruel lie. How often friends had criticized them for making their two boys the entire focus of their lives.

517

If they were guilty of anything, it was their excessive devotion to their children.

•

In describing what happened shortly after the Rosenbergs had been locked into their cells, Terry recalled what Julius had subsequently told him. Ethel had suddenly become anxious about her husband's silence down at the other end of the cell corridor.

. . . She wanted desperately to assure him that she had not been crushed by Kaufman's icy last words. She wanted to assure him that she was not feeling "down," that they must not lose hope, that their case was not ended yet, that during their appeals to the higher courts the truth would gradually become known of how they had been framed. And that, despite the black silence of fear, despite "the lies and smears," despite everything, once the facts were made known, there would be people who would take courage and help . . .

All this, she wanted to tell him, but in a very personal way, as Ethel to Julie. . . .

In the New York *Times* account of what followed the sentencing, there is only this terse description of what "the United States Marshals guarding the Rosenbergs reported" that afternoon:

Mrs. Rosenberg, who once studied voice, sang "One Fine Day" from "Madame Butterfly," and the popular song "Goodnight, Irene." The husband sang "The Battle-Hymn of the Republic," the marshals said.

And that was all. The reporters evidently made no inquiry concerning this unique behavior in that strange locale and mentioned no reasons for the choice of these songs.

It was, of course, the message of hope from Puccini's opera which Ethel chose to sing to her husband. She sang the famous aria in the original Italian, "Un Bel Di Vidremo" (One Fine Day He Shall Return). And, according to the account given by Terry, she sang it without the slightest tremor or quaver.

Suddenly Julius was heard calling to her, "Ethel, sing the other aria too!"

She did so promptly; it was "Ah, Dolce Notte!" from the same opera. And Terry recalled that she sang so beautifully that he almost thought he was attending a concert rather than being locked up in the "bull pen" in the basement of the Foley Square Courthouse. And this is what he witnessed immediately after the second aria.

One of the deputy marshals standing near Julius' cell walked over to the bars and said impulsively—almost as though it "just popped out of him":

"Julie, they've marked you upstairs a low-down son-of-a-gun. But down here you're the luckiest man in the world—because no man ever had a woman who loved him that much."

In the nearby cells, as Terry recalled, there was a kind of hush broken a moment later by Julius' quiet but bitter reply:

"Look, I'm supposed to be a big shot in an espionage ring. I pass out $1,000 here, $1,500 there, toss $5,000 to my brother-in-law—but I never had the money to train that voice. I never had the money to do anything for her. Think about that."

In the meantime, their fellow-prisoners had asked for encores, and to please them as well as to keep up their own spirits, Ethel sang "Goodnight, Irene," and kept on singing until the two were taken back to their different prisons an hour later.

But before their parting Julius, too, had selected a song of faith and hope; one that had inspired a nation to its highest sacrifice:

> He hath loosed the fateful lightning of his
> terrible swift sword:
> His truth is marching on. . . .
> He is sifting out the hearts of men before
> his judgment-seat:
> O, be swift, my soul, to answer him! be
> jubilant, my feet! [16]

•

When the prison van dropped Ethel off at the Greenwich Avenue jail and Julius waved good-bye to her, it was the last time they saw each other outside the death house in Sing Sing prison. But there, in the next two years and two months, although they were kept apart in different wings of the death house, they felt at least that they were under one roof again, and somehow this, too, helped them through the long ordeal—until they were finally joined on the nineteenth of June in the year 1953.

NOTES AND REFERENCES

1. The hearing of June 8, 1953. Dr. Urey, who was present, described Kaufman's conduct as, among other things, "incredible."
2. Miller v. U.S., 120 F. 2d 968, 972 (C C A 10th, 1941).
3. These page numbers correspond to the Record, pp. 678–685.
4. Also, in his charge to the jury, Kaufman had stated: "I believe it is my duty as a Judge to help you crystallize in your minds the respective contentions and evidence in the case. . . ." (Record, p. 1554.)
5. In his charge Kaufman had placed special emphasis on the presence of "a state of tension," a prejudicial error objected to by the defense. (Record, pp. 1550, 1568.)
6. Brothman Record, pp. 1160–1161.
7. See New York *Times* of March 17, 1954. See also article by *Times* science editor Waldemar Kaempffert, concerning the "minor importance" of the alleged espionage of the Rosenbergs. (New York *Times*, March 6, 1955.)
8. Bernard O'Donnell, *The Old Bailey and Its Trials*, Macmillan, New York, 1950.
9. This execution date was automatically stayed by the first appeal. See *Chronology of Events*.
10. From an appeal for clemency by Chief Juistice Wolfe, Supreme Court of Utah, to President Truman.

11. From an address at a clemency rally for the Rosenbergs held at Triborough Stadium, New York City, on May 3, 1953.
12. *Columbia Law Review*, pp. 228–233.
13. Morton Sobell was released on January 14, 1969, after 18 years and five months of imprisonment, with five of those years served in Alcatraz. *Note:* Although his parole was to end in 1981, it was terminated (by telephone) by the Parole Board on June 24, 1976, apparently to prevent him from using newly released evidence as a basis to set aside his conviction as "tainted."
14. David Greenglass was released from prison in November, 1960, having served 10 years.
15. From interviews with Helen Sobell and Emanuel Bloch.
16. "Battle-Hymn of the Republic," by Julia Ward Howe.

ADDENDA

Concerning the jury's state of mind on the morning of its verdict, one cannot overlook the sensational Hiss trials of 1949 and 1950. The first had ended in a hung jury with four jurors voting for acquittal. These were excoriated by the other eight as "blockheads" and "Communist sympathizers," and they received anonymous threats of death and warnings to "go to Russia." In Washington, Richard Nixon was making noises indicating that these jurors might be subpoenaed by the House Un-American Activities Committee. The lesson was not lost on the second Hiss jury which voted for conviction. Six months later came the Korean War and by March, 1951, the political and emotional views of the Rosenberg jurors were hardly conducive to an objective examination of the evidence. (See article "What The FBI Knew and Hid" by John Lowenthal, *The Nation*, June 26, 1976.)

•

Concerning Kaufman's death sentences, FBI files released in 1975 have disclosed these items:

1. On March 16, 1951, Raymond Whearty, a Justice Department official, stated that he thought Judge Kaufman would impose "the death penalty." In the same FBI memo, Whearty is further quoted: "I know he will if he doesn't change his mind." This was reported during the *midpoint* of the trial, five days *before* Julius testified and almost two weeks *before* the jury had considered the evidence.

2. From an FBI memo to the "Director" (J. Edgar Hoover), dated February 19, 1953 (exactly four months before the Rosenbergs' executions), we learn that Kaufman was urging that Attorney General Brownell "expedite Supreme Court action on the Rosenbergs' appeal rather than let the case go past a June recess until that autumn." ("Push the matter vigorously. . . . Not in the interest of the government to permit a delay in this matter.")

3. The significance of Kaufman's urging is directly related to another FBI memo dated June 17, 1953, two days before the executions. The wave of national and international protest was mounting daily. By autumn, the Supreme Court might very well agree to review the record and find the trial had been unfair. There was also the danger that the high court might find that the Atomic Energy Act of 1946 was applicable, in which event, Kaufman's death sentences under the Espionage Act of 1917 would be ruled as illegal. A new trial with all the new evidence exposing the frame-up would be disastrous.

Thus we learn of a secret meeting between Attorney General Herbert Brownell and Chief Justice Fred Vinson taking place at 11 P.M. on the night of June 16, *anticipating* Justice Douglas' famous stay of execution made the next day. (See *Chronology of Events* on p. *xvii*.) The stay must be vacated "immediately" even if it means summoning back to Washington all of the justices already on vacation. In this June 17 memo, we see that Vinson, yielding to Brownell's pressure, as well as that of Kaufman and Hoover, agrees to call the full court to an unprecedented special session "immediately." Whereupon, Brownell phoned Kaufman the very next morning to reassure him that the Douglas stay would be vacated. This is clearly implied in the memo, wherein we learn that Kaufman had "very confidentially advised" the FBI official making the report of what had been planned the previous night. (See New York *Times*, June 11, 1976.)

Thus, Kaufman was now satisfied that his urging of

Brownell begun back in February had been successful, and that the Rosenbergs' executions, which he had ordered for the week of June 15, would not be delayed more than another forty-eight hours. Indeed, this was the primary reason for the extraordinary special session on June 18, because the next day was Friday, June 19. And while the end of the week, technically, was Saturday, June 20, this would be the Jewish Sabbath and, therefore, Kaufman would have to set another date for execution, meaning another delay of possibly three months, during which anything could happen. (*Note:* All this frantic haste should be seen against the background of the tidal wave of protests, indicated in the *Epilogue.*)

Hence, on June 19, with the Douglas stay vacated by a vote of six to three, the executions took place that same evening and the travesty was ended.

Three days later, in Justice Frankfurter's dissenting opinion to the decision, he concluded, "But history also has its claims."

It is the opinion of this writer who attended that special session of the Supreme Court, that historians will, one day, describe it as the most unfortunate episode in its otherwise creditable history. But at the same time, they will eulogize Justices William Douglas, Hugo Black and Felix Frankfurter for their courage in dissenting against "the compact majority."

EPILOGUE

June 19, 1953

"The last moment belongs to us—that agony is our triumph."

—*Bartolomeo Vanzetti*

There was mounting tension all that day. It kept increasing steadily until the hour of execution when it reached its peak. Perhaps it was that so many new precedents had been established by this world-shaking case. Not the least of these was the unseemly haste of the Supreme Court in vacating the stay granted only two days before by Mr. Justice Douglas.[1]

Indeed, the rush in official circles to execute the condemned couple was of such magnitude that it swept up even the President, for his denial of clemency came less than thirty minutes after the Supreme Court's fateful announcement.

So excessive was the haste that the electrocution was moved up from the traditional hour of eleven at night to just before sundown. Reportedly done to avoid desecration of the Jewish Sabbath that Friday night, the change was all the more shocking to most religious people, both Jew and Christian. For it had been expected that the execution would be delayed until after the Sabbath to avoid ushering in the day with the shedding of human blood. Many were reminded of the High Priest Caiaphas and his frantic haste with the Roman soldiery to end the last agonies of the crucified before sunset in order to preserve the sanctity of that other Sabbath night.

Throughout the day commentators interrupted broadcasts to report on the hour-by-hour bulletins from the death house. The constantly repeated question was: Would the condemned finally confess to their espionage activities and thereby save their lives —or would they go to their deaths with sealed lips, still insisting on their innocence? It was exceedingly strange that few of these commentators considered the possibility that if the couple were indeed innocent, they could scarcely be privy to the secrets of an espionage ring.

•

There was considerable tension in official quarters that day. In Washington, D.C., the Attorney General remained in his office until the very end, for he had arranged an open telephone line direct to Sing Sing in the event of a last-minute confession. In New York City, in his chambers, the judge who had imposed the death sentences waited for word of final submission. More than once since the trial he had indicated his certainty that only the threat of the electric chair would force the convicted pair to recant and name their co-conspirators. How many execution dates had he set for them and how many times had last-minute reprieves cheated him? This time, however, one of them must break—if not the husband, then the wife.

Two long years he had waited for "proof" that he had been right—that they had had their full day in court, had received a just sentence. Their endurance had been the greatest possible strain on him. It had been a terrible war of nerves but he had held firm despite all the unfair vilification, despite all the appeals from the duped and the do-gooders. Now the world would see—it was only a question of the breaking point—it could be any minute now.

•

There was very great tension throughout the world that day, but for other reasons than those offered by the commentators. Catholics in many countries had implored the Pope to intervene in behalf of the Rosenbergs and he had tried three times, to no avail. They could not comprehend how a civilized nation, professing belief in Christian ideals, could permit such torture and felt with His Holiness that to do this to a young mother of two small children was nothing less than abhorrent. From London, Paris, Rome, Vienna, Dublin, and Melbourne came reports of mounting anger, shock, and dismay expressed by millions of all religions, of all political shades of opinion.

In the Place de la Concorde, tens of thousands gathered at midnight, but the American Embassy had called for a cordon of steel-helmeted poilus armed with machine guns and tear gas to keep the protesting throngs at a safe distance. In London, as the minute hand of Big Ben neared the hour of one o'clock in the morning and the great crowd of people gathered before the entrance to 10 Downing Street, suddenly a man sang out in the stillness the refrain from "Joe Hill": "I never died, said he . . ."

It was a unique thing—no two children in the entire world had become so known, so pitied, as the two little Rosenberg boys. In Chicago, Los Angeles, in Milan, Buenos Aires, and even in places as far off as New Zealand, thousands gathered in prayer vigils that night, to pray for them and for the lives of their father and mother. In the United States many thousands had written hopefully to the President for mercy or clemency and now that it had been refused they were numbed with the shock of disillusionment. For the Rosenbergs had become a symbol. The sparing of their lives had come to express long-stilled hopes for moderation, for a lessening of world tension rather than a continuance of the suicidal arms race, for civilized negotiation rather than atomic diplomacy, for peace rather than war. And now that the death knell was tolling, it tolled not only for the Rosenbergs but for the symbol.

•

Within Sing Sing Prison itself there was also tension. Outside its walls, barricading all approaches, was a veritable army of State troopers, police, and unknown numbers of undercover men. They were under stern command to prevent any public demonstration such as had taken place twenty-six years before in Boston, the night Sacco and Vanzetti had been executed.

Inside their cell-blocks were some two thousand other convicts waiting for the "grapevine" reports. All of them were acutely aware of the "dance party" to take place shortly. It was the first daylight execution in the history of the prison. For more than two years they had been conscious of the two "C.C.'s"—Condemned Convicts 110,510 and 110,649—"sweating it out" over in the death house. Many felt a strong empathy with them, not merely as fellow-inmates, but as victims of stool-pigeon evidence. Very few concerned themselves with the legal question of guilt or innocence. Most were troubled by the moral question: How could the newspapers eulogize an informer as a patriot? How could such testimony be trusted at all? Most revolting was the idea of a brother sending his sister to the electric chair.

Many of them had followed the case over the prison radio. They had heard of the Vatican's appeals for clemency, and yesterday they had heard about the appeal from the President of France. They had never known of such international great intervening in behalf of an American prisoner. Under such extraordinary circumstances, they felt certain a reprieve must come—had to come. Their tension was simply the waiting for it.

•

In the visitors' room were packed thirty-eight reporters. Three others, representing the major wire services, had been selected to witness the executions and then brief the rest on the macabre details. Waiting, restless, they had little to do but chatter speculatively about which one of the pair would weaken first. Almost all fell to writing clichés about the burning sun setting inexorably over the Hudson and the ominous prison clock ticking away.

A few, however, had been waiting since early in the week. And, somehow, these four or five days of waiting had given them an inkling of what the two years must have meant to the condemned, especially to Mrs. Rosenberg, who had been kept in virtual solitary confinement. These few tended to remain apart from the general chatter. Instead they had begun to discuss some of their increasing doubts. There was all the new evidence, never examined by the Supreme Court. There was the disturbing factor of accomplice testimony. Above all, there was the unusual severity of the sentences—not approved by any of the upper courts, not recommended by the original jury or even by the prosecutor, but imposed solely on the judgment of one man, the sentencing judge.

> "Julius and Ethel Rosenberg . . . went to
> their deaths with a composure that aston-
> ished the witnesses."
> —*New York Times, June 20, 1953*

There was only one place where there was any semblance of calm that day. It was in the women's wing of the death house, where husband and wife were permitted to spend their final hours together, talking quietly through a fine mesh screen wheeled in front of her cell.

At 7:20 o'clock Julius Rosenberg said farewell to his wife by touching the tips of his fingers to hers through the mesh. He was then led to the special execution cell where the guards made final preparations—the slitting of the trouser leg, the shaving of the top of the head. Both were described as so extraordinarily calm that the most hardened prison officials were amazed.

It was precisely 8 o'clock when Julius began to walk his "last mile" along that short, narrow corridor leading to the death chamber. Just ahead was the young rabbi intoning from the 23rd Psalm:

Yea, though I walk through the valley of the shadow of death, I will fear no evil; for thou art with me; . . . Thou preparest a table before me in the presence of mine enemies. . . .

. . . Nearby, Julius saw the United States marshal, still watching for any indication of compliance. He knew about the choice now being offered them officially, about the two FBI men stationed at the open telephone line. And although they had not told him he was the first to go he knew that too. For if Ethel had been scheduled to precede him, she would have had to pass by his execution cell.

. . . All he needed to do then, to save both their

530

lives, was to nod his head to the marshal and mumble the few words admitting the "truth" of the accusations. It would be so easy. "Names" would be suggested, as well as places where he had conspired with the "names." What names? Any at all—Comrade X, Soviet Consul Y, Scientist Z—anything to keep the ball rolling. For "names" had become the vital grist for the vast propaganda mill—to keep up the scare headlines, to keep up the national temperature of feverish suspicion and contagious mistrust. "Names" had become the magic formula to keep the ball rolling. And was not this their real crime? They had stopped the ball rolling, had stopped the endless game. . . .

Now they were opening the heavy door to the death-chamber. The rabbi was intoning, "Thou annointest my head with oil; my cup runneth over."

. . . Had it been anything like this for that young rabbi, Yeshua ben Yussuf, on his bitter path past Golgotha, the place of skulls? Had it been like this when he had faced *his* false witnesses, faced his judges who had charged his silence as blasphemy—his teachings as rebellion against Caesar? Had it been this way, too, when the multitudes had stood by, not daring to question—when even Peter had thrice failed him?

It was 8:02 o'clock. The witnesses said later that he had seemed lost in thought, gazing calmly ahead, as the guards strapped him down.

. . . Ah, there was the Tempter standing against the wall, still waiting for the nod. And there, the three newsmen waiting to report with clinical accuracy any reflex that might denote fear. Or did they perhaps expect a final statement, the traditional last favor extended to him about to die?

. . . Now, as the guard approached with the mask, now, if any time, was his last chance to repeat their three-year cry of innocence. But, why repeat the wearisome refrain? So much had been offered, yet most of it had met with a conspiracy of silence. What had the press printed of the scathing opinion of the trial, written by the Chief Justice of the Supreme Court of Utah? Or even those urgent appeals from the heads of state, from the twenty-three rabbis of Jerusalem, from

the three thousand Protestant ministers? All—all had
been scornfully dismissed as "Communist-inspired."

. . . No matter what he might say, they would
describe it only as fanatical defiance or "a compulsion
for martyrdom." No. One did not dare risk this last
precious instant "in the presence of mine enemies."
Rather let the eloquence of silence ring out the truth
to all who would listen . . .

> Lord, who shall abide in thy tabernacle? . . .
> He that . . . speaketh the truth
> in his heart . . .
> He that sweareth to his own hurt, and
> changeth not . . .

•

It was 8:08 o'clock when they led in Ethel Rosenberg. The rabbi was reading the psalms she had requested. And there were the two doctors waiting self-
consciously for their fee; and somewhere the electrician,
poor man, waiting so long to earn his. And there, too,
the waiting marshall, still hopeful.

. . . Yes, of course, she *knew*. For she had just
passed his *vacant* cell. But she had known it in her
heart the instant it happened, just as she knew the reasons why they had held her to the last. On the one
hand, they had calculated that with the man out of
the way the woman would no longer be under restraint
or feel the shame of betrayal. On the other hand, they
had reckoned that since she was the frailer sex the
confrontation of actual death would finally shatter her
will to resist. Undoubtedly, too, they counted strongly
on the pull of her children.

. . . Ah, my precious ones—at least you are innocent. And yet, what have they not done to you? You
are already fatherless and I am a widow and soon
you will be orphaned. But would you want me to
befoul now your father's life? You know, despite all
that was done to him, the depth of his faith in the
power of truth. And now at the last, to have his own
wife play the role of harlot to political procurers! Oh,
no, my sons, you would not want such a mother . . .

In thee, O Lord, do I put my trust;
    let me never be ashamed . . .
For I have heard the slander of many:
    fear was on every side:
While they took counsel together against me,
    they devised to take away my life.

. . . And now the scribes were scribbling down how they dressed for death—in ill-fitting cotton and shuffling felt—how she might yet falter, or recoil, or freeze fast. Oh, you cynical ones—I ask how any of you would feel if you and your beloved were torn from the arms of your children and from each other, accused of a vile crime you did not commit? What answer would you give your tormentors? Would you be so forgiving as to relieve them of their guilt? Would you become their willing creature and ready tool? Would you, or could you, consent to a bargain of abomination? Would you betray every moral principle, conviction, and life-cherished ideal? And would you, in branding yourself, compound hideous crime, and brand your own children forever as the sons of spies and traitors?

Let me not be ashamed, O Lord; for I have
    called upon thee: let the wicked be ashamed . . .

. . . It was 8:10 o'clock. There was the chair, its thick, black straps, its dangling wires—the device designed to send her crawling, terrified, to the feet of these agents of the Grand Inquisitor, to wring from them the "mea culpa" that would turn them into a pair of puppets to be carted from courtroom to courtroom to mouth falsehoods against other heretics. There was the diabolical prod to make them toss terror-stricken each night with the dread of its proximity and scream out finally, "We'll talk—we'll talk!"
. . . But oh, you scribes—did you hear any guilt from the lips of Socrates, Bruno, or Joan? Or from Dreyfus, or from Sacco and Vanzetti? All through the bloody history of hatred of the dissenter, you have tried to ease your consciences by calling them would-be martyrs. But, oh, you smug ones—in the judgment of

history, who were the innocent and who the guilty, who the defeated and who prevailed . . . ?

•

Later, the witnesses reported that she had a wistful smile as they had led her to the chair, a Mona Lisa sort of smile. Perhaps it was this apparent resignation that made what happened thereafter appear so startling, because:

. . . Just before she reached the chair, Ethel Rosenberg held out her hand to the prison matron, Mrs. Helen Evans. As the latter grasped it, Mrs. Rosenberg drew her close and kissed her lightly on the cheek.

Although this simple act, taking place only a minute before a woman turned to face her death, has been variously described, none of the witnesses seemed to have grasped the significance of its profound message.

In all the nation's press, thousands of words were devoted to the most morbid details of the executions—the sizzling sounds that issued from the writhing flesh of the dying, the quantity and duration of jolts of electricity, the color of the smoke that plumed upward from the seared bodies—but not one word of under-standing or the willingness to understand that final act which

. . . startled the guards and witnesses more than any-thing in the entire electrocution.

And yet, consciously or intuitively, many millions did understand—that that last embrace was a sacred covenant made with all who shared faith with them that "brotherhood and peace" were worth fighting for, and could be won. For with that firm handclasp and tender kiss, Ethel Rosenberg was passing on her un-dying faith to all who treasured truth and justice, to all who could understand or come to understand what they had lived and died for.

NOTES AND REFERENCES

1. The documentation for the *Epilogue* is from the New York *Times* of June 15–20, 1953. In addition, this writer interviewed Warden Denno of Sing Sing, Ethel's matron, Mrs. Helen Evans, and the New York *Post* correspondent assigned to report the executions.

   Those portions dealing with Judge Kaufman's views on the executions are based upon statements made during motion to reduce sentence and requests for stays of execution. Those portions dealing with the Rosenbergs' reactions to the coercive measures to make them "confess" are based upon the letters they wrote on this subject, published in their *Death House Letters*.

ADDENDA

As indicated in the *Addenda* of Chapter 16, these are the highlights of my own recollections of the final three days of the Rosenberg tragedy:

On Wednesday, June 17, 1953, following the news of Justice Douglas' stay of executions, I flew to Washington to confer with Mr. Bloch on my proposal to release to the press the crucial significance of the Hilton registration card and the timetable; to demonstrate that the card was an FBI-Gold forgery and that the timetable provided documentary proof that Gold had testified falsely; and to emphasize, moreover, that these and other of our findings pointed strongly to the possibility that Gold was an FBI puppet used knowingly by the prosecution.

However, Mr. Bloch, confident that the Supreme Court in its hearing the next morning, would uphold the Douglas stay, decided that the release of these facts would have more impact with his next move—a motion to obtain a hearing for a new trial on the basis of this and other new evidence. As a lawyer, he felt it wiser to hold back our trump card until after he had prepared his motion thoroughly. He also feared that our charge of outright frame-up to the press would be resented by the conservative majority of the Supreme Court and hence jeopardize the Douglas stay.

Unfortunately, he was unaware at this time of the secret machinations of Kaufman, Hoover, and Brownell to prevent the airing of any such charges by getting the Rosenbergs executed with no further delay.

On Thursday, June 18, I attended the historic special session of the Supreme Court. And, although Bloch presented in his argument various legal issues, he was still chary of offending the Court with any frontal attack on officials of the Department of Justice. Later, as indicated in the conclusion of Chapter 16, he regretted bitterly that he had not done so.

On Friday, June 19, having flown back to New York City, there came the announcement that the Supreme Court had vacated the Douglas stay by a vote of six to three and that the executions would take place that same day before sunset.

As the fateful hour drew near, this writer hurried to Union Square where some 15,000 people had gathered spontaneously, both as a final protest and to wait hopefully for a last-minute reprieve from President Eisenhower, or for any other miracle. It did not come.

(*Note:* In the interview for the PBS television documentary previously mentioned, I was asked about my feelings as we waited for the dread announcement. As I recall, seeing all those thousands of agonized faces, it occurred to me that perhaps I was the only one there who knew the Sing Sing death house firsthand as the result of research on my play *The Last Mile* produced back in 1930. Indeed, I had derived my title from the little corridor along which I knew Julius and Ethel would be led to the death chamber.

On Sunday, June 21, at the funeral of the Rosenbergs, seeing Julius and Ethel in their coffins, it seemed a bit ironical that it should be the first time I had ever "met" them.

Perhaps more ironical and quite revealing of that traumatic period was this incident: Standing by me during the impassioned eulogy in which Mr. Bloch denounced the "murderers" of the Rosenbergs, was the weeping chairman of the Los Angeles branch of the National Committee to Secure Justice in the Rosenberg Case. In Los Angeles, he had often given me the latest items on the case. Quite naturally, I told him about my recent findings. However, about a year and a half later, following a nervous breakdown, he confessed in open court that he had been "a paid FBI informer" all along. During recess, in the corridor, he asked my forgiveness. His tears at the funeral, he claimed, had been sincere. Nonetheless, since he had infiltrated the Los Angeles branch at the request of the FBI and was being paid, he had felt obliged to report what I had told him concerning the Hilton card and the timetable.

On June 22, 1953, after the burial of the Rosenbergs, I resumed the writing of this book.

APPENDIX 1

Rogge memo re discussion between David Greenglass and attorney H. J. Fabricant concerning interrogation by FBI.

MEMO

TO: FILE	11:45 a.m.
FROM: HJF	6/16/50

Re: DAVID GREENGLASS

After conferring with OJR and the subject's brother-in-law Louis Abel, this morning at our office and pursuant to telephone call made by OJR, I visited the offices of the FBI on the 6th floor of the Federal Building where I spoke with Mr. Whelan, apparently the Agent in charge.

He told me that Greenglass was down the hall and that I could see him and that he had signed a statement indicating that he had met Harry Gold and that he had transferred information to Gold.

He further told me that the matter was being taken up with the Department of Justice and that the probability is that a complaint will be filed in Albuquerque, New Mexico charging conspiracy and advised me that I could see Greenglass if I wished. . . .

Greenglass confirmed that he had given a statement that he had met Gold for an hour, that he had given him some information concerning the names of people who would be sympathetic but he thought that Japan was the enemy and Russia was an ally and there was no reason why information could not be given. He had told the FBI that he received $500 from Gold.

He told me that he had made a number of confusing statements purposely in order to confound the FBI and to draw attention from his wife who is in the hospital. His wife apparently originally told him that his brother-in-law, Julius Rosenberg, had suggested this (and so I fail to see how his mind operated in connection with keeping his wife out of the picture).

He told me further that Julius Rosenberg is apparently very close to this whole situation. Julius Rosenberg had once introduced him to a man in a car somewhere in New York who apparently made this request. He does not know if the man was a Russian and told the FBI that he didn't know.

APPENDIX 2

Handwritten statement by David Greenglass to Rogge office reporting his interrogation by FBI; dated June (17), 1950.

Saturday
June 1950

These are my approximate statements to the F.B.I.

1. I stated that I met Gold in N. M. at 209 N. High St. my place. They told me that I had told him to come back later because I didn't have it ready. I didn't remember this but I allowed it in the statement. When he came back again I told them that I gave him the envelope with the stuff not expecting payment and then he gave me an envelope. Later I found that it contained $500.

2. I told them that on a visit to me in Nov. 1944 my wife asked me if I would give information. I made sure to tell the F.B.I. that she was transmitting this info from my Brother in Law Julius and was not her own idea. She was doing this because she felt I would be angry if she didn't ask me.

I then mentioned a meeting with a man who I didn't know arranged by Julius. I established the approximate

538

meeting place but no exact date. The place was a car an Olds owned by my father-in-law, at somewhere above 42nd St. on 1st Ave. in Man. I talked to the man but I could recall very little about which we spoke. I thought it might be that he wanted me to think about finding out about H.E. lens's used in experimental tests to determine data on the A bomb.

I made a general statement on my age etc. you know the usual thing.

I mentioned no other meeting with anyone.

One more thing, I identified Gold by a torn or cut piece of card, but I didn't tell them where or how I got it. Also I definitely placed my wife out of the room at the time of Gold's visit.

Also I didn't know who sent Gold to me.

I also made a pencil sketch of an H. E. mold set up for an experiment. But this I'll tell you I can honestly say the information I gave Gold maybe not at all what I said in the statement.

APPENDIX 3

Rogge memo re conference between Ruth Greenglass and attorney R. H. Goldman concerning her husband's arrest.

MEMORANDUM

TO: FILE
FROM: RHG
June 19, 1950

Re: David Greenglass

OJR and I visited Mrs. Greenglass at her home, 285 Rivington Street, Brooklyn, New York, at 4:00 P.M. Sunday, June 18, 1950. She was in bed as she had just returned from the hospital.

We first discussed the question of arranging a meeting of various relatives at our office to discuss financial problems. . . .

There was subsequently present during the conference: Issy Feit, Sam Greenglass, Bernard Greenglass, and Louis Abel.

Mrs. Greenglass discussed her visit to New Mexico. She was there between March 1945 and March 1946. They had been married in 1942. She feels that New Mexico is a very bad place to try the case since the citizens did not like GI's because of the big boom and then the big slack, because of anti-semitism and because the local citizens all felt bitter about the wives of the GI's taking jobs there. She was employed in Albuquerque by the OPA and temporarily by the Soil Conservation Office.

As to her husband, she stated that he had a "tendancy to hysteria." At other times he would become delirious and once when he had the grippe he ran nude through the hallway, shrieking of "elephants," "Lead Pants."

She had know him since she was ten years old. She said that he would say things were so even if they were not. He talked of suicide as if he were a character in the movies but she didn't think he would do it. They had been under surveillance by the FBI for several weeks. In particular, they had noticed a car of the Acme Construction Company, 1400 First Avenue in Manhattan. She ascertained there was no such Company. (There is an Acme Construction Company at 1402 Fulton Street in Brooklyn.) She was interviewed at the hospital by two FBI men, Mr. Tully and Mr. Wood. One was tall, ruddy and dark. The other she described as toothy and short. They assured her that they had nothing against her. She described her stay in Albuqerque and stated that she could not remember all of her addresses. Since it was difficult for GI's to get rooms for a long period, they had lived in five or six places. She had only been to Los Alamos to a party for a few hours one time. She had remembered no visitors at her house. She had notice of the project and signed an affidavit for it. She knew her mail was censored. She would not have allowed her husband to bring anything home after Hiroshima had disclosed what the project was. She intended to raise a family and did not want that kind of material around. In the future she will refer everyone to her lawyer.

She pointed out Dave did not ask for the job; that he was going overseas; that they have been watched constantly, and feels as if they are the object of presecution. Shortly before their accident the FBI asked if they had a speciman of uranium in the house, in the course of what they call a routine investigation. One of their friends had a similar experience.

People in the neighborhood want to raise a petition.

Note: All errors are preserved as in the original photostats.

All newspapers are to be referred to her lawyer.

People keep flocking in the house to offer support and advice including that perhaps a right-wing lawyer should be selected. The Jewish Daily Forward, which is certainly not a leftist newspaper, is very excited about the anti-semitic issue and has offered a lawyer. Mrs. Greenglass urged OJR to try to get a court appointment for himself and he agreed to try. OJR pointed out that if Dave was innocent he should talk; that if not it would be advisable not to talk but to let the Government prove its case. The third course was that of cooperation. That was also discussed at length.

There was a long discussion about JR.

Questions to be looked up:

1. Was the arrest valid—was he held in detention before the complaint issued?
2. What is the effect of the complaint?
3. What do the cases hold on the intent to harm the Government?
4. Statements of Co-Conspirators.
5. Venue.
6. Joinder.

APPENDIX 3A

Rogge memo re transfer of David Greenglass to the "11th floor" of the Tombs.

MEMO

TO: HJF

FROM: RHG   7/20/50

Re: Greenglass

Saypol called me today and I returned his call. He stated as follows:

"I have made arrangements to have your man Greenglass transferred to the Tombs Prison, 11th Floor, where he will be more comfortable and also because it is desirable to take him away and keep him separated from Rosenberg. I assume you agree."

I stated that it seemed perfectly agreeable to me and asked whether Greenglass had been told about the reasons.

Saypol said he was not sure whether he had but seemed to indicate that he would be told.

Saypol requested in referring to where he is stationed, if we did refer to it, we simply mentioned the Tombs and not mention that it is the 11th floor.

APPENDIX 4

Rogge memo re discussion with Ruth Greenglass concerning "suspended sentence" for David Greenglass.

MEMO

TO: OJR

FROM: RHG   8/21/50

Re: Greenglass

I spoke to Ruth Greenglass this morning. She is feeling better and so is Dave apparently about the fact that they were not named as defendants. From Helen I learned that she may have been a little upset about it originally but now she feels the thing is moving smoothly.

However, Dave is worried about something else which I was able to reassure him through Ruth. Some of his cellmates in the Tombs have been telling him horror stories about the treatment he will get. I told her that we were happy to say that few of our clients went to jail but those who did had never had such a complaint. I further assured her that Saypol would not permit any mistreatment. But the thing that impressed her most however was that I told her that you were on friendly terms with Bennett, Director of Prisons. This impressed her because she feels that Dave may not get a suspended sentence and is worried about the kind of treatment he will get. I assured her that if he does go to jail for a period of time that you would certainly not hesitate to speak to Bennett and to make sure that Dave got good and fair treatment.

APPENDIX 5

Rogge memo re "deal" for David Greenglass.

MEMO

8/23/50

FROM: RHG
TO: . FILE

Re: Greenglass

Lane, the Assistant U.S. Attorney, called me at 1:00 o'clock and told me that something important had come up with respect to New Mexico and would I and/or Fabricant see him this afternoon. I told him that I could and HJF would come with me.

Lane wanted to know when OJR would return and I told him that we had expected him and in fact were trying to ascertain exactly when he would return. HJF and I went over to see Lane at 4:00 o'clock. He told us that Bloch had earlier in the day argued to the judge at the arraignment of his clients that they were absolutely innocent and that from the fact that Greenglass was not indicted but merely named as a co-conspirator in the New York indictment, it looked to Bloch as if the government had made a deal with you as Greenglass' attorney. Lane felt that we would now have to consider the question of whether it was OK that Greenglass be indicted here in a superceding indictment and not merely named as a co-conspirator. He would then be a defendant and be tried here in New York but would testify against the others. (See also the newspaper clipping)

The New Mexico District Attorney, acting on instructions from the Attorney General's office, with whom Lane had been in touch, would agree to such a procedure. Lane pointed out that he thought it was obviously advantageous for both sides for the matter to be decided in New York. HJF told Lane that if there was no hurry we would not want to give a definite commitment but that it would seem that such an arrangement would probably be approved by OJR.

543

I thought at least that I should make a purely off the record inquiry as to whether Dave could not testify as a co-conspirator in New York but not as a defendant and that the question of his plea be postponed. But Lane said that something should be done on this before September 6th and reiterated again it was to our advantage not to take any chance of getting before a judge in New Mexico, clearly indicating that he felt that in a small state like New Mexico they might well prefer to give a good stiff sentence (of course he added he did not want to sell us on anything, and so forth).

There was no indication that Ruth is to be indicted and neither Herb nor I wanted to raise the point. I had the inference that they were not planning to indict her but I could be wrong and I didn't even want to ask the question, though you may desire to do so.

Lane also informed us that he believed they found nothing on the bag in the way of fingerprints.

> There was some discussion between HJF and Lane on the question of Sobell but Lane did not know what Sobell planned to do.

> I think it best not to discuss this with Ruth until you return as she might get somewhat excited about it and at any rate we don't have to do anything before September 6th.

(*Note:* The following is transcribed from a handwritten postscript.)

Friday

We learned today that Lane thinks Dave [Greenglass] should agree to a plea in N.Y. on the New Mexico indictment; the New Mexico papers would all be sent here and then there would be the N.Y. indictment.

Also, I had lunch with Ruth, Pilat, and HJF [Fabricant]. We looked at Pilat's articles. They look O.K., but HJF as a precaution, told Lane previously he would insist Pilat, who already had 2 conferences with Saypol, showed the draft of the articles to Saypol or Lane.

APPENDIX 6

Rogge memo re "deal" for Max Elitcher.

MEMORANDUM

TO: OJR
FROM: HJF   March 19, 1951

Re: ELITCHER

In connection with our conversation this morning wherein I told you of Elitcher's particular problem concerning which you suggested that it would be profitable to speak with MacInerny, the following is a thumb-nail sketch of the client.

He was a City College classmate of Rosenberg, Sobell, Perl, et al. . . .

As appeared from the trial, with the Rosenbergs and Sobell, Elitcher had joined the Communist Party and was on the fringe of the spy apparatus created by Rosenberg. Elitcher never gave any classified material or other information to Rosenberg. However, he was constantly sought out and urged to participate in the espionage activities of the latter. . . .

In July, 1950, Elitcher was interviewed by the FBI and even from the inception of this interview to the present time, he and his wife have cooperated fully with the government in connection with their prosecution of the aforesaid espionage ring. As you know, Elitcher and his wife testified before the grand jury not only in connection with the conspiracy indictment but subsequently in connection with the indictment of Perl for perjury.

The importance of Elitcher's cooperation cannot possibly be underestimated since he was the government's lead-off witness and provided the testimony which links Rosenberg and Sobell.

Shortly before the spy trial got under way, it was suggested to Elitcher by Reeves that it would be best if he resigned from his employment with Reeves Instrument Co. Elitcher did resign effective as of the last working day prior to the beginning of the trial.

He has never been named as a defendant or as a co-conspirator in any prosecution and it is reasonable to assume he never will be. It is equally reasonable to assume that his cooperation in subsequent prosecutions by the government will be essential to the success of said prosecutions and it is also apparent that Elitcher will continue to cooperate.

At the present time, Elitcher . . . needs a profitable employment and preferably in the field in which his qualifications are tops, to wit: fire control work.

It is evident that he will not be employed until his loyalty and security status is cleared up. . . . In other words, if Elitcher could be assured that when he sought employment either in classified or other electrical engineering work, that the appropriate authorities would come forth at some future time when his security investigation was under way and state things of commendatory nature such as the circumstances would permit, then to some extent, the initial obstacle to employment would be overcome.

It is to this end that I think your talk with MacInerny could be helpful. If the Department of Justice or the FBI were to furnish Elitcher's prospective employers with a letter stating that they would be willing to appear or give testimony in his behalf at any future security investigation, it would be a most desirable achievement.

APPENDIX 7

Affidavit of Bernard Greenglass re "sample of uranium" taken by David Greenglass from Los Alamos Atomic Project. (*Note:* The following is transcribed from the handwritten affidavit.)

State of New York
County of New York S.S.

My name is Bernard Greenglass. . . . I am the brother of Ethel Rosenberg and David Greenglass; Ethel is my elder sister and David is my younger brother.

Some time in the year 1946 my brother David told me he had taken a sample of uranium from Los Alamos without permission of the authorities. . . .

. . . Sometime before David's arrest in June 1950,

David told me that he had thrown this uranium into the East River.

About a month ago . . . David Rosenberg, Julius Rosenberg's brother came to my home to discuss the case of Ethel and Julius. There was also present Ruth Greenglass, and my mother Tessie Greenglass. The subject of uranium came up. I told Dave Rosenberg the same story that I am stating here.

Ruth, David's wife said "David took a sample of uranium but he threw it into the East River."

I told this same story about the uranium to my sister Ethel during my visit to her about a month and one half ago . . . at the Sing Sing death house.

I also told the same story to Rabbi Koslowe at his home in Mamaroneck, N.Y. in the presence of David Rosenberg on the evening of May 25, 1953.

I have voluntarily related this story again to Emanuel H. Bloch at his office at 401 Broadway New York, N.Y. on this 31st day of May 1953.

The above is true,

[signed] Bernard Greenglass

sworn to before me
this 31st day of May 1953
[signed] Gloria Agrin
Notary Public State of NY
Com. Exp. Mar. 30, 1954

APPENDIX 8

Telegram re Sobell, translated.

UNITED STATES OF MEXICO
NATIONAL TELEGRAPHS
DTO NU-49   NUM 32.50/s   OFFICIAL (CR)
NUEVO LAREDO, TAMPS., AUGUST 19, MEXICO, D.F. 10.50.
[TO]: CHIEF OF THE OFFICE OF MIGRATION
         DEPT. OF STATE
         MEXICO, D.F.
NUMBER 1920. MEXICAN CONSULATE, LAREDO, TEXAS, INFORMS ME ON DEPORTATION FROM MEXICO TO UNITED STATES OF AMERICA OF

THE NORTH AMERICAN, MORTON SOBELL WHICH TOOK PLACE 3:45 A.M. YESTERDAY BY SECRET SERVICE AGENTS OF THE CAPITOL [Mexico City] WHO EVADED THE VIGILANCE OF THE MIGRATION SERVICE. I PASS THIS ON FOR YOUR FULLEST INFORMATION.
RESPECTFULLY
　　　　　MIGRATION.—RAFAEL ARREDUNDU CES

APPENDIX 9

Reply to telegram re Sobell, translated.

GENERAL DIRECTOR of POPULATION
DEPARTMENT of MIGRATION
BUREAU OF PROMOTION
CLASSIFIER
2
From the Files

35563

To the Chief of the Office of Population
Nuevo Laredo, Tamp.

I acknowledge to you that this office was duly informed via telegram, Number 1920, on the date of August 19th past, that Agents of the Secret Service deported the North American Morton Sobell, evading the vigilance of the Migration Service. As of this date, efforts are being made before the Chief of the aforesaid Service to the end that in the future the requirements of migration will not again be omitted.

Courteously,
Effective Suffrage, No Reelection
Mexico, D.F., Sept. 6, 1950
The Assistant Chief of Department
(signed) Enrique J. Palacios

(official stamp "Despachado
Sept. 11, 1950)
co.c.p. Rev. y Orft. de Doom.—Control.—
amb/gvr.
Tel. s/n.s/exp.

APPENDIX 10

Letter re investigation of illegal seizure of Sobell and sending of Laredo Times, *translated.*

CONFIDENTIAL

Secretariat
  of
Foreign Relations

Branch Office GENERAL DIRECTORATE OF
THE CONSULAR SERVICE OF THE
DEPARTMENT OF MIGRATION
Serial No. IV/230(73-26)/112414
                                  624537
Re: MORTON SOBELL and wife their
  exit from Mexico.
Mexico, D.F., Sept. 13, 1950.

Department of State
Bureau of Population
Department of Migration
Mexico City

The Consulate of Mexico in Laredo, Texas, in official document 2746, of August 18th just past, reports to this Bureau the following:

"This Consulate via the Office of Migration in Nuevo Laredo, Tamps., was informed that yesterday before dawn there was delivered to the North American authorities of the FBI (Federal Bureau of Investigation) at this border, a person who had been residing in the Capital (Mexico City).

This same Office of Migration in Nuevo Laredo, Tamps., asked this Consulate to investigate the identity of the person handed over to the aforementioned authorities, as well as the means by which he was delivered.

Today in the afternoon, I commissioned Hector Rangel Obregon, Chancellor assigned to this Consulate on my behalf to carry out the investigations required in this case. Having presented himself before the North American

Office of Immigration in this city (Laredo), he obtained the information which is supplied below:

'At 3:45 A.M. today, there was delivered to the authorities of the FBI (Federal Bureau of Investigation) as well as to the Immigration authorities of this country (U.S.A.), Mr. Morton Sobell and wife Hellen Sobell, both North American citizens by birth, the former having been born in the City of New York, N. Y., U.S.A. on March 11, 1917. The delivery of these persons was made by the Agents of the Secret Service Police of the Federal District, as it will be found recorded in the files of the Office of Immigration in Laredo, Texas. The two said persons were brought from the capital of the Mexican Republic.'

"As additional information, it is known that the authorities of this country (U.S.A.) were searching for Mr. Morton Sobell, accusing him of espionage. Attached to this letter, I take the liberty of forwarding to you a clipping from the newspaper The Laredo Times of this city, containing information concerning the seizure of the North American Morton Sobell. The above information was supplied to the Office of Migration (Mexican) in Nuevo Laredo, Tamps., today at 4:30 P.M."

Allow me to draw your attention to the enclosed newspaper clipping which was mentioned in the above quoted report, and I repeat the assurances of my courteous consideration.

> Effective Suffrage; No reelection
> By the Office of the Sub Secretary
> in Charge of the Office of the
> Sub Director General.
> (signed) Antonio Canale Urueta

JAC/crg.-47446
(signed): "Joe."

APPENDIX 11

Santa Fe Railroad Timetable of June, 1945.

(*Note:* The daily trains, *The Chief* and the *California Limited,* were the only two trains traveling east from Albuquerque on Sunday, June 3, 1945. In his testimony, Harry Gold claimed to have taken the *California Limited.*

Relevant portions of the timetable are extracted here and presented in larger print. The full photostats also are in Appendix 22 in the original edition of this book.)

STATIONS	Daily	THE CHIEF
Lv. Albuquerque	9:00 AM	Sun., etc.
Ar. Chicago	1:25 PM	Mon., etc.
STATIONS		
	Daily	CALIFORNIA LIMITED
Lv. Albuquerque	8:30 PM	Sun., June 3
Ar. Chicago	7:30 AM	Tues., June 5

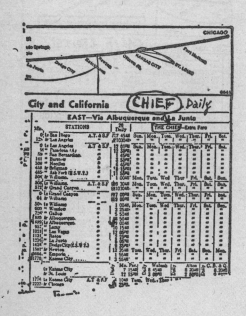

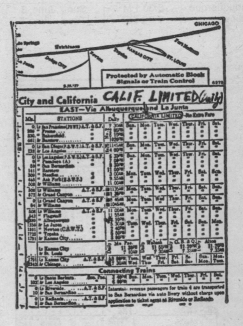

Index

ABEL, DOROTHY, 429
Abel, Louis, 113, 432-33
Adomain, Lan, 429
Albuquerque, Ruth Greenglass and, 300-301; security measures, 329-30
Albuquerque *Tribune*, 116, 118
Allen, Charles, 165
Alsop brothers, 278
American Airlines, 165
American Jewish Committee, 246
American Student Union, 131
Anti-Semitism, *Daily Forward* on, 123; and Kaufman, 233; *Jewish Examiner* on, 510; in New Mexico, 117; in Rosenberg trial, 243, 244; Rosenbergs' awareness of, 228; in selecting jury, 245-46
Army-McCarthy hearings, 53
Associated Press, on Sobell, 277-78
Atomic Energy Commission, 372. *See also* Joint Committee on Atomic Energy
Attlee, Clement, on Fuchs case, 60

Attorney General's "subversive organizations" list, 246-47

BAIL, DENIAL OF, 143, 214
Baney, Ralph S., 62
Bautista, Dora, 455
Beckerly, James, 372, 507
Bennett, J. V., 106, 165
Bentley, Elizabeth, background, 440-43; and Brunini, 224, 443; did not know Rosenberg, 408; and Elitcher, 274-75, 278-79, 408; and FBI, 449-50; and Gold, 209-13; and Golos, 367; and Remington, 223, 443; role in trial, 444; Saypol's reliance on, 223-24; testimony analyzed, 440-51; testimony never corroborated, 428; testimony questioned, 441-43
Bernal, John D., 374
Bernhardt, George, 434-35
Birkby, Fred, 87
Black, Hugo L., 425-26
Bloch, Alexander, 224, 242
Bloch, Emanuel, appeal to Supreme Court, 255; argument for new trial, 201; on coaching of Greenglass, 202; courtroom

strategy, 371; cross-examines Greenglass, 106, 366, 368, 371, 385, 387-88, 405-406; Elitcher testimony, 187-89, 237-38; engaged by Rosenberg, 135-36, 142; examines Rosenberg, 389-90; on FBI, 435; on frameup, 355; on Greenglass, 405-406; and Jello box, 354-55

Bohr, Niels, 301

Boyle, Kay, 173

Brothman, Abraham, bail denied, 214; conviction, 214; and Gold, 73, 464; sentencing, 214; trial, 75-81, 235-37; and Yakovlev, 349-50

"Brown paper," 411, 432

Brunini, John, 224, 443

Bureau of Standards, Rosenberg at, 265

CATHERINE SLIP, 271-79

Chambers, Whittaker, 92, 236-37; on informers, 182, 185, 189, 191, 193

City College of New York, 131, 160, 182-83, 453

Cobb, Chandler, 455

Cohn, Roy, altered photographs, 53; background, 288; 443; on Bentley, 442-43; Brothman case, 75; and "eleventh floor," 221; examines Greenglass, 340, 367, 382, 411-12; on Matusow charges, 419-20; pressures Perl, 223; responsibility for Rosenberg conviction, 419-

20; coin-collection can, 468

Columbia Law Review, on conspiracies, 512; on Elitcher testimony, 260-61; on Govt. witnesses, 428; on Govt's purpose, 443-44; on Greenglass testimony, 288-91, 292, 338; on political atmosphere, 56, 215; on Sobell, 456-57; on Supreme Court, 426

Communist Party, attempt to implicate, 153-54, 164, 208-209, 293, 443-44, 462; Fuchs' "membership," 59, 60; membership issue in trial, 444-45; Rosenberg not member, 472-73

Console table, 138, 141, 385-95, 436-38

Consolidated Edison Co., jurors employed at, 247-49

Conspiracy, legal status of, 255-57, 263

Cooke, Alistair, 465

Court of Appeals on Greenglass testimony, 160

Cox, Evelyn, 394-95, 435-37

Crowther, James, 374

D DAY, 266, 267, 281

Daily Forward, on anti-Semitism, 123

Danziger, William, 166-67, 453-55

Darrow, Clarence, 255-57, 263

"Davidson, James," 59, 64, 98